Advance Praise for *Facebook Marketing: An Hour a Day, 2nd Edition*

Are you looking to grow your business with Facebook marketing? If so, you need a trusted guide. Facebook Marketing: An Hour a Day *is not just any book on Facebook marketing. It happens to be carefully crafted by two of the world's leading Facebook marketing authorities: Mari Smith and Chris Treadaway. Study it. Digest it. Then watch how your business thrives.*

> —MICHAEL STELZNER, author of *Launch* and founder, Social Media Examiner

Facebook has become a fundamental marketing platform and, thanks to this book, you'll learn exactly what you must do in order to get the most from it.

> —JOHN JANTSCH, author of *Duct Tape Marketing* and *The Referral Engine*

Chris and Mari have created the Holy Grail, a book where nearly every page is worthy of an underline, highlight, or dog ear. With some companies posting to Facebook twice a month, and others posting banalities four times daily, the content strategy guidelines alone make this book indispensable. It's the definitive guide to doing Facebook right.

> —JAY BAER, co-author of *The NOW Revolution: 7 Shifts to Make Your Business Faster, Smarter, and More Social*

The social media world is full of people saying they know this tool or that tool. But there's a reason "Mari Smith" is the first name people think of when they think "Facebook marketing." This book show you how the world's largest social network can be leveraged for your business. And it's written by one of the few people out there who actually has shown companies how to succeed on Facebook. If you're trying to leverage Facebook to reach your customers, this book should be on your shelf. It's on mine.

> —JASON FALLS, Social Media Explorer

Chris & Mari have provided the roadmap to help you succeed with Facebook marketing. This is the one book I'd recommend to anyone who needs to launch and measure a great social marketing campaign.

> —BRIAN GOLDFARB, Director of Product Marketing, Windows Azure, Microsoft Corporation

Mari and Chris take the very complex and sophisticated paradigm of social marketing and present it in a way that anyone can understand and, more importantly, put into practice.

> —BRIAN SOLIS, best-selling author of *The End of Business As Usual* and *Engage*

Facebook®
Marketing
An Hour a Day

Second Edition

Chris Treadaway

Mari Smith

John Wiley & Sons, Inc.

Senior Acquisitions Editor: WILLEM KNIBBE
Development Editor: KIM BEAUDET
Production Editor: LIZ BRITTEN
Copy Editor: KIM WIMPSETT
Editorial Manager: PETE GAUGHAN
Production Manager: TIM TATE
Vice President and Executive Group Publisher: RICHARD SWADLEY
Vice President and Publisher: NEIL EDDE
Book Designer: FRANZ BAUMHACKL
Compositor: CHRIS GILLESPIE, HAPPENSTANCE TYPE-O-RAMA
Proofreaders: LOUISE WATSON AND SCOTT KLEMP; WORD ONE, NEW YORK
Indexer: TED LAUX
Project Coordinator, Cover: KATHERINE CROCKER
Cover Designer: RYAN SNEED
Cover Image: © DMITRIY FILIPPOV/ISTOCKPHOTO

Dear Reader,

Thank you for choosing *Facebook Marketing: An Hour a Day, Second Edition*. This book is part of a family of premium-quality Sybex books, all of which are written by outstanding authors who combine practical experience with a gift for teaching.

Sybex was founded in 1976. More than 30 years later, we're still committed to producing consistently exceptional books. With each of our titles, we're working hard to set a new standard for the industry. From the paper we print on, to the authors we work with, our goal is to bring you the best books available.

I hope you see all that reflected in these pages. I'd be very interested to hear your comments and get your feedback on how we're doing. Feel free to let me know what you think about this or any other Sybex book by sending me an email at nedde@wiley.com. If you think you've found a technical error in this book, please visit http://sybex.custhelp.com. Customer feedback is critical to our efforts at Sybex.

Best regards,

Neil Edde
Vice President and Publisher
Sybex, an imprint of Wiley

For my wife, Kim Toda Treadaway, whose support and encouragement mean everything to me. I love you!

—Chris

For our reader—sit's an honor to blaze this trail with you!

—Mari

👁 Acknowledgments

Writing several hundred pages of content on any topic is a huge undertaking by itself. But it's even tougher when it's about something that changes as rapidly and as often as Facebook. The authors, editors, and supporting staff have to respond on a dime to changes, updates, and new issues that arise. Kudos to Mari Smith for again being a thorough collaborator on this book. Her expertise far exceeds the celebrity status she's earned over the years.

Special thanks also goes out to the world-class team at Wiley that I've had the pleasure of working with for five years now. In particular, I should mention Ellen Gerstein, Jennifer Webb, Katie Feltman, and others at Wiley who, among other things, encouraged me to write this book. It was a great and humbling honor to be asked to write the second edition. I'd also like to thank the editorial staff at Sybex. Without hands-on help from Willem Knibbe, Kim Beaudet, Gary Schwartz, Pete Gaughan, Liz Britten, Kim Wimpsett, and countless others, this book would have been obsolete by the time it hit the shelves!

I'd like to thank all the people at the hundreds of clients that I've supported in the years that I've done consulting work. Interactions with you have made this book a better product and a true "practitioner's guide" to using Facebook for marketing purposes.

Thank you as well to everyone who contributed ideas to this book—either through collaboration or via participation in our sidebar Q&As. Your unique perspectives are the lifeblood of the industry, and you're continuing to lead the way. Keep it up!

I'd be remiss if I didn't thank the different people who have taught me valuable school and life lessons along the way. In particular, I'd like to thank teachers from St. George Catholic School in Baton Rouge, Louisiana, and Northwest Rankin High School in Brandon, Mississippi. They all, in their own ways, instilled enthusiasm, confidence, and (tough as it may have been at times) grace in me throughout the formative years of high school.

In addition, I'd like to thank friends and colleagues for being supportive—each in your own way: Tommy Perkins, Rick Wittenbraker, Van Baker, Joseph Guthrie, Barry Willett, Damon Cali, Michelle Cali, Jason Chenault, Josh Jones-Dilworth, Isaac Leonard, Jason Jaynes, Alec Cooper, John Cooper, Kathryn Rose, Kris Fuehr, Lauren Lamb, T.J. McLarty, and Q Beck. Thanks to you all.

Special thanks also to my business partner at Polygraph Media, Robert Starek, who has been patient and supportive despite long hours of writing, editing, and improving this book. And also to Paul Groepler, advisor and friend, who is never too busy to talk. That means the world to me.

Most importantly, I'd like to thank my parents and grandparents for raising me in a healthy, happy, and supportive home; without your sacrifices for and undying confidence in me, I'd be ill-equipped to deal with life's difficulties, and I wouldn't be the person I am today. I'd like to thank my wife, Kimberly Toda Treadaway, for her love, support, and patience. I love you dearly. And finally, I'd like to thank God for all the opportunities and blessings he shares with me every day.

—CHRIS

⤫ ⤫

Thank you so much to my wonderful coauthor, Chris Treadaway—it's truly a joy to know you! I'm also grateful to the amazing team at Sybex (especially Willem Knibbe).

A special thank-you to my friends and fellow social media professionals, whom I admire greatly for setting quality standards in the industry: Michael Stelzner, Gary Vaynerchuk, Chris Brogan, Guy Kawasaki, Jeremiah Owyang, Ann Handley, Scott Monty, Robert Scoble, Neal Schaffer, Viveka Von Rosen, Marsha Collier, Steve Rubel, Charlene Li, Amy Porterfield, Brian Solis, Lee Odden, Pete Cashmore, David Armano, Erik Qualman, Liz Strauss, Jason Falls, Jay Baer, Dave Kerpen, Louis Gray, Jesse Stay, Nick O'Neill, Laura Fitton, Paul Dunay, and Beth Kanter.

My deepest gratitude goes to my spiritual mentor, Esperanza Universal, who continues to support me unconditionally in all my endeavors.

And, to my dear Facebook and Twitter community—it is a true blessing to be connected with you.

If I missed anyone here, it was unintentional; send me a tweet or write on my Facebook Wall, and I'll happily acknowledge you!

—MARI

About the Authors

Chris Treadaway is the founder and CEO of Polygraph Media, a social media data mining and analytics company. Prior to his work at Polygraph Media, Chris spent almost four years at Microsoft Corporation, where he was the group product manager for web strategy in the Developer division and the business lead on the first launch of Silverlight. Chris has worked in the Internet marketing field for more than 15 years and in two other startups, Infraworks and Stratfor, where he built the company's first portal, which was profiled in *Time Magazine* and other international publications. He has a master's degree in business from the University of Texas at Austin and a bachelor's degree from Louisiana State University. He blogs regularly about entrepreneurship and social media issues at http://treadaway.typepad.com and on Twitter at www.twitter.com/ctreada.

Mari Smith is one of the world's leading Facebook marketing experts and social media marketing consultants. *Fast Company* describes Mari as "A veritable engine of personal branding, a relationship marketing whiz and the Pied Piper of the Online World." Both Forbes and Dun & Bradstreet Credibility recently named Mari as one of the top 10 social media influencers in the world. She is also an in-demand social media keynote speaker and trainer, and she runs her own vibrant social media marketing agency, specializing in helping businesses of all sizes increase their profits through social media integration. Mari has an impressive online network comprised of well over half a million fans, friends, followers, and subscribers. Connect with Mari on her website and blog at http://marismith.com, on her popular Facebook page at http://facebook.com/marismith, on her active Facebook Timeline at http://facebook.com/maris, and on Twitter at http://twitter.com/marismith.

Contents

Introduction

Over the past seven years, the social media business has grown from a sleepy, sophomoric way for college kids to communicate to the future of how people all over the world will share information and bring their offline lives online. It's incredible to see how much the Internet business has evolved as a result of Facebook, Twitter, Google+, and the many startups that are currently jockeying for position in order to advance our experiences further. I (Chris) originally took a great interest in social media in business school at the University of Texas in 2003. A classmate, Cory Garner, and I had just heard of this new thing called LinkedIn, and we were instantly captivated by the possibilities. Social relationships were becoming more and more transparent, and they were moving online. We worked like crazy to encourage classmates to get on the social network. Our fear, at the time, was that we would lose the opportunity to get people to sign up, and in so doing we'd lose our captive audience. We succeeded in the "membership drive" of sorts, but it didn't turn out to be that important in the end. We had no appreciation for the fact that social media was a tsunami that would eventually encourage just about everyone to create a profile and establish relationships—even the Luddites in our class.

That same tsunami hit consumers in 2006 with MySpace and later with Facebook. I was at Microsoft running Web 2.0 developer strategy and messaging when Facebook had a mere 40 million users. Even then, it was apparent to me that this Facebook thing was poised to redefine the Web, Internet advertising, and possibly even web development. I worked aggressively inside Microsoft to shed light on the new paradigm. I looked around and saw a variety of business opportunities in and leveraging social media. So, I left Microsoft to start a new company in March 2008, where I could spend all my time thinking of new business opportunities and helping clients with their social media problems.

Over the past several years, I've interacted with countless entrepreneurs, visionaries, and managers and executives of large corporations in an attempt to learn about how people view and want to utilize social media. That experience alone has been rewarding—the best and brightest people from a variety of disciplines are redefining the Web in their own little ways with social media at the forefront of those changes.

Interestingly, since leaving Microsoft, I've also reviewed and edited books on Facebook and social media marketing. The one common theme across all these books is that, to date, they've all been heavy on the ideas, the theory, and the trends that social media brings to bear. That's great, but now there are perhaps far too many books that explain social media marketing from an "academic" perspective.

Conversely, there aren't many books that actually tell people how to conduct a social media marketing campaign. I looked around for books that would help people with the day-to-day tasks associated with Facebook marketing, and I was disappointed to find very little that would help a panicked middle manager navigate the breadth of the Facebook platform. So, I had a quick conversation with the people at Wiley, who I had helped with their Facebook presence, and next thing you know, I, along with Facebook marketing expert Mari Smith, was writing this book for Wiley.

It is in that sense that this book is written strictly as a "practitioner's guide" to Facebook marketing. Mari and I wanted to get down on paper all the tips and tricks that we employ when marketing products and services for ourselves or for clients. We specifically did not want to create a feature walk-through like those that appear in so many other Facebook marketing books. We also did not want to write another book about the shift to social media, what is possible in the future, or what it means for society. This book is about the here and now and what you can do for your organization using Facebook today.

This book is a collection of thoughts and ideas from hours upon hours of experience spent with clients who have different interests, different motivations, and different levels of expertise. While it's an impossible task to cover everything to everyone's satisfaction, I think we've done a good job summarizing what it takes to be successful. Ideally, this book sparks your creativity so you can use the tools and processes to advance your marketing goals.

This book is a summary of all the little things necessary to make a marketing campaign work. It's specifically for people who get a mandate from a manager, investor, or whoever who says, "This Facebook thing is important—go figure out how to make it work for us!" Those can be stressful situations, and the last thing you need is pressure along with a vague directive and no idea of how to make it work. This book does not provide the creativity necessary to resonate with your customers in clever and unique ways, although we do provide examples in different parts of the book to give you ideas and show you how other people have solved tough problems.

—CHRIS

I will never forget the defining moment in my life when I pulled up www.facebook.com in my browser. It was May 4, 2007 (I know the exact date thanks to Facebook's new Timeline format!). I was a bit of a holdout at first, because I had been using all manner of social sites for several years prior without much real traction—sites such as Ryze.com, Ecademy.com, LinkedIn.com, Plaxo.com, and Friendster.com. I never did "get" MySpace.com; in fact, my head would hurt whenever I visited the site with all the wildly animated images and morass of jumbled-up content. Plus, the teens and 20-something audience wasn't a match for my networking objectives.

Now, when I say traction, I mean in the sense of yielding any business results. Granted, I probably wasn't really optimizing my time on LinkedIn back then. See, I'm a very gregarious person and am an excellent networker. (In Malcolm Gladwell's book *The Tipping Point*, his definition of a "connector" fits me to a *T*.) I never really felt the "need" to add an online social network to my marketing arsenal because I was so well connected in my local community.

However, like I say, Facebook for me was a defining moment. It was love at first sight. I had been asked by a friend of a friend if I'd like to beta-test a new Facebook application, called Podclass. Facebook had not long opened up its API to allow developers to create third-party apps. The founder of Podclass (Gary Gil, who has since become a great friend) was ecstatic to have just been accepted as a Facebook app. So, in order to beta-test Podclass, I had to create a Facebook account. Well, something magical happened that day: I loved the beautiful, simple layout; the white space; and the ease with which I could instantly befriend people whom I'd long admired, people whose books I had on my shelves, and people whose seminars I had attended. Suddenly well-known leaders, authors, speakers, musicians, and even a few celebrities were my Facebook friends, and we began interacting on a regular basis. I was like a big kid in a candy store. I couldn't believe that we all suddenly had this common platform about which everyone was extremely excited and could hardly wait to spend time there. I instantly became Facebook's top evangelist!

Interestingly enough, right from that very beginning moment, I have always seen Facebook from a strategic business point of view. Because, quite simply, there was life before Facebook. We connected with friends, family, and other loved ones via phone, email, Skype, even regular mail, and, of course, in person. Sure, Facebook has helped spark millions of personal friendships around the globe. There have been more family reunions and school reunions in the last six years than there have in the previous 60 years...because of Facebook! But, just like the line in the movie *The Social Network* goes, "The Internet is in ink, not pencil." So, I'm very cautious (and strategic) about what I share online, even under the tightest of privacy settings. (I belong to and run many secret Facebook groups, including one for my immediate family, so we can connect "behind the scenes" without being concerned about who's reading what on our Walls.)

There's absolutely no doubt that Facebook has fundamentally changed the way we communicate and do business on the planet. It has become part of our daily habits. Wake up, brush teeth, shower, check Facebook. (OK, for many people, those daily habits are in reverse order!) And, when something becomes an ingrained part of our day-to-day lives, there is a massive opportunity for you—as a businessperson and a marketer—to position yourself as the number-one choice within your industry in front of your target audience during prime time. This is very exciting news. Throughout this book, Chris and I will lead you through all you need to know to consistently capitalize on the world's number-one social network. We've seen a massive amount of change and growth on Facebook over even the past couple of years, which is why we're thrilled to bring you the second version of our popular book!

—MARI

Who Should Read This Book

This book is for anyone who is charged with the responsibility of owning some part of Facebook marketing for an organization, whether it be a business, a nonprofit, a government agency, and so on:

- A middle manager who needs help executing a marketing campaign on Facebook
- An employee who needs ideas for how to best utilize Facebook for marketing purposes
- A business owner who wants to engage better with customers but doesn't have a lot of time to learn on their own
- A manager or executive who needs to know the possibilities and the challenges that employees face when executing campaigns

Much of the content of the book is geared to the tactics of building, measuring, and monitoring a Facebook marketing campaign. People who are not directly responsible for executing a campaign will also learn about the possibilities of Facebook and other social media products.

What You Will Learn

Facebook has attracted almost a billion users in less than a decade. This book will help you learn how to tap into this wealth of consumers for whatever marketing purposes you have. You may need to drive traffic to a website. You may want to use Facebook to drive awareness of another type of marketing campaign. You may just want to get the word out about your own Facebook presence in what is an increasingly crowded space. This book will teach you how to mine Facebook for the very people you need in order to have a successful marketing campaign, regardless of the goals.

What You Need

Although we cover Internet marketing basics throughout the book, it will be easier for you to pick up the skills and demands of effective Facebook marketing if you have a basic understanding of Internet marketing metrics and measurement. The only other thing you need is something to market—a product, a service, a brand, and so on. Without it, you won't be able to run a real campaign.

What Is Covered in This Book

Facebook Marketing: An Hour a Day is organized to turn you into a social media marketing powerhouse while attracting people in your target market to your organization cost-effectively.

Chapter 1: Welcome to the Post-Social Era Walks you through the evolution of Internet marketing, from closed services to portals to search and now the mainstream adoption of social media.

Chapter 2: Understanding Social Media and Facebook Summarizes the Facebook phenomenon, the basics of how Facebook works, and how Facebook fits into the social media landscape.

Chapter 3: Marketing and Business Success on Facebook Helps you frame your approach in terms of how people approach social media and success metrics that will drive your work and inevitable adjustments to your campaign.

Chapter 4: Month 1: Create the Plan and Get Started The first chapter with "hour a day" content, designed to create your first Facebook marketing campaign. We also discuss social media policy, some basic organizational planning issues, how to use the Facebook profile for marketing, and other valuable features of Facebook.

Chapter 5: Month 2: Establish Your Corporate Presence with Pages Summarizes the primary means by which organizations create an "official presence" that is used to communicate with consumers and other target audiences. It includes information on content strategy, editorial calendar, posting multimedia content, page promotion, and culture.

Chapter 6: Month 3: Create Demand with Facebook Advertising Highlights the wide range of opportunities in promoting a website or Facebook presence using Facebook's self-serve advertising system, one of the best values in Internet marketing today.

Chapter 7: Month 4: Beyond Pages: Groups, Apps, Social Plugins, and Mobile Includes information on a variety of Facebook platform extensions and features designed to help the marketer create better and more engaging social network marketing campaigns.

Chapter 8: The Analytics of Facebook Summarizes all the metrics that are discussed throughout the book to make it easier for you to understand how to keep score and monitor success.

Chapter 9: Addressing Common Marketing Problems Offers solutions to the most common and toughest challenges that marketers have shared with us when promoting products and services on Facebook.

Chapter 10: Unique Facebook Marketing Scenarios Helps frame Facebook marketing opportunities, risks, and threats as they pertain to specific types of organizations that see the opportunities in Facebook.

Chapter 11: Facebook in the Future Presents interviews with the leading experts on social media about where they think Facebook is going.

Contacting the Authors, and Companion Websites

One thing is constant with Facebook and life alike: change. The Facebook platform is, to be polite, a moving target. The behavior of Facebook changes, the rules for communications/notifications and the News Feed change, and developers are allowed to do things today that they aren't allowed to do tomorrow. Facebook makes changes rapidly and sometimes without warning. So, if you'd like to keep up with these changes, feel free to check out one of the following:

www.facebookmarketinganhouraday.com is the Facebook fan page for this book and includes information on the book, links to destinations on Facebook, links to blog posts that will cover hot issues, contact information for any questions you may have, and information on vendors that can help you with sticky social media marketing problems.

www.twitter.com/FacebookMktg links to interesting articles and developments in Facebook marketing, case studies, statistics, and so on.

Sybex strives to keep you supplied with the latest tools and information you need for your work. Just visit www.sybex.com/go/facebookmarketinganhouraday, where we'll post additional content and updates that supplement this book if the need arises.

Final Note

This book is really one part social media marketing, one part Internet marketing. As hot of a topic as social media is, in some ways it is just the next iteration of things that have evolved over the past 15 years. It is Internet marketing with social context. Throughout the next several hundred pages, we will do our very best to help you learn what you need to know to succeed with Facebook marketing. Good luck, and let's get to work!

Welcome to the Post-Social Era

1

In just a few short years, we've gone from being relative neophytes in social media to having a vast majority of our personal connections and brand affinities captured in Facebook. Facebook is now the dominant player in social media. No other company comes close to Facebook's market penetration and the rich set of data it has been able to collect. However, the initial wonderment of social media is now gone. People have discovered long-lost friends, have met new people, and have interacted in ways that were unimaginable before Facebook. What was once cool is now mainstream. What does that mean for Facebook users and the marketers who are so desperate to reach a mass audience?

The Humble Beginnings of Social Marketing

We all enjoy life through a series of defining experiences with friends and loved ones in our social circles: people who attend the same school, live on the same street, work in the same company, or root for the same team. The jeans they wear, the phones they use, and the brands they favor to some extent encourage us to think positively or negatively about ourselves and others. They're consumers just like us, and they shape our thoughts and opinions in profound ways that we rarely notice.

All of us have been pitched products in advertising from memorable spokespeople: Spuds McKenzie, Joe Isuzu, the lonely Maytag repair guy, Max Headroom, the Geico gecko, and the California Raisins, to name just a few. We remember catchy sayings like "Every Kiss Begins with K(ay)," "Where's the Beef?," "Just Do It," and "Calgon, Take Me Away!" We respond to their honesty, their humor, and their brute force, and we take on their marketing messages by making subtle, subconscious changes to how we live, what we consume, and what we think.

For years, experiences were lived largely "offline." Our interactions have been in person, in front of a television, or through headphones. But times are different. Internet technologies and social media have enhanced our online experiences. We enjoy interactivity, video, audio, and pictures just as much from computer screens as from offline experiences. We want to learn, share, and interact from the comfort of our computers and mobile devices more than ever.

For me (Chris), it started when my parents bought a Commodore 64 in 1984 along with a 300 baud modem. Connecting to other users in the "online world" was a novel concept at the time—it was 1984, after all! But I wanted to experience the future firsthand. My first taste of social computing was on a service called Quantum Link (see Figure 1.1). Quantum Link was one of the very first online services that combined electronic mail, public file sharing, and games. It was fascinating. To play games, I didn't need to get permission from my parents to invite people over. I could do it from the comfort of my own bedroom and at any time of the day or night. The only problem was the pesky usage fees. Mom and Dad didn't seem too excited about a big bill for "plus" services. Nonetheless, I got my first taste of social computing on Quantum Link.

Figure 1.1 Quantum Link home page

Online Services v1

Three major competitors—Prodigy, CompuServe, and America Online (AOL)—evolved over the following years. All three took online services to an entirely different level with improved user interfaces made possible by advances in computer hardware and operating systems. Some of the first real-time online services were made available via Prodigy (a joint venture between CBS, IBM, and Sears) in the early 1990s—news, sports scores, weather, and so on. Prodigy also offered premium content from the Mobil Travel Guide and Zagat's Restaurant Ratings, to name a few. But perhaps most important, Prodigy had a very well-integrated message board and email services that allowed people to meet, discover similar interests, and communicate with one another. These were the "killer apps" behind the growth of the Internet in the early 1990s. They were, in effect, the first generation of modern social networks. Figure 1.2 shows the Prodigy login screen, which may be familiar to early pioneers of the Internet era.

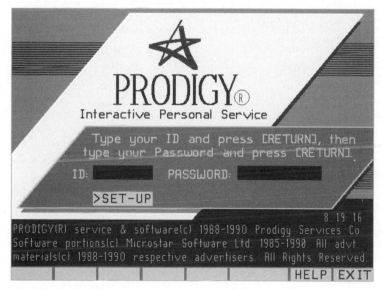

Figure 1.2 Prodigy login screen

While Prodigy, CompuServe, and AOL were pioneers in the online services business, they were not particularly interesting channels for e-commerce or Internet marketing. Most notable was Prodigy's classified ad experiment with *USA Today*, whereby Prodigy offered advertisers the opportunity to reach parts of the Prodigy user base for as little as $60/month for an approximately 250-character text advertisement. Prodigy also made screen space available to advertisers through *teasers*, or what would be viewed today as banner advertising, at the bottom of each screen. If a consumer was interested in the advertisement, they could click the advertisement to get more information via a larger version of the ad and then buy the product or service being offered. But neither advertising option became sufficiently popular and effective for Prodigy or any other online service. Internet advertising was only a $55 million industry world-wide in 1995; it was just too early for people to respond well to the advertising of goods and services on the Internet. Compare that to the $25.7 billion Internet market-ing business in 2009. Because Internet advertising was so ineffective early on, Prodigy, CompuServe, and AOL focused primarily on growing consumer subscription revenue by increasing subscribers in the mid-1990s.

Emergence of the World Wide Web

The proliferation of proprietary first-generation online services came to a stunning halt with the emergence of Mosaic, the first widely available web browser. In 1994, with Mosaic and a web connection via an Internet service provider (ISP), a user could spend an unlimited amount of time surfing the Internet and sending an unlimited number of email messages. This was a departure from existing services that relied upon tiered hourly service rates and other usage upcharges for profitability. Fueled by the wealth of new online services, applications, and a proliferation of websites, consumers moved to the World Wide Web en masse starting in 1995.

As users flocked to the Internet, the first experiments in Internet marketing were already underway. *Hotwired*, an online web magazine, was the first company to sell banner advertising to corporations, in late 1994. Figure 1.3 shows the first banner ad ever sold, an AT&T advertisement. Banner ads were long, rectangular advertisements, usually 468 pixels wide by 60 pixels tall, with information and/or graphics designed to entice a reader into clicking them to visit another website. They were sold for a flat rate per 1,000 impressions or views, which is now referred to as *cost per mil* (CPM). Around the same time, a number of experiments popped up to guarantee clicks and not just impressions. The idea was that advertisers wanted visitors and not just views.

Figure 1.3 The first banner ad ever displayed on the Internet

The mid-1990s were revolutionary for the Internet, as millions of people got online. The possibilities were endless, as were questions about how advertising could be used to build new businesses, new opportunities, and new communities. How would people interact with each other? How much would the Internet change purchase behav-ior? How would business be conducted differently in the age of the Internet? What new business opportunities would be possible? All of the possibilities led to an unprec-edented level of entrepreneurial activity from both new companies and established cor-porations. Everyone wanted an opportunity to participate and reap the spoils.

As a result, the Internet advertising business grew tremendously through ban-ner advertising. Sites could devote a certain amount of space to banners to generate revenue. It was a good deal for advertisers as well because, at the time, it was the best way to reach people and get them to learn about another site on the Internet or a product, service, or other offer. For no less than five years, banner advertising was the best Internet marketing opportunity available to people who wanted to connect with consumers on the Web. This dynamic led the developers of many early popular websites to turn their sites into *portals*, that is, sites that would help users get a wide range of information that would be helpful in a personal and sometimes professional context. By building an effective portal, a company could create a thriving and growing web property that would generate revenue and profits through banner advertising.

Search and the Decline of Banner Ads

The number of websites continued to proliferate well beyond people's expectations. Consumers needed a way to sort through all the noise to find exactly what they needed at any given time. A number of companies built sites to help with this exact problem. Publishers eager to cash in on the craze even created books that offered all the links to the Web you could possibly want—in *print*, of all things! Yahoo! indexed sites by subject matter and added a rudimentary search function that helped users find resources quickly. Other sites didn't rely on a proprietary directory but instead depended on scanning the full text of web pages to determine the relevance of a particular search term. Popular search engines from this period included Magellan, Excite, Inktomi, AltaVista, and Lycos. Later, other search engines, such as MetaCrawler and Dogpile, emerged, combining search results from individual search engines to provide more accurate and complete results to users. Over time, these search engines became the "starting point" for many users. Rather than logging into a portal like Go.com or MSN to get information, users began to frequent search engines.

Before long, it became apparent that users preferred an effective, powerful search engine to all other means of finding relevant information on the Internet. Enter Google. I (Chris) remember the first time I used Google in early 1999. I was stunned by how it so easily and quickly pointed me to the exact information I needed at the time and, more important, how consistently effective the search engine was regardless of the search term I used. It took just a few tries for me to realize that Google was revolutionary. Like a lot of other Internet users, I ditched every other search engine I had used before and converted to Google. Contrary to popular belief, Google did not immediately revolutionize Internet advertising. It was primarily a great search engine for several years while the company experimented with a variety of business models.

The world continued to buy and sell banner advertising as the primary means for generating demand on the Internet, although banner advertising certainly peaked in the late 1990s for a few reasons. For one, the proliferation of websites meant that the number of advertising options increased significantly. More options = lower prices. Negotiating power shifted from the publisher to the advertiser, who now had more available options for ad spending. Second, the novelty of Internet advertising wore off to some extent. Click-through rates on banners dropped from as high as 2% to well below 0.5%, and with that drop came a reduction in prices. No longer were companies blindly sinking thousands of dollars into banner advertising. Advertisers demanded results, which increasingly worked against banner advertising. Third, consumers experienced some level of banner ad fatigue. These ads were everywhere on the Internet by 1999, which also made them somewhat easy to ignore. This created an environment ripe for the emergence of a new, effective, and trackable way to reach consumers.

The Rise of Google and Click-Through Ads

Around this time, Google emerged as perhaps the world's greatest and most accurate search engine. In just a few years, it launched a search engine that was superior to rivals such as HotBot, AltaVista, Lycos, and others. It quickly gained market share but, ironically, launched an impression-based advertising business in 2000.

Advertisers were tired of spending a lot of money on ineffective banner ads, and consumers were ignoring them. Realizing this, Google abandoned its impression-based advertising program in favor of experiments with *click-through advertising*: text-based ads for which the advertiser would pay only if a user clicked the ad (see Figure 1.4). This invention was named Google AdWords, and the rest is history.

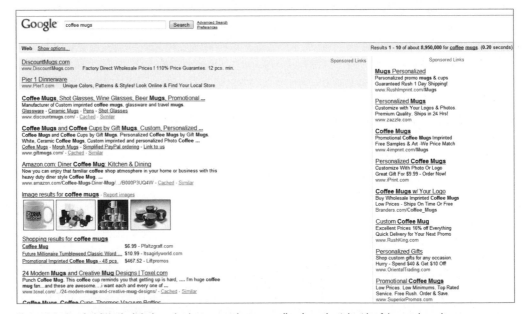

Figure 1.4 Google AdWords click-through ads appear at the top as well as down the right side of the search results pages.

Google AdWords was a self-serve advertising service similar to services offered around the same time by competitor GoTo.com, later renamed Overture by Yahoo! Advertisers would enter the text for a relevant ad that adhered to style guidelines and character limitations. The advertiser would then add the search terms that would trigger these ads, along with the highest bid they would be willing to pay for the click. The final step was setting a daily budget; without a budget, a lot of money could be spent on these ads! Using an automated auction system, Google would serve ads based on the total bid and the amount remaining in the budget for each bidder.

It may seem simple now, but this was a revolutionary shift in Internet advertising for a few reasons. First, an advertiser could effectively guarantee traffic to a website by simply bidding high enough and devoting enough budget on a daily basis to the advertisement. Now this wasn't particularly difficult in 2002—many click-through ads cost as little as a nickel apiece, so 100 new visitors to website per day could cost as little as $5. Not a bad deal. More important, however, Google realized that the folks clicking these ads weren't just any users. They were highly targeted users because they had searched for a specific term in a search engine. This was in stark contrast to banner ads, which generally were not targeted to specific users looking for specific things. In summary, Google took an increasingly large audience and made it available to advertisers on a relatively inexpensive, self-serve basis. It was pure genius.

As with any auction model, prices increased significantly as more people jumped in. I (Chris) remember first getting into Google AdWords in the fall of 2002 with my third startup, a lead generation business that found qualified leads for consumer products from Google. I could buy tons of clicks, send these visitors to a website where I qualified them and converted them to leads, and then resell them to customers who wanted incremental business for 5 to 10 times the cost of generating the leads. In less than a year, however, I started to see the bids increase substantially as larger corporations, ad agencies, and other entrepreneurs discovered this "new" opportunity. This trend continued for years as Google maintained and grew its search share. From 2003 to 2008, Google was the one place to go to tap into large numbers of Internet users interested in a particular subject matter.

The Emergence of Social Networks

As Google asserted its click-through dominance, a number of social networks began to emerge and reach mainstream consumer audiences. There wasn't anything particularly new about social networks. Online communities had formed at every turn in the evolution of the Internet, dating back to well before the emergence of the World Wide Web. The difference was that, by 2003, people had grown increasingly comfortable with interacting with one another on the Internet and, at times, in plain view of other users. Social networks, after all, work better with a larger number of engaged users sharing more and more details about themselves.

The first notable companies from the social networking era were Classmates h.com and Friendster. Classmates.com allowed people to associate themselves with certain graduating classes to keep in touch with friends from various schools and points in their lives. The concept of *profiles* on Classmates.com was very basic, and many features of the site were ultimately hidden behind a paid subscription.

Friendster emerged six years after the launch of Classmates.com, and it exposed more features to users. Friendster was the first social network to integrate the profile concept successfully, whereby a user could enter personal data, preferences, and so on. Friendster grew aggressively just after its launch in 2002, but it endured a number of technical problems that disenfranchised early adopters and new users alike. Further, Friendster exposed profile data and actions to people within several degrees of separation from a user, which later, more-successful social networks did not do. Despite the fact that neither Classmates.com nor Friendster achieved mainstream worldwide success, both sites continue to operate today, each with a large user base. Table 1.1 summarizes the top social networks from 2000 to 2009—note how the early pioneers have faded as Facebook now dominates the social media market.

▶ **Table 1.1** Popular social networks 2009 vs. 2012

Social network	# users in July 2009	Audience
Facebook	350 million	800 million active users (have returned in the last 30 days)
Twitter	75 million	More than 300 million
LinkedIn	55 million	135 million
Friendster	90 million	116 million as of April 2011
Google+	Did not exist	62 million (December 2011)
Classmates.com	40+ million	10.3 million active users (December 2011)

Source: Official statistics released by each company

MySpace, in many ways, was the beneficiary of Friendster's inability to turn into a mainstream global phenomenon. The service launched in mid-2003, not as a new startup but rather as a side project of parent company eUniverse. With support and resources from a larger company, MySpace was able to scale from a handful of users to several hundred thousand very quickly. MySpace and Friendster had many of the same features, such as profiles, friends, blogs, and comments, but MySpace did not always share data with friends of friends. A direct friend connection was required to view specific information about a person. Care over sensitive data created an environment in which users were much more willing to add personal information to profiles. MySpace also allowed users to customize their profiles with different types of information, special layouts, and unique background images.

All of this had the impact of fueling the growth of MySpace in a relatively short time. MySpace went from launch in mid-2003 to being the most popular social network in the world in 2006. It became very popular with younger demographic groups in that period of time. comScore estimated that more than 60% of MySpace users were younger than 34 in 2005. As such, it became an essential marketing tool for musicians and bands that sought to engage with fans through the site. Over and above that, users of MySpace got more and more comfortable with the idea of living their lives online— communicating important life events and mundane details to friends on the Internet. See Figure 1.5 for a sample MySpace profile.

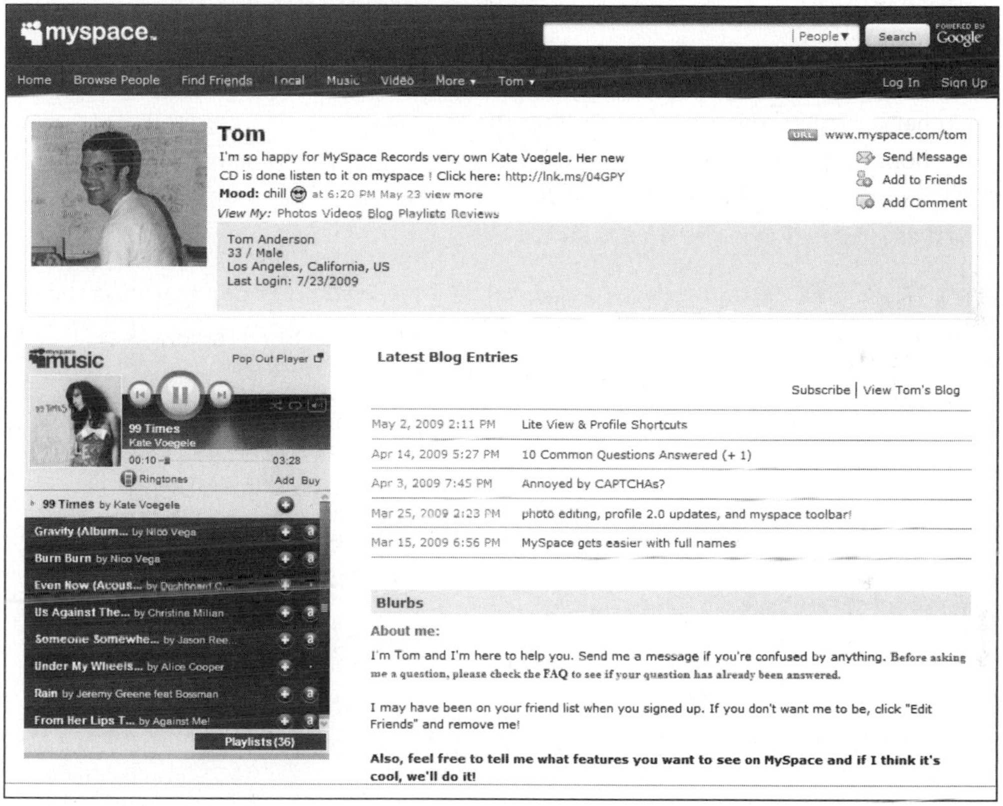

Figure 1.5 Sample MySpace profile

Having collected information about users through profile data, MySpace became the "next-generation" way to target consumers. Google pioneered learning about consumer interests through search. MySpace did the same in 2006 to 2008 through information such as profile data and interests. Think for a moment about the types of information available through a social media profile:

- Hometown
- Current home
- Date of birth
- Interests

- Likes and dislikes
- Hobbies
- Marital status
- Activities

- Education
- Political views

Access to this amount of information about a person is a marketer's dream! All of it was unlocked by social networks that created a relatively safe and fun environment in which people were encouraged to share this information willingly with friends. This data has not, to date, been used by advertisers to communicate directly with individual users, but it has been used in the aggregate to target groups of people interested in a certain thing. For example, through social networks, a marketer can do the following:

- Send banner ads to the 47,000 users interested in bowling in Ohio
- Update 2,809 fans of the (fictional) band Orangebunny Wahoos about a new concert tour
- Tell 13,287 single New Yorkers interested in kite flying about an upcoming event in Central Park

For more information on this phenomenon, read the following articles and blog posts. Clearly, privacy issues related to social data are becoming a big issue that the major platforms are encountering, both from consumers and governments.

`www.technewsworld.com/story/69158.html`

`www.danah.org/papers/talks/2010/WWW2010.html`

`http://bits.blogs.nytimes.com/2011/09/27/as-like-buttons-spread-so-do-facebooks-tentacles/`

Emergence of Facebook

While MySpace continued to grow between 2004 and 2008, Facebook emerged as its chief rival in dominating the consumer social network industry worldwide. Conceptually, Facebook was very similar; it had just about the same profile data as its predecessors. But it did not allow data and profile backgrounds to be customized by users as MySpace did. This had the impact of providing some standardization to data and the overall experience of browsing profiles. Facebook did offer users a rich set of tools to limit or expose data to only certain people: friends or people in their particular networks. But aside from this, the design philosophy behind Facebook was to make user experiences consistent. Users could expect similar data and the same look and feel when browsing profiles.

Facebook initially launched at Harvard, where its founders originally used it to encourage classmates to get to know each other better. Check out Figure 1.6 for an early Facebook home page. At that time, many colleges actually provided printed "face books" to students that included biographical information, interests, areas of study, and so on. After getting half of the undergraduate class at Harvard to create profiles, Facebook expanded to other Ivy League schools. The company later expanded to other colleges and universities, high schools, and finally major corporations before releasing to the general public in late 2006. This strategy of exclusivity in the early years gave Facebook the advantage of gaining critical mass within networks of people who were likely to keep in touch with one another. A high concentration of people interacting inside Facebook provided great insight into what people would do and how they would share information with one another; most important, it provided an idea of the features and enhancements that would help Facebook compete with rivals. Later, the early growth of Facebook would be chronicled in the acclaimed movie *The Social Network*. It's a fascinating look at how the company was founded and how it dealt with growth in its early days.

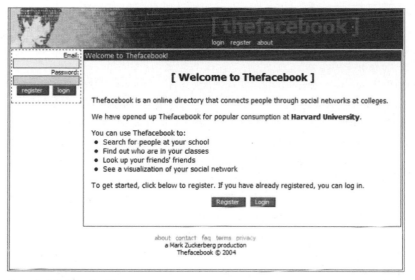

Figure 1.6 Early Facebook home page

The battle between Facebook and MySpace became yet another chapter in a long line of "Coke vs. Pepsi" battles throughout late 2006 to 2008. In early years, MySpace had a loyal following in younger demographics, but Facebook slowly gained the attention of college students. The visual customization aspects of MySpace made some profiles very difficult to read, while the lack of data standardization meant that users could say anything they wanted without necessarily making it readable for the viewer. Others believe that the Facebook/MySpace preference fell along class lines. One such critic was danah boyd, a fellow at the Berkman Center for Internet and Society. In her June 2007 essay, "Viewing American Class Divisions through Facebook and MySpace," Boyd argues that Facebook's origins in Ivy League schools and its original "by invitation only" method for signing up new users set it down a path to be the preference for affluent, upper-class early adopters.

www.danah.org/papers/essays/ClassDivisions.html

MySpace was positioned as a place for young people interested in bands and those who were not particularly popular or into extracurricular activities in high school and college. MySpace users were not likely to become Facebook users because their friends were not on that network, and vice versa. *Forbes* and other major publications covered Boyd's observations in great detail. It was, and remains, a compelling argument.

www.forbes.com/2007/07/20/facebook-myspace-internet-tech-cz_ccm_0723class.html

After expanding beyond education, Facebook slowly began to eat into MySpace's market share for a few reasons. Applications such as Photos, Notes, and Gifts were easy to understand and very well executed—and all three helped encourage users to interact with one another. Status updates and News Feeds gave users the opportunity to keep in touch with friends passively. Perhaps the most important development, however, was the May 2007 release of the Facebook Developer Platform, a framework that allowed developers to write custom applications that ran inside Facebook.com and took advantage of each person's unique *social graph*; that is, the broad collection of people, places, and interests that make us individuals (more on this in chapter 2). All of a sudden Facebook made its audience available to third-party developers. This opportunity led to a quick proliferation of new applications on Facebook. Games were most popular, but all sorts of applications were created over the subsequent 12 months. Two main things contributed to Facebook's success in this arena: valuable supporting applications and the elegantly executed strategy to encourage developers to write applications for Facebook. Finally, in early 2009, Facebook overtook MySpace in several key usage metrics and was poised to be the dominant player in social networking.

The Social Media Revolution Takes Over

What a difference two years makes!

When we started writing the first edition of *Facebook Marketing: An Hour a Day*, Facebook had fewer than 150 million users worldwide. It was taking the world by storm as an interesting and innovative website where people could share details about their lives with each other. Social media, as an industry, was in its early days, and few companies were actively using it for marketing purposes. Its user base had just eclipsed that of MySpace, its chief rival, and the company had turned down a number of big acquisition offers, most notably from Yahoo! A number of us who had worked in and around social media thought Facebook was going to be successful, but the world hadn't quite realized it yet.

Contrast all of that to the present day. Facebook is *the* dominant social media property in the world. Competitors such as Orkut, MySpace, Hi5, Friendster, and others either are out of business, are about to be out of business, or have focused their businesses in other areas. Twitter is a distant second place, and it has not significantly evolved in the social graph itself, focusing its attention on real-time data and feedback from the crowd. A cottage industry of next-generation social networks, such as Foursquare, Gowalla, and Color, have emerged around location and photo sharing specifically—two mere features of Facebook. No company seems to be well positioned to mount a serious challenge to Facebook. In a sense, Facebook is currently the "winner takes all" of social media.

Facebook has more than 150 million users just in the United States, has more than 200 million on Facebook Mobile, and is closing in on 1 *billion* users worldwide. It is easily the world's most addictive web property—users spend hours of time on Facebook every month, and the numbers just keep on improving. In fact, there is now an official disorder for people addicted to Facebook!

> http://socialtimes.com/facebook-addiction-disorder-the-6-symptoms-of-f-a-d_b60403

Many businesses are now putting a link to their Facebook page on television advertisements and marketing collateral. Think about it—major brands (including some of the more conservative marketers in the world) are diverting attention *away* from their websites and pointing people to Facebook! This is despite the fact that, in a lot of cases, the company websites have taken years of investment and are much more mature than their Facebook Pages. This only makes sense because, from what we hear, businesses are diverting significant amounts of money to social media investments today. Businesses are attracted to the promise of the social graph and, more importantly, the audiences of consumers who spend hours each day on Facebook.

Let's look for a moment at usage patterns over time on Facebook. As time has passed, the masses of Facebook users have used the site more and more. As of June 2011, users are on Facebook an astonishing 15+ hours per month. This is a function of a few things—a bigger network of people, more businesses doing more things on Facebook, social plug-ins that help people share web experiences inside Facebook, and social gaming. The last two are phenomena that have really taken hold over the last few years. Social plug-ins make it easy for people to see what their friends are doing across both the Web and Facebook. Social games help many of us pass the time and escape into our own little world of our online family, our NFL franchise, our farms, and our virtual worlds. You could very much make the case that Facebook wouldn't be as powerful as it is today without these extensions that had little to do with Mark Zuckerberg's original vision. But then again, what startup stays true to exactly what it set out to do from the beginning?

Those of you who read the first edition of *Facebook Marketing: An Hour a Day* may also remember that we talked about how important it is for major technologies to own "the first place people go" on the Internet to start their days. Now, more than

55% of Facebook users log in every day—it isn't inconceivable to think that Facebook is how people start their days. People are using the Facebook experience to read articles of interest to them, to find out the details of their friends' mundane lives, to plan social events, and to keep up with their farms on Farmville. Facebook is the social "operating system," much like Microsoft Windows was the original operating system that democratized the computer revolution and like Google was the search "operating system" that brought about the search revolution.

The Technology Evolution

As a technology, Facebook has morphed from a social media website to critical social infrastructure. Not long ago, Facebook was merely Facebook.com—just another destination on the World Wide Web. Now it is not only the most addictive web property in the world but also the most pervasive.

How? Before our very eyes, Facebook transformed itself into a true social platform. At the f8 conference in April 2010, Facebook made two big announcements that really set the stage for this—the collection of personal profile information in the "Open Graph" and the availability of Facebook social plug-ins for web developers to use to integrate social features into existing websites.

These were, in effect, an extension of Facebook Connect—the company's first release of social tools in May 2008 that allowed developers to create applications that would interact with Facebook. But the Open Graph and social plug-ins were far easier to integrate. To some degree, this extension of Facebook was a lot less intimidating to users, because people had become accustomed to sharing personal information and activity on social networks over the preceding few years. Cultural norms had shifted with the times.

At the f8 conference, Facebook CEO Mark Zuckerberg called these changes "the most transformative thing we've ever done for the Web," and he was probably right. The ambition behind these moves was to map activity taking place on the Web broadly and combine it seamlessly with the Facebook experience and profile data. Facebook was banking on the simplicity of this strategy and the allure of its large audience to attract companies and large organizations that operated websites with significant reach.

The strategy undoubtedly worked. Marketers accepted social plug-ins as a way to extend actions taken by its users on websites to Facebook, and vice versa. Developers liked how the simplicity of the new changes made their jobs easier. A developer no longer needed to understand the idiosyncrasies of Facebook Connect to embed Facebook comments, likes, and authentication into websites. Simplicity for web strategists and web developers was the key to accelerate adoption and become a real "standard." At the time of the writing of this book, more than seven million apps and websites had integrated Facebook using social plug-ins.

Social plug-ins are used by web developers to add comments and authentication and as a channel to encourage sharing of content and experiences with friends. Not surprisingly, almost two-thirds of all web traffic referrals in November 2011 came from Facebook, according to Net Applications, a marketing analytics company.

www.techweb.com/news/232200657/facebook-utterly-dominates-web-referrals.html

Facebook Mobile has more than 200 million users worldwide, making it arguably the world's second largest social network. Relatively young features such as the Wall, News Feed, Places, Credits, and Questions have become integral parts of the overall experience. Of course, there remains a thriving developer ecosystem of companies and individual developers building innovations with Facebook applications and social games.

The underreported story about Facebook, the technology marvel, is its server farm—its technical infrastructure. The scale necessary to collect the world's social graph reliably, power social plug-ins, and ensure site reliability is truly amazing. The only thing that rivals Facebook today in terms of technological scale is Google. Remember, there are millions of users on Facebook, many of whom spend hours a day on the site and a majority of whom log in every day. These users want Facebook to be up and running at all times—spikes in the day or server outages notwithstanding. Disruptions are bad for Facebook's business, which is why you don't hear about problems nearly as often as you hear about outages from other social networks.

Facebook has spent significant resources developing homegrown tools, technologies, and protocols based on open source software to handle the massive load of personal data, connections, photos, videos, and other content. It has hired some of the best programming talent in the world from Google, Microsoft, and other industry leaders. It's probably why there has been a bit of an ongoing war for tech talent. In 2011, it was announced that Google paid massive bonuses to top developers just to stay at the company, all in response to job offers from Facebook and Twitter. For those of you gearheads interested in learning more about Facebook's technical achievements, check out this article on Facebook's peer-to-peer data management system, Cassandra:

www.facebook.com/note.php?note_id=24413138919

In addition, Facebook operates server farms all around the world to handle the workload and make data redundant in case of hardware failure. It may seem a bit heavy-handed, but it takes quite a bit of infrastructure to store the world's social graph and make it reliable for the world's users and websites. *Time* magazine's photo essay of a Facebook server farm is probably the best illustration of everything that happens behind the scenes to ensure that your data and your social graph is there when you want it.

www.time.com/time/photogallery/0,29307,2036928,00.html

Novelty Gone in the Post-Social Era

We've rapidly gone from having little or no social context for the Internet experience to being surrounded by it seemingly at all times. We've found hundreds of friends and acquaintances on the Internet. We've connected with friends and "frenemies" alike. Businesses, nonprofits, causes, celebrities, and even governments have jumped in.

Now what? Is it all going to continue? Will we continue to play out our lives online and in the real world simultaneously? Will social context be a bigger part of our lives five years from now, or will there be a backlash against all of this? And has the novelty worn off?

Welcome to the Post-Social Era—a new and distinct phase in social media characterized (at a high level) by the now widespread and mainstream character of Facebook, its rivals, and its complements by a large and worldwide consumer market. In business, it's the acknowledgment even by laggards and Luddites that social media is a serious yet at times hard to understand marketing channel. In many cases, people have interacted with each other and with brands for several years now using social media. In fact, users now in their mid-20s may have come to Facebook while in college and may have been using social media for as many as eight years. That's an eternity in technology.

Pardon the analogy, but Facebook has grown from toddler to adolescent to young adult rapidly, and people around the world are adjusting. That's really what the Post-Social Era is about—and we're just at the beginning of it. We are at a point in time now when the bloom is off the rose just a bit, and social media is arguably just another way consumers spend time interacting in an increasingly interconnected world. The prodigious child of Facebook has grown into an adult overnight, and expectations are as high as ever.

The Post-Social Era is characterized by a few new realities:

- Ubiquitous social context
- Curated social experiences
- Evolving social etiquette and expectations (international culture)
- Shifts in usage patterns among different demographic groups
- Dramatically increasing business/marketing investment
- Democratization of community management (sophistication)
- Immature yet critically important legal frameworks

Let's go into these in a little more detail.

Ubiquitous Social Context

It may seem a little obvious today in 2012 to point out that a social layer exists on the Web and enhances, at minimum, our entertainment experience. However, as recently as five to six years ago that layer simply did not exist. If you wanted to ask your friends what they thought of something, you'd have to grab a beer or coffee with them. If you needed to catch up with a friend, you didn't have Facebook status updates to keep you informed. You'd need to have lunch or catch up on the phone (perish the thought!).

The same phenomenon is going on in the entertainment business. Most major celebrities have a Facebook page or Twitter account. If you look at the top Facebook Pages ranked by audience at www.fanpagelist.com, you may notice that most at the top of the list are artists, musicians, actors/actresses, and television shows. NBC's popular hit show *The Voice* and many others integrate live Twitter feedback on the screen during the show. Commercials for popular consumer products now communicate their Facebook page URL as often as they include their website address—just to get people to "join the club." Heck, even Shaquille O'Neal retired from professional basketball not on television or in a press conference, but rather using social media.

Consider also Facebook's social plug-ins that allow web developers to offer authentication, commenting, and other features inside websites. So, instead of building this code or using another service for this functionality, Facebook offers it for free. These social plug-ins are tied directly to Facebook, so comments appear both on the website itself and on the Facebook News Feed of friends of the commenter. As you can imagine, this provides a tremendous marketing benefit to people concerned about page views and site traffic. Through social plug-ins, Facebook's presence has extended to hundreds of thousands of websites around the world.

In a few short years, social media has become a mainstay in our lives and in the media we consume every day. Millions of people around the world have flocked to Facebook and other social media platforms, and now that experience extends to everyday websites as well. Marketers around the world have taken notice. Our friends and the brands that we love are all contributing to the conversation that is increasingly taking place online, on Facebook, and everywhere in between.

Curated Social Experiences

As our friends and interests have flocked onto the world's largest social network over the years, we now have more content than ever before that should interest us on Facebook. It should interest us because either we have opted into an affiliation with a page or we've accepted a friend relationship with another person. Naturally we'd like to hear what those with whom we associate have to say, right?

Well, for a lot of people, there are simply too many friend and fan page relationships for us to maintain effectively. For example, let's assume you are pretty extroverted; you now have 800 friends, and you "like" 200 pages on Facebook. We know that, using the most recent estimates, as many as 55% of Facebook users log in on average at least once per day. Using that estimate, can you really consume status updates, shared links, and social game updates from 550 of those folks every day?

Fortunately or unfortunately, Facebook has responded to this with Edgerank. Edgerank is an algorithm that decides what to show users when they first log into Facebook in the News Feed. This algorithm takes a few things into account—your history of interaction with friends and pages, how engaging the particular piece of content (status update, photo, link, and so on) is to other people, and how old it is. In a sense, Facebook is using behavior to decide what to put on your News Feed when you first log in. It is curating your content experience to show you precisely the things you are most likely to enjoy.

Edgerank was announced at the f8 conference in April 2010, just as the first edition of this book was being printed. We'll talk a lot more about it in Chapters 3 and 5. It's an important concept to achieve success with content marketing of your Facebook page.

Evolving Social Etiquette and Expectations

For many of us, Facebook's ability to capture our social graphs has changed how we interact with people we know on an interpersonal level. We can pay latent attention to what people are doing, saying, and thinking just by reading their status updates, viewing their pictures, seeing who they've friended, checking out articles they share, and knowing the events they are attending. Our opinions are shaped and influenced by our friends, but we no longer have to see them or talk with them regularly for this to happen. It's one part interesting, one part voyeuristic, one part scary—all at the same time.

As these trends continue, we're all grappling just a little with how we should deal with situations—from the routine to the uncomfortable. Take, for example, one of the interesting patterns to emerge in social media over the past few years—applications, games, and business processes built around incentives for drawing in friends. These tactics were once used by companies like Amway, Tupperware, and multilevel marketers like the fictional Confederated Products, featuring sales pitches by Officer Burke and Irene from the hilarious 1999 movie *Go*. Some of the world's most successful social applications to date have similarly grown rapidly by helping friends recruit friends—to earn coupons, to get a stronger Mafia in the popular Facebook game series Mafia Wars, or to grow their farms faster in Farmville.

The trouble is that our social etiquette has not evolved rapidly enough to offer answers to simple questions:

- How much should I ask my friend Jane to maintain my farm on Farmville?
- Should I post coupons to Facebook so that my friends will see and buy them and I'll get one free?
- Why wouldn't I be Facebook friends with my co-worker or business contact?
- Is it appropriate to use bad language on Facebook?
- Can I post risqué pictures to Facebook without offending people?
- Why shouldn't I talk politics or post links about a presidential election?
- What is an appropriate or inappropriate Facebook profile picture?

The fact is that there really are very few answers to these questions today. Each individual user makes their own decisions about sharing information—status updates, Wall posts, pictures, video, and so on, on Facebook. There isn't an "Emily Post" publishing etiquette guides for the social media world. Thus, there is no one way you should behave, and there are certainly no guidelines for sharing, oversharing, friending, and overfriending.

Add to that complication the fact that Facebook brings together people from pretty much every culture in the world. Those of you who have friends of different cultures may already realize that what is common practice for one person may be offensive or inappropriate to another. We all live in an increasingly shrinking world where we have greater transparency than maybe we ever wanted.

Shifts in Usage Patterns

As mentioned previously in this chapter, Facebook is a maturing platform. Facebook usage has matured as well, especially among demographic groups that can be described today as veteran users—people who have been active for five to six years or more. Even people who joined Facebook as recently as 2008 or 2009, when it truly became a mainstream phenomenon, are now three years or more into it.

Just about anyone who is a repeat user of Facebook at this point continues to frequent the site for reasons different from why they joined in the first place. Old friends have been found and are back in our lives. We now know who has gotten married to whom, who looks great, where we all have settled, what we're doing professionally, and (sorry to all you parents out there) how little baby Johnny looks in his 17 outfits. Finding people is becoming rarer and rarer these days—most people who want to be on Facebook are pretty much there—at least in the United States.

So, why do people keep coming back? Facebook is in some ways our "digital watercooler." It's the place where we spend a little time to talk about the affairs of the day. It's also the mechanism by which people share things they find funny or interesting. Instead of saying "Did you see that funny clip on YouTube?" people are just sharing a link from their profile. One can argue that it's highly impersonal, but welcome to the Post-Social Era.

The Facebook experience has evolved significantly over the last five to six years as well. Groups are more or less gone in favor of pages. Facebook has added Places and Deals. Apps have improved significantly as a few major players have emerged and taken mind share from the collective masses of small companies and individual developers who owned the platform in its early days. Games are arguably the stickiest feature on Facebook today and guarantee daily, if not hourly, logins by some users.

For people not interested in new features or social games, Facebook is at risk of fatigue. People who came to the site originally to find friends and relive the past have probably done that by now. What is going to keep people who don't play social games and who don't have time for the watercooler coming back? This fatigue issue is already playing out in younger demographic groups. I (Chris) was speaking recently to a group of college students at a major public university. Most people in the room were younger than 25 years old. I asked two questions. First, how many had used Facebook since 2006 or earlier? Nearly every hand was raised. I then asked, how many use Facebook now more than a year ago? Only two hands went up in a classroom of more than 100. Several cited Facebook fatigue as the primary reason but also admitted that once they left school they would probably use Facebook to learn more about the people around them.

Consider also parents who spend their free time with their kids. They are probably engaging in hobbies if they have free time, not spending spare moments on Facebook. Busy professionals have the same issue—if you spend a lot of time working on a computer all day, you probably need a break.

All of this brings up an interesting point, however. If Facebook carries data about us and maintains it, is Facebook more useful for people on the move? Once you know people in your social circle, does it get less interesting unless you are playing a game? For people who don't care about expanding their social circle, is it useful at all? The next few years should clarify usage patterns among different demographic groups and will tell us how much Facebook must continue to innovate to capture people's attention...and if it can.

Dramatically Increasing Business/Marketing Investment

As the Facebook user base has grown significantly, so has attention from brands, enterprises, and agencies. It's really been a self-reinforcing cycle. Agencies wanted to bring the latest and greatest marketing opportunities to their clients in big brands. Facebook was cool and had not only a great platform for marketers but also a large and growing worldwide audience. The next thing you knew, every major brand in the world established a Facebook presence.

It doesn't take much investigation to see that brands are putting significant resources into building interesting Facebook Pages. Most consumer brands have a custom landing tab on Facebook for first-time visitors, oftentimes encouraging people to "like" the brand to get more content, coupons, or access to more information. Some are inventive and on-brand, like YETI Coolers, a high-end cooler company that engages with fans about issues of interest to their outdoorsman/sportsman customers.

www.facebook.com/YetiCoolers

Some run campaigns in a totally unrelated area, such as IKEA attracting more than 20,000 fans to its IKEACats page.

www.facebook.com/ikeacats

Others, like Chef Boyardee Club Mum, focus on community—giving people an opportunity to find others who enjoy their products.

www.facebook.com/ChefBoyardeeClubMum

And then others are just mysterious because they can be. Coca-Cola currently has the largest fan base of any brand on Facebook. But its page is cryptic at best (see Figure 1.7). It must be nice to be a Coca-Cola marketer.

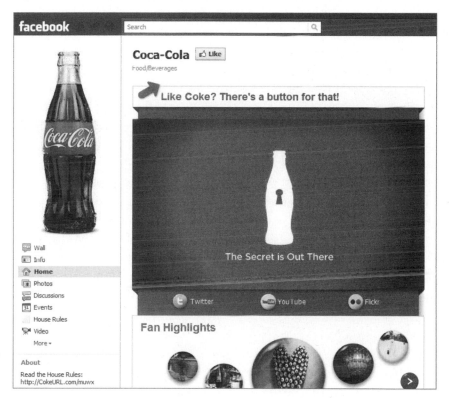

Figure 1.7 Coca-Cola Facebook page

Facebook has gone from a novelty to a place where many brands treat the page much like they'd treat a website. It's how to make a good impression on people who are there to make a snap decision to like a brand and establish an ongoing relationship through the News Feed. Fail, and you can't build your fan base as quickly. So, it stands to reason that brands would pump money into these assets to grow them. It's also why brands are a lot more prominent today in Facebook advertising—relatively small advertising budgets can buy a lot of Facebook ad impressions and clicks.

But while brands, agencies, and, of course, Facebook have been the biggest winners in this, it has gotten a lot harder for smaller companies to differentiate themselves.

Competing for attention with the world's most recognized celebrities and brands is as tough on Facebook as it is in the real world. On Facebook, smaller companies initially understood it and utilized it faster than bigger brands. But that has changed, and the playing field has swung wildly in the other direction.

Democratization of Community Management

The blogging/self-publishing revolution has been fantastic at breaking down barriers between customers and companies. However, it has also created a lot of work in the process. Think about how things have changed for a moment. It's an inevitability that consumers may have a problem with a particular product or service. In the past, an aggrieved consumer would write a letter to the customer service department for resolution or call a complaint hotline. Needless to say, it's a lot different today. Consumers can take their gripes to social media, where the complaint and the company's subsequent reaction are there for everyone to see. If you really want to get a good laugh on a rainy day, run a quick search engine query on "social media customer service disasters." There are some great stories out there.

As communities have come together on Facebook and other social media properties, members of those communities have developed new expectations for the companies, products, and organizations they love. One of our favorite studies to have been released over the past few years comes from, of all places, the American Red Cross. It commissioned a study in 2010 of more than 1,000 U.S. citizens age 18 and older to understand better what people think of social media as it relates to emergencies and disasters. You can check out the report for yourself here:

www.redcross.org/www-files/Documents/pdf/other/SocialMediaSlideDeck.pdf

The study is loaded with fascinating data points, but one question really sticks out: "If you posted a request for help from a social media website, how long do you think it should reasonably take for help to arrive?" (See Figure 1.8.)

A whopping 75% expected someone to respond to an emergency! The idea that someone is listening is not just taken for granted but ingrained in the experience of Facebook and other social media properties. Unreal.

Customers are now projecting these requirements onto brands. According to some research conducted by Lightspeed Research in the United Kingdom, in early 2011, 65% of customers surveyed expect a response to a Facebook complaint within a single day. Customer expectations in the survey were higher for Facebook and Twitter than the company's website. For more information, check out the summary of the report:

www.krishnade.com/blog/2011/social-crm-research-lightspeed/

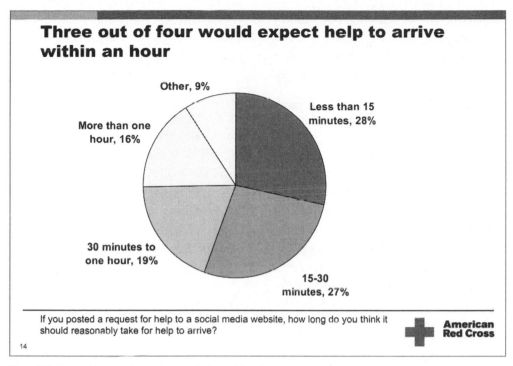

Figure 1.8 Expected response to emergency posted on social media

IBM has similarly done some good research on the topic, which it has released to the public in a summary report located here:

ftp://public.dhe.ibm.com/common/ssi/ecm/en/gbe03391usen/GBE03391USEN.PDF

Customer demands have made enterprises and brands get increasingly sophisticated about managing feedback from global audiences—understanding how content makes people engage, gauging responses to issues and customer services requests that arise, and so forth. The bar has never been higher.

Some companies do an exemplary job. Take Dell, for instance. Dell has invested in a social media listening center that has been profiled in the press as a best-in-class solution to the growing volume of customer feedback. It makes sense. When you are a global brand like Dell, customers are communicating their needs and disappointments in real time—all the time. That's a huge opportunity. Other companies, which have not committed to a command center like Dell has, nonetheless have dedicated managers on staff to watch what people are saying and then reply on behalf of the business to whatever issue a customer or prospective customer may have.

Community management is everywhere today, and it is becoming an essential part of the marketing function at companies all around the world.

Immature Yet Critically Important Legal Frameworks

Unfortunately, this discussion wouldn't be complete without briefly mentioning the legal issues associated with social media activity—not that we have anything against attorneys! It's just that in our experience lawyers tend to tell marketers that they can't do something, not without thousands of words of legal jargon and disclaimers to protect a business from anything that could possibly go wrong. Boring!

But in all seriousness, because social networks are relatively young, case law surrounding what people and companies do on Facebook is relatively immature. And what about companies that use Facebook data? What are the legal issues surrounding user data from the Open Graph? What about social plug-ins? What happens in the event of a data breach or security issue? What happens if there is service outage? How does this affect companies that build products and/or services on the Facebook platform?

We don't mention these things to scare or paralyze you. But the reality is that the legal frameworks and case law are young, just like the social etiquette, best business practices, and everything else surrounding Facebook. If that is a concern to you, have a good conversation with your attorney to understand your legal obligations and vulnerabilities.

Summary

All of these things have implications for the rest of us who desperately need to reach audiences and have them carry our marketing messages with them on the world's leading social network. This is the new reality of the Post-Social Era. Most people in the developed world know about social media now. Most sophisticated marketers have a plan, at the very least, to take advantage of Facebook and its peers, and most businesses targeting consumers are executing their plans. We've come a long way over the past few years. Now what do we do about it?

Understanding Social Media and Facebook

Social media and Facebook have evolved significantly over the past few years. The competitive landscape has simplified dramatically. Facebook has fundamentally changed into an infrastructure that is redefining the Internet experience, and major players across a wide range of industries have taken notice.

Chapter Contents

Social Networks, Social Media, and the Social Graph Defined

Before we discuss the other websites that we want to call to your attention, it is important that you understand some nuances in the vocabulary that we will be using when covering these topics. In particular, we will discuss a few terms: *social media*, *social networks*, and the *social graph*. Figure 2.1 is an illustration of how all of these fit together.

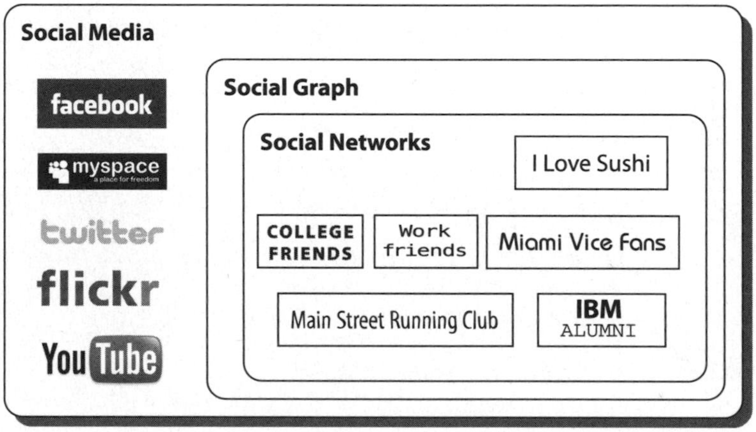

Figure 2.1 Social media, social graph, and social networks

Social media refers to the collection of technologies that captures communication, content, and so on, across individuals, their friends, and their social networks. Examples of social media include social networking sites like Facebook and Twitter; blogging technologies like TypePad, Tumblr, and WordPress; crowdsourcing products like Wikipedia; and photo- and video-sharing sites like Flickr, YouTube, and others. These technologies help users easily create content on the Internet and share it with others. Social media is the infrastructure that helps users become publishers of content that is interesting to them and their friends.

Social networks are groups of people, or communities, who share a common interest, perspective, or background. As much as we like to talk about social networks in the context of popular online services such as Facebook, these networks exist offline just as much as they do online. They have for many, many years—the only difference today is that these communities are easier to find, and communications are done interactively via social media. So, whether you are talking about Pink Floyd fans, people who attended the University of Texas in 2004, people who enjoy fly-fishing, or Brazilians, these networks exist regardless of whether the individuals in them share information and life experiences on social media.

The *social graph* is the broad collection of people, places, and interests that makes us individuals. It's how and why we're connected to other people. Think about it—a lot of who we are is defined by who we know, the associations we have made over the years, the schools we've attended, the interests that captivate us, and so on. Before social media, information about our social graph was largely difficult to find—gone when we moved to a new place, lost touch with old friends, or stopped participating. Social media keeps us connected to our interests, our past, and our old friends. For this reason, many experts believe that Facebook may emerge into a "next-generation social operating system" similar to Windows and the Web. Logging into Facebook and other social networks is the first thing a lot of people do every day, and it will get only more important as it attracts more users, more friends, and more data on the social graphs of individual users. Facebook CEO Mark Zuckerberg popularized the term *social graph* in 2007 when first describing why the company was able to grow so rapidly.

For example, we are entrepreneurs, so we are part of the social network of entrepreneurs. But because I (Chris) worked at Microsoft for three and a half years, I'm also a member of the social network of Microsoft alumni. I am a member of hundreds of networks from various associations in my life to date, and I'll likely join others in the future. The collection of my networks is my social graph, and it is as unique to me as my own fingerprint. All of the information across my social graph, including the social networks to which I've subscribed, is captured in social media sites such as Facebook and Twitter. These sites collect, organize, and disseminate that information to me and other users in consumable ways, through our news feeds and other features we use every day.

The Social Landscape 2012

In just a few short years, the social media landscape has matured significantly. Facebook and its rivals started with fairly limited functionality but grew, both as user needs became apparent and as developers in each company moved from making their platforms stable to working on new, exciting, and more immersive features.

As competition shook out, social media followed a pattern similar to that of many other software businesses over the years. It starts with an opportunity everyone sees and a cast of startups offering mildly differentiated products with a goal to get adoption quickly. But as time passes, consumers make choices based on convenience, which service provides the best user experience, and other criteria. This process usually takes a long time, but it's accelerated just a bit with social media because, well, social media is inherently…social. You won't get much out of Facebook by interacting with yourself—friends are necessary. Interactions are necessary; otherwise, a visit to a social media site is like walking through a graveyard or having a conversation with yourself. Boring.

For this reason, consumers made their choice over a much more condensed period of time. Winners like Facebook and Twitter grew very rapidly, while the losers declined rapidly. It was a much different situation than, say, the word processing software market that took 10 years or more to get resolved in the 1980s and 1990s between Microsoft Word, Lotus WordPro, and WordPerfect. To give you an idea, we profiled 10 major social networks in the first edition of this book, which released in 2010—and some of them are already out of business!

In the early days of the social era, MySpace was the largest social network in the world. Facebook was the underdog. Now MySpace is an afterthought. Its traffic dwindled to the point that it was acquired for a mere $35 million in June 2011 by Specific Media and Justin Timberlake. Even so, now MySpace has a huge uphill battle to fight to be relevant again. So to say that social media moves quickly would be grossly stating the situation.

The highly fragmented social media business of the early days of the industry coalesced somewhat around Facebook, Twitter, and LinkedIn. Facebook is the place where people casually interact with their friends, acquaintances, and "frenemies" (people who you friend primarily out of courtesy or social pressure more than a real relationship). Twitter is the place where people monitor what interests them by following people—perhaps a business expert, a celebrity, an athlete, an anthropomorphized representative of a brand/product, or all of the above. LinkedIn is a business-oriented social network—an online resume, job bank, and career resource all in one.

Google+ is a relatively new entrant offered by Google, the world's leading search engine. It has many of the same features of Facebook: a Stream that mirrors Facebook's News Feed functionality, pages for companies, and the ability for people to "like" content that is manifested with a "+1" button. The biggest difference, however, is the concept of Circles, which allows users to classify friends based on the type of relationship they have with the person. Google+ provides a number of default Circles— Friends, Family, Acquaintances, and Following—that can be used to categorize friends. In addition, people can create custom Circles to further slice friends as they see fit. Adding someone to your Circles does not require a "two-way" friendship as it does on Facebook, which is another subtle difference between the two services. Google+ is available worldwide, and a new account can be created using an existing Google login and password.

Paul Allen Predicts Google+ Network Effect Will Continue

Paul Allen made a fortune as a cofounder of Microsoft and in a variety of other tech business ventures. So, it was notable when Paul Allen announced that he expected Google+ to grow significantly, citing its rapid user growth and numbers following its June 28, 2011, release:

```
https://plus.google.com/117388252776312694644/posts/ZcPA5ztMZaj
```

Except…it wasn't *that* Paul Allen who made the predictions. It was Paul Allen, Utah entrepreneur, founder of Ancestry.com and unofficial Google+ statistician. Nonetheless, the numbers are stunning. Google+ grew from no usage on June 27, 2011, to 62 million just six months later to become the fastest-growing social network ever. It's an important innovation in the sense that Google+ gives users more

The use case is also shifting for each major player as people increasingly use the Web and social media on mobile devices and tablet computers. While each social media destination has its own mobile apps on the iPhone, Android, and other devices, the user experience for each is still more or less optimized around using a computer. Technically, tablets are really just mobile computers that don't use a mouse for navigation and interaction. But the form factor is different; specifically, there is no keyboard or mouse for someone to use to navigate in and around the social network. Screen size also requires each company to prioritize the things that matter most to both the user and each business. For example, you don't currently experience Facebook ads in the Facebook iPad app (although by the time you're reading this, you may very well do so). Social media sites, like all businesses, are currently grappling with the rapidly changing world of mobile devices. You'll have to watch for these changes—both the devices and the social networks that run on them—to best optimize your social media and Internet marketing approach.

Startup Social Media Platforms

Every few years, a new class of startups gets enough traction to warrant inclusion in a discussion of social media. This market moves so quickly, our next edition just may include 100 pages or more about a startup that simply didn't exist a few years earlier. It's hard to say, though, if startups compete with the major social media companies or if they will just engage in "coopetition" through partnerships or merger and acquisition activity. A vibrant industry of startups has emerged around the proliferation of smartphones and tablets. For the sake of limiting this conversation, we'll focus on just those that ask users to establish a profile.

Much as it redefined the experience of listening to music, Apple redefined the mobile phone experience with the iPhone. Now just about every mobile phone manufacturer has a stunning device that features a world-class user experience. In fact, that experience has become the ante in really everything related to websites and applications today. It can be argued that the Apple revolution was, and continues to be, one of user experience that just moves from one platform to the next.

A cottage industry of smartphone applications began to litter the landscape. One area of innovation has been in location-based services. Location-based services are applications that enhance a user's experience by providing rich, location-specific data to the user of the application. As such, there are several types of location-based services. Some provide information about the businesses around you, like Yelp. Others provide users with information on nearby experiences, as Gowalla does. Others, like Foursquare, are more based around the concept of "checking in," i.e., telling other people and local businesses where you are. Facebook has even gotten into the fray, offering users an opportunity to "check in" to their location and have that information propagate to the user's Facebook profile, and, ergo the News Feeds of friends.

Quora is a social network based on asking and answering questions. CaringBridge is a social network designed to help people deal with grieving a loss or terminal illness. Last.fm is a social network for music enthusiasts. Meetup helps people get together in real life (IRL). myYearbook is a social network that appeals to tweens and teens—instead of "poking" another person on Facebook, a user can take almost 100 different actions. Now that's a diverse set of options for flirting with romantic interests! Quepasa is built on cultural grounds, targeting primarily Latin Americans all around the world. Tumblr, like Twitter, is a social network built around the ability of users to publish content to the Internet rapidly and with few technical skills. You could argue that emerging fitness tracker MapMyFitness is a social network that allows people to share details of their workouts with friends. Instagram is a social network built around iPhone photo sharing, and Pinterest is doing the same thing with photos published anywhere on the Web. There are hundreds of other services that we'll probably profile in the next edition of this book in a few years, and many will evolve in different areas.

The Future: Niche, Fragmented Social Networks?

For all that Facebook has done over its brief history, it could be argued that the trend is actually moving toward specialized social networks. LinkedIn, for example, currently shows no signs of losing momentum, yet it has no designs on being anything more than a professional social network. Path is one of Silicon Valley's hottest startups, and it's focused on being the destination for people to share more intimate details about themselves with a much smaller circle of friends.

Many of the social networks mentioned earlier are focused on building social communities around specific, less ambitious social commonalities that Facebook would likely consider to be too "niche" to innovate. Facebook is the big player in the business and is the go-to destination for a broad set of social experiences. But it may ultimately be threatened by companies that provide a tremendous user experience for people in niche communities and specific, less mainstream social situations. Facebook's biggest threat, therefore, is probably not something that looks like Facebook does today but rather a combination of other communities that may collectively do a better job of capturing users' attention.

Another area that has seen significant advancement over the past few years is in the curation, user experience, and consumption of content. *Curation* is just a fancy word for "filtering out all the noise so you don't have to surf the Web to get the content that interests you delivered to you conveniently." Instapaper was one of the first curation products; it would simply let a user save an article for reading later by downloading the article and making it available via an Instapaper login or by accessing Instapaper through an iPad, iPhone, or Kindle. Flipboard and paper.li mine articles that are shared by your Twitter followers and repackage them into a beautiful UI on tablets and the Web, respectively.

The greater point is that innovation continues, despite the rapid growth of the three market leaders. If you want to see the future of social media and consumer experiences, all you have to do is pay attention to new and emerging social media products and technologies. All three current market leaders watch innovation for ideas they can bring along to their social media properties, either by building those features into their products themselves or by acquiring them.

A good, relatively accurate list is maintained on Wikipedia here:

http://en.wikipedia.org/wiki/List_of_social_networking_websites

Seven (Plus Two) Truths of Social Networks

While mainstream use of social networks is only a few years old, we already know a lot about how consumers use them. Besides, a few years is a generation in Internet parlance anyway. Here are seven truths of social networks that you can rely upon. If you are going to bookmark one page of this book, bookmark this page because these truths should guide your thinking regardless of what you do with social media:

1. Social media is a preferred way for people in younger demographics to communicate with each other. Only text messaging from mobile devices is in the same ballpark.

2. Social media is based on the concept of friends, but that term today is very loosely applied. Similarly, profiles are loosely defined and can be used in a variety of ways by people, companies, brands, and so on.

3. The more active a consumer is on the Internet, the more likely they participate in multiple social networks. Oftentimes, these people are influencers within a circle of friends and have a tremendous impact on the opinions of others.

4. Once information is shared on a social network, it is out there and can't easily be contained. Everything is out in the open and largely visible for other people to see, even if it is deleted after the fact. Always assume you're being watched and scrutinized. The bigger you are, the more likely people are just waiting for you to slip up.

5. Social media is best applied in addition to existing Internet marketing programs and alongside other web assets. When building a strategy, you must think comprehensively. That isn't to say you should do everything you can in a disjointed manner. Customers need to understand where to go for what and why.

6. The rules are still being made. Social media "etiquette" is still relatively immature. Tread carefully.

7. The seventh truth involves the factors that contribute to social media usage. Everyone on social networks is motivated by some combination of the following human needs:

Love Finding love, keeping up with loved ones, and so forth

Self-Expression/Emotion Sharing life's details with friends

Sharing Opinions/Influencing Friends Using social media as a platform for influencing opinions—usually about politics, religion, or other things we don't typically debate in person

Showing Off Sharing life's successes and/or achievements with others

Fun/Escapism/Humor Using social media to get a good laugh

Memories and Nostalgia Catching up with old friends and sharing old stories

Making Money Using social networks primarily to support professional pursuits

As you can probably tell, the motivation for using Facebook varies significantly depending on your customer. Most companies with mature marketing departments spend a lot of time on customer personas to understand who customers are and how they behave. While this can, at times, trap a business into oversimplifying its customer base, this is one case where developing personas can be especially effective even for a smaller business.

Let's think of this in practical terms. For instance, single people might be interested in finding a love interest using Facebook, while happily married people in their 40s are more likely to use Facebook to keep up with relatives and loved ones. A grandmother will be more interested in sharing pictures and stories about loved ones than her grandchildren will be. If you are going to create a successful marketing campaign, you're going to have to identify the people you are trying to reach and exactly how you can reach them more effectively. Figure out who your customers are and what their motivation is for using Facebook. That exercise will help you craft a much better campaign for your target market, and it will also inform your ad copy and creativity. We'll talk more about building the right social media campaign for your target audience later in this chapter.

Truth #8: Our Attention Is Split across a Rapidly Homogenizing Social Media Experience

All three market leaders (Facebook, Twitter, and YouTube) are social media destinations, yet they carry different meanings and different contexts for their users. But time is limited, right? Our attention is fragmented across multiple social services and the Web at large—and that's just when we're online. We also have busy offline lives to lead as well. Our response to date has been that we'll happily create social media accounts on multiple services and not give much thought to why we're doing it or how we'll keep up with it all. This behavior is particularly common among white-collar and information workers who spend 8 to 10 hours a day on computers every day at work.

If we're so busy, why do we invest time to monitor and maintain accounts on three different social media properties?

Inconsistent Social Standards Different people treat their social media profiles in different ways. Some will friend anyone who comes along on any social network. Others want Facebook to have "real friends" and LinkedIn to have "real business contacts." As we suggested in Chapter 1, there is no "Emily Post" of social media today, so we're all in the dark about how other people view their privacy and their participation. This is one factor that drives us to use different social networks.

Distinct Features Allow Different Types of Communication Let's say you want to get to know someone online or want to establish a relationship for some reason. Something as simple as the process by which each social media site allows this causes people to use one over another. Facebook relies upon friending an individual's profile or liking a page for a relationship to be established. The former requires a two-way acknowledgment of a relationship, while the latter can be initiated by any Facebook user. LinkedIn is two-way but does offer a few features like LinkedIn Introductions that make an unsolicited request for a relationship at least somewhat socially palatable. Twitter is entirely one-way; two-way relationships unlock the potential for direct communications between people but little more.

Access to Private Information In addition, Facebook, Twitter, and LinkedIn grant access to information differently based on simply how they operate. I can follow Kim Kardashian on Twitter without her consent and find out all the things going on in her life. But to get her personal status updates from Facebook, I'd have to hope she posts them to her Facebook page—and that I see the status update on my News Feed, assuming she has good Edgerank on her page. Alternatively, she can just accept a personal invitation from me to be her friend. The latter is very unlikely. In this respect, Twitter lends itself to ambient monitoring better than Facebook. The same can be said for business information on LinkedIn.

Consider a common scenario—you are a 30-year-old woman working in an office with a group of people with different interests, from different backgrounds, and of different age groups. A superior working near you, but not your boss, friends you on Facebook. What do you do? Do you accept the friend invitation? The experience people have with their parents joining social networks has since permeated the workplace over the last few years. Will you offend someone by not friending them on Facebook and LinkedIn? What does it mean if you don't accept their invitation? And will you open a Pandora's box of concerns about people in your workplace intruding in your personal life, off-hours?

While some people are doing a great job of keeping work networks distinct from their social networks, an increasing number of people have ceased to make these distinctions. As such, we're seeing that friend lists across the three major social networks often include the same people—just in a different context (work, social, shared content).

Truth #9: All of This Is Getting Exhausting

So, as all this "socializing" (if you could call it that) is taking place online, a practical reality has emerged. It takes real time and effort to maintain social profiles. Sure, a status update every now and then is not all that tough to enter. But you have to remember to do it, and you have to want to do it. And as we've previously discussed in this chapter, it's easy to have accounts on half a dozen social networks or more. Consider also that you may have separate accounts for yourself and your business, and the number of things that you have to maintain can very quickly get out of hand.

As a result, we've seen a number of behaviors evolve. First, even though statistics tell us that people are spending more time on Facebook, they are not necessarily there to share more information. Rather, people are using Facebook as a place to entertain themselves, to catch up with what other people are doing and saying, and to play free social games. Profile data used to be a lot richer—containing detailed information on what made individuals unique. Now people are removing vital information from their profiles.

Social mores have evolved as well, and some folks are being more careful about posting status updates and about sharing content and offers with one another. It is probably a result of introspection to some extent—users find that someone is "loud" or wants to broach controversial topics like religion, politics, or selling products or services all too often. Not wanting to be "that guy" or "that gal," people limit what they are doing or saying on Facebook. This is probably a good thing—perhaps the lack of stated "etiquette" has made people consider how their thoughts and actions on Facebook may negatively impact others.

Along these lines, people are also increasingly accepting friend requests to "keep the peace" and to avoid awkward social circumstances. In that sense, Facebook is becoming the hub of all the interpersonal relationships that a person has. One might consider this a good thing, but it actually can have a detrimental effect on how often people use Facebook, the personal information they share, and the observations they make. But isn't that what Facebook is for? To have fun? Now many of us have to think about the mishmash of friends, acquaintances, business contacts, "frenemies," and the like, who can so easily keep up with what we are doing and saying.

At one time not long ago, we all used to be able to do and say the things that we wanted without having to give it any thought. But now it's becoming something that we have to think about.

Social fatigue is a real challenge for Facebook as it continues to become a social utility. A quick anecdote illustrates this: at a recent speaking engagement, I (Chris) asked an audience of young professionals if they were getting tired of Facebook. Almost all raised their hands. I then asked if they used Facebook less than they did a year ago. Almost all hands were raised again. One of the attendees cited hating to "have to think about what was posted to Facebook and Twitter." She went on to say, "Facebook used to be the place for me to escape. Now I have to think about everything I do there. It sucks."

All of this is not to say that Facebook is a lost cause for marketers. It remains the richest data set in the world for us to access and use to reach consumers with the offers, messages, and products we want them to enjoy. But people are using social media sites in new ways just because we've all learned from using this system over the years. Social media usage is evolving all the time. It's something to keep in mind as you plan marketing initiatives on Facebook and other types of social media.

Facebook, the Evolving Organism

Let's turn our attention specifically to Facebook, the evolving organism. To stay relevant and on the cutting edge, Facebook has added new and richer features over its relatively short life. Some changes are a function of practicality. Some are Facebook's response to innovations from other companies. Some are simply because Facebook has been continuing to develop its platform as time has passed and user patterns have emerged. Remember, this is the era of the Web and not packaged computer software— things can change overnight and without warning or even a friendly announcement. And with Facebook, they often do.

We'll focus on specific changes to Facebook and how to use that to your advantage when marketing later in this book. But for now, let's think a little higher level. Strategically, what is Facebook doing with their platform? Where are they going? And where have they been?

As we mentioned in the first edition of this book, Facebook started as a way for people in college to connect with each other and meet people with similar interests. Facebook very quickly outgrew this original vision as it moved beyond the hallowed walls of Harvard and permeated colleges around the United States. Early-adopter college students became young professionals and brought Facebook with them inside the firewall of corporations around the world. As it conquered the business world, Facebook started enjoying growth internationally and among people in the Baby Boomer and retiree demographic groups. See Figure 2.2.

| Harvard | Colleges | Workplaces | International | Older Demographic Groups |

Figure 2.2 How Facebook's audience has evolved

Today Facebook appeals to a mass market of consumers and business users with a wide set of needs and desires. It has conquered a high and unrivaled market share in each of these groups. Now the business problem for Facebook is that it must continue to appeal to each. As you can imagine, that's pretty complicated. You need your social media property to stay fun for college users and the broader consumer audience while being increasingly important to businesses. All the while, rivals are nipping at your heels and innovating a little more every day. Competitors would love nothing more than to migrate a large number of users from Facebook to their new platform, be it a social network, a mobile app, or something in between.

So, what has Facebook done to respond? And how does Facebook view itself and its users today? For your reading pleasure, we've summarized where Facebook is today in the Seven Immutable Laws of Facebook:

1. Facebook is the one, true social platform. No other social network shall come before it. Facebook sees itself as the market leader and is motivated to stay on top at all times.

2. Data and algorithms are king. Statistics drive the content that is displayed to users on their News Feeds, how ads are served, and when changes are considered for the Facebook platform.

3. Power to the people. Individual users can do whatever they want, post as often as they want, hide people and pages from their News Feeds, and take advantage of Facebook however they see fit.

4. Power to the business. Law 3 notwithstanding, controls for businesses, nonprofits, and other types or organizations are the order of the day. Organizations can run effective ads, can get more control over pages, and can watch comments made on pages more easily than ever before.

5. Don't steal Facebook's branding thunder. People and businesses are prohibited from using Facebook's name and branding in advertisements—they simply won't pass approval, so don't try.

6. Facebook is the people and places of the world but with structure for the Internet. And that structure can and does scale effectively, as evidenced by worldwide adoption.

7. Always build and reconsider the Facebook product. Incremental change is a constant. Major changes are occasionally necessary.

Like it or not, Facebook is constantly tweaking itself to evolve. Sometimes it is to set the agenda in social media. Other times, it's a response to a competitive threat or an opportunity that has surfaced. The more you think of Facebook as a living, breathing organism, the better off you'll be. As such, tried-and-true tactics for marketing success can and often do change very rapidly.

Facebook Basics

Now that you have a good idea of what is happening in the broader social media business, you can turn your attention to some of the basic features of Facebook, including setting up an account, accumulating "friends," and using the News Feed.

Account Setup

The entire setup process at www.facebook.com is designed to be as simple and intuitive as possible for the user. With almost one billion accounts worldwide, Facebook gets tons of user behavior data that is helpful when considering how to evolve the platform and streamlining the process of getting started. On the home page, Facebook asks users for the basic information necessary to create an account/profile: first name, last name, email address, password, gender, and full date of birth. (We recommend that once your profile is set up, you then edit your personal information to show only your month and day of birth in your profile for security purposes.)

For the sake of creating examples in this book, we'll use this as an opportunity to create an account (Figure 2.3). Notice how this account creation step has not changed significantly over the last several years. It is short and simple.

Figure 2.3 Facebook home page and account setup as of November 2011

After the user creates a profile, Facebook walks them through a process that is designed to make their experience richer and more interesting. First, the user is prompted to enter their email login credentials. This allows Facebook to scan the user's inbox to see whether any friends already have a Facebook account. This is mostly self-serving for Facebook; it is a way to help people invite new people to Facebook more than it is a tool to help a user immediately find friends already on the social network.

Second, the user is asked to enter information about schools they attended or the company where they work. It's handy for a few reasons: most of our personal connections are made in either school or the workplace. For Facebook purposes, it's especially handy because it is used as a way to help people find old friends or colleagues. And remember, one key to Facebook's success is the ability of people to discover something interesting or new there every day. So, for Frank W. Furter, we're going to enter a high school, Northwest Rankin, and a year, 1992. But here's where it gets interesting. After we enter the information, Facebook presents us with a list of people from that graduating class! We can now choose friends from the list and make them part of our "circle" on Facebook. We'll talk more about what that means later. You wrap up by adding a profile picture or importing one from a webcam.

That's it. It took about 5 minutes to go through the process of establishing a Facebook account and profile. The rest of the profile includes ways to enter additional information and expose it only to certain types of Facebook users. We'll go into more detail on that later, too. For now, what are the main takeaways for a marketer?

- It's a simple process that takes only a few minutes. Just about anyone with basic computer literacy can become a Facebook user.
- Everything in the setup process is geared toward helping users find friends on Facebook and build their network.
- An extraordinary amount of personal information is collected in the setup process, but it really is just the beginning. Users can provide a lot more information about themselves through Facebook after the profile is created. (And, keep in mind, you can choose how much or how little your Facebook friends can read about you via Facebook's granular privacy settings.)
- It's also stunningly easy to set up a fake profile. With simplicity and ease of use comes the ability for people to misrepresent themselves. Now there are some cases where this is valid, not to mention maybe even the right thing to do even though it is against Facebook's terms of use to maintain multiple accounts. More on that later. The takeaway here is to remember that it is very easy for people to set up a Facebook profile with any persona they would like.

Friending

The News Feed is an aggregate of your friends' activity that you'll see every time you log in. Facebook uses algorithms to choose what they deem that most popular. Profiles, friends, and the News Feed are the key components to understanding how Facebook works and how information is shared across Facebook users. Friends are people who have the right to see information about you as well as anything you post.

You can probably tell how much someone uses Facebook by the number of friends they have. It isn't because Facebook is a tool for popular or outgoing people. But the more friends you have, the more active you'll be on Facebook and the more time you'll spend. It's a cycle that Facebook has perfected. Today, Facebook is the most popular destination on the Internet measured by time spent on the site. More than 50 billion minutes per month are spent on Facebook as of October 2011, according to Nielsen Online. That's almost 8 hours per month, per user, or 15.5 minutes per day. And a staggering 163.2 million Americans—more than half the population of the United States—visited Facebook in that month.

http://mashable.com/2011/09/30/wasting-time-on-facebook/

Building an active network of friends is the key to becoming someone who uses Facebook every day. But why exactly is that the case? What interactions does Facebook simplify or make more convenient?

Keeping Up with Old Friends and Acquaintances Passively There is no more efficient way to keep up with people who aren't in your life on a regular basis. Facebook gives you the opportunity to know what is happening with old friends and acquaintances without having to call them, send a letter or email message, or chat on an instant messaging service. This can be one tremendous benefit, especially if you are a social butterfly and are on good terms with a lot of people.

Learning Things You Didn't Know about Friends Profile data, status updates, and vocal support for other people, groups, or entities on Facebook can tell you a lot about people. Sometimes you find out good things and commonalities. Sometimes you learn things that result in disappointment. Either way, some people just really like knowing as much as they can about the people around them. Facebook makes it easy to communicate and snoop around to see what friends are saying and doing.

Commenting on Friends' Opinions, Shared Links, and Random Thoughts Facebook gives users the opportunity to share links, status updates, and random thoughts with friends. More important, any friend can comment on things that are exposed by another friend on Facebook. These are conversations that, in the physical world, often take place over lunch, happy hour, or dinner with friends. While users can't necessarily have a good deep conversation on Facebook as they can in person, they can interact with basic off-the-cuff reactions to things they read and see.

Socializing through Photos, Events, Playing Games, and Social Applications Sometimes the basic features of Facebook don't allow for specific types of social interactions that people would like to engage in with their friends. Third-party applications have filled the void in many of these cases, while Facebook has also built additional features into the platform to make these social interactions possible.

None of these kinds of interactions, viewed on their own, is particularly significant. But collectively, they represent the value proposition of Facebook for an individual user. Nowhere else on the Internet can a person find more old friends and former colleagues in one convenient place. Friend someone, and they are in your circle. In the end, you'll be able to keep up with that friend as much as you'd like. If you're as busy as we are, you probably need this to appropriately manage your social life and prioritize your time.

The News Feed

The News Feed has emerged as probably the most important part of Facebook. It's the first thing users see upon login—a running list of the latest updates across the user's unique social graph. But it includes far more than updates from friends. The News Feed also includes updates from fan pages and third-party applications installed by the user. Items in the News Feed can include status updates, photos, events, and links to other sites or articles on the Internet. Friends or other fans can comment on any of these things or choose to "like" them, so it is possible to see how people you don't even know react to updates.

So, why is the News Feed so critically important to mastering Facebook? We spoke earlier in this chapter about Facebook becoming a "social" operating system of sorts. Traditionally, we've used operating systems to help us start our work day, write a paper, build a financial model, or pursue some other productive activity. But as computers and social networking get more intertwined in our lives, it is possible that we'll start our day not with work but rather with casual social interaction with friends on Facebook. The jumping-off point for us won't be the traditional "desktop" but rather the Internet browser running Facebook.

This is especially possible as the News Feed becomes more and more useful. Consider when the News Feed first appeared as a Facebook feature. It primarily contained updates on friends with very little intrusion by brands, companies, artists/musicians, and all the other interests people cared about. But now, it is the filter through which we get content that interests us from all over the Web, from companies, businesses, or brands that interest us as well as from our friends and business colleagues. It includes comments our friends make on websites, recommendations about products and services, and other content deemed relevant by our stated interests and social relationships. As you can tell from Figure 2.4, it can become almost a full-time job to keep up with everything that is going on!

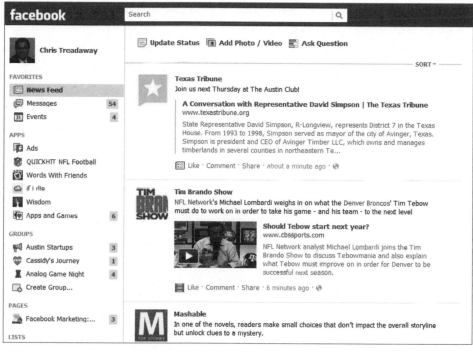

Figure 2.4 Updates on the Facebook News Feed

That's why being in the News Feed is so important. Breaking into the News Feed is currently the easiest and most important consideration for brands and companies looking to establish a presence and identity on Facebook. Your biggest fans, not to mention future customers, are on Facebook every day. If you aren't in the consciousness of prospective customers on Facebook, odds are your competitors are or will be. The one thing all of them see is the News Feed.

We are currently in a period when a lot of companies and brands have recognized that they need to have a presence on Facebook. Most of the time, this is in the form of a fan page, Facebook's preferred type of landing page/presence for companies, organizations, and nonprofits. More and more, brands engage with customers on another form of media (TV/radio commercial, email campaign, Twitter, and so on) and ask them to "like" a page on Facebook. We've always found the nomenclature a little clunky when it comes to some brands or products. It makes more sense if you're talking about Willie Nelson, a favorite college football team, or Reese's Peanut Butter Cups. It's probably why a lot of people still refer to Facebook *fans*—the term originally given to supporters of a product, service, brand, or artist on Facebook.

As the News Feed remains the primary means through which users experience content, Facebook has adapted in several meaningful ways— all of which have implications for the everyday marketer. Probably the biggest change to the News Feed has been the increased importance given to Edgerank. Edgerank is the algorithm Facebook uses to determine the exact updates that are visible for a given user in the News Feed upon login. An *edge* is a piece of content—a post, a comment, a "like," a note, a link, a tag in a photo, and so on (see Figure 2.5).

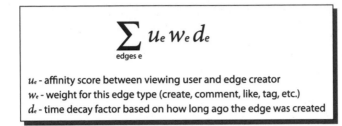

$$\sum_{\text{edges } e} u_e \, w_e \, d_e$$

u_e - affinity score between viewing user and edge creator
w_e - weight for this edge type (create, comment, like, tag, etc.)
d_e - time decay factor based on how long ago the edge was created

Figure 2.5 Edgerank algorithm

Edgerank consists of the following three main components:

Affinity Score Between edge User and Edge Creator This is a measurement of how often you engage with the person, group, page, or person you've subscribed to who created the content.

Weight for This Edge Type This is the score Facebook gives each type of content simply based on what it is, because different types of content are more or less meaningful to the average user.

Time Decay Factor This is when the edge was posted, with credit given to items posted more recently over those posted at a later time/date.

Edgerank is thus personalized for each user based on their real interactions on Facebook—decisions that are made every day to ignore content from some people and read content from others. Facebook stores all those interactions for the purposes of improving its users' News Feed experience—to make the News Feed items as relevant as they can possibly be. So, if anything, presence on the News Feed has gotten more important. But now more than ever, it requires a real, established history of social interactions taking place through Facebook. In other words, what was nice to have for marketers to be successful on Facebook a few years ago is a must-have today.

But Facebook uses Edgerank for more than just the News Feed. Facebook also uses Edgerank to prioritize the people who show up in your Chat screen as being available. Figure 2.6 illustrates a Facebook Chat pop-up, which is accessible from the bottom right of the screen. You'll notice a list of people at the top—most of whom we have significant and regular interaction with. The "More Online Friends" section includes a vast group of friends with whom we have not interacted frequently. It's both accurate and just a little scary to know that Facebook knows us so well.

In the fall of 2011, Facebook introduced Ticker—another feature designed to deal with an unintended consequence of having too much data for the News Feed. The Ticker is a real-time update of everyone's status updates, links, photos, and the like. Items move in and out of the Ticker immediately as friends post updates to Facebook. It's a direct response to the complaint that Edgerank isn't always perfect; some users complained that Edgerank was too aggressive about filtering out too many status updates. The Ticker gives equal standing to everyone that a user maintains a relationship with on Facebook. The only catch is that, for most computers, the Ticker is currently "beneath the fold." In other words, a user is required to scroll down on the screen before discovering it. For marketers, the implication is relatively clear. If you haven't broken into the News Feed for a user, all hope is not lost. You can still reach people through the Ticker, but it's tough to convert them from there. Figure 2.7 is an example of a Ticker that is visible on the main News Feed page upon login to Facebook.

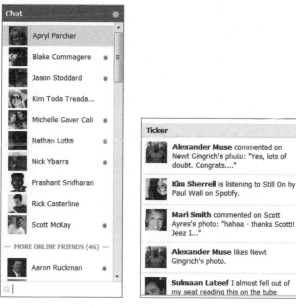

Figure 2.6 Chat window   **Figure 2.7** The Ticker

Campaign Ideas

It's now time to consider how you can use Facebook and other social networks to improve your business. Opportunities are not just in the marketing arena. Social media technologies help people with similar interests or behaviors find and meet each other and share problems and solutions. You can use social media to improve efficiency in any customer or internal corporate communication. While these technologies are applicable to a variety of areas of your business, you are likely to make the biggest and most immediate impact by launching something in the marketing arena.

The key to success with social media marketing is mapping your business goals to the social networks that can make you most successful. How do you assess this? Ask yourself a few key questions when putting the plan together:

- Are there enough people in your target demographic on the social network?
- Is it common for people on the social network to say good things about your company or brand?
- Are there other ways for people on the social network to approve of your company or brand?
- Does your product fit the needs of your target demographic?
- Can you turn positives or negatives about your product into a viral marketing success?

But perhaps the most important question in any major corporation is about risk. Is your company willing to take a chance on social media marketing? We're not talking necessarily about dollars and cents or coping with success. Is your company a cultural fit for the experimentation necessary to make social media work? For reasons outlined before in this book, social media is both hot and new. Facebook, Twitter, and other social media properties have been covered extensively in business magazines and other publications. Management at your company may see this as a huge opportunity or a potential for embarrassing failure. Like other examples on the Web, those who experiment ultimately win.

What types of things can you do with social media from a marketing perspective? We like to think of any new social media marketing project in terms of the sales funnel. After all, as marketers we are making sales easier, right? You'll need to figure out where your priorities lie in the sales funnel. Identify what is broken and fix it.

Prospecting How do we find people with a stated or latent need? How do we introduce them to our product or service for the first time? Or if they've heard of us already, how do we remind them about how great we are?

Customer List Building They are as good as gold—lists of qualified customers who want to hear from us. Where can we find more people willing to listen to things we have to say? Can we get clever with social media to expand our reach?

Communicating with Qualified Customers Now that we have customers, how does social media make it easier for us to reinforce our message with them regularly? Are you able to produce the types of content that work best in social media?

Lead Generation and E-Commerce Do our efforts reinforce the sales process either by generating leads or by facilitating e-commerce purchases? If this is our main priority, are we able to measure the outcome and return on investment (ROI), and have we elegantly integrated it in a way that doesn't anger our customers?

Customer Relationship Management Social media affords opportunities to make your company or brand considerably more personable than the old ways of communicating via an 800 customer service phone line and postal mail. It's also a Pandora's box of complaints that people are probably sharing via social media today.

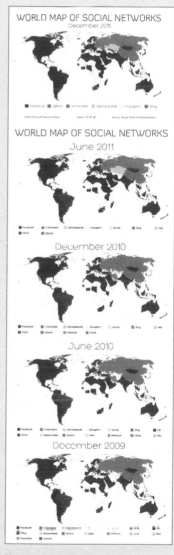

Facebook Takes Over the World

In the first edition of this book, Facebook was the leading social network in a number of countries. But it was not yet dominant worldwide. Fast-forward to 2012, and Facebook is the winner-take-all pretty much anywhere on Planet Earth. Check out the maps in Figure 2.8 from Vincenzo Cosenza, author of *Social Media ROI* (Apogeo, 2012). The first map is from June 2009, and the last is the most recent. Slowly but surely, Facebook is becoming the world's biggest and most used social network.

Figure 2.8 World maps of social networks

Most of these things require good social media campaign execution, but in all likelihood doing some of them well will also require cooperation from colleagues who manage your website, email mailing lists, advertising budgets, or customer service department. This probably isn't a big deal for those of you in smaller companies. But in larger companies, each of these is often run separately by managers with different interests and goals for their teams. We've seen it happen too many times already—the lucky person who manages social media for their company is often the "object of everyone's affection," meaning that they will take a lot of negative feedback even in the best of circumstances. Only you will know if you should upset the apple cart or move things forward incrementally as you go.

Social media is the ultimate cross-functional discipline for a company. While it is most closely identified with marketing, it is truly more of a shift in information flow. If harnessed appropriately, social media can become a competitive differentiator for your business. If not, it will attract enemies and fail. You need to take charge of the situation to ensure that you get the most out of Facebook and other social media properties for your business. In the next chapter, we'll discuss exactly how you can do that.

What You Want: Viral Marketing

Executing an effective viral marketing concept is the dream of many marketers today. We all dream of taking a great idea, a few hundred bucks, and a camcorder and turning that into an Internet sensation with a huge return on investment. Some people call it *viral marketing*; others call it word-of-mouth marketing. Whatever you call it, social media is the infrastructure that makes all of it far more possible today than ever before. With the codified relationships in social media and the canvas available for viewing interesting things, it isn't out of the question that you can reach a lot of people as long as you catch lightning in a bottle and create the right thing. One person's experience or recommendation can easily be entertainment for hundreds if not thousands of people. This is a cycle you obviously want working for you, not against you.

We've all seen things spread like wildfire over the Internet—jokes, chain letters, you name it. Remember the dancing baby (www.cnn.com/TECH/9801/19/dancing.baby/index.html) from the early days of the Internet in 1996? We all felt the new technology taking the world by storm, but there was just something about that three-dimensional dancing baby that made us want to send it around to friends through email. Today, most of us don't send jokes and such to friends on email unless the content is really interesting, really funny, or relevant to someone's work or social life. Social media is far less restrictive, and it gives everyone a loudspeaker. Therein lies the opportunity for marketers. Anything you do or say, as well as anything your consumers do or say about you, has the potential to spread uncontrollably. People have the power to comment on your brand, product, or company and get the word out to a great number of people much more efficiently through social networks.

Burger King's Subservient Chicken campaign for the launch of the Tendercrisp Chicken Sandwich in 2004 and 2005 was an example of an effective, albeit well-funded, viral marketing campaign. Burger King launched a commercial with a guy on his couch, directing another person in a chicken suit to act in various ways. It simultaneously launched a website at www.subservientchicken.com with a video of a man in a chicken suit (Figure 2.9). The chicken could be controlled by visitors, who would enter in a text box commands such as sit, fly, lay egg, even "march like a German soldier." The site and marketing effort created significant buzz. People hit the site repeatedly to figure out what commands they could give to the chicken. *Adweek* later reported that the site received more than 14 million unique visitors through March 2005. Why? The campaign was creative, fun, and innovative, yet it required visitors to participate and discover new things. Most importantly, it resulted in a successful launch of the Tendercrisp Chicken Sandwich, increased store traffic, and increased revenue for Burger King.

Figure 2.9 Subservient Chicken does the YMCA

Negative publicity can also spread like wildfire. United Airlines had a public relations disaster on its hands with the *United Breaks Guitars* video of July 2009. A disgruntled musician whose guitar was broken on a flight posted a video on YouTube (www.youtube.com/watch?v=5YGc4zOqozo) that got more than three million views in the first two weeks. It was terrible publicity for United Airlines but great for the musician. On a smaller scale, you'll often see that disgruntled customers are willing to share negative experiences they've had with companies on the blogosphere, Twitter, and Facebook. Empowered customers, especially active users of social media, know the power of complaining in public, and they're starting to use social media to get what they want.

None of this is exactly new. We have been exposed to new ideas and new business opportunities for years. Our grandmothers attended Tupperware parties. We've all seen the pink Cadillacs from Mary Kay. Maybe you attended a college swarming with Amway representatives. Perhaps your first experience with multilevel marketing was Burke's "Confederated Products" pitch over dinner in the movie *Go*. While these pitches can, at times, be uncomfortable, multilevel marketing companies have done a fantastic job over the years of preaching their marketing message in an efficient manner. Now, we're not suggesting you turn your company into a multilevel marketing business, nor are we saying that you should annoy social media users into becoming evangelists for your company or product. But we do think we have a lot of history we can reference when considering how to be effective on social media.

What is new today is that all the interpersonal relationships are exposed online. We can keep up with friends, new products, companies, and brands in real time. We can share the experiences we have, good and bad, more efficiently than before. More of our lives than ever before—our choices, our problems, our successes—are recorded, communicated, and shared. In that sense, it challenges all of us as marketers to use social networks as a channel for customer engagement and for being more understanding, more human, and arguably more subtle.

You Can't Force Viral

Viral marketing tends to just happen. It can't be forced. When it is forced, it comes off as insincere and has the opposite effect of what you likely intended. If you want to create your own viral marketing campaign, think about the assets you have that are naturally funny or entertaining. Why do they resonate with people? Then make sure you can capture and reproduce that magic in an ongoing campaign.

Other Opportunities in Social Networking

Aside from viral marketing campaigns, social media affords you other opportunities to engage with customers. Some of these are regarded as traditional marketing functions, while others may be in a different part of your company managed by other people. This is why later we'll discuss organizational dynamics and why it's to your long-term career benefit to become a social media evangelist inside your company. But for now, what types of things can your company or brand manage more effectively with social media?

Complaints It's becoming more and more common for people to use their loudspeaker to complain about bad customer service or bad experiences with products and services. You can't stop people from saying whatever they'd like, but you can aggressively work to remedy the situation and turn the unsatisfied customer into a satisfied one.

Praise It's rare for your customers to praise you, but in the case of especially good service or experiences, it does occasionally happen. This is a great opportunity for you to reinforce your attention to detail and customer service, as long as you tell people the good things about what you are marketing.

Lead Generation/Business Development Social media is the "great democratizer"—that is, people are far more accessible than they were 10 years ago. They are blogging, commenting on different social networks, and making their thoughts and feelings known. As a salesperson or business developer, you have access to all the information you need on sales and business development targets. This is one of our favorite applications of social media.

Recommendations While Amazon.com was one of the first pioneers in this area, it has become common for companies to adopt their own recommendation strategy for products and services. Think *Consumer Reports* but in the form of individual testimonials. Some companies are more active than others in "managing" feedback.

Outbound Communications/Updates/Mailing Lists Skeptics say that social media is just a modern-day mailing list. That would be true except that social media provides ample opportunity for people to share and comment on things they receive. It raises the bar for effective marketing communications. If you want people to talk about you positively in social media, you have to say something pretty compelling.

Fan Clubs Your most passionate supporters will likely be willing to identify with your brand. In the past, clubs have been created to allow marketers to communicate regularly with fans. Now, using social media, costs are reduced to the amount of money it takes to produce your content. It's time to get creative.

> **Note:** Don't be ashamed to reach out to businesspeople on Twitter and the blogosphere. Social media is a perfect icebreaker for conversations with prospective clients, customers, or partners. Just be sure to start a conversation, and don't sell until you've established some common ground.

Some of these things may be better executed inside existing social networks. Some may require you to add social features to existing websites. Others may require recalibration of your team to respond to and engage with customers proactively. You'll have to consider all of these things when putting together a comprehensive social media campaign that gets people to act.

Marketing and
Business Success
on Facebook

One of the best things to come from the Internet marketing revolution is that we can measure things. Page views, unique visitors, and transactions have been measured for quite some time now. With social marketing, we can now measure interactions more effectively. But is it all a red herring? Is measurement just setting us up for disappointment? What are the right metrics? When should they be achieved? Are there things that we perhaps shouldn't even measure?

This chapter will summarize the different ways you can measure success so that you can establish a framework that will work for your business and the expectations you have of the social channel.

Chapter Contents

Right-Brain vs. Left-Brain Thinking

Neuroscientists have struggled for many years to understand the differences in how we think. Some people are comfortable with numbers, while others think of spending a few minutes in a spreadsheet as a circle of hell. Similarly, others are natural artists, but don't ask a spreadsheet jockey to be the next Rembrandt.

Data suggests that *hemispheric dominance* is in play for all of us. We are born with either right-brained or left-brained tendencies; in other words, we favor one side of our brain over the other. Education and other environmental forces also play a major role in how we view the world, how we see events, and how we experience life. According to Carolyn Asbury of the Dana Foundation, a private brain research philanthropic group, most people are left-brained: 97 percent of right-handed people and 70 percent of left-handed people. Table 3.1 summarizes the differences between right-brained and left-brained people.

▶ **Table 3.1** Common elements of left-brain vs. right-brain thinking

Left-brained	Right-brained
Truth through logic, facts, math, and science	Truth through feeling, symbols, and images
Natural skeptic	Natural believer
Detail-oriented	Artistic
Perceptive to order/patterns	Emotional
Reality-based	Presents possibilities
Strategic thinker	Impulsive, risk taker
Practical and safe	Prefers fiction, fantasy
Prefers nonfiction, history	

SOURCE: VARIOUS SOURCES, "LEFT BRAIN, RIGHT BRAIN" BY DAN EDEN, http://viewzone2.com/bicamx.html, www.perthnow.com.au/fun-games/left-brain-vs-right-brain/story-e6frg46u-1111114517613

A great example of how we view the world differently is in the personality traits of the two authors of this book. Chris is a typical left-brained thinker who loves numbers and lives in spreadsheets. Predictably, he enjoyed chemistry in high school, he loves the History Channel, and he reads biographies for fun. He even majored in history in college. Mari, on the other hand, is a right-brained thinker who is energized by positive feedback from members of the social media community. If you've ever scanned Mari's posts on Facebook and Twitter, you'll see that she's quite clearly right-brained.

World-class marketers recognize that right-brained and left-brained people fundamentally see the world differently. But this applies not just to the consumers you're marketing to but also people inside your company who may run your social media marketing activities or judge them. Success takes all types. The ideal person running your social marketing campaigns will be someone who can flip between the two effectively. If only you could combine a right-brained thinker who can establish real, emotional connections with a left-brained thinker who is naturally fluent in metrics. All your problems would be solved! But people who have developed that capability are very hard to find. If you have one, give them a hug!

In some cases, your brand may already have made some choices about how it positions itself. If people can be right- or left-brained, why can't companies or brands? Take, for example, the cases of Microsoft and Apple, two tech giants. Microsoft has positioned itself as a "left-brained" brand in a variety of ways. Launches of its software products are generally not "flashy" (Xbox excepted) but rather consist of product features, detailed demos, and technical specifications. Executive briefings focus on value and the practical application of the suite of products. The marketing and branding are designed to get the attention of left-brained business decision makers. Like Microsoft or not, it's pretty effective positioning in the market when people say things like "Nobody ever got fired for choosing Microsoft!"

Contrast that with Apple and its product launches under the late Steve Jobs. He'd wear the same stylish black turtleneck and pair of jeans to every launch event. Its products were sleek and elegant. They were demonstrated with few/no technical details, in a manner designed to create an emotional attachment and connection with the viewer. Style was at the forefront of every Apple product launch, and it was part of every detail of every major iPhone and iPad launch until Steve Job's unfortunate passing. That's marketing to the "right-brained," creative segment that was the "apple" of Apple's eye.

Interestingly, that very attention to detail is inherently a characteristic of the left-brained marketer. Apple recognized that its early adopters were likely to be artists, creative people, entrepreneurs, and the like—many of whom are right-brained. The company effectively reinvented a moribund market by understanding the differences between right-brained and left-brained thinkers. Apple combined the two to revolutionize an industry.

Now let's apply this to your marketing problems. Use the following questions to help you think through your organization, your customers, and your capabilities:

- Is your business right-brained or left-brained? Looking at this in the simplest way, does your organization and its products or services appeal to practicality? To charitable causes? To art or style?

- In your other marketing channels, do you communicate in a right-brained or left-brained manner? Do right-brained or left-brained marketing communications result in the best outcomes? If you don't know, ask your colleagues what they think.

- Are your customers more right-brained or left-brained? What will people in your target audiences respond to best? Facts or ideas? Hard data or stories? Will they engage in unbridled cynicism, or will they "believe"?

- Is your marketing team right-brained or left-brained? Is it dominated by people with a specific orientation? Idea people can't dominate, because you would have a hard time establishing success metrics and quantifying success. Similarly, numbers people would make a Facebook presence or ad campaign about as boring and clinical as it could be.

None of this will tell you the precise steps you should take to market yourself on Facebook, but it will give you an idea of the tone you should take, the types of content that will appeal to your audience, and the people who are guiding the work. Facebook is unique as a platform in the sense that success really requires you to think in both right-brained and left-brained ways. You have to entertain your fans while getting them to interact with you and each other on an ongoing basis. You must appeal to logical people who want "just the facts" just as well as those who respond more emotionally. And you have to quantify what you're doing to ensure that you're getting better all the time. Let's dive into these two things now in more detail.

Overview of Social Marketing Metrics

It stands to reason that as social marketing matures, marketers have higher and higher expectations of how Facebook will move meaningful business metrics. Larger companies are spending more time and resources on social media, and sooner or later those dollars have to help the business. Small businesses are perhaps even more efficient. They're usually run with a lean, small staff, if one exists at all beyond the owner or manager. There usually isn't a "marketer" assigned at many small businesses. There might be a consultant, or the owner may take a special interest in promoting their business beyond the traditional means that have worked for many years. Nonprofit organizations and government agencies are jumping into the fray now as well, often attaching social marketing to the responsibilities of an eager but maybe overworked employee who wants to pitch in.

All too often, thoughtful analysis of the success or failure of social marketing initiatives these days is replaced by one increasingly asked question:

What incremental return on investment (ROI) are we getting for our social media activities?

That is, how much more money are we making because we're spending so much time on "engagement?"

Perhaps social media is a great target for finance and accounting types, but ROI is not just a measure of direct, incremental revenue. Return includes both incremental revenue and cost savings. Social media allows you to acquire customers more easily than traditional alternatives. It is a cheaper way to keep people informed about your business, and it is a very effective way to plant subconscious and occasional reminders into the psyche of friends and fans alike.

An obsessive focus on social media ROI is paradoxically both an intelligent and a naive stance to take. It's intelligent because all marketers should be held accountable to an ROI standard. It's naive, however, because few things in marketing today can be measured and tracked solely by an ROI standard. Look around—exactly what aspects of marketing today are tracked to ROI and strictly held to that standard or else they are cut from the marketing mix?

Tip: ROI is fantasyland for people who are not in marketing, yet want so desperately to understand it. If you focus on using metrics to help you get smarter and not necessarily prove ROI, you'll do better than most of your peers.

Don't take this the wrong way. It would be great to spend marketing dollars and resources on precisely the things that are incrementally profitable to your business. However, wouldn't it be even better to know the specific things that you did that turned out to be big money losers?

Unfortunately, business is a lot more complex than that. Nobody knows all the exact levers that result in a profit. We all have judgment calls to make. All the things that marketers do to drive attention to a business, a product, or a service are not equal in driving traffic to the store and customers to the cash register. Some work, and some just don't. Moreover, if you held all your business operations to a simple profit and loss metric, would you kill the ones that were unprofitable?

Our guess is that you wouldn't do it. It's unrealistic, not to mention a heartless and relatively inhumane way to operate a business that requires interaction with real people in order to make money. Businesses offer loss leaders all the time to get foot traffic in a store. Think of the "convenience stores" on a busy corner that sell their gasoline at cost just to have a shot at selling higher-margin items like soft drinks, snacks, and beer.

Sure, we should hold our marketing activities to a high standard. But typically someone who is ultra-concerned only about financial return on investment from social media is either a short-sighted thinker, a cash-crazed accountant, or maybe someone who read last week's *Business Week* on a recent flight. Remember the old saying about advertising: "20 percent of my money is well spent. I just don't know which 80 percent to cut!"

We all want return from investment, but strict dollars-and-cents accounting isn't the only way to know that your efforts are valuable. Furthermore, it isn't even appropriate for certain uses of social media where return on investment is elusive and may show up in other areas, such as customer satisfaction, reduced costs to the business overall, and the likelihood of recommending your company's products and services in the future.

Marketing Metrics and Your Organization

Meaningful marketing metrics in Facebook depend on your organization's specific situation. Consider for a moment that you were dropped into two different situations: marketing your neighborhood pizza place and marketing Barbie. Those are undoubtedly two vastly different business and marketing situations where your boss would have different expectations and where you'd be under different pressures. Your organization's specific marketing metrics will depend on the following:

Type of Organization Are you marketing a recognized brand? A small business? A celebrity?

Type of Product or Service that You Sell Organizations of all types sell something to people, even if there is no financial transaction implicit in the relationship. Organizations sell products, services, information, causes, people, concepts, and so on.

Your Marketing Priorities As such, marketing priorities—especially as they relate to social media—may not be obvious. Earlier in this chapter, we discussed the obsessive focus on financial return on investment for social activities. But some marketing initiatives may be optimized for other goals, such as branding, getting awareness of a product/service in a particular demographic, and so on.

Resources You Have Available No matter how small or resource-constrained you may be, you have resources at your disposal to use to help you engage with customers using social media. What are they? People? Content? A budget?

Nature of the Relationship with Your Customer Is the relationship between you and your customer an inherently personal one? Do you know your customers personally? Is that feasible, or would the scale of getting to know each of your customers be cost-prohibitive? How do your customers typically interact with you?

Also remember the role of emotion when it comes to success in social media. Most marketers want to tap into emotion because they know that passion is an indication that someone is emotionally invested. Put another way, you don't just want fans; you want lunatics who will support you, share your content, interact with you, and also tell their friends. Later we will expand upon this when we discuss customer service opportunities in social media.

These considerations should drive exactly what you want to get out of social media marketing as you build your plan.

Defining Your Facebook Presence

It seems like a relatively simple concept, but a lot of companies struggle in defining exactly what their presence on Facebook and other social media will be. Should you lead with brand? Product? Information about your business? Newsletter content? What will resonate with customers in a meaningful way that will compel them to listen to you and share your wisdom with their friends? If you are struggling with this, you aren't alone. It isn't easy to translate your assets into a social media success story.

When helping clients with their social media problems, we've been most successful when starting off by thinking about the exact reasons a consumer interacts with a company. What is the value proposition of your company or product? What does the product provide that competitive products don't? Do you spend more time marketing the actual benefits of your product, or do you market a lifestyle to which people aspire?

Facebook won't cure problems with a product or brand, but it will give you an opportunity to reach out in new and interesting ways that, to some extent, reinforce what people already think. Therefore, it's pretty important to think through your most successful customer campaigns and find commonalities across them. If you are trying to establish a campaign that highlights differences between your products and those of your competitors, you should probably undertake the same exercise for them as well.

It sounds almost elementary, but you really need to think critically about your business, where you fit in, what you have (or should have) learned from past campaigns, and how you can sell your vision in the context of social media.

Understanding Who Your Customers Are

Empathy with target customers is another key part of the brainstorming process. What do they want from you and your company? More important, what *don't* they want from you? Product stewards (product managers, marketing managers, evangelists, executives, and so on) like you put your life into improving products, marketing efforts, sales performance, and so on. As such, however, you can be too close to empathize with customers who get marketing messages at every turn, many of which are annoying, intrusive, or flat-out offensive. They come in commercials, Internet advertising, product placement, email, social media...you name it. Good Facebook campaigns will enhance a customer's life in a meaningful way.

Those of you in larger companies have probably spent a fair amount of time or resources thinking through customer segmentation and personas. *Personas* are a way to humanize a customer segment by making some generalized assumptions about how individuals in certain segments live, what they do, how they think, and so on. The sample personas in the featured case "Sample Personas for Acme Foods" illustrate the personas of a fictionalized frozen food company.

Personas are great for kick-starting the creative process. Although they can sometimes become a crutch used to oversimplify thinking, they can be very helpful in considering customer engagement.

Featured Case: Sample Personas for Acme Foods

Acme Foods is looking to understand different segments of its market by creating personas that reflect the reasons customers are interested in their products. Here are a few examples:

Debbie is a 41-year-old woman in Cedar Rapids, Iowa. She is married, has three children younger than 8, and cares for her aging mother, who is being treated for lung cancer. Her husband travels for business three days a week. She is responsible for all the household chores, cooking, and meal planning, so she doesn't have much time for the Internet, although she is a regular email user. Her family eats at home six days a week. Her children are overweight, so she is increasingly concerned about nutrition and portion control.

Brock is a 22-year-old college graduate in Palo Alto, California. He is single, and he just entered the workforce after graduating with honors from Stanford University. He just rented his first apartment, and now he is learning to cook and prepare meals on his own. The only problem is that he is now busier than he has ever been. He buys food at the grocery store mostly based on convenience. His refrigerator is empty, but his freezer is full. He keeps up with friends on Facebook, and he watches more YouTube than live television.

Annie is a 66-year-old retiree currently living in Savannah, Georgia. She enjoys playing golf, spending time at the beach, catching up with old friends, and visiting with her 11 grandchildren. Her husband is now diabetic, so they don't enjoy dining out as much as they did years ago. Annie has never enjoyed cooking—she looks for shortcuts in the kitchen wherever she can find them. The retirement community provides packaged meals three times a week. She now frequents the computer center to learn how to use the Internet.

Jill is a 31-year-old attorney in Bristol, Connecticut. Now that she's settled into her career, she has taken up cooking as a hobby. She likes using fresh ingredients whenever possible, but she always has backup ingredients in her freezer just to be safe. She has read about the health benefits of frozen foods, but she remains a skeptic. She aspires to open a restaurant later in life. She just found Facebook, but she's afraid of sharing personal data on the Internet.

Mapping Customer Needs to Effective Tactics

Some tactics will resonate well with certain personas, and others obviously won't. This is an important consideration—social media and Facebook campaigns can't be expected to (and likely won't) solve your problems across all customer segments. Pick and choose opportunities, and make sure you are reaching those customers in friendly, helpful ways that map to your brand or product.

Some tactics will work, but others may offend your customers. Don't be so close to your social media effort that you fail to see when your tactics actually bother the customer. Facebook and social media are interesting, innovative ways to reach out to your customers, but poor execution can certainly backfire on you. Think customers first and your business second, and you'll probably be more successful.

How does this work as a practical matter? Let's think through a few examples. A local home builder wants to take better advantage of social media. So, start by asking these primary and critical questions:

Q: What do customers of the home builder want?

A: They want the best house they can get according to their prioritized purchasing criteria: size, neighborhood, convenience to work/play/children/family, price, and so on.

Q: How will they find this house?

A: There are a lot of ways people can find houses. Maybe they hear about houses from a friend, perhaps they drive by properties in a certain neighborhood and find what they want, perhaps they find a great deal in the newspaper, or maybe a friendly real estate agent has suggested properties for them.

No matter what, it's fragmented and oftentimes difficult to find a great deal. So, the customer's main motivations in this case are convenience, knowledge, time savings, and assistance with a very important purchasing decision.

Keeping the home builder in the back of your mind, now think about a different example—a popular local restaurant that has a unique local flair.

Q: What do customers of this restaurant want?

A: Occasionally, they want a great meal at a great price. But the restaurant is more to local customers than just another place to eat. It's a lifestyle and a part of the fabric of that city that makes it a special place to live. It's a popular brand, and association with it speaks volumes.

Thus, the customer's main motivation to engage with this restaurant is one of affiliation, personality, and appreciation for local business.

These are two totally different cases where customers are motivated differently and where appropriate and effective Facebook marketing tactics will differ. Customers for houses want totally different things than people showing support for a unique local business. Perhaps more important, people make a one-time decision to purchase a home, whereas they may eat at the same restaurant 30 times a year. So, the characteristics of the business—transaction cost, transaction frequency, local differentiation, and brand affinity—all have a significant impact on the tactics that would make sense. You'll see this in more detail as we walk you through the different marketing elements that Facebook provides.

Note: When in doubt about your customer, keep asking questions. Whether you're in the brainstorming process or in the middle of a focus group, it doesn't hurt to keep asking questions until you get answers that clarify the motivations of others.

Your Social Media "Product"

One thing that is common across different social media campaigns is that each has a fairly well-defined set of rules by which they operate. The social media presence is, in effect, an interactive online "product." The medium is a combination of Facebook, Twitter, other social media destinations, and the Web. All of it is consumed by a computer, a mobile phone, or a tablet device. Each of these experiences is different based on each form factor and what users are able to do conveniently therein.

Customers, fans, and followers are found for the "product" through a variety of means, such as viral marketing, Internet marketing, email marketing, social network marketing, and word-of-mouth marketing. There is an implicit contract between the company and the customer that the "product" will perform as expected and that the company won't violate the terms under which the customer was first attracted to the product. Your thinking should assume that your social media presence is a product of its own that needs care, maintenance, and performance metrics that will help guide decision making. This social media "product" enhances a consumer's experience with the product or service you are trying to sell or the brand you are trying to manage.

Different situations in business require different tactics. Some tactics are off-limits to you as a marketer of a certain kind of product, while others are fair game. You shouldn't get too critical of yourself or of your company, and you shouldn't significantly change what your product, service, or brand represents to the marketplace. Translate what you do to the social media context and experiment on the edges. The "Quick-Start Guide for Social Media" sidebar should kick-start your creativity and guide your thinking as you brainstorm project ideas.

Quick-Start Guide for Social Media

Maybe you are approaching social media for the first time, maybe you have inherited a failed project, or maybe you are resurrecting some old ideas. Whatever the case, sometimes you need quick answers to help you see opportunities and make quick decisions.

Get good answers for the following 10 questions before you decide how to engage. We highly recommend this exercise before getting, started regardless of whether you will run your first project in-house or with the help of a consultant.

- What is most recognizable about your brand? This can be a person, a place, a logo, a jingle, and so on.

- Does your brand have a spokesperson or character who "is" what you are trying to sell? If not, are you open to creating one?

Quick-Start Guide for Social Media *(Continued)*

- What is the goal of your project? Sales/e-commerce? Improved image in your market? Better customer service and satisfaction?

- What specific metrics will you use to measure success?

- When discussing the opportunity in social media with executives at your company, do they view social media as an opportunity, a risk, or an unknown?

- Does your company or brand have official policies for blogging, employee activity on social media, and outreach to customers? Is it centralized or decentralized?

- What types of content do you have that would be interesting to share with social media users?

- Are you willing to share interesting content from third-party sources on the Web with your customers?

- Creating your campaign, maintaining it, tracking metrics, and making adjustments will take time and expertise. Do you have interested people in your company who are willing and able to do this work?

- What is your backup plan in case the social media project fails or doesn't meet the goals of your organization? Who can you call for an objective third-party opinion if you have a problem?

What You'll Get in Return: The Hard and Soft Benefits of Social Media

When you succeed in social media marketing, what do you get in return? As we've suggested earlier in this chapter, you will get a combination of immediately measurable and ongoing marketing benefits. If you're in a retail business, you'll hear the cash register "ring" as a direct result of your actions, but you'll also get customers whom you can't track to a specific marketing action or tactic. If you execute well, you'll be top-of-mind the next time customers think of you and your competitors. That's what makes social marketing both refreshing and frustrating at the same time.

Let's shift gears and talk about all the benefits that you may earn by doing a great job with social media marketing. Remember that *how* you use Facebook and other types of social media will impact the benefits you get and the type of business you are marketing. An e-commerce retailer will have different success criteria than a local bricks-and-mortar business, which will have different objectives than a multinational consumer packaged-products company.

Here are some of the benefits of good social media marketing:

Revenue This is the holy grail of all marketing. If we could translate small marketing investments into increased revenue through sales, donations, contracts, and so forth, we would do it all day long.

Qualified Leads You gain qualified leads by using social media and all its features to find people with specific needs that may make them worthy of a sales call or additional marketing activity designed to turn them into customers.

Fans/Email Subscriptions This involves a direct association someone makes with your organization for updates. In the context of Facebook, it's fans. For Twitter, it is followers. For YouTube, it is subscribers. The email marketing industry was the original, digital means for marketers to reach consumers and keep them informed, but that is being enhanced and in some ways replaced by social media.

Clicks This is the number of people who see something in social media (article, advertisement, and so forth) and click the related hyperlink to get more information. This is typically an indication of interest and an intention to learn more.

Testimonials Because social media is an opportunity for everyone to publish to the Web (not just you marketers), it's also a great customer feedback vehicle. For example, customers use review sites such as Yelp (www.yelp.com) and Angie's List (www.angieslist.com) to assess local businesses. Customers similarly use review functionality on existing websites to provide feedback to other people who may purchase an item. These testimonials may happen with or without your direct intervention, and they can be a positive or negative force for your business depending on your online reputation.

Customer Service It can be very costly to handle all issues related to your organization with a personal phone call or in-person visit. As organizations continue to look to more cost-effective ways to scale their operations, some have turned to social media as a way to provide good, cost-effective customer service to resolve the conflicts and issues that inevitably rise.

Retention and Loyalty Many industry experts have observed that social media can be an ideal platform for customer retention and loyalty programs for businesses of all sizes. If, as we mentioned, a social media fan/follower relationship is a good proxy for being a loyal customer of a business, why not use social media to develop a connection between a customer and an organization further?

Cheaper, Faster, and More Targeted Ad Campaigns Executing email, direct mail, and traditional yet targeted ad campaigns can be costly and can involve quite a bit of lead time. Facebook advertising is a great way to execute a new customer acquisition campaign quickly and cost-effectively.

Information Consumption Sometimes, you just need to get the word out about something—an event, a sale, a fundraiser, and so on. Email tends to be a high-investment way to do it. Even with email marketing tools from MailChimp (www.mailchimp.com) or Constant Contact (www.constantcontact.com), it may take a lot of setup time and hand-wringing about whether people open their email. Social media is very quick and requires a low investment by comparison. Just update your status, and instantly your message will show up on your friends' and fans' Facebook News Feeds.

Branding/Name Recognition When you hear the word *cola*, do you instinctively think of Coca-Cola? Don't worry, most people do, as Sheena Iyengar suggests in her great best seller, *The Art of Choosing* (Twelve, 2010). Execute any type of marketing well over a long period of time, and you'll get instant name recognition, which translates to purchase affinity and long-term success. Maybe this is what you're after, and social media can help provide it.

Influence/Access Social media is democratized access just as much as it is democratized publishing. Everyone's profile is online and available, and most people can be contacted, or at least reached, by virtue of the information they share about themselves.

Specific Applications of Facebook Marketing

Facebook offers several options and features for marketing your product or company. But the two main marketing tactics that have emerged and are most widely used are pages and advertising. Pages are effectively the "basic presence" most organizations have on Facebook, while advertising is the primary demand-generation vehicle for companies that want to do social network marketing. While we're discussing how to develop your social media product on Facebook, it is helpful to take a look at how some other brands, companies, and organizations have utilized these features.

Pages

3M (www.3m.com) used many of the features of Facebook Pages in its marketing strategy to launch the Scotch Shoe, a tape dispenser designed to look like a Mary Jane shoe.

Although many in the company were excited about the launch of this new product, targeted at a predominantly female market, budget constraints put traditional media out of reach and made promoting the product a challenge. Although many in the organization were skeptical, the 3M marketing team chose Facebook as the channel to launch this unique product. Despite the promise of Facebook, 3M nonetheless had to harness the value of the social network to specifically create product awareness and generate buzz for the new product.

> *We have the sales and market share, but with a product like tape, it is difficult to get your consumers passionate about your product.*

> BRIAN STEPHENS
> *E-Marketing Manager*
> *3M Canada Consumer and Office Division*

3M chose to market the Scotch Shoe on Facebook for a few different reasons. Facebook is Canada's most popular social networking platform. At the time of the launch, Facebook was home to more than 12 million active Canadian users and boasted 7.5 billion impressions per month.

While marketing on Facebook is free, there are, of course, costs involved with ad creation, copywriting, design, marketing, planning, execution, campaign and community maintenance, and more. But creating a business fan page costs nothing on Facebook. When you are on a budget, it's hard not to at least investigate free options.

3M created a Facebook fan page. This gave its customers and fans a targeted destination for free, which allowed 3M to not worry about designing and developing a new product page on the 3M website, saving scarce financial resources for better use elsewhere. On the fan page, 3M provided fans with all the relevant information about the product, such as images and videos, store listings, and product availability. The Facebook page also allowed 3M to conduct surveys, post discussions to facilitate dialogue, develop and nurture relationships with community influencers, and collect feedback about the product.

3M also produced and promoted contests to drive traffic to its fan page. One contest incentivized users to become fans by offering a gift card for a shoe store. Another contest awarded the winner a free Scotch Shoe. In both cases, the contests were directly targeted to the product's key demographic. This, in turn, encouraged interaction and engagement on the fan page. To enter the contests, users were required to enter commentary and feedback about the Scotch Shoe on the fan page, thereby dramatically accelerating the amount of exposure the fan page received via the social media ecosystems of the product's fans. Remember, any time a user entered a comment on the fan page for the Scotch Shoe, that comment was potentially exposed to every person who followed that user via their News Feed, which shows up on the home page of every single person who is Facebook friends with the Scotch Shoe's fan page member.

3M launched three different Facebook ads during this campaign. As part of the marketing strategy, 3M closely monitored the performance of its ads and adjusted the rotation and targeting on a regular basis. The result? The Scotch Shoe sold out almost immediately in every store that stocked the product. The Scotch Shoe Facebook page has more than 21,000 fans and thousands of Wall comments. According to MarketingProfs, the engagement ads created for the campaign delivered more than 1.5 million impressions and 300,000 clicks.

3M didn't have big marketing dollars to execute this campaign. Scotch certainly isn't one of the sexier brands like Apple, BMW, or Nike, but it was still able to run a successful Facebook marketing campaign and hold contests that engaged its customers without giving away prizes that would have been cost-prohibitive. The 3M marketing team used Facebook as an effective, low-cost platform to launch a product successfully and create new relationships with its customers.

The Scotch team replicated its success on other properties that now lead the way for the company. Check out several of its pages today at the following links:

www.facebook.com/Scotch

www.facebook.com/ScotchBlue

www.facebook.com/ScotchDuctTape

Advertising

When Charlene Li was an analyst at Forrester Research, she produced a series of case studies where she showcased the differences between traditional marketing and social media marketing. The key takeaway from the series of case studies is that marketing on Facebook requires communication, not advertising. That's true to a point.

Advertising of any kind requires some method of interruption. This can come in the form of a commercial interrupting a television show or radio program, a billboard interrupting the landscape on your commute home, a large decal on the floor in the grocery store interrupting your shopping experience, or any of a myriad of other creative techniques advertisers have devised to turn your attention from the content or task at hand toward a message from a client who wants your attention.

When Facebook first introduced ads, one of the challenges of advertising on the platform was the relatively low response rates from users. Although Facebook's pay-per-click model of advertising offers competitive rates when compared with similar platforms on Google, Yahoo!, Microsoft Advertising, and others, Facebook users have been consistently obstinate when it comes to responding to advertising on their profile pages. As an advertiser/marketer, Facebook offered a unique challenge. It has an extremely large, desirable, and targetable audience that is not interested in clicking ads.

To be sure, there are plenty of options for you as a marketer to consider when it comes to purchasing advertising on Facebook. For instance, as with most sites, you can purchase standard ad units across the Facebook.com domain as targeted users check out the News Feed, profiles, and pages and while they play games. Click-through rates vary significantly based on the type of advertising you are running (CPM impression ads vs. CPC click-through ads) and the historical performance of your ads.

Companies and organizations also have the option of creating Facebook ads. Facebook ads (previously called Facebook flyers) are nothing more than self-serve advertisements that you can create at www.facebook.com/advertising/. Advertising with Facebook ads allows users to make their own custom-designed ads on Facebook at low prices. Users have the option of creating Facebook ads on either a cost-per-click (CPC) or cost-per-thousand (CPM) model, and the ads appear throughout Facebook on the right side of the screen. Figure 3.1 shows a few examples.

These are just a few of the ways that people experience advertising on Facebook.

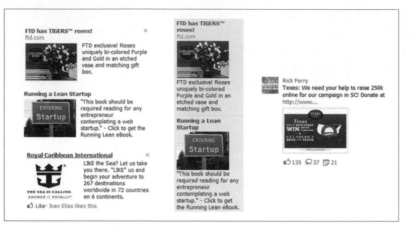

Figure 3.1 Facebook ad types: standard sponsored ads, ads as they appear on the Facebook Timeline, and sponsored page ads

Your Facebook To-Do List

Now turn your attention to execution. What are the specific tasks required to establish and maintain a successful presence on social networks? Figure 3.2 shows the basic workflow for social network marketing.

Figure 3.2 Social media workflow

The first thing you may notice is that the decision to create a campaign kicks off a work process that is iterative. Welcome to the Web! At each stage of the process, you really should have the next step in the back of your mind. It's rare that one of these steps takes a significant amount of effort, but the aggregate can get time-consuming, especially if you are running or managing multiple campaigns or if you are taking advantage of several social networks at the same time. Let's go through what each part of the social media workflow really means.

Set Up Campaign

The entire workflow starts with a concept—an idea that will drive the execution of the work along with the tone of the project. So, it's safe to say that when you are getting started, you are squarely in creativity mode. As you define your "product," what will the experience be for an end user? Can you do something special that will inspire your audience? Take the Subservient Chicken example from Chapter 2, "Understanding Social Media and Facebook." What does Burger King have to do with a man in a chicken suit taking orders from an Internet user? Not a lot, unless you want your brand to be fun and lighthearted.

Of all parts of the process, this is the one best suited for outsourcing to creative agencies. Creative professionals can really help by contributing unconventional ideas that may resonate unexpectedly well with your customer base. If you are going to go this route, *don't* interfere with the creative process, but *do* make sure you task the agency to come up with a variety of ideas for you to consider. Nobody succeeds every time out—baseball players, quarterbacks in football, or creatives—so don't look for one great idea but rather a few concepts that can drive your final decision. Remember, *you* are the one making the decision. At the end of the day, you are the customer. You need to be able to execute on the idea you choose, and that idea has to fit what you intuitively know about the brand or product you manage on a regular basis.

Procure Content

Content is the linchpin to successful social media. With all the noise out there, you need to have an interesting or useful voice, and you have to communicate regularly enough to stay relevant. This can be in the form of articles, essays, status updates, podcasts, videos, music, and so on.

Fortunately, norms on the Internet have evolved in such a way that you don't have to create your own unique content every time you want to say something. So much content is available on the Internet that you can sometimes just point to content produced by others. Alternatively, you can use existing content that you've created for other reasons. You can commission new content for use on social media.

There are a lot of strategic considerations here that we'll cover later in this book. For now, understand that you'll need to find, repurpose, or create new content (pictures, video, podcasts, status updates, blog posts, and so on) if you're going to engage with customers effectively via social media.

Update Content

Having the content certainly isn't enough. You need to make sure you use the content effectively. Since social media is truly interactive, you're going to get both direct and indirect comments and feedback. How will you keep content updated and respond to feedback? Who will manage this process? These questions certainly need to be addressed well in advance of launching your Facebook campaign. You need at least an understanding that guides the social media presence—the hierarchy of people who are allowed to make updates, what they are or are not allowed to say, scenarios they are not allowed to address, and so on. Without understanding across your organization, you are implicitly creating a situation that turns the social media effort into a political minefield. This is particularly important given that social media is at the intersection of sales, marketing, business development, customer service, and customer satisfaction.

Track Metrics

Someone, somewhere in the process needs to update the daily metrics that are created as a result of your activity. Some of this already happens when metrics are generated for activity on your website. In all likelihood, your team is already using one of a number of statistics or web analytics vendors (Omniture (www.omniture.com), Core-metrics (www.coremetrics.com), Webtrends (webtrends.com), or even Google Analytics (www.google.com/analytics). These products track unique users, page views, and other important data that tells the tale of how your websites are used.

The use of social networks similarly creates a rich data set that tells you how customers receive your social media presence and campaigns. Some of it is readily available just by scanning a fan page, a group, or a profile. Other data can be found in Facebook Insights. And a litany of third-party social analytics companies have emerged to answer deeper questions. One thing is certain—critical data is located in a number of places. In some cases, these reports will be suitable for your business needs. In other cases, you may need to pull appropriate raw data into a spreadsheet so that you can analyze it appropriately and create charts, graphs, and data visualizations to help you both understand and communicate the meaning of the data. We'll look more closely at the importance of tracking metrics in several places in this book and in detail in Chapter 8, "The Analytics of Facebook."

Analyze and Revise

After you've established your social media presence for a period of time, you'll have a rich set of data that can tell you whether your effort is succeeding. Success may be an absolute goal, such as 2,500 Facebook fans or an additional 5,000 unique visitors for a website during a month, or it may be a trending goal like 10 incremental fans per day after 90 days. Progress against these goals will need to be judged based on all the relevant data. For instance, maybe you are getting a lot of traffic coming to your Facebook presence, but it mostly comes from paid advertising when you need something a little more "viral." So, you've achieved your goals, but you've done so in a way that isn't sustainable and won't make your boss happy.

Revise: Set Up Campaign, Take Two

Once you determine whether you can improve or whether you've maxed out the benefits of your efforts, you'll know what you need to change. Changes can come in the form of increased/decreased advertising, demand generation from email marketing or other sources, more/less regular communication, better coordination with other web properties, or a different type of messaging altogether. Revisions are OK and a natural part of the process. Rarely does a social media presence launch without any revisions. You should expect to go through a few rounds of the entire process before you figure out the sweet spot where customers respond to your efforts.

It takes a special person to know how to do all of these things well, especially considering that success relies upon both creativity and proficiency with data analysis. Usually people are *either* right-brained or left-brained but not both! It's an important dynamic to understand. People who naturally complement each other generally run these projects best together.

Diversity of Opinion and Strengths

Most successful marketing projects are well executed across several criteria. The campaign meets customer needs or wants, and it is true to the core values of the business. The value proposition of the product or service is communicated effectively. The design of the campaign is well done, and the brand elements are elegantly integrated. Communication with customers is effective, and it fits the needs of the campaign. Numbers are captured to reflect the success of the campaign, and your colleagues instinctively know how and when to act to make modifications.

What we've described is, in simple terms, a successful marketing campaign. Yet few people have skills across all these areas to be a one-person marketing machine. Why? It takes a variety of different skills, and they rarely appear in a single person. Some of it is education; for example, you don't typically expect educated engineers to be the most fun at a cocktail party. Similarly, you'd never want a born salesperson to brand your company—different people have different skill sets. By tapping into a variety of people with different strengths, you'll do two things:

- You'll get some overlap of responsibility so that no one person can take down your marketing campaign.
- You'll get a diversity of opinion that can make the entire project run more smoothly.

Now that you know the basic requirements for a Facebook marketing campaign, it's time to make your plan consumable in your organization and get started.

Month 1: Create the Plan and Get Started

4

Now that we've gone through all the basic background information you need, it's time to get started on a project. Getting your colleagues comfortable with social media and all it entails—the good and the bad—is a key factor for organizational buy-in and ultimately success. Remember, these projects involve a lot of trial and error. Your company and your management team have to be comfortable with that dynamic if you are going to have the flexibility you need to find a successful social media marketing strategy for your organization.

Chapter Contents

Week 1: Lay the Groundwork

Early in any project, you really should be in fact-finding mode more than anything else. You should research what other people have done and look for examples of companies that execute well. Read everything you can about successful and failed campaigns. Remember that there are a lot of examples of both out there. You can find them by just searching to see what popular brands and your competitors are doing. The best and worst cases tend to get covered in the blogosphere. Week 1 is all about doing due diligence without even getting into the details of what Facebook or other social media services can do for you. Find out what your colleagues think and what people in the industry are saying about customer engagement via social media.

Monday: Set Project Goals

At the highest level, what are you trying to achieve with Facebook? How does it fit into the marketing plan you are already executing? We talked about a few of these opportunities earlier in the book—additional sales, increased revenue, lower marketing/customer engagement costs, improved customer service, collecting feedback quicker, and so on. Most of the time, you and your management team will want all of them, but you'll really need one or two. It's better to be selective about your goals and nail them than it is try to solve every problem for every constituent in your business. Table 4.1 presents some of the types of things you can do with a social media campaign, how you would measure it, and examples.

▶ **Table 4.1** Examples of opportunities in social media

Goal	Metrics	Example
Increased sales	Incremental revenue	Social media campaign launched specifically to sell/market products; URLs set up to identify social media as channel that found the customer
Improved customer service	Increased number of service queries handled, faster response time	Facebook fan page and Twitter account established for customers to ask questions of your business
Save money on marketing or advertising	Lower cost/touch vs. other marketing options	Facebook advertising campaign run to compare costs with traditional marketing efforts
Earn more blogger, journalist, or analyst attention	Number of blog posts mentioning the organization or product / Number of articles written / Number of analyst mentions	Informal engagement 1:1 with people active in social media (Facebook, Twitter, and so on) to inform them of a new product, service, or event

Then there is always the concept of *buzz*, which is the amorphous term used to broadly describe a palpable increase in the positive responses to a product or company in social media. You know that you're getting good buzz when you find that people are saying a lot about you and you haven't really done anything to force it. You may also find that you're getting good buzz when customers just magically appear, seemingly out of nowhere. We find that people use the term when they like what they see but don't quite understand why there is a positive response from customers or pundits in the marketplace. This isn't a criticism—you may conduct a campaign that doesn't immediately result in significant increases in your metrics only to find that, for whatever reason, there is considerably more buzz several weeks or months later. Social media is a handy and relatively inexpensive way to introduce a concept to people well in advance of a product launch or a major marketing push. Buzz is the indirect, and often immeasurable, benefit of those efforts.

Overall, if your company has been active on Facebook and social media, your company is probably more sophisticated at setting goals and measuring success. The bar to achieve success may be pretty high. If it's your first project, the goal may just be as simple as learning what to do and what to expect in the future. Learning is a perfectly reasonable goal, especially if you keep your costs low and your tolerance high.

When working with clients, we often ask them to visualize the 15-minute presentation they are giving to superiors to update them on the status of the project. How will that meeting go? What numbers will support your success? What specific results will help them understand that the project has been a success based on your strategy, your recommendations, and your effort? You know your management chain better than anyone else—it's best to think through their expectations at the beginning of a project so you can guide it to success.

Tuesday: Analyze Stakeholder Needs

Ideally, you'd take a full day here to understand impacts to your business as you enter the world of social media marketing. Interview key stakeholders to understand their perspectives. But if you're short on time, you may be able to learn just as much by putting together a questionnaire that your colleagues can answer easily via email. Make a list of all the people who may be impacted even peripherally by your work on Facebook and social media. Be as inclusive as you can when compiling your list: people in your management chain, colleagues who work on different products, people in organizations that support the marketing or sales effort, and so on. The last thing you need is to be blindsided by influential colleagues who think they were not adequately consulted. They can be your harshest critics.

Start by putting a list of questions together. You want to understand how they view you, your project, your organization, your product, and the nature of the work. Some relevant questions to ask include the following:

- What does the person think of social media?
- Is the person an active Facebook or Twitter user?
- What are some of the company's best offline campaigns for dealing directly with customers?
- What opportunities does the company have to improve its customer engagement?
- What should your company be doing on social networks?
- What would social media success mean to them?

Then there are questions you probably don't want to ask directly but can impact the landscape of your project:

- If the person is an influencer on marketing decisions, does the person think that it is a waste of time?
- How will this project increase their workload? If so, are they aware of it, and are they prepared to deal with it?
- Does the person truly want to see the project succeed? Will the person be difficult when you need help advancing your project?
- Will you get the benefit of doubt from this person in executive or management reviews?

You're doing a few things with the stakeholder analysis. First, you are comparing your assumptions on project goals/priorities to the perception of your colleagues. You may find that the goals you have set for the project are significantly different from the goals that other people have for the project. This is your opportunity to confront the differences and make a course correction if necessary. Second, you want to learn who your friends are within your company. Let's face it—all companies are in some ways political. Some people have authority; others either want it or think they deserve it. It's the nature of business today. You're probably aware of the political minefield in which you work, but it's better to extend the olive branch to as many people as you can as early as you can. You don't want to find out that certain people in your company have a political aversion to your work at the time when your success or failure is being judged. We generally advise middle managers to do what they can at this stage to build consensus around the project. It's a great way to give yourself enough time to learn as you go and get the benefit of the doubt should anything go sideways.

Wednesday: Analyze Customer Needs

Your work earlier this week to determine project goals and the motivations driving or influencing the project inside your company should begin to give you some ideas about campaigns. Now it's time to take all of that to the very people you rely upon to turn your idea into a marketing success. Granted, as a marketer, you should always be engaging with your customers to learn about their needs. But translating that to social media success can be a bit tricky. You'll need direct feedback from relatively disinterested customers in your target demographics to further understand the opportunities and limitations.

The best way to do this doesn't generally involve a lot of money. Do things that are relatively simple and almost immediately actionable. Find people you already know in your target demographics, and give them a cup of coffee or ice cream in exchange for a 30-minute chat. It's essentially your own focus group. If you'd rather have a larger set of opinions, create a survey on SurveyMonkey or a similar service. It's easy to get paralyzed by not having resources to conduct a professional, statistically valid study, and sometimes there are good reasons to conduct such things. But this probably isn't one of those places. As we've mentioned in this book, the Web is the land of experimentation. Users will vote with their presence, and you'll see the results in the number of fans or followers you have, page views, unique users, comments, and so on. Your strategy should be to act on imperfect or incomplete data early in the project and be more reliant on mountains of data as the project matures.

When you get access to your subjects, you're going to have to ask them a lot of questions:

- What do they do on social networks?
- How much time do they spend on Facebook? How often do they log into Facebook? And what do they do once they get there?
- What annoys them about Facebook?
- Are they a Facebook fan or Twitter follower of companies? If so, which ones?
- Have friends shared recommendations on social media? If so, which ones stand out and why?
- What types of content, information, and so on, from the company would you be willing to share with your friends?

There are many more that are applicable to your specific situation. Before sitting down, come up with another three to five questions that can help validate ideas from you or your colleagues. Try not to let your own perceptions of the project or of feedback you've received get in the way of your learning. Be humble, and listen as best you can. Also leave some time for free-form feedback or suggestions. Oftentimes, some of the best ideas don't originate with your company but rather with your customers.

We should mention one other cautionary note here. It's really easy to take customer feedback and run with it full speed. After all, when we hear something from a customer, it's valid and "straight from the horse's mouth," right? Although that is true for the most part, you can't always trust that verbatim feedback to represent what customers really want. You have to map feedback to promises you can keep, both profitably and sustainably. And sometimes you have to jump out on a limb and make assertions that you know what the customers want more than they do.

Note: It's dangerous to listen too closely to what customers say they want. Remember the old Henry Ford quote: "If I'd asked my customers what they wanted, they'd have said they wanted 'a faster horse.'" Customers may not be aware of how technology can help them in new and innovative ways. It's your role to translate their feedback into new and interesting offerings that they'll love.

Thursday: Determine Work Roles

By now you've set your goals, and you've gotten feedback from internal stakeholders and customers. It's time to think through the operational mechanics that will make your Facebook marketing project sing. Regardless of the size of your business, you have to figure out "who does what," and most people have a full-time job managing the roles and responsibilities they were originally hired to do. Branding, messaging, design/creative, e-commerce, product management, website management, IT, and others all may have some role in the success or failure of your project. In small businesses, these roles may be filled by one or two people. But in corporations, you can have entire teams that work on one element of what you need. Like it or not, these people won't necessarily have the same priorities you have. So, you have to get them on your side.

The "Necessary Skill Sets" sidebar illustrates how the role of social media champion is suited for people who are well regarded inside their company. You'll regularly need to get the cooperation of your colleagues to do things they aren't necessarily resourced or equipped to do, oftentimes on short notice. The job is one part visionary, one part marketer, one part politician. Do what you can to give people as much time as you can to help you. You have probably heard the quote "Failure to plan on your part does not constitute an emergency on my part." If you limit your emergencies to times when it's truly warranted, you'll gain the respect of your colleagues, and you'll probably get what you need more regularly.

For each of the roles mentioned, make sure you have a point person available to take requests, feedback, and so on. You really don't want the responsibilities to be ambiguous either—talk through the requirements, what people will need to do, and what the deadlines will likely be. You have to know who will do what, when, and what the rules of engagement will be. Smaller organizations may have a single person handling all of this. That's OK and very common—hey, we don't all have unlimited resources at our disposal. If you are in a larger corporation, your work will likely be handed to a junior member of the team. But don't let that fool you: you'll have to keep that person and their manager happy to get their undying cooperation and love. Earlier in this book, we mentioned that you're truly building a social media product when you create a Facebook campaign. You're the product manager here, so you'll have to manage relationships as much as you'll have to manage the end product.

Friday: Set or Review Social Media Policy

As you navigate the political waters of your organization, you'll undoubtedly face questions about the organization's official policies regarding the execution of social media products. We're talking as much about who does what as who can edit Facebook on behalf of the company, who can comment on success or failure, who can access statistics and summary reports, and who is in the room for executive reviews.

If you are in a large corporation, odds are that you may already have some loose guidelines for blogging set forth by public relations people. This can be a good start—because such guidelines tend to reflect a company's treatment of risk, customer advocacy, and interaction. Put another way, some companies simply put more trust in their employees to make judgment calls that may ultimately reflect on the business. Others prefer a more centralized communications structure that closely manages company positioning. Smaller companies tend to have less complex rules about customer engagement for a few reasons. They tend to be scrappier and more action-oriented. In our experience, this has a lot to do with the fact that larger companies are generally more risk-averse because they are "under the microscope" more than their smaller brethren.

What you really want to do here is make sure your team is on the same page across blogs *and* social media. Although we're not huge fans of "makework" (that is, unproductive work done primarily for the sake of satisfying process), an email or document that summarizes the basics can be very helpful to keep you from having arguments or misunderstandings as your campaign evolves. Here are a few questions to consider when putting together your company's policy on social media:

- What are the official social media accounts for the company?
- Who manages them?
- How often will you post updates from the different accounts?
- What types of content will be shared from the different social media destinations?
- Will the social media account engage in conversation with users?
- When posting news and updates, which accounts have priority?
- What are the loose rules for how the Web, blogs, and social media interact?

Now, you know your organization a lot better than we do. Some companies manage their brand and outbound communications very closely, while others have a more decentralized approach. Think Proctor & Gamble on one hand and Southwest Airlines on the other. It really comes down to philosophy for a lot of businesses. Where your company or organization stands will drive a lot of other factors:

- Whether you will need a stated policy for information shared via social media
- Whether you will communicate with customers directly via social media
- Whether the Facebook presence is managed in-house, by a trusted vendor or consultant, or by a combination of both
- The degree to which updates to the Facebook presence must be approved in advance because of fear of offending parts of the customer base—either accidentally or on purpose
- Whether you should promote your product, your brand, or your company

We have worked with organizations that first spend a lot of time on an "official social media policy" that drives what they can and can't do. And we've worked with others that simply shoot from the hip and worry about problems as they come along. If you don't have such a policy, spend an hour today to create a basic framework that establishes some rules. Think of a few difficult situations you may encounter—a difficult customer, a question you don't want to answer, verbal abuse, and so on—and think about the most appropriate response that fits your company's culture. Make your Facebook marketing project fit the cultural norms of your organization, lest your misunderstanding cost you professionally.

If you don't want to spend time developing your own social media policy, all is not lost. There are plenty of resources available on the Web today to help you either take a few shortcuts in the process or just look at what other people have done.

http://socialmediagovernance.com/policies.php lists several hundred social media policies that have been developed for organizations around the world. We do not condone copying these verbatim, but they can give you a good idea of what other people are doing and how they direct employees to behave.

Inc. Magazine has a great rundown of other considerations for your social media policy at http://www.inc.com/guides/2010/05/writing-a-social-media-policy.html.

And if you want to fill out a quick questionnaire to get a customized policy, visit http://socialmedia.policytool.net/. But be sure to read their disclaimers and have your attorney read the resulting policy very carefully to ensure it works for you.

Week 2: Draft and Present the Plan

You've spent the last week gathering information from your colleagues, customers, and management. By now you should know your limitations for the project, and you should begin to see some specific opportunities. You must put your thoughts into a coherent package that can help you start the project.

We've alluded to this several times in the book, but we can't overstate that success relies on your ability to set up a structure by which you can experiment. No two marketing situations are alike—what works for your brand may not work for someone else's, and vice versa. The problem is that you won't know going into your project if your approach will be naturally viral, if it will require demand generation via advertising, if your lighthearted approach works with consumers, or if you need to deliver "just the facts." You may have a hunch of how things will work, but you need freedom to learn and react to customer feedback. Smaller companies or companies operated by an owner/manager who don't have a management structure should still use this as an opportunity to vet the plan with advisors, peers, other business owners, or anyone familiar with the business and its operations. This is the time for a sanity check—it's time to get outside opinions on what you think will work.

Featured Case: Bad Reactions to Social Media Policy from the Sports World

Sometimes, the reaction to an organization's social media policy can take on a life of its own. Take, for example, the case of ESPN in August 2009. ESPN released a social media policy that is by all accounts pretty fair. ESPN reporters are, in fact, as much representatives of the network as they are individuals—and their social media policy was set accordingly. But one commentator, NBA analyst Ric Bucher, sent a message via Twitter that said ESPN had "prohibited [employees and commentators from] Tweeting unless it serves ESPN." The result was a PR nightmare for the "total sports network," and it sent its PR team into quick action the same day. Nonetheless, the blogosphere lit up with a number of critical posts suggesting that the network doesn't care about fans and wants to control the sports industry. Check out http://mashable.com/2009/08/04/espn-social-media for the full text of the policy along with ESPN's official response.

Continues

Featured Case: Bad Reactions to Social Media Policy from the Sports World
(Continued)

Also in the sports world, the Southeastern Conference of college athletics in the United States released a similarly restrictive social media policy later in August 2009. According to the policy, ticketed fans can't "produce or disseminate (or aid in producing or disseminating) any material or information about the Event, including, but not limited to, any account, description, picture, video, audio, reproduction or other information concerning the Event."

Uproar against this policy ultimately led to its revision 11 days after the policy was released.

What is the reason for all the wrangling over social media in the sports world? Two words: money and control. The only problem is that attendees and consumers today are the same people who insist on sharing their experiences with friends through social media. The consumer is an active participant in social media culture. Keep that in mind as you craft your own social media policy for your employees and your customers moving forward.

Monday: Research Best Practices and Success Stories

Although Facebook is relatively young as a platform, in 2012 and beyond you have the advantage of hindsight. A lot of companies have gone before you to create a Facebook presence. Some have failed; others have enjoyed wild success. Some companies have done very well by letting their communities manage themselves. Before you put pen to paper, you'll want to know more about what has been done in the past. You have to know as much as you can, because these stories oftentimes reach the newsstands, the popular business periodicals, and the blogosphere. You'll get a lot more credibility in your company if you are the expert and not a colleague who just keeps up with business news.

A variety of sources keep up with innovations in Facebook and social media marketing. Some of our favorites are listed here. You'll want to look for sources that can keep you up-to-date on the latest creative uses of Facebook or social media. We cover some of these in this book and on our Facebook page, but you'll want to keep up with a few sources so you can bring the world's best work to your specific situation.

Facebook Marketing: An Hour a Day: www.facebookmarketinganhouraday.com

Mashable: www.mashable.com

AllFacebook: www.allfacebook.com

Inside Facebook: www.insidefacebook.com

Social Media Examiner: www.socialmediaexaminer.com

Government 2.0: www.govloop.com

Enterprise 2.0: www.web-strategist.com

It's handy to read observations and commentary from practitioners in your field. Ironically, Facebook isn't the easiest way to get familiar with content from bloggers and other industry pundits who you did not know previously. Industry magazines, business magazines, trade shows, Twitter, and search engines are good ways to help you discover some of these people. Once you start digging, you'll find that a lot of experts are grappling with the same issues you face every day. Most are relatively open with their experience and their advice—and they share it at low cost or free on the Internet and on their blogs. Thank God for the Web!

Tuesday: Assess the Social Media Activity of Competitors

Before launching your own presence, you really should know exactly what your competitors are doing on Facebook and other social media sites. If you're going to comprehensively analyze your competitors' activities, consider staying on top of the following:

Features Keep track of all the elements of the competitors' presence that appear to be run or officially sponsored by them. You need to know whether they are maintaining a profile, Facebook fan pages, Twitter accounts, blogs, or other social media accounts. Since social media sites typically rank high on search engines, you shouldn't have any trouble finding these sites with a search engine.

Commitment Monitor the quantity and quality of social media updates. Is the competitor truly committed to social media for customer outreach, or does it appear to be more of an experiment? Objectively speaking, would you consider their effort a competitive differentiator, or is it just the bare minimum necessary for a company these days?

Popularity Keep track of the number of customers who appear to be communicating with your competitor. This can be a simple metric such as the number of fans/followers/friends/participants they've attracted, or you can dig deeper to see how much "conversation" they have with their customers via social media. This is good to give yourself a benchmark for performance—either as a stated goal or as a personal goal.

PR/Coverage Analyze how much your competitor's social media work is discussed through articles, in popular periodicals, by bloggers, and so on. It's been said that there is no such thing as bad publicity. We guess that depends on your risk tolerance. A good campaign or strategy can get a lot of people saying good things about a company. When looking for this, be sure to discern between a competitor's own employees talking about the social media effort and seemingly disinterested third parties doing so. It's far too easy to appear anonymous on the Web—sophisticated competitors will plant moles around the Web to say good things about themselves to make it all more impactful.

A chart that summarizes all this data is a helpful and important resource that you can use to both benchmark yourself and monitor the playing field in the future. If you've effectively gathered the data, you've built the scorecard as it relates to your competitors. Now, your management may not hold you to that high a standard or your competitors may not be executing well, so the numbers are largely irrelevant. But as long as you know where your competitors are, you'll be much more informed when setting goals and positioning your progress. Spend a little time to put this chart together with as many hard metrics as you can find. Leave the subjectivity to perhaps only your assessment of PR. You'll need a snapshot at the beginning of your project and the commitment to update it regularly. Add your performance to the chart to be honest about how you stack up.

 Tip: You can save time by buying a report on your competitors as opposed to creating one yourself. Polygraph Media offers reports on other people's social media assets, just as Compete.com offers reports on the traffic on other people's web pages (www.polygraphmedia.com).

Wednesday: Assign Metrics

As you're finalizing your proposal, you need to spend some time thinking about score-keeping. How will your superiors know with confidence that you are successful? This comes down to a few things—what numbers you'll share with them, how often you'll share updates, and how you'll manage expectations.

It always starts with the sophistication of the people ultimately responsible for the effort and what they expect to see. Ideally, you spent time last week talking with them in detail. Getting everyone on the same page is important—so it's probably a good idea to go back to the most influential stakeholders to get feedback on your plan. Give them an opportunity to own part of the project through suggestion or advice, and they'll be easier on you when times are tough.

Choosing metrics for your scorecard is one part art, one part science. You certainly want to fill it with numbers that you know you can affect, but your management chain will likely want to tie the scorecard to meaningful business metrics: return on investment, low customer acquisition cost, number of fans/subscribers, how you do relative to your competitors, and so on. A good scorecard will have elements of both that will easily demonstrate a few things: maintenance, capturing opportunity, efficient advertising spend, competitive environment, and customer interaction. Figure 4.1 shows a range of popular metrics and how easy or difficult they are to affect today.

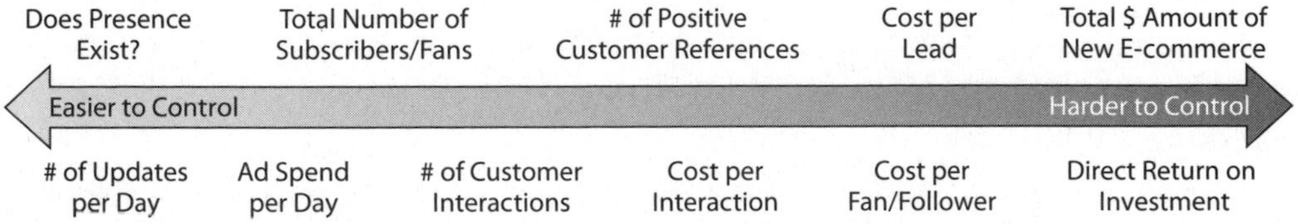

Does Presence Exist?	Total Number of Subscribers/Fans	# of Positive Customer References	Cost per Lead	Total $ Amount of New E-commerce

← Easier to Control   Harder to Control →

# of Updates per Day	Ad Spend per Day	# of Customer Interactions	Cost per Interaction	Cost per Fan/Follower	Direct Return on Investment

Figure 4.1 The continuum of social metrics

Table 4.2 shows an effective scorecard for a simple Facebook marketing campaign that utilizes Facebook fan pages and Facebook advertising. The first two metrics are entirely based on effort and measure simply whether the project manager did their job. The third metric, number of fans added, is a measure of the overall effectiveness of the effort as measured by incremental fans. Advertising spend tells you whether the manager stayed within budget. The number of customer interactions per week is a measure of how engaging the effort is and whether there is sufficient follow-up with customers. Advertising cost per fan is a customer acquisition cost metric that determines whether the ad spend is effective. This is an admittedly simplistic measure—we'll talk in Chapter 8 about isolating the exact impact of advertising dollars. Finally, the ratio of total number of fans to a competitor's total number of fans tells you how you compare to other companies in your market.

▶ **Table 4.2** Example of a basic Facebook marketing scorecard

Metric	Last week	Goal	This week	Goal
Daily updates of scorecard/metrics	Yes	Yes	Yes	Yes
Number of updates or posts/day	0.7	1.0	1.1	1.0
Number of Facebook fans added	77	80	106	90
Advertising spend	$37.28	$40.00	$39.15	$40.00
Number of customer interactions per week	13	25	19	30
Advertising cost per fan	$0.484	$0.50	$0.369	$0.44
Ratio of our total number of fans to competitor's total number of fans	1.03:1	1.0:1	1.07:1	1.05:1

You should know two additional things about metrics and your scorecard. First, you and your management team should consider all of this to be somewhat fluid, especially early in the process. As you work on the project, you may determine that some metrics matter more to you and others matter less. This is a learning experience for many people who take on such projects for the first time—it's OK to make a mistake or course-correct as you learn.

Second, the spirit of the scorecard isn't that you necessarily get locked into doing things just because they're on a scorecard but rather that you get in the habit of recording and analyzing relevant data about your efforts. These projects generate mountains of discrete pieces of data, and you can use this data to help drive decision making as long as you commit to recording it regularly. It can be tedious, but it's very worthwhile. Some data is available to you long-term, but Facebook discards other types of data such that you can't go back to get it if you forget to record it. Use spreadsheets to record progress and analyze data, and collect as much of that data as you can, even if you don't think it will be immediately helpful. You never know what you'll want to use later.

Thursday: Set Reporting Strategy

Now you'll turn your attention to the how and when of reporting metrics to your superiors. The funny thing about Internet marketing is that even in 2012 a lot of managers aren't experienced enough to know the ins and outs of reportage. As a result, every statistic that you report could turn into a potential black hole of debate that may be totally unproductive. This may also make people question your work or how you are analyzing progress.

Getting out in front of these issues is key to managing perceptions, and education is the way to do it. Take the time to educate people on what key metrics are and why you are measuring them. It will go a long way toward improving your internal credibility. It also shows people that you have nothing to hide, which will come in handy especially if you do have some metrics that you need more time to improve. At the end of the day, you want people to understand that you can measure your progress, you can be self-critical, and you know how to fix problems that emerge.

When establishing the reporting cadence, think through the ongoing reporting need and the frequency of management reviews. You will probably need to share updates with some of your colleagues on an ongoing basis so they are always in the loop. This is most efficiently handled on a weekly basis, although we have seen cases where a small team gets daily updates on progress. Management reviews should be scheduled monthly at the most—otherwise, you won't have time to see the outcome of inevitable changes or corrections to your strategy and tactics. The frequency and depth of your reporting will be driven by management requirements and how critical the project is in your company.

If you communicate proactively and openly, you're doing everything you can to manage expectations and reactions to your work. We see people run into problems in their company all the time when they hoard information or don't ensure that management understands the goals, the measurement, and the process of establishing a healthy social media campaign. Deal with issues directly as they occur, and be open to feedback. Distrust is created when people don't communicate—you have a leadership role to play as the manager of the social media project.

Friday: Present the Plan

You've spent most of the last two weeks gathering information, negotiating with stakeholders, and preparing a plan to help your company take better advantage of Facebook and social media. Now it's time to sell it. We've talked at length about the value of metrics and the importance of communication to get cooperation from your colleagues. Here are a few other potential potholes that you should consider as you summarize your thoughts and wrap up your plan:

Management/Mitigation of Unintended Consequences Good executives at major corporations are trained to mitigate risk wherever possible. You'll need to show that you've thought through all the potential negative situations that may arise from your effort and that you have a plan for dealing with problems and unintended negative consequences.

Organizational Fit Are you the right person in the company to run the project? Would this cause a political problem in your company that will create problems for the management team? Have you reached across organizational lines proactively to make the project run as smoothly as possible? Will the project be at odds with other major initiatives inside the company? You don't want to compete with your colleagues unless there are good reasons to do so.

Fit with Corporate Culture/Norms Are the things you are proposing a fit for the way the company communicates with customers, partners, and so on? If so, is that a good thing? Management may have a different perspective on this than the rank and file. Be sure to understand how superiors see the opportunity in advance of your presentation.

Future Commitment Will this project cause the company to take on a future financial or head count liability that it currently does not have? Do you have a handle on the costs associated with the effort and how that may change over time? Are you creating work for an agency in the future that isn't worth the perceived benefit? Could backing out of such a commitment cause customers significant consternation and create negative perceptions about the company or brand?

If they are balanced and fair, your superiors will likely ask you for a good balance of metrics that you can control and stretch goals that will make you really work. That's OK. Remember, you are trying to learn what will work and what has worked on Facebook. ROI is certainly the toughest metric to guarantee today when we talk about what managers and executives should demand of employees who run social media projects. We will talk more about ROI in Chapters 8 and 9.

> ## One Final Point for the Day of Your Presentation
>
> Be sure to keep your cool when you present your ideas. Not all of your ideas are going to necessarily work. That's OK. React calmly and professionally to feedback. It's the best way to make people confident that you can take feedback and you can do the job!

Week 3: Establish a Presence with the Facebook Profile and Friends

Congratulations! Now that you have a plan and you've taken feedback from the firing line of your management team, it's time to execute! You're probably already very familiar with the basics of Facebook, but you may never have looked at all the opportunities from a business perspective. We did a quick walk-through of the basics of the Facebook profile and friending in Chapter 2, "Understanding Social Media and Facebook." Now we'll talk about these features with an eye toward marketing opportunities. We'll avoid feature walk-throughs as much as possible here and focus on how different elements of Facebook help you create a campaign that your customers will appreciate. Also, note that Facebook now refers to the profile as a Timeline, so we will use both terms interchangeably in the book.

Monday/Tuesday: Learn about Data in the Facebook Profile and Security Settings

As we've discussed previously, everything about your identity is summarized in the Facebook profile. There, you have the ability to say as much or as little as you want about yourself. Table 4.3 summarizes the personal information users may expose about themselves. It is a ridiculously rich set of data, most of which is accessible to marketers for better targeting through Facebook advertising, which we will cover in detail in Chapter 8, "The Analytics of Facebook."

▶ **Table 4.3** Facebook user information

Category	Data listed
Basic Information	Gender
	Birth date
	Hometown
	Neighborhood
	Family members
	Relationship status
	Significant other
	Languages spoken
	Time zone
	"Interested In"
	Work history
	"Looking For"
	Political views
	Religious views
Personal Information	Activities
	Interests
	Favorite music
	Favorite athletes
	Favorite games
	Favorite teams
	Favorite TV shows
	Favorite movies
	Favorite books
	Favorite quotations
	Biography

Category	Data listed
Contact Information	Email
	Instant messenger screen names
	Mobile phone number
	Land phone
	Address
	City/town
	Neighborhood
	Zip
	Personal website or blog
Education and Work	College/university
	Graduation year
	Concentration/major
	Degree attained
	High school
	Employer
	Position
	Job description
	City/town
	Dates worked
Groups	Facebook groups to which the user belongs
Pages	Facebook Pages for which the user is a fan

The downside to collecting all this information is that it may make a user nervous. Think about it—if the Facebook profile is totally filled out, it contains quite a bit of personal information that is often used in sensitive situations such as when you've forgotten your password for a credit card or when old friends you haven't seen in years want to reconnect. It's perfect for criminals who may want to steal someone's identity or use profile data to impersonate that person or act maliciously on behalf of that person—especially now with the new Timeline design where anyone can easily zip back through years of posts and glean all manner of information about users.

Facebook established a rich set of data privacy controls with privacy settings for limiting exposure of certain types of information to certain people on Facebook—friends, friends of friends, people in certain networks, nobody at all, and so on. All of this was done to make users more comfortable when adding life's personal details into the social network. Figure 4.2 shows the available privacy options. Users can also customize the privacy they want on a user-by-user basis if they are particularly concerned about certain individuals. Facebook truly has done a remarkable job of simplifying a user's management of personal data, although it continues to evolve.

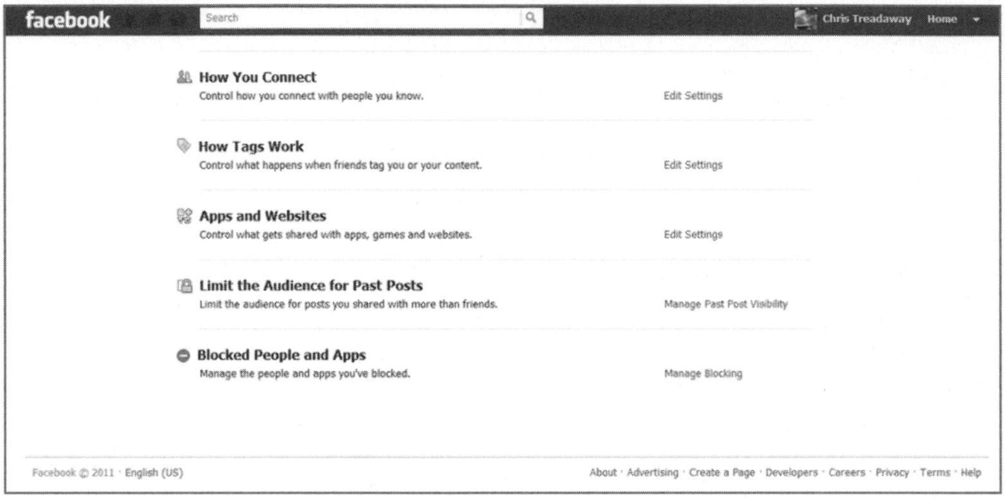

Figure 4.2 Facebook privacy settings

All of it means a few things for marketers:

- You simply won't be able to access some people who are more careful with the data they share on Facebook.
- However, most Facebook users, by virtue of adding self-identifying data to their profiles, are by default exposing themselves to marketing offers.
- Facebook has an unbelievably rich set of demographic and behavioral data on its users, and that data plays a major role in Facebook advertising and marketing on the platform.

In the sense that Facebook can gather accurate and up-to-date demographic targeting data from users, Facebook has only a few rivals (Google, Yahoo!, Twitter, maybe Microsoft, and a few others).

But ironically, the increasing prominence of Facebook in our lives is having an increasingly negative impact on the amount of information users are sharing. Younger demographic groups, which have been the least concerned about sharing information through the young history of Facebook to date, are beginning to understand the impact of "oversharing."

http://articles.cnn.com/2010-03-29/tech/facebook.job-seekers_1_facebook-hiring-online-reputation?_s=PM:TECH

This trend certainly warrants watching over the next few years.

Wednesday: Decide How You'll Use Your Facebook Profile

In September 2011, shortly before the f8 conference, Facebook announced an exciting change to personal profiles: the Subscriber button. When enabled, this new feature allows anyone on Facebook to sign up to start receiving your publicly shared posts in their News Feed. Fortunately, the Subscribe feature is entirely optional. However, we have found it to be one of the most exciting and rapidly developing features on Facebook. I (Mari) watched my subscriber numbers rapidly skyrocket past my total fans. It took me 4 years to build up 60,000 fans, and only 4 months to build up more than 120 subscribers—and currently growing at approximately 1,000 new subscribers per day. This is unprecedented territory on Facebook. Facebook has always limited the number of friends you can have on a personal profile to 5,000. But what the Subscribe button now does, in essence, is lift that limit to unlimited. And, so long as you're not blatantly overly commercial in your use of your profile, turning on your Subscribe feature gives you a whole new marketing channel. (One word of caution: you may need to keep a closer eye on the comments you get on your public posts. We did notice a significant uptick in the amount of spam/inappropriate comments, but it wasn't anything that couldn't be managed. It's easy to block users on Facebook, too, if needed.)

When Facebook introduced the Subscribe feature, some users became concerned about privacy and exposing content they didn't want to show publicly. But all content shared publicly was always visible to anyone on Facebook anyway. It's just that before users would have to come directly to your profile to see the public content; now they may see your public posts in their News Feed. We believe where the confusion came up is that Facebook's label for "public" posts was "everyone," and users could easily mistake thinking they were posting something to all of their *friends*—meaning "everyone." Many users did not realize that "everyone" actually meant the entire population of Facebook. When Google+ launched in the summer of 2011, Facebook quickly began introducing more and more seemingly minor changes. One such change was changing this term "everyone" to "public." There are icons on every piece of content on Facebook that indicate who can see the post. In Figure 4.3, you can see the various icons. A little globe is always public. (All posts on fan pages have this icon.) A silhouette of two people means friends only. And a little cog or gear icon means "custom," which indicates the person who made the post published to a friend lists, for example. If you're ever in doubt as to who can see what content, check the little audience selector icon.

So, as we mentioned earlier, you may choose to use your personal profile for a mix of both business and personal. This can easily be accomplished even with the Subscribe option enabled. Just always double-check to whom you are posting your content. Also, make good use of the friend lists option so you can choose to share specific content with specific friends/contacts. My (Mari) personal philosophy on Facebook is to share 90 percent of my content publicly so I can take full advantage of the growing number of subscribers.

Figure 4.3 Audience selector visibility icons

Assuming you already have a Facebook profile, you can create a fan page for your company while logged in to Facebook, and your profile then serves as the administrator account for the corporate presence. You should never need to share your Facebook login with anyone else. Facebook has evolved over the years when it comes to administering fan pages and protecting users' safety and privacy. To ensure your fan page can always be accessed by more than one admin, we also strongly recommend adding one or more additional admins to share the "load" of accessing and managing the company fan page. Even though Facebook insists on connecting a personal profile to a fan page, they are still treated as two entirely separate entities, and no one would ever know you are the admin, unless you want to showcase that fact. When it comes to posting content on the company fan page, you should usually choose to do so when switched to "page mode." Otherwise, you would be posting to the fan page as your own profile and perhaps drawing unnecessary (and unwanted) attention to your personal profile. Don't worry so much about data flow, getting on News Feeds, posting pictures, and so on, right now because those are not unique benefits to the Facebook profile. This is really about whether you want to use the Facebook profile to include a personal touch complete with personal details and relationships that develop over time with real people. Facebook allows users to have up to 5,000 friends on their personal profile. You may end up being friends with a wide range of people, including your own immediate and extended family members, real personal friends, colleagues, prospective customers, industry experts, media contacts, and more. Make sure that your choices regarding the Facebook profile fit what you need to achieve and, if applicable, the brand assets you already have and the commitments you are willing to make in the future.

Machiavellian types may be thinking by now, "Facebook exposes so much data that I can use it to learn about people I work with or those I want to target." Customers, partners, or other types of business contacts often share a lot of information about themselves through Facebook. If they've friended you directly, you can see most of this information. Similarly, data is available if you've worked at the same place in the past and you both are on the same company network.

There are also more circuitous ways to get access to content people share on Facebook. If they've posted a picture on one of your friend's profiles, depending on how the two parties have their privacy settings configured, you could go through all the pictures in that particular photo album. If they've posted a status update, you can find it using Facebook's Status Update search, which was developed as a means to compete with Twitter's search (`http://search.twitter.com`). Despite the wealth of privacy and security settings in Facebook, there are still a number of workarounds like this that allow unintended people to see personal profile data. A great salesperson can use little things found in the Facebook profile to better empathize with a sales target and ultimately win them over. Facebook provides the vehicle by which people share a lot of information that can be used as business intelligence for a business advantage.

Similarly, you can also use the Facebook profile to create whatever persona you want. There are thousands upon thousands of organizations to follow, groups to join, and links to post. Everything you do, say, and associate with paints a picture of who you are—and those little things can certainly impact how business contacts perceive you. If you have friended customers, partners, or other types of business contacts, your Facebook presence can be used to keep them up-to-date just like you do for friends. Similarly, you can share articles, photos, or other types of content that you think may influence them in some way. In essence, you can deliberately manage how your Facebook community at large perceives you. By being mindful and strategic about what you share, you may find yourself making friends with very key contacts and deepening your relationship with these individuals. It's really up to you to determine just how aggressively you'd like to use your own Facebook profile to talk about your business or market yourself to prospective customers. We do recommend making use of friend lists to manage how you filter your own News Feed and who gets to see which posts via your privacy settings.

Thursday: Set Up Your Profile and Make Friends for a Consumer Campaign

We briefly discussed friending in Chapter 2 to make you familiar with the basics of how people interact on Facebook. Now we'll talk about it as it relates to a consumer campaign. You really have two options when it comes to creating a Facebook profile to support a consumer campaign. You may want an actual person to be the focal point of a campaign to personalize your organization and to give the appearance of humanity and being approachable. If so, you'll have a fairly loose policy about friending, and you'll want to watch activity on the Wall to ensure that people don't abuse the privilege of communicating directly with you.

One such example of this that took place in social media was the rise of Robert Scoble. Scoble was an early blogger and technical evangelist employed by Microsoft to showcase the company, its products, and its people. His blog, Scobleizer (`www.scobleizer.com`), became a tremendous hit and a "must read" for anyone wanting to keep up with startups and new Internet technologies. But just over three years after taking the job at Microsoft, Robert Scoble announced he was leaving the company to join a startup. The face of Microsoft's technical evangelism efforts was all of a sudden gone.

On one hand, Scoble's efforts worked really well to personalize Microsoft and soften the software giant's image. On the other hand, it also exposed a real weakness in allowing a single person to have such an influential role. When a single person has such a significant impact as the face of an organization, it can be devastating when that person leaves. The person can take with them the brand that has been created and the audience that follows religiously.

The second option you have is to establish a fictional character for a campaign. A fictional character on Facebook appears and acts just like a real person who can travel, update their status, share pictures, comment on current events, and so on. Similarly, that character can "friend" individual Facebook users and also accept friend requests. When a user becomes a friend of another Facebook user, a notification appears on the News Feed of each person's friends. It's a quick and viral way for people to find out that a new friend from a previous social context has joined Facebook.

Actions taken by the fictional character will appear on friends' News Feeds, where they can be acted upon, commented on, shared, or "liked." When friends of your fictional character do any of these things, a notification will appear on their profile and the News Feed of their friends. It doesn't take a lot of imagination to realize that this can be one heck of a viral benefit to you. What product manager at McDonald's wouldn't want the ability to establish the Hamburglar as a living character on Facebook with thousands of fans eager to hear about how he's going to get his next McDonald's hamburger? Sadly, this is exactly what Facebook is trying to avoid by restricting the presence of fictional characters on the News Feed. We're a big proponent of testing the limits—what's the worst that can happen? Facebook will shut you down? Well, it actually happened, as described in the "The Hard-Knock Life of Dummies Man" case study.

Featured Case: The Hard-Knock Life of Dummies Man

In the summer of 2007, Ellen Gerstein, marketing director for Wiley Publishing, had a great idea for marketing the *For Dummies* books. She thought she'd create a Facebook profile for "Dummies Man" to make the brand and *For Dummies* books more personal. She was totally unprepared for what happened next—Facebook shut down the Dummies Man account not long after its launch. Here's a quick Q&A with Ellen, where she shares her experience:

Q: *So, what exactly happened when you tried to create a profile for Dummies Man?*

A: The idea to create a profile for Dummies Man came about when I was working with Joe Laurino, our summer intern, on some Facebook marketing ideas. I casually mentioned that it would be fun for Dummies Man to have a Facebook persona. Joe ran with the idea and created a profile for him based on his likes (helping people learn new things), dislikes (idiots), and so on. He also added a bunch of information about our publications in there as a way to showcase some new books. It seemed really fun, and we got a lot of people at work curious and interested in Facebook as a result.

Featured Case: The Hard-Knock Life of Dummies Man *(Continued)*

Q: *What were you trying to achieve with a Dummies Man profile that you couldn't achieve with a Facebook page?*

A: The idea was to make Dummies Man accessible to readers in a way that only social media allows you to do. You can connect with him, share book ideas with him, and even throw sheep at him! We wanted to take this to readers in a very personal way that we had not tried before.

Q: *Did you ever get a chance to make your case directly to people at Facebook regarding the profile?*

A: One day, I tried to log into the account and was denied. After a fair amount of legwork, it showed that the profile was suspended because the person who set up the account (me) was not using her real name. I tried reaching out to a few contacts at Facebook but was directed to write to the automated customer service email addresses on the site.

Although I may have felt this wasn't fair, I totally acknowledge that this was within Facebook's right as laid out in its terms of service agreement. It's their sandbox, and if I don't like how they are playing, my recourse is to pick up my pail and shovel and go home. I understand that. What did anger me was that Dummies Man was singled out, while others having profiles not under their real names were not shut down. Not to pick on him, as I am a fan, but the example I brought to the attention of Facebook was that of Fake Steve Jobs. How can you say that "Fake Steve Jobs" is someone's real name? How was he (Dan Lyons) allowed to keep that account and not Dummies Man? I wasn't trying to bring down Fake Steve Jobs but rather to make the case that we both had a place on Facebook.

Q: *In retrospect, do you think that all of this proved to help your company? Or was it harmful?*

A: I think both the benefits and the damage were minimal. We got some play in the blogo-sphere about it and were able get a bit more press out of it when Robert Scoble's profile was removed from the site (`http://scobleizer.com/2008/01/03/ive-been-kicked-off-of-facebook`). I think it showed most of all that Wiley cared enough about social media as a means of connecting with customers that we were trying something new, even if it ended up being something we got our wrists slapped for, however lightly.

Q: *How does it feel to pave the way for other companies to put their fictional characters on Facebook?*

A: I think Facebook has lightened up and made it easier to have that presence, while still maintaining the overall feel they intended to have. As long as you are generally respectful of what Facebook is trying to do, I think it's great to have fictional characters on there. It's what social media was made for!

For more on social media and observations on the publishing industry, check out Ellen's blog at `http://confessionsofanitgirl.com/`.

That isn't always a positive, however – it's just as easy for someone to hijack your brand by creating a phony profile that you *don't* control. Figure 4.4 is an example of the search results for profiles of "The Most Interesting Man in the World," a fictional character that was the face of Dos Equis marketing in 2008–2009. Presumably few of these are not endorsed or managed by our good friends at Dos Equis. Imagine for a moment what a malicious person can do by managing such a profile, friending a large number of people, and saying whatever they want in an effort to propagate messages virally on individuals' News Feeds. This may horrify you, but sadly there isn't a lot you can do about it short of contacting Facebook or any other social network where your fictional character is hijacked. It certainly warrants monitoring at minimum, and fortunately this can be done rather easily by friending rogue accounts to make sure they aren't misusing your character. But you may want to go to the extent of shutting down people who create these accounts entirely. Your company's philosophy on its brands will be a good guide for how you should treat these situations should they emerge.

Figure 4.4 Search results for "Dos Equis"

Overfriending means different things to different people. It could be getting too close to perfect strangers. For others, it could be a matter of accepting or sending in the region of more than, say, 50 friend requests a day. Facebook doesn't publish these limitations, but anecdotally we have found sending no more than around 20 outgoing friend requests per day keeps you under the radar. If you're including a personal greeting (which we recommend), try changing up the wording a bit, as Facebook's bots are looking for repetitive, verbatim wording.

One solution to growing a friend base quicker is to use other marketing mediums to ask people to friend you. There's no limit to how many incoming friend requests you can have. Internet marketer, John Reese, holds the record for reaching the 5,000 friends max in the shortest amount of time: a mere five days. How did he do it? He simply sent a message to his sizeable opt-in email list asking his subscribers to add him as a friend on Facebook. Of course, this brought in a flood of new accounts to Facebook as many of these people did not yet have Facebook accounts. There are pros and cons to asking your existing database to friend you: if, like Reese, you have a sizeable database, you may use up your friend "slots" with people already in your reach. So, you might want to save some of those slots to establish relationships with new people.

Watch Out for "Overfriending"

Chris Treadaway's retiree father, Clifford Treadaway, developed quite an addiction to Zynga's popular Facebook game Mafia Wars. He played every day for months, gradually building up his character and the size of his "family." In the course of doing so, he started begging his immediate Facebook friends to join his Mafia. But that wasn't enough, so he relaxed his rules for friending people on Facebook. Before long, he started friending random strangers on Facebook just to have a bigger and better Mafia.

One day, Facebook decided to shut down his account. No reason was given—he just couldn't log in to Facebook with his email address and password any longer.

Weeks turned into months until he finally got a response from Facebook. His account was suspended because of "suspicious friending activity." Facebook reluctantly activated his account again but not without a bit of anxiety and frustration.

What's the moral of the story here? Don't "overfriend." Facebook is watching, and it'll shut down an account that appears to be overzealous. But if you do want a loyal Mafia Wars member on your team, go ahead and friend Clifford Treadaway.

Friday: Repurpose a Profile for Business

Alternatively, your interest in Facebook may be to sell products or services on a business-to-business basis, or you may be selling products to consumers that involve a longer sales cycle and require more consultation. That's the realm of business development, where relationships built over a long period of time matter. Business development tends to imply more "strategic sales," in other words, higher touch, more surgical, higher-stakes interactions with people who make big decisions that can impact your success or failure. Social media is a fantastic tool for business development. It breaks down communications barriers that were the rule of the day just 10 years ago. It gives you low risk and potentially helpful excuses for interacting much more casually and much more regularly with prospective partners. It also exposes the social side of our lives, which may be helpful in a sales context. Not only that, but it can help you learn more about the very people you are trying to sell to—their thoughts, concerns, likes/dislikes, and so on.

First things first, you need to decide whether this is a good opportunity for you and your organization. Will your customers or partners be willing to engage with you on Facebook? How will they view your friend request? Will they be threatened or amused by your occasional comments and activities on the social network? By creating friend lists and adjusting your privacy settings to your liking, using these friend lists (for example, determining who can and cannot see what content), you can easily control how your business-related posts and personal sharing are propagated. Using your Facebook profile for business development is dangerous because unless you use a duplicate profile for business activities or you carefully sanitize everything you say and do on Facebook, you're going to mix business and pleasure. (Note that it's actually against Facebook's terms to have more than one account/profile.) Some individuals have an aversion to mixing business and pleasure; in fact, many people hesitate to get too involved with social networking on a wider scale because they are afraid of having to "live in a glass house." This is perfectly natural; most people like to have an element of privacy to their lives.

You may choose to have a completely open policy and only share content—both business and personal—that you're totally OK with being found in a Google search, possibly featured on the front page of a mainstream newspaper, or archived for years. One distinction we've found helpful over the years is to think of our experiences as falling into one of three categories: professional, personal, and private. Since the prevalence and popularity of social media, the line has become rather blurred between our professional and personal lives. Typically, people are interested to know a bit more about you behind your "work self." Sharing about hobbies, travel, family, and interests is actually interesting to most people. However, here's where you get to maintain control: you still may have a private life and simply never share anything online that you don't want out in the open.

Before friending someone, get a sense of whether they'd appreciate it. We wouldn't necessarily be pushy about this—some people draw lines in various parts of their lives, and your intrusion may be seen as inappropriate. If you have a business contact who requests to be your Facebook friend, you're probably in good shape with that particular contact. Before accepting the request, be sure to review your profile critically to ensure you don't have anything there that may be embarrassing to you. You can be sure that a business contact who wants to know about you will check every picture you've posted, pictures where your friends have tagged you, comments on your News Feed, who your friends are, and conversations you've had in the past.

If you've used Facebook's security settings to keep different parts of your life separate, now would be a great time to double-check the settings and public visibility of your profile. If your profile is open to the public, assume the worst—that your business contacts will do due diligence on you before deciding to trust you or do business with you. You may need to make some changes there, so you don't hurt yourself as you try to build your business and earn a customer's trust through a Facebook friendship. Here are a few other steps you can take to ensure your profile is appropriate for business contacts:

Sanitize Your Profile Go through the effort of reviewing status updates and pictures to ensure you don't share anything that may be embarrassing or potentially offensive to your new professional friends. Good news: with the latest settings on your Timeline (profile), you can actually go back through and retroactively change the visibility of any past post.

Avoid Ongoing Political, Religious, or Other Controversial Commentary These are things that you should truly avoid to keep from offending people, assuming you aren't affiliated with political or religious organizations. You may even choose to not fill out your own political and religious views on your Info tab. Some individuals may have strong opposing beliefs and actually choose not to do business with you because of this. On the other hand, it's possible those who resonate with your beliefs would want to do business with you all the more.

Remove Controversial Groups or Facebook Pages from Your Profile Groups and pages imply a level of support that goes well beyond an occasional comment. Remove anything that will damage your credibility with business development contacts.

Stay Vigilant Sometimes your friends can post some things that are off-color or potentially embarrassing. Once you see things like this, be sure to remove them or disassociate them from your profile.

Note: People share an amazing amount of information on popular social networks. Create a social graph of all your primary targets. Learn everything you can about them from Facebook, Twitter, Flickr, LinkedIn, blogs, and so on. You know that empathy and knowing your customers' needs can help make the difference between a sale and a lost opportunity. Use the social networks to make you smarter.

Week 4: Use Basic Facebook Features to Promote Yourself

Odds are that you are already a Facebook user and you already know the basics of sharing information with friends through your profile. But how should you think of your options in the context of promoting a business? This week, we'll walk you through the different options you have on Facebook and how you can best utilize them.

These features are available to you if you've set up a profile or a fan page for your business, which we will discuss in more detail in Chapter 5, "Month 2: Establish an Effective Corporate Presence with Pages and Groups."

Monday: Post Status Updates

Status updates are in many ways the backbone of the "real-time data" revolution. These are generally short-form messages of a few hundred characters at most that share one of life's mundane details, an observation, a random fact, or a link to something else on the Internet. Although Facebook and MySpace have both had status updates for a long time, Twitter has popularized them and to some extent taken status updates "mainstream." That said, Facebook status updates can be considerably more impactful in certain situations.

Let's look at how status updates are presented to other users on Facebook. Status updates, along with other types of notifications on Facebook, appear on the News Feed. As we discussed earlier in this book, the News Feed is the feature that all Facebook users see upon logging in. Because so many status updates are entered by a user's friends, they can quickly appear and disappear in favor of more recent updates from different friends. Figure 4.5 shows the Facebook status updates from some of our friends. Users have some options for seeing status updates as well. They can filter out everything else to see just the updates their friends have shared by clicking the Status Updates link in the upper-left corner of the News Feed screen, as shown in Figure 4.6. Users can also opt to hide status updates from particular friends, which you can also see in Figure 4.6.

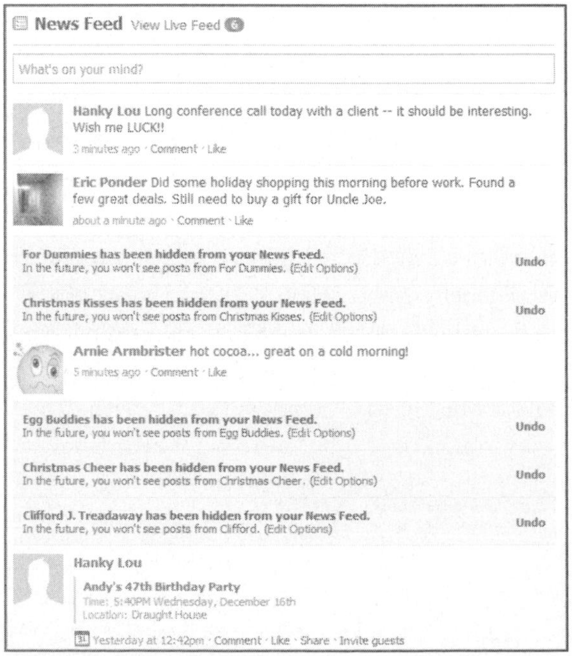

Figure 4.5 Facebook status updates

To post a status update, you do so in what's called the Publisher, and you have a whopping 63,206 characters, which is a huge increase from the previous limit of 420 and then 5,000 characters. (Facebook seemed to increase the status update character field in response to Google+'s extensive publishing limits.) However, usually less is more when posting content. Now Facebook users of all types have the opportunity to publish short-form thoughts similar to what you can do on Twitter all the way to something more resembling a blog post. The Publisher at the very top of your Facebook home page can be accessed by clicking the Update Status link. This will post to your personal profile. In addition, there is a Publisher on the Wall tab of your Facebook page. This allows you to publish updates to the Wall of your page instead. Facebook also recently released a few additional features to give users control over who can read status updates they share. Figure 4.6 illustrates how you can target posts to specific groups that you've established. We'll have more on creating groups later in this book.

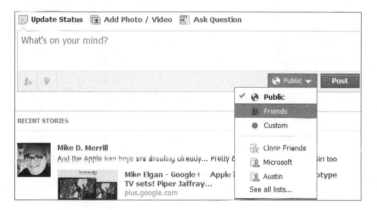

Figure 4.6 Status update targeting to specific groups

What are the implications for marketers and business developers? For one, anything you post as a status update can be seen by the groups that you choose to publish to. So, if you've chosen the Public to view something that you've posted, anyone in the Facebook community at large can see it. So, be careful, be relevant, and be entertaining if that is your goal. Stay out of political or religious rants and observations, strong language, or polarizing statements if you are using Facebook primarily for business purposes. You are likely to offend someone with whom you could do business. It's an unnecessary risk. Also remember that you can be "hidden" from view on a friend's News Feed. Some percentage of people who you have as a friend will not hear from you once they make the decision to hide you. So, your message will not quite go out to as many people as you think. That's yet another reason to proceed with confidence but also with caution.

Tuesday/Wednesday: Share Links, Events, Photos, and Videos

You may have noticed in Figure 4.6 that you can upload a photo or video where you enter your status update. You may also insert a hyperlink to an article somewhere on the Internet. In previous iterations of Facebook, they provided icons to allow users to add links, events, photos, videos, and other content to a status update. Now that process has been streamlined in the user interface. Don't worry—all the features that have always been there are still available to you.

These features add an entirely new dimension to the types of things you can share. Not only can you comment on something, but you can embellish that comment with content to make the experience around the status update more engaging.

Take, for example, links in a common scenario we see for clients; a company wants to post a link to a web page from a Facebook profile or fan page. The idea is that they want to share specific web content—news stories, press releases, YouTube videos, blog posts, and so on—with Facebook users. In this case, the status update is truly secondary, although it makes sense to add a comment or something to appropriately frame the shared content and plant a seed in a user's mind about how they should view/ feel about the content. As you post your link, Facebook pulls in a series of thumbnails from the web page that can be shared alongside the link. You'll have the option to cycle through a selection of thumbnails and choose the one that best represents what you're posting: "A picture says a thousand words." This is particularly handy if you are sharing content from your own property and if Facebook picks up your brand's image. It's a free impression that is there for all your friends to see.

You can similarly share events with friends using this process. Events are great calls to action and are used to keep people informed about things that are happening. Figure 4.7 is an example of an event.

Figure 4.7 Event summary

Think of Facebook events as a supercharged version of Evite. They have all the same features—event details, maps, contact information, photos, and guest management tools—but they allow invitations through the Facebook social graph. These events can be shared among friends, and they can be promoted through the Facebook News Feed. We've seen bands and comedians do a great job at this by publishing their tour stops on Facebook as events. Marketers are increasingly doing the same for trade shows, product launches, and so on.

Photos and videos can also be shared through the Publisher, as well as through specialized apps that Facebook runs for every user. You have two options with photos and videos. You can store them on Facebook, or you can link to libraries or individual photos/videos on third-party sites such as YouTube, Vimeo, Flickr, and others by sharing links to that content. When posting a YouTube link, for example, Facebook actually pulls in the embedded video with the player, and users can play the video right in their News Feed or on your Wall without leaving Facebook.

Thursday: Install Third-Party Apps

Of the tens of thousands of third-party Facebook apps, you may find only a small number of them serve any great use from a marketing standpoint by adding to your personal profile. Many popular apps tend to be lighthearted or game-type apps. Sure, you may meet like-minded individuals or potential customers while playing FarmVille, Bejeweled, or Mafia Wars...but it depends on how you want to invest your social networking time.

In the context of profiles, apps are ways to play games and do other things inside Facebook. But in the context of pages, apps are a great way to help you customize your Facebook page however you'd like. So, if you want your page to have features that are a little different from the standard fare on Facebook, third-party apps are your friend. Many are free, while others require you to make a nominal investment. For many businesses, it's very much worth it.

Friday: Understand Other Aspects of the Facebook Platform

The last day of this week is a good time to become familiar with the other ways Facebook allows users to interact with friends both inside the social network and on the Internet. Here is a quick summary of a few of them; they are listed in order of most commonly used by marketers to least commonly used to date:

Badges Facebook allows users to create small widgets that can be put anywhere on the Internet and summarize basic Facebook profile data—usually a picture, first name, last name, and other basic data of the user's choosing. Badges can be created for both profiles and fan pages and can inform users of a website or an organization's Facebook presence (www.facebook.com/facebook-widgets/profilebadges.php). Chapter 5 includes more detail on badges and creatively using the Facebook fan page.

Applications/Games Facebook Applications are third-party apps that use the Facebook social graph and provide some functionality to users over and above the basic Facebook platform. In certain cases, these applications can propagate messages to the Facebook News Feed, but only after the user agrees. You should run a few Facebook Applications to get an idea of how companies use the functionality and get game content to be present on users' News Feeds. We've listed a few recommended apps in the preceding section and will talk more in-depth about applications and branded games in Chapter 8.

Notes This is Facebook's attempt at a simple social blogging platform. Users can type whatever they'd like in a note, tag certain friends because they are part of the story or because they want attention, and share it on Facebook where it can be found on a News Feed and commented upon. If you've used WordPress or TypePad, it won't take you long to realize that Facebook notes are far less sophisticated. But Facebook Notes is really more about helping people share thoughts as they would in a blog, but inside Facebook. You can import any RSS feed via the Notes app—most commonly, your blog feed.

Marketplace Facebook allows individual users to sell items, services, and so on, to other Facebook users through the Marketplace (`http://apps.facebook.com/marketplace`). It is similar to Craigslist, a modern version of old-fashioned classified ads, or other services that allow people to sell or barter with each other. Marketers may have trouble coming up with scenarios that fit the Marketplace, so we won't spend a lot of time discussing this particular Facebook feature. Marketplace was originally a default feature of Facebook; then in March 2009 Facebook teamed up with Oodle—a classified ads service—and re-launched Marketplace with a much more commercial spin.

Month 2: Establish Your Corporate Presence with Pages

Facebook fan pages have grown over the past several years to become one of the most effective ways to build community with consumers. Because of the sheer volume of users on Facebook, businesses of all sizes—from small entrepreneurs to major corporate brands—focus on fan pages as the top destination for their online presence with the ultimate goal of keeping consumers informed.

Chapter Contents:
Week 1: Research Pages, and Set Up Your Own
Week 2: Determine Your Content Strategy
Week 3: Add and Experiment with Content
Week 4: Promote Your Page and Engage with Fans
Week 5: Monitor and Modify the Plan

Week 1: Research Pages, and Set Up Your Own

Facebook's rules stipulate that users can have one *personal profile*, and it has to use their real name. Facebook provides *fan pages*, also known as *business pages*, specifically for establishing your commercial presence on the platform, connecting with prospects and customers, and marketing your products and services. There is no limit to the number of fan pages a user can create. If, for example, you have multiple locations or different divisions of your business, you could certainly create a fan page for each location or division.

Advantages of building and maintaining an active fan page for your business include the following:

- Garnering an *unlimited* number of fans
- Adding custom applications
- Split-testing ads by driving click-throughs to the unique URL of a custom tab
- Running special promotions, contests, sweepstakes, and giveaways from a custom tab
- Increasing search engine optimization (SEO) because fan page content gets indexed on Google
- Gaining tremendous insight into the needs and behavior of your target market
- Accessing detailed metrics to help you improve your posting quality, boost engagement, and improve overall page performance
- Posting on other business pages as your own page for added visibility

Monday: Observe a Successful Facebook Fan Page

The best way to learn the elements of an effective fan page presence for your organization is by observing the work of others. Very little is new or novel, and Facebook contains a wealth of examples of good fan pages that you can review to give you ideas of what would work in your specific situation and with your target customers.

One such example of a successful Facebook fan page is EasyLunchboxes. Founded by entrepreneur Kelly Lester, EasyLunchboxes makes reusable food containers and cooler bags, and it is the best-selling lunch box on Amazon.com. Check out Kelly's fan page in Figure 5.1.

When you first go to EasyLunchboxes' fan page, you'll see a bright, colorful custom cover image that immediately communicates what the company offers. You see a big, bold photo of the product, which is crucial for any product-based fan page. The main purpose of a cover image is to communicate to the visitor instantly that they are in the right place. You'll also see a friendly photo of Kelly Lester holding the product,

Plus, the four main apps displayed under EasyLunchboxes' large cover image clearly display Photos, Likes, a Welcome page, and the fact the company is on Pinterest too.

Figure 5.1 EasyLunchboxes' Facebook fan page

- On the Wall, EasyLunchboxes consistently shares quality, relevant information with its fans, and the page owner is very prompt and responsive in engaging with fans (see Figure 5.2).

Figure 5.2 EasyLunchboxes' Facebook Wall posts

More on Succeeding with Pages: An Interview with George DeCarlo of Woobox

George DeCarlo founded Woobox in early 2010 and serves as CEO. Woobox has become one of the most popular social media promotion application suites for marketers on Facebook. Woobox was built with the focus of making engagement and fan growth easy and delivering data-driven results to maximize promotion conversion and viral sharing rates for brands, agencies, and small businesses. Prior to Woobox, George founded the domain registration and hosting company Dotster in 1999.

Q *Your company, Woobox, helps companies customize their Facebook Fan Pages with landing tabs, coupons, sweepstakes, and other enticements. Why do you think marketers want to customize the Facebook experience?*

A Facebook Pages create a tremendous opportunity to engage with fans and potential fans where they are, on Facebook. Fortunately, Facebook's platform provides endless possibilities to customize Pages so that marketers can better engage and grow their fan bases. Facebook is great at providing base capabilities, but their platform allows companies like Woobox to provide many more options that are built to be viral and achieve results that can't be achieved without customizing and adding apps to Pages.

Q *How have marketers evolved their thinking about Pages over the last few years?*

A As Facebook has continued to open up their platform and create more integration points to connect with fans, third-party developers like Woobox along with marketers have taken advantage of the new capabilities. What's possible has changed dramatically in the last few years and marketers have come to expect more from the user experience on their Pages.

More on Succeeding with Pages: An Interview with George DeCarlo of Woobox (Continued)

When Woobox first launched a giveaway app that allowed users to enter completely on a Facebook Page, it pushed the limits of what was possible at the time. When Facebook made the switch to new technology on Page tabs, many capabilities became possible. It's not good enough to put up a simple form and a share button. Marketers need and demand apps that deliver measurable results and are built to be viral and maximize sharing and friend involvement.

Q *What is the biggest missed opportunity for marketers in social media? What do you think marketers understand the least about Facebook marketing?*

A For many offline businesses, in-store promotion is a big missed opportunity. For everyone, getting your existing customers and newsletter subscribers to connect with your social network accounts is a must, but frequently missed. Staying up with the latest technology changes and opportunities is also difficult for most marketers, yet some of the biggest opportunities are also the newest. Application usage has exploded, but many marketers are still not taking advantage of tools designed to improve fan growth, engagement, and management.

Q *From your observations, how is Facebook doing to solve the needs of marketers?*

A Facebook clearly has a focus on driving usage among brands to connect with their audiences. Instead of trying to create all of the tools to solve the needs of marketers, they've created and are constantly innovating the platform that fosters an ecosystem of solutions. In most situations, actions you can perform directly on Facebook, such as advertising, can be done more effectively using one of several third-party tools competing to be the best solution. That's smart for Facebook and provides marketers with multiple solutions. Whether scheduling messages or making promotions viral, these third-party companies also enable needed capabilities that are not possible using Facebook's tools. Lastly, Facebook is always innovating new technologies such as Open Graph actions that help marketers reach larger audiences.

Q *Last question, looking in your crystal ball for a moment: what do you think the future of social media promotions will be?*

A Many marketers are currently in a building phase. There is a land-grab for fans, and the most focus seems to be placed on metrics related to fan growth. The future will be in how those fan bases can best be utilized to further business goals. Marketers will be looking for solutions to monetize fans and better leverage those fans to increase brand awareness and drive commerce socially. Social promotion applications will be an important part of that shift, and Woobox will continue to innovate solutions to accomplish those goals.

Tuesday: Become a Fan of Successful Fan Pages

Let's start by reviewing an effective Facebook fan page. Log into Facebook, pick a brand or a company you really like, and enter it in the search box in the upper part of the screen. In the search results, click Pages, and then click the fan page you'd like to see. Pages with a higher number of fans are obviously doing something better than those with fewer fans, so you should opt for those pages that have been more successful as you seek examples. (Alternatively, you may want to browse the index of all Facebook fan pages in their respective categories. Here is the direct link to the directory, which is not easy to find on Facebook: `www.facebook.com/pages/?browse`. Or, two other sources are `www.socialbakers.com` and `http://statistics.allfacebook.com/pages`.)

Which elements of a Facebook fan page will help your business? If building a good Facebook fan page is one part technical skills and one part relationship skills, then how can you emulate success for your own business page? Here are a few ideas:

Design What is your first impression of the fan pages? Is the type of business clear and obvious? Can you instantly tell what products and services the page owner offers? Is the cover image visually appealing? Do the cover image and app thumbnails compel you to want to click the Like button and join the page?

Content Once you join the page and view the Wall, what types of content do these fan pages share? Do the posts always seem on-topic, or do the page owners intersperse off-topic posts? As you view your own News Feed, which pieces of content catch your eye the most? Do the page owners always post the same types of content, or do they mix it up with a variety of updates, photos, videos, and links? What kinds of content seem to work best to encourage interaction? Do the posts include clear calls to action from time to time?

Frequency How often do the page owners post content? Does it seem about right, or is it too seldom or too often? As you view your own News Feed, does one particular page's posts dominate it?

Engagement Does the fan page owner respond to fans' Wall posts? Once the fan page owner posts their own content, do they return to respond to the comments made by fans? Does the fan page owner encourage fans to interact with each other?

Creativity What elements of the fan page really catch your eye? Does the page include elements that are a clever extension of the brand that makes it more acceptable or more interesting to the target market?

Informing How is the fan page used to communicate business information to customers? Is it too frequent, or is it used appropriately?

Soft-Selling Does the page have a commerce app that displays their products or services? Whether the page has a commerce app or not, is it clear to fans how to purchase from the page owner? In the Company "About" section, are there plenty of links and descriptions explaining what the company offers? Does the page owner make periodic offers on their page Wall with clear calls to action?

As you investigate success stories, consider becoming a fan of a half dozen or so fan pages and observe how they communicate with you over time. You're looking for your snap reaction when you get a communication from a fan page—are you annoyed, or are you happy to hear from them? Little things like this can have a big impact on how your fan page will be received. How will this differ by demographic group and for your particular situation? Remember, some demographic groups accept a more or less frequent amount of communication from popular brands. Observe and remember to empathize with your customer base. Don't impose your standards on the market-place—misreading what would or would not be allowed could cost you.

File all this knowledge away for the future when you begin to build your company's Facebook fan page.

Wednesday: Complete the Fan Page Checklist

First, apply the POST method to your fan page planning. (The "POST" method was created by Forrester Research and is detailed in the book "Groundswell" by Josh Bernoff and Charlene Li.)

What PEOPLE do you want to attract to your Facebook fan page? This is your target market. When describing these people, include their age, gender, geographic location, career, average income, buying habits, interests, and so forth; the more you know about your target fans, the more customized you can make your fan page.

What is the primary OBJECTIVE of your Facebook fan page? Some possible objectives include engaging with customers, furthering brand awareness, building a loyal fan base, generating leads, increasing sales, gathering intellectual data from your marketplace, monetizing your content, enhancing your customer service, increasing event registrations, and creating buzz with contests and giveaways.

What STRATEGIES do you plan to implement? This will depend on your main objectives for your Facebook marketing. For example, your strategy to begin building your fan base might include a rolling launch with ads, a contest, free giveaways, in-store incentives, direct mail campaign, and email broadcasts.

What TECHNOLOGIES will you use? For example, by using third-party platforms such as HootSuite, Argyle Social, or Post Planner, you can schedule content to augment your manual updates. In addition, you'll want to familiarize yourself with the Facebook mobile app for your smartphone or tablet of choice. Likely, you'll want to have the flexibility of updating and moderating on the fly.

How will you MEASURE your results? We added this fifth element into the POST method—think of it as the POST method. (Refer to Chapter 8, "The Analytics of Facebook," for more in-depth information on measurement.) It's important to be thinking about tracking and measuring your results even before you get started on your fan page. Measurement can take many forms; the number of fans is just one yardstick. You can also measure the click-through rate (via tracking links), traffic, traffic sources, new subscribers, new registrations, purchases, increase in brand sentiment, increase in customer satisfaction, decrease in returns, and more.

Next, go through this checklist and jot down the main elements you plan to include on your page:

☑ Title—person's name vs. company name

☑ Include a tag line? (additional keyword rich text)

☑ Category

☑ Subcategory

☑ Images to include

☑ About section (255 characters on the left side)

☑ About sections (depends on category chosen)

   ☑ Websites

   ☑ Company overview

   ☑ Mission

   ☑ Products

   ☑ Other fields

☑ Import your blog

   ☑ Recommended app: Networked Blogs

☑ Custom apps (iFrame):

   ☑ Primary purpose?

   ☑ Title: (*Examples*: Welcome, About Us, Be Our Fan, Contest, Free Tips, Free Download, Free Stuff, Our Blog, and so on)

   ☑ Content

   ☑ Graphics

   ☑ "Fangated?" (nonfans see different content than fans)

Thursday: Set Up Your Page

Before we dive into specific instructions for setting up fan pages, it's important to note that Facebook forces users to connect fan pages to a user's personal profile. Many businesses balk at this and have, in fact, run into challenges because of this enforcement. For example, say a staff member creates the company fan page while logged into their own personal account. This means that person is the primary administrator for the fan page, which is fine. However, if they do not assign any other staff members as admins and they leave the company at some point, the fan page could end up sitting in limbo with nobody to administer it if the ex-staff member can't be tracked down. Unfortunately, this has happened to many businesses. The key, therefore, is to give careful thought as to which staff member will be the initial admin for the company fan page. Then have that person immediately assign at least one additional staff member as an admin.

Facebook treats your personal profile and your fan page as two totally separate and unique entities. Admins can choose whether to become a fan of any page they create.

An alternative is available for any business owner who does not want to have a personal presence on Facebook. It is called a *business profile*. If an individual (or company) wants to have a Facebook fan page but currently does *not* have a personal profile on Facebook, it is possible to create a fan page that is connected to this very limited business profile. It's impossible to view and experience even a small fraction of the features Facebook offers via these business profiles, so we don't recommend this approach. (See www.facebook.com/help/?faq=12850.)

With your checklist in hand from the previous lesson, it's time to dive in and begin setting up your first Facebook fan page. The good news is that you can build the page behind the scenes before actually publishing it and making it live.

First, go to http://facebook.com/pages/create.php. Select from the six main categories (see Figure 5.3).

Figure 5.3 Six primary fan page categories

On each of the six main sections, there is a subset of categories from which you'll need to choose. Next, depending on the title of the page you want to have, enter your name or the name of your brand, business, band, or cause. Check the box to agree to the Facebook page terms, and click the Get Started button. *Voila*. You're on your way!

What comes next is typically a three-part wizard that you simply follow (Figure 5.4):

- *Step 1:* Add a profile photo.

- *Step 2:* Get fans.

- *Step 3:* Enter your basic information.

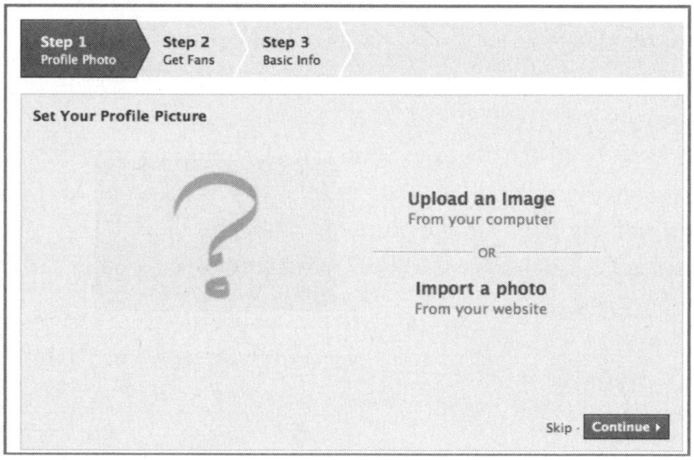

Figure 5.4 Facebook fan page three-step process

You'll certainly want to complete step 1; just upload an image from your computer or import one from your website. Or, you can skip this section and come back to it (see the Skip link next to the Continue button).

We recommend skipping step 2 for now; it's best not to go through the process of inviting friends, importing contacts, posting the page on your personal profile Wall, or liking the page—all these actions obviously bring attention to the page, which is what you want. However, you've barely laid the foundation so far, and it's better to wait until you have a much more impressive page before flipping the switch, so to speak.

Fill out step 3, which is simply your website and a short About section (255 character maximum). You'll have plenty of opportunities to edit these fields later.

At this stage, your page is created and is live right away. To place it in a temporary unpublished state, click the Edit Page button at the top right and, on the first section (Manage Permissions), check the button Only Admins Can See This Page at the top. Then click the Save Changes button. Now you can make all the edits and additions you want to implement before unveiling your shiny new page to friends and your community at large.

The Edit Page button is always visible to administrators of the page at the top right. Click this button anytime to get to your settings and make edits.

At this stage, fill out all the categories under Basic Information. Leave blank any field that does not apply to your business. Blank fields won't show on the live page. Be sure to click the blue Save Changes button at the bottom of the section.

The Edit Page button (which is located at the top right of your fan page) provides some features that you'll want to explore. It is really more a collection of settings that govern the use of your fan page. On this screen, you should see a menu on the left column with the following options (Figure 5.5):

- Your Settings
- Manage Permissions
- Basic Information
- Profile Picture
- Featured
- Resources
- Manage Admins
- Apps
- Mobile
- Insights
- Help

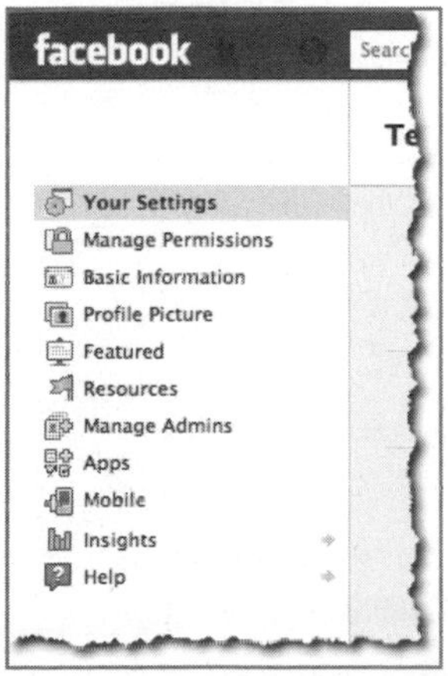

Figure 5.5 List of admin settings under Edit Page

Familiarize yourself with the various options by clicking through to each section.

Some of the specifics that you can edit include the following:

- Who can or can't become a fan (age and country restrictions)
- Whether or not fans can post directly to the Wall
- Settings for other applications that you run

Your decisions about these settings will determine quite a bit about the user experience for your fan page. Your page settings drive the type of audience that you target and the level of interactivity for which you're aiming.

You can share upcoming events through the Events app, photos through the Photos app, blog posts through the Notes app, links through the Links app, and videos through the Videos app.

You'll need to try a few things and see what other page administrators are doing to make their Facebook presence more engaging. Most activities that are edited or shared by an administrator on the Facebook fan page will appear in fans' News Feeds. As you investigate new features and opportunities, test the outcomes with a Facebook profile so you can see how other fans will experience your page.

Friday: Add Design Elements

The primary design elements of a Facebook page include three main components:

- The cover image
- The small page image (avatar)
- The four app thumbnails under the cover image

Each of these three areas can be customized to provide a consistently branded look, feel, and experience for your visitors and fans.

Let's start with the cover image The dimensions are 851 pixels wide by 315 pixels high.

The cover image is intended for showcasing your brand/business; however, it may NOT contain the following:

- Price or purchase information, such as "40% off" or "Download it at our website."
- Contact information, such as web address, email, mailing address or other information intended for your Page's About section.
- References to user interface elements, such as Like or Share, or any other Facebook site features.
- Calls to action, such as "Get it now" or "Tell your friends."

Facebook encourages brands and businesses to change their cover image often to reflect activity in your business and spark engagement.

Dimensions for your profile picture (the small Page image) are 30px by 30px. Facebook recommends not changing this image that often. We strongly suggest your profile picture is simple your logo. Or, if you're a personality based brand or solopreneur, then use a good headshot.

You may also wish to add an array of custom apps to your Facebook Page. These apps include simple blank fields into which you drop your code, such as the Static HTML app, or user-friendly "drag-and-drop" interfaces, such as the one provided by TabSite.com. Plus, there are plenty enterprise-level solutions available from the likes of BuddyMedia.com and Involver.com. It's important to discuss the branding elements you want to extend to your fan page with your marketing department. With the latest major change to Facebook Pages (late February 2012), you can add up to 12 apps, but can only display the first three apps under your cover image, next to Photos which cannot be moved. Apps not displayed on the first row are visible to anyone viewing your Page by simply clicking on the small down arrow on the right side.

Adding additional apps may or may not spark engagement among your fans. However, an important point to note is that each app has its own unique URL and you can always post that link on your wall to drive your fans to, a contest app, or registration app, for example.

Week 2: Determine Your Content Strategy

Fan pages are a great way to establish a presence on Facebook for your company. But your page will be lifeless, not to mention pointless, without content that is updated for your fans to consume on a regular basis. We have seen many examples of companies that spend significant time, resources, and money building a fancy Facebook fan page but have pages that lack regular, fresh and relevant content. The right combination of content plus engagement is the lifeblood of any successful social network presence, yet companies often don't match the time and resources spent on excellent design with a content strategy that keeps the fan page lively, vibrant, and worth visiting on a regular basis.

Monday: Develop a "Product Strategy" for Content

We've talked a few times in this book about the importance of getting on users' News Feeds every day. The only way to do this without annoying people is by providing new and interesting content at least once a day. So, the Facebook page that you use is merely the container or the infrastructure that holds your presence. The content is the product that users either accept or reject with their continued support.

We've also mentioned the value of mapping your social media presence to your customers' needs. What do they want? What motivates them? Do their needs change at certain times of the year? Why would they recommend your site, product, or social media presence to their friends? What would make them comment on or interact more with your Facebook presence? You will hit the mark if you think carefully about the needs of your different market segments and then meet those needs with content.

When we think of any new social media presence for a new client, we instinctively think in terms of magazines. Facebook helps every company, brand, or organization become a publisher of their own online, interactive "magazine." You can look at the benefits of this and say, "Sure, I'd love my own interactive magazine!" But it comes with a lot of responsibility. You have to maintain your "magazine." Stop publishing information to it, and you no longer have a publication. People will lose interest if you fail to maintain it.

Your "magazine" has a perspective on the world—think through the perspective you want to have and don't deviate significantly from it. If you do, your fans may get upset with you. But perhaps most important, give people things they can't or don't get anywhere else. This doesn't necessarily mean that your content has to be extraordinary or unique. Your target markets may just consume information primarily through Facebook—and you could be the one to provide a very simple yet helpful service!

Don't Over-advertise Yourself

The next time you are at a bookstore, pick up a few different types of magazines. Pay attention to how much they advertise themselves. Aside from the necessary insert that falls out of the magazine, you won't find too many "house ads." Remember this when establishing your own Facebook presence—people don't need a lot of advertisements for your business when they are already a fan, friend, follower, or member of your group. If you over-advertise, you run the risk of people getting dissatisfied. Focus on the needs of your customer and not the needs of your marketing department.

Tuesday: Talk with Colleagues about the Use/Reuse of Content

The good news is that most organizations—large and small—already have mountains of content that would be perfect for sharing through social media. The bad news is that it is likely unorganized or used for entirely different purposes. Thus, you have a few major problems that you'll need to resolve if you want to use or repurpose content from your colleagues:

Cultural Issues You'll need to help your colleagues get comfortable with repurposing content for sharing through Facebook. Some people will be very happy to share information with you, while others will not. Some of the people may want to share information that isn't appropriate for your social media presence—and some information is just simply uninteresting.

Sourcing and Sorting the Data You'll need access to information/content, and you need to organize it to build your library. Some of it may already be online, but the real gems may be offline. You need to learn what is available, and you need to organize it so the content you share covers a wide range of topics and doesn't bore your customers.

Operational Realities Ensure you can update your social media presence frequently enough to keep your customers happy. This means that you need a person to make sure that everything is updated as necessary.

In addition to producing your own relevant content for your customers, including reusing and repurposing good content, you'll want to share third-party content that reinforces your company's point of view. This is what we call Other People's Content (OPC). It's perfectly acceptable (and often expected) that companies will share and promote content from sources other than their own. It's important to properly screen all such third-party content to ensure quality, relevance, and noncompetition. Of course, you never want to simply copy and paste other people's content; rather, share the link to the content on your Facebook Wall. Or, you can post an image and then include the link and also an "@ tag" to the company's Facebook page. Few companies are in a position to produce unique content for social media. Most use a hybrid strategy of sourcing their own content and pointing to the best available content on the Web to maintain sites and social media.

As you talk to your colleagues about these issues, you'll get a clear sense of how your organization views sharing and producing content. From this feedback, you'll be able to create a strategy and some requirements for keeping your Facebook presence fresh and up-to-date. You'll know the language you should use and the amount of third-party content you can rely upon either on an ongoing basis or on slow days.

Note: Remember that social media makes everyone a publisher of content that reinforces their perspective—be it personal or professional. Individual users have the ability to share content with thousands of people with just the click of a mouse. Take advantage of the fact that everyone is a publisher to get the word out about your campaign.

Wednesday: Set Editorial Policy for Content

Let's review where we are—your social media presence is, in essence, a 21st-century form of journalism. You are a publisher of sorts, as are your customers. Success is driven by interactivity, not by an antiquated measurement of how well you "shout." Customers are free to interact with your content and your presence, and their reactions can be seen by hundreds or thousands of people. Facebook gives you some opportunities for controlling the flow of information, and you've probably given a lot of thought to how you can use these controls to make Facebook work for your company.

Editorial policy is very important to ensure that the customer experience with your Facebook presence is consistent and valuable. It is the set of rules that govern what you post, how often, and when. We're not proposing that you go to the effort of creating an editorial policy for the sake of making work. We think it's a handy way to make sure that everyone associated with your social media presence knows what to do and knows the behaviors that should be avoided. You should have multiple people involved, if for no other reason than to mitigate the risk of losing a single person to vacation, illness, and so on.

So, what elements are required for a good editorial policy? The following are a few to consider. Answers to these questions should drive a succinct document that you can circulate to ensure that you don't have mistakes and to help make tough decisions when they arise:

Purpose Why do you have a Facebook presence? Who are you trying to reach?

Types of Content What are the primary types of content that you'll share? How will you "mix it up" so that consumers can get a variety of experiences (and not just status updates or links)?

Tone/Language What is the best way to communicate with your customers? Formal language/informal language? Do you joke around? Are you serious? Informative? Authoritative? Will you use third person or first person or a mix of both?

Subject Matter What will you share? From what sources (internal/third party)? What won't you share? What topics are taboo? Will you change the types of information you release based on circumstances (time of year, the economy, current events)?

Communication Will you engage in a conversation with users through Facebook? Will your presence help people communicate with one another? If it is important to you, how will you use the site to gather customer information?

Organization Can people find what they want easily? If their needs can't be met through your Facebook presence, can they easily be diverted to your other properties (online or offline)?

Frequency How often will you post? Daily? Five times a week? Twice a day? What is an acceptable range for your posts (low and high)?

Advertising Will you advertise your own products/services through your Facebook presence? If so, how? How often? Will you allow third parties to advertise through your Facebook presence?

Clear communication will help everyone on your team succeed. Remember, you don't want to create a massive infrastructure to post to Facebook and monitor social media, but you do want redundancy and consistency. Know who your "editor-in-chief" is, who that person's backup will be, and who will support them.

The editor's job is to provide a product that customers love and one that they'll enthusiastically recommend to others. You also want to be so in tune with customers' needs that you can intuitively drive the future of your Facebook presence by commissioning new types of content, changing editorial policy, and helping solve problems in other areas of your business.

Finally, it's good to have ways to involve other people in your company in the execution of your social media strategy. Fellow employees may have great suggestions for content, campaign execution, creative, and so on. The lessons of "crowdsourcing" have taught us time and time again that great ideas can come from anywhere—you just have to be open to the possibility. If you can create a system to triage suggestions and ideas quickly, you'll probably get a great idea or two you may not have considered. You'll look better when you are able to humble yourself enough to know that you may not have all the answers.

Thursday/Friday: Perform Your Content Audit

If you're going to do a good job posting content, you need an idea of the assets that you have and those you are willing to share via social media. These can be items that have never been shared with customers or content that is already out there for the world to see on your website. It's OK to post content that is already available—many people have been very successful with Facebook by simply exposing fans to existing content that is available elsewhere on the Web. (You're essentially doing your fans a service by aggregating good content for them!)

Start by classifying the types of content that you have based on whether it is already online. You should have enough content nearby that has already been produced for online consumption—it's your lowest-hanging fruit that probably doesn't require much additional work. Make sure, though, that the content is interesting for your customers. It's better to take a little extra time to get the content right.

Keep in mind also that your users may want some variety in the types of content you post. You need different types of things (articles, blog posts, charts, graphs, numbers, third-party articles of interest, videos, podcasts, and so on) to keep things fresh. You'll also need a good mix of product information, commentary that supports your company or brand, events, sales/offers, and so on. Keep your voice consistent but your content fresh and compelling. This audit should ensure that you have a variety of different things to post and that you're able to see how different types of content encourages fans to interact and share with friends more often.

Crowdsourcing Content

In big organizations, the effort required to collect content to reference or repurpose on Facebook may be substantial. The most efficient way to do it is to spread the work. Set up an easy system for people to submit content or suggest ideas for your social media presence. It takes a lot to explain to people what you need, but it takes far less if you can summarize your plan in an email message.

After you have created a list of content for sharing on Facebook, you will likely notice that you have some gems—great content that you know your customers will love. There are two schools of thought about gems. Some people prefer to lead with their best content so the first fans or followers become rabid and enthusiastic evangelists for your brand. Others prefer to hold their best content for later, once a loyal following has been established. There are really no right or wrong answers for this. We usually advise clients to share their best at both times to get the best of all worlds.

Week 3: Add and Experiment with Content

Now it's time to move from ideas to execution—the day-to-day process of keeping your social media presence alive. You have two main options when it's time to publish. You can enter a simple status update, or you can share content. Status updates are good for direct albeit lighthearted interactions with your customer base, while content (in the form of links, photos, videos, imported blog posts, events, and so forth) is typically used to share interesting things you want them to see or experience.

Monday: Publish Content to the Wall

Sharing content through Facebook is simple, and the same interface is used for both pages and profiles (see Figure 5.6). To post a status update on your fan page, begin typing in the composer (publisher input field). This field is very similar to the publisher on your personal profile. Then click the Share button. To share content other than a plain status update, click the icon for posting a photo, link, video, or question.

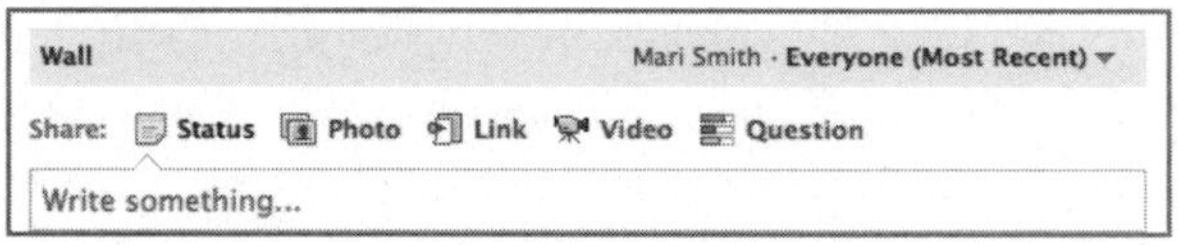

Figure 5.6 Interface for posting content to pages

As you experiment with posting different types of content, you may notice some subtle differences between the different things you post. Links shared through Facebook are reformatted to include the following:

- Title of the link, pulled from the `<Title>` tag of the web page being referenced.
- A brief summary of the link, pulled from the `<Meta "description">` tag of the web page being referenced.
- A thumbnail picture that represents the link that is chosen by the poster. (With most posted links, Facebook pulls in several thumbnails, and you can cycle through to select the most appropriate one to post.)

This content can also be targeted at specific users, although Facebook currently allows only geographic and language-based targeting. You can edit the title and summary by clicking either and changing the text—but be sure you do this *before* you click the Share button. Once you click the Share button, you can't edit the post any longer; you can only delete it.

Tuesday: Correct an Erroneous or Embarrassing Post

It's an inevitable reality of publishing to the Web—no matter how careful you are—that you are going to make a mistake now and then. Maybe you've posted content to the wrong place. Maybe you said something that you shouldn't have said. In these cases, it's important to stay calm, don't panic, but act fast. If you posted a piece of content on your fan page that you want to remove, you can delete it by going to your page and hovering over the post. A small cog or "gear" appears at the upper-right corner of the post. Click it, and then click Remove Post; the content will be removed from your fan page and the News Feed of your fans.

With photos or videos, the good news is that the narrative you share with these types of content can be edited. At any time, click the link to the photo or video and look for the Edit button. As you edit the text part and save your changes, the post automatically updates in the News Feed of your fans.

You can't stop people from seeing any erroneous posts in the time it takes you to remove them, but you can minimize the damage of your mistake! In certain cases, it makes sense to acknowledge the mistake and apologize openly to people who associate with you. In other cases, it's just better to let a sleeping dog lie. You'll have to make a judgment call to determine exactly how and if you should address mistakes that you inadvertently publish.

Fortunately, mistakes are not discoverable long-term unless they're so bad that someone took a screen capture of your mistake and decided to share it somewhere on the Web. Search engines are beginning to catalog data shared via social media for discoverability and to make search engines more accurate. But as of now, there isn't a "Wayback Machine" (www.archive.org) for social media, though there are third-party services springing up that back up social media sites—such as SocialSafe.net and Backupify.com—so you never know what's being kept on a backup.

Wednesday: Post Videos and Photos

You can share individual photos, create an album to commemorate photos of a certain theme, or take new photos with your webcam. As with other types of content sharing on Facebook, this process is also very simple—uploading a photo requires you to browse for it on your hard drive and click Share. For an album, you simply give your album a name and a location. Then you upload the pictures you'd like to put into that album. You can add a description to albums and individual photos; plus, you can tag friends who appear in photos and other fan pages. Other options include the ability to select a specific photo for the album cover, reorganizing the order in which photos appear in an album, and posting the album (and/or individual photos) onto your profile using the Share button.

Posting a video is a little more confusing. Facebook gives you two main options for dealing with video—either you can record a video with a webcam or you can upload an existing video from your hard drive. A webcam can be an interesting way to "personalize" your brand or company, but most companies will probably not use this feature for marketing purposes. Most will instead opt to upload a video from a hard drive that has been edited in some way. It usually takes some time for Facebook to process your video, so don't expect it to post to your profile or page immediately. After it is uploaded, you may want to "share" your video again from your profile or page. Uploaded videos don't always make it to the News Feed, so it may be helpful to share it again to be safe.

What about YouTube, you ask? Well, at this snapshot in time, you will need to share YouTube videos as links. Interestingly enough, YouTube videos that are shared within Facebook can play inside the Facebook profile or fan page. So, a user doesn't have to go outside Facebook to see a video that is shared. How nice of Facebook! YouTube provides significant search engine optimization benefits, so this is an excellent way to optimize your presence and links of different types across popular web properties. People can still "like" or comment on your YouTube videos just as they can "like" or comment on other links you share.

Thursday: Experiment with Content

Experimentation is key throughout any Internet marketing project, but it's particularly interesting early in social media marketing. Why? Well, when you start, you have no idea at all exactly how customers will react to you. The beginning is in some ways the scariest part of the project whether you are a marketing manager, a consultant, or just a friend giving free advice. You've sold the benefits of social media, and you've sold people on your abilities. You probably also showed examples of successful companies and how they were able to succeed with social media. If management has agreed to a project, they're probably expecting it to produce.

Don't fret—the answer lies in truly becoming expert in how the little things you do impact performance as measured by fans, friends, and so on. For example, you can learn the following:

- What happens when you post a link, photo, video, or note?
- How do customers respond differently to different types of content?
- How often should you post new content?
- How do customers respond to unique content that is unavailable anywhere else on the Web? Is the response different from when you post content that exists on your website? Third-party content?

- Are customers disappointed if you don't post an update frequently enough?

You can measure it by the following:

- Increase/decrease in fans
- Sign-ups to a newsletter or other lead generation mechanism
- Number of comments
- Number of "likes"
- Increase in traffic to your website
- Increase in referrals from Facebook.com web pages to your website

Remember that every action you take has a reaction from your customer base. The best practice for capturing this information is to keep a spreadsheet with details on what you post and outcomes over the subsequent 24 hours. Don't rely on memory or anecdotes for this information. If you get into a habit of recording the data for outcomes, you'll have a great resource that you'll use in a variety of ways you can't possibly predict in advance. Refer to Chapter 8 for more on monitoring and measurement.

Rising Tides Raise All Boats

As your numbers grow, you'll probably notice more and more interaction on your properties. This is a great thing—congratulations! But remember that with increased numbers, you should expect increased interaction. Hold yourself to higher standards as you generate a larger following.

Friday: Fill Your Presence with Content and People

All week, you should have been gradually adding content to your presence according to the editorial policy and cadence that you set previously. A Facebook presence that is not maintained on a regular basis runs the risk of losing supporters. Sure, it's difficult to maintain something that is so public, but it's the key to your success.

You really need to fill the presence with content so that you don't have white-space in the Wall and other places where people will be viewing your presence and making judgments about your organization. The minimum bar here is to fill available space with information and to do so often enough to communicate that you've made a commitment to the presence and that it is valuable. In most cases, you'll need to answer the basic organization profiling questions in the About section, and you'll need at least half a dozen pieces of content, status updates, videos, links, and so on, on your Wall.

After you've achieved the minimum bar, you're ready to tell more people about your Facebook presence. This would be an appropriate time to invite people—employees, partners, friends, family, and so on. Just as with content, you'll need supporters for your presence to communicate to other people visiting for the first time that you are relevant and interesting. The more people you have willing to associate with your organization, the more it appears to be a seemingly unbiased third-party endorsement to strangers and other people who you'll also need to be successful.

Featured Case: Shashank Nigam, CEO of SimpliFlying

We had a chance to catch up with airline marketing industry guru, Shashank Nigam, CEO of SimpliFlying, which is a company that specializes in helping airlines and airports engage travelers profitably. We asked Shashank the following five questions about his opinion and experience of marketing on Facebook:

Q. *Overall, what opportunities do you think Facebook brings to marketers in the air travel business?*

A. Airlines can now use the "wisdom of friends" to influence decision making. People spend a lot of time on Facebook, and airlines need to use the social graph to engage customers and drive specific goals like revenue and loyalty.

Q. *What do you think customers want from air travel companies in social media, and how does that differ from other marketing options?*

A. Customers are looking to seek customer service during and before travel from airlines in social media. Eighty-eight percent of all tweets to an airline are customer service related, according to Eezeerdatalab. This is due to the real-time nature of the medium, which is lacking in other marketing mediums.

Q. *Do you see any common mistakes that marketers make when engaging with customers on Facebook?*

A. Many airline marketers create a Facebook fan page and then expect customers to come to them. But a typical person on Facebook spends almost half his time viewing the activity feed from his friends, rather than on an airline's page. There needs to be a compelling reason for them to be on the airline's page. And that needs to go beyond just discounts and special offers, as that's unsustainable.

Featured Case: Shashank Nigam, CEO of SimpliFlying *(Continued)*

Q. *What are the most forward-thinking companies in this business doing well or better than their competitors?*

A. Delta Air Lines replies to all customer service queries on Twitter within 10 minutes and aims to resolve them within 24 hours. KLM forms the real-world connection with their fans, but surprising them at airports with little gifts and even painting a plane with photos of its Facebook fans. Estonian Air has just launched the world's first social loyalty program, which has racked up 1,000,000 impressions on Facebook while the airline carries only 800,000 passengers a year! It's the first loyalty program to reward for advocacy.

Q. *How do you see this evolving over the next three years?*

A. In the next three years, social media will form the fabric of an airline's interaction with its customers. Travelers will explore new destinations and plan holidays on Facebook, seek flash sales on Twitter, and share their memories on Flickr and YouTube. And airlines and airports will be a part of this process.

Shashank's company, SimpliFlying, has created a very attractive and informative infograhic (Figure 5.7) on how the future of loyalty programs is social. You can find the infographic and additional information here:

`http://simpliflying.com/2011/infographic-the-future-of-loyalty-program-will-be-powered-by-social-media/`

Plus, see the accompanying presentation for further study on loyalty programs and social media here:

`http://simpliflying.com/2011/presentation-why-the-future-of-loyalty-programs-will-be-social-media-based/`

Figure 5.7 The future of loyalty is social.

Week 4: Promote and Engage

Now that you have your foundation in place with a compelling design and regular content that reflects your brand, it's time to open the floodgates to bring in the fans! There are myriad ways to promote your fan page inside Facebook, on the Web at large, and by using traditional marketing and in-person methods. In this section, we'll explore a variety of ways to get the word out about your Facebook business presence. Then, once the fan count begins to build, you'll want to be equipped properly to interact with your fans on a regular basis and build the engagement.

Monday: Promote on Facebook and the Web

You can easily create anywhere from moderate to extreme visibility for your page inside Facebook and potentially reach hundreds of millions of prospective fans. The following are ways to promote inside and outside of Facebook. We suggest you select one or two to test at a time. This is a meaty section, and you'll want to come back to it time and again for more ideas.

Try Facebook Ads and/or Sponsored Stories You'll definitely want to experiment with Facebook ads—this is the most targeted traffic your advertising dollars can buy. For an in-depth guide on making the most of ads, see Chapter 6, "Month 3: Create Demand with Facebook Advertising."

Make Use of Tags These are often referred to as @ *tags*, because you used to have to type an @ symbol first to get the list of pages to show up. Now you just type an uppercase letter and begin typing the name of the page you want to tag, and you'll see a drop-down menu from which to select.

You can easily gain tremendous visibility on highly trafficked fan pages by coming up with legitimate reasons to "tag" them in your updates. By legitimate, we mean having a good reason to give credit or acknowledge a page owner. The one disadvantage of tags is that, on the tagged page's Wall, the only option is View Post, so this limits engagement with your content on the other page. However, this can also be a strategic advantage because fans of the other page may well click through to your page and become a fan.

When you make posts with tagged pages, your post will appear on the other page's Wall and provide you with an opportunity to be seen by a different audience. Use this practice with great care and always think about how the post will come across to the other page owners. See the example in Figure 5.8 where I (Mari) tagged Social Media Examiner's fan page and, in fact, owner Mike Stelzner had shared the same post a few hours prior. Mike often removes tagged posts to keep his Wall clean; however, he and I have a strategic business partnership and frequently cross-promote one another. It all comes down to intent, really.

Figure 5.8 Example post with tagged page

Run a Contest Running a contest, competition, sweepstakes, or drawing are great ways to generate buzz and bring traffic to your fan page. Just keep in mind the number one rule to which you need to adhere is using a third-party app. We suggest checking out the apps offered by Wildfireapp.com, Strutta.com, and LikeOurBusiness.com along with companies that offer suites of apps such as NorthSocial.com and Involver.com. There is a plethora from which to choose. You might need to do some research and a get a free trial account to find the app you like best. To run an effective contest, make sure you plan everything out well in advance, from the prize, administration, promotion, judging and selecting and announcing winners. We don't recommend running a promotion until you have, say, at least 500 fans. You might not get as much traction and value for your money otherwise. For more on the subject of successful Facebook contests, see these two helpful blog posts:

www.socialmediaexaminer.com/facebook-promotions-what-you-need-to-know/ **and**

http://spiderworking.com/blog/2012/02/08/how-to-run-competitions-on-facebook-by-the-rules/.

Place Social Plug-ins on Your Blog Facebook offers a variety of widgets to place on your website to drive traffic and engagement back to your fan page. These plug-ins include the Facebook Like button, Like box, Comments plug-in, and more. See Chapter 7 for more information about how to integrate these tools on your website and blog.

Use Other Plug-ins On Your Blog We like the toolbar created by Wibiya.com. The bar sits on the bottom of each page of your blog, and you can easily customize the buttons to include a pop-up for your Facebook fan page. In addition, WordPress.org has an extensive variety of plug-ins pertaining to Facebook. Check out Sexy Bookmarks too, and place the Facebook option toward the beginning of the plug-in.

Write a Blog Post Assuming you have a reasonably sized platform/subscriber base on your blog, go ahead and write a blog post announcing the launch of your new fan page and outlining some of what you plan to cover on the page. You can easily embed the Like button for your fan page and/or Like box into the middle of the post!

Add Your Facebook Link to Your Email Signature Be sure that you always promote your presence on Facebook in your email signature file. Include buttons and links to your Twitter, LinkedIn, Google+ profiles, and more. The handy email extension for web-based mail by Wisestamp.com works great for this purpose.

Include Your Facebook Link in Ezines If you write a regular email newsletter, be sure to add the Facebook logo and a link to your fan page with a good call to action. Try ideas such as "come write on our Wall" or "let's be Facebook friends."

Promote Facebook on Your Other Social Profiles Include a note of your Facebook page URL on your Twitter background—this is prime real estate because you never know how many people are visiting your Twitter page. You might consider placing your Facebook page URL in your Twitter bio link. And, of course, be sure to tweet about your page on a regular basis. You can sync your Facebook posts with Twitter and automatically post each update as a tweet. See `http://facebook.com/twitter`.

Tuesday: Promote Offline

Depending on your particular type of business or industry, there may also be plenty of opportunities to create great visibility for your business offline.

Print Media On any print media, add your social links including your Facebook page URL. This media would include business cards, letterhead, envelopes, brochures, flyers, coupons, postcards, and other direct mail material.

Product Packaging It may even be feasible to add your primary social profile links on product packaging. We are seeing a significant increase in this practice among major brands and some smaller ones too. Corona Tools now includes the Facebook and Twitter logos on its product packaging with links to its profiles.

QR Codes You may have heard of QR codes. These are "quick response" codes with a two-dimensional graphical pattern that is recognized by QR code readers, apps, or scanners. More and more smartphone users are willing to try QR codes, and marketers are including these codes in more creative and strategic ways.

Menus If you are a restaurant, bar, café, or coffee shop, think about how you could prominently place links to your social profiles on the menus! That is prime real estate. Every customer who looks at your menu is a potential fan of your Facebook page.

Deals If you have a Place page for your local business, you can also take advantage of Facebook's Deals. (You'll know you have a Place page because there is a Bing map in the apps section.) Place pages function in the same way as business pages (fan pages), except your fans can "check in" to your place and take advantage of deals that they see on their mobile devices only when they come in to your premises. To set up Deals, go to Edit Page and then look for Deals. See this section on Facebook for more: www.facebook.com/deals/checkin/.

Wednesday: Follow Engagement Best Practices

One of the biggest fears business owners have when it comes to setting up an active Facebook page is that they will get negative comments and spammer posts and not know now to deal with them. Fortunately, Facebook has a handy "moderation block-list," where you can proactively add keywords so that any post made containing those keyword(s) will be hidden from view. In addition, Facebook's own spam algorithms are rather tight, and you'll end up with a number of fan posts sitting in the Hidden Posts area. As a best practice, you'll need to check this area regularly to moderate posts, because often they need to be unhidden. To do this, hover over each post, and you'll see a little gear icon in the upper-right corner. Click and select from the following options: Remove Post, Remove Post And Ban User, Unhide Post, and Report As Abuse.

We recommend you assign a minimum of one additional admin to your fan page. Then, create a schedule for who will moderate your page on what days and times. You might even post this schedule in your About section or on a custom app.

When you have to handle a negative post, this is a golden opportunity to demonstrate stellar customer service right out in the open. In most instances, you may be able to turn around a disgruntled customer into a customer for life and, in the process, pick up new clients too. You'll need to make a judgment call and decide if the post is by someone who is out to attack and make a fuss for no good reason, in which case those types of posts should be deleted, or whether the person has a legitimate reason to be upset. For the latter, this should be included in your overall company social media policy where you have predetermined how to handle such situations. It may be that a bit of homework is needed to ascertain what happened and what to do to remedy the situation. However, time is of the essence. The faster you're able to post at least an interim reply, the quicker you'll be able to nip any negative situation in the bud.

For a list of sample social media policies, refer to this helpful directory:

http://socialmediagovernance.com/policies.php

For great examples of posting guidelines, see the About sections on the Facebook Pages of PETCO and Skittles:

www.facebook.com/PETCO?sk=info

www.facebook.com/skittles?sk=info

Observe other fan pages from the list you created at the beginning of this chapter. From small businesses to large brands, see whether you can get a sense of how other page admins handle negative comments and spammers.

Thursday: Build Your Page Culture

We have found that the best way to mitigate spam and possible negativity drastically is to engender a strong culture of mutual respect. There are certain specifics you can easily emulate, such as ensuring your default Wall visibility is set so that posts *both* to the fan page and by fans are visible. Many businesses set their Wall either to display their own posts by default or to completely turn off their Wall for fans, meaning that fans can only comment on the page posts, not make their own. To us, this sends a subliminal message of "them and us." It seems to say that the business cares more about what they have to say and doesn't want to hear from fans.

To create ongoing mutual respect, always build up your fans, acknowledge them, and reply to fan posts with the person's first name wherever possible. Also, if your fan page is in the name of a business or brand (vs. a person's name), always sign off your posts with your first name. This is particularly important if you have multiple admins.

Take a look at apps that allow you to display leaderboards off your most active fans. This helps inspire and empower your fans to want to give more: to step in and help out other fans by answering questions and to remember to come back to your page often to share.

Two apps in this genre to check out include Fangager.com and Booshaka.com. Using these apps, you can easily identify your "superfans" and come up with ways to honor, recognize, and reward them. The good news is that, because you use a third-party app, you can run a contest and be compliant with Facebook's promotions guidelines.

You might also simply select a fan of the week and announce this on your Wall or display their photo on your main fan page image. Many brands and businesses practice this on a weekly basis. For example, see Zappos' fan page: `http://facebook.com/zappos`.

Friday: Spark Engagement

As of the time of writing, Facebook is still using its complex algorithm called Edgerank to determine what content goes into the News Feeds of users. Some studies have shown that as much as 90 percent of fans do not return to your fan page once they have clicked the Like button. Your fans see and interact with your content only in their News Feed. Therefore, you need to become skilled at "News Feed optimization," that is, ensuring your fan page content gets seen in your fans' News Feed! See the helpful reports from Buddy Media for more stats and facts on getting your content seen: `http://buddymedia.com/resources`.

Some suggestions to help optimize your visibility and engagement include the following:

Include Specific Calls to Action For example, when you actually say something like, "We love Fridays here at the office. Click Like if you agree!" you will get more people liking that post than if you did not include the request to click Like. Equally, include a call to action to add a comment, thoughts, or feedback and see whether your engagement rate increases.

Keep Updates Short and Simple Some studies show that posting status updates of less than 80 characters gets the best News Feed visibility and the highest engagement. This can sometimes be difficult, but just observe popular pages like Mashable, The Huffington Post, and *The Ellen DeGeneres Show*, and you'll see their style of updates is typically very short.

Try Posting Outside Business Hours Many Facebook users are on the site during the evenings and weekends. Friday is one of the most popular days, and Facebook even has a "Happiness Index" showing the spikes in activity on Fridays and public holidays. Take advantage of early mornings, evenings, weekends, and even holidays to boost your engagement.

Host Expert Hours Set aside a regular weekly time to host an expert who answers questions for your fans. Fridays are a great day to host expert sessions. Be sure to promote the upcoming session on your page Wall and through all other channels. Then keep to a designated one-hour window, and have your fans post questions rapid-fire on your page Wall while the guest expert answers. Here's an example session I (Mari) lead for SiteSell:

> www.facebook.com/notes/sitesell/live-qa-with-mari-smith-collection-of-questions-answers/226320474083008

Test Making Off-Topic Posts Typically, most of your fans will want you to stay totally on topic, that is, only share posts pertaining to your business's area of expertise. However, experiment with throwing in a few off-topic subjects. For example, "What's everyone doing to celebrate Labor Day weekend?" (assuming most of your fans are in the United States and Canada).

Host Live Webinars People love to interact with a live person, especially if that person is on camera. There are several webinar and live video streaming platforms available that can be integrated with your Facebook Page. Take a look at platforms such as Livestream: http://facebook.com/livestream, Ustream: https://apps.facebook.com/ustream_live, TinyChat: https://apps.facebook.com/tinychat/, and Linqto: https://apps.facebook.com/linqtomaster/.

Week 5: Monitor and Modify the Plan

At this point, your project should be in full swing. You've set up your fan page, and you've started posting content to fill out your presence. You have an editorial understanding, you have a voice, and you are committed to posting content on a regular basis to keep your customers happy and informed. Although you are only a week or two into the campaign, the only things you haven't done are Facebook advertising and detailed reporting/analytics—things that are more appropriate later in the campaign. Some parts of the project are proving to be easy, but others unfortunately are not; this is the time to fill gaps in your operational plan.

Monday/Tuesday: Reassess Your Progress

In Chapter 3, we discussed the discrete tactical tasks necessary to produce your Facebook presence effectively. In Chapter 4, "Month 1: Create the Plan and Get Started," we talked about a few things to consider when assessing your competitors. You've learned a lot about what it takes to get the job done and the challenges you face. So, now let's make sure you can do the job.

Figure 5.9 shows a simplistic view of the cycle of work for any Facebook marketing campaign. While you're always doing a few of these things simultaneously, you start with a theory on the types of content that would be interesting to your customers. You post that content on a reasonable cadence and with an editorial policy and voice that fits both your brand and your customer segments. You monitor results and feed a reporting mechanism that will give you time-trending data for later analysis. This analysis feeds revisions to your plan and your approach, and the cycle refreshes. It's rare for this cycle to go around only a few times—you'll iterate repeatedly learning the entire way.

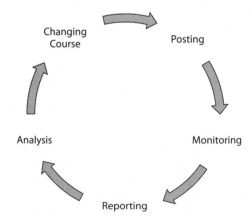

Figure 5.9 Facebook marketing cycle

After a single week, it's probably too early to make dramatic changes to your approach—you want enough data to make informed decisions. How much data is enough? Typically, a few weeks will smooth out such things as three-day weekends, holidays, vacation schedules, and other types of seasonality that can dramatically impact results. So, let's hold off on data for a few more weeks—we'll cover analytics in detail in Chapter 8, "The Analytics of Facebook." For now, let's focus on the operational issues that you face, for example:

- Are you handling the workload, or are you overwhelmed by the project?

- Are you confident in the choices you've made regarding your social media presence (Facebook, Twitter if appropriate, and elsewhere)?

- Is your effort comparable to, or, better yet, better than, your competitors'?

- As a result of your efforts, are customers interacting with you and other fans, friends, and followers more?

- Do you have enough interesting content to keep customers engaged, or are you already finding it difficult to source interesting content?

- Do you think you're doing the right things, or do you intuitively believe that you are missing out on some opportunity?

- Do your colleagues support you and the effort? Are you getting necessary management support?

Be honest with yourself—there is no point in lying to yourself or your superiors. We find a very interesting and effective forcing function is a meeting with a friendly senior colleague to assess progress. Have this "mentor" of sorts give you honest feedback on what you're doing well and what you're doing poorly. But make sure it's a friendly person who won't cause problems! After all, you do need time to iterate and succeed.

Wednesday: Get Help Where You Need It

If you are doing a great job and you're on the way to meeting goals, feel free to skim this part of the chapter or even skip ahead. But if any part of this project is too difficult or time-consuming, it may be an indication that you need help from someone with the expertise or time to manage the process.

We always recommend that companies first look internally to find colleagues who may be able to offer assistance. Oftentimes, companies have a good person or group willing and able to assist right around the corner. Besides, these projects tend to be interesting—so you may get more cooperation than you expect. Keep in mind that if you're the one responsible, you are the primary person to get the job done. This isn't an opportunity or justification for you to get your colleagues to do work for you. But if, for whatever reason, you can't find help or if it doesn't fit your company's culture to share responsibilities across different groups, you can always get help from people who specialize in Facebook marketing or social media.

When assessing third parties who can help with your social media project, first know exactly where you need help. Draft a list of problems you want a third party to solve for you. Make sure you're assessing people against the likelihood that they'll solve your problems first. Oftentimes, consultants will want to do a different part of the project, so you have to stand firm. You should always be open to suggestion, but you should also make sure you hold third parties accountable for the exact help necessary to advance your campaign. The right person to help with the day-to-day maintenance of a social media presence may be different from the right person to help with high-level strategy. Get the right person for the right job.

While doing your due diligence on consultants, consider that the world has spawned a lot of "social media experts." Scrutinize people, and consider a few other things as you make your decision:

Background Does the person or the principals of the consulting business have a track record of optimizing new technologies and running successful campaigns?

Fit Is the consultant able to do the things you need them to do? Are they a strategist, someone who can roll up their sleeves and get the job done, or both? Strategy and implementation are two different things—many consultants like to gravitate to the sexy strategy work when you may not even need it, and then you're still left with the need for implementation. Clear communication is key.

Expertise Can the person truly do the job for you? Have they or the company done projects for clients similar to yours? Does the person ask you a wide variety of relevant, fact-finding questions? (The more thorough a third party is in their initial intake process, the more likely they'll do a good job for you, assuming they also have the track record to back this up.)

Validation Have third parties validated their or their company's expertise? Are former clients willing to share success stories or references?

Training is critically important. Once set up, a lot of Web 2.0 projects can run on autopilot if someone on staff is able to monitor success and failure. Hold consultants to a high standard that includes training and an exit plan. You don't want to pay a consultant *ad infinitum*, and you shouldn't have to if you've hired the right person or company.

Thursday/Friday: Produce the First Reports and Analysis on Your Progress

In your company, it may have taken a committee to decide to approve your Facebook marketing project, or it may have taken just a single person. In either event, sharing the things you've learned early in the campaign is a handy tactic to reinforce the decision and to set the right tone for the future. This would be a great time to share initial findings with interested parties.

What constitutes a good report? We've always had success by sharing data on effort and outcomes, including what has taken place and what happened as a result—all in the language of numbers. But you can't stop there; a good report will also have some seemingly objective analysis. You're the one writing the report, and you'd be remiss not to take the opportunity to offer your interpretation of the numbers and what they mean.

Start slow and try to focus on a single metric or two in the early phases of the project. Figure 5.10 is an example of a good, simple page views graphic provided by Facebook Insights that would be perfect to share early in a campaign. Add a simple commentary to something like this, and you have your first report! Your colleagues are not nearly as expert as you are on Facebook marketing, so reporting will need to reflect important data points that can be both easily understood and explained. Over time, you'll have the opportunity to get more complex as people learn alongside you.

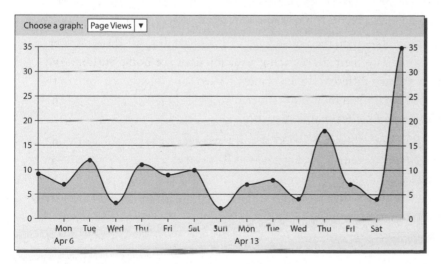

Figure 5.10 Basic early campaign report for fan page

You won't have a lot of time-trending data early in the project, but that's OK. Show what you can, and make sure you manage your colleagues' expectations. Learning often is a huge benefit when companies decide to do social media work in-house. Focus on what your effort has taught you and how it informs future decisions.

Month 3: Create Demand with Facebook Advertising

Facebook advertising remains one of the best deals today in Internet marketing; nowhere else can you target users as precisely as you can on Facebook. Better yet, you can do it for a fraction of the cost of the same targeting on other Internet properties and offline outlets. Even so, you should paradoxically temper your expectations. Just because you can target people inexpensively doesn't mean that mastery is simple. Users respond differently to Facebook ads, and depending on demographics and social norms, some ads work better than others. Success with Facebook advertising requires aggressive monitoring, experimentation, patience, and creativity.

Chapter Contents

Week 1: Learn the Basics of Facebook Advertising

Before we get started with a campaign, we'll review some basic concepts of Internet advertising. All Internet advertising campaigns set out to influence consumer behavior in one way or another. Campaigns range from simple awareness to image building to specific calls to action based on the manager's goals. These goals are determined based on the context of a specific situation within an organization: a company may be looking to improve its image, a nonprofit may be looking to expand its volunteer base, or a government agency may be looking to inform users of a new site that will improve their operating efficiency. Regardless of the intent, Internet advertising, if properly harnessed, can help achieve those goals. For more information on Internet marketing metrics and derivative statistics, please skip ahead to the metrics section of Chapter 9, "Addressing Common Marketing Problems."

Monday: Review Opportunities in Facebook Advertising

Facebook advertising can help with a variety of problems when you decide to hit the accelerator on creating demand for whatever Internet properties you are marketing. Specifically, Facebook advertising is great if you want to do the following:

- Create more traffic or visibility for your Facebook page or a custom landing tab on your page.

- Test the effectiveness of a change or addition you've made on your Facebook page or application, and see how effective that change is at converting traffic to something more meaningful (fans, friends, group members, leads, application users, and so on).

- Tap into the Facebook audience to promote an external website, campaign, or landing page.

Note: If your organization wants to use Facebook advertising in the future for a large campaign, you may want to learn on a lower-priority project. It's better to get a feel for it without pressure to perform. Just make sure you measure it and learn from the process.

Whatever your motivation, Facebook advertising can help with any or all of these things if you have the budget to pay for the impressions or clicks and if you have the wherewithal to do the work necessary to effectively monitor your progress. If you have the budget to do the work but you won't have the time to learn how to analyze the data, you are wasting an opportunity to get smarter and become more efficient with your ad spend. That is not to say that you have to optimize your own ads, but it's the best way to make the most of the money you're spending.

Facebook employs two different advertising models. If you have $5,000 per month or more, you can work with a Facebook ad representative directly. But for most businesses, the best and easiest way to begin experimenting with Facebook ads is through its self-serve advertising model. You can access the self-serve interface by clicking the Ads link under Apps in the left sidebar of Facebook after you log in (Figure 6.1).

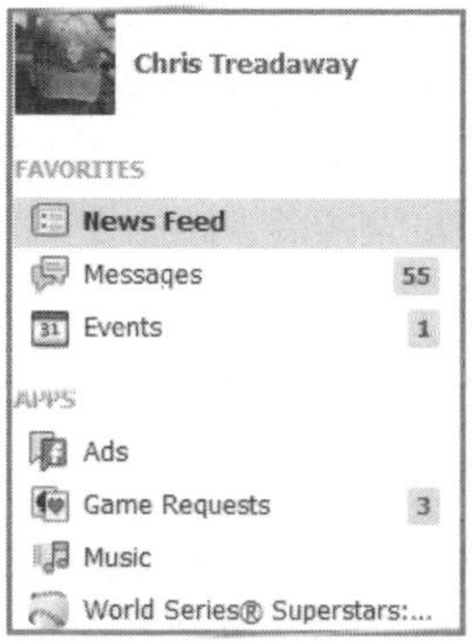

Figure 6.1 Facebook ads menu option on left sidebar

With a little patience, you can learn how to turn it from something seemingly esoteric in the beginning to a ship you can steer to generate demand for your product or service with remarkable precision. This is probably also an ideal time to be honest with yourself to determine whether you have the time and energy to run your own ad campaigns. If you think you'll have time for experimentation and you'll have the discipline to monitor your own success or failure, proceed. Otherwise, consider reaching out to a local agency or a specialized ad management service to do the heavy lifting for you. Either way, you really can turn Facebook into a machine where you put money into one end and get traffic and attention from customers on the other end. That's the goal here.

The Business Case for Facebook Ads

There are a lot of reasons why Facebook advertising makes a lot of sense for most businesses:

Low Cost to Start   Facebook ads are accessible to anyone who has $1 a day or more in terms of budget. It doesn't take very much money if you're going to run your own Facebook ads to actually try it. It does take money to optimize and do well with Facebook ads, but you can actually get your foot in the door and start learning without blowing a ton of money.

Demographics   It's the richest demographic targeting opportunity that currently exists in the world for advertising when you consider that Facebook has 800 million+ profiles that it can read from. It can pull the demographic data out of the profiles that people have made available on Facebook and make that available to advertisers as groups of people that you can advertise to.

continues

The Business Case for Facebook Ads *(Continued)*

Targeting The combinations and permutations of targeting are really unbelievable and still relatively inexpensive. If you target an audience of about 100,000 people or more and you're doing the self-serve advertising yourself, you can get the clicks for as little as about $1.25 each—and sometimes lower—which ends up being a lot cheaper in most cases than Google click-throughs. And you can currently get the impressions for a CPM at about $0.25 to $0.30 a piece or less. It does get more expensive as you do more aggressive targeting, but this is roughly what you can expect to spend if you end up running the campaigns yourself.

Tuesday: Choose Success Metrics

Facebook is not unlike any other Internet marketing effort you may undertake. First you determine your goals for the effort. Make sure you can measure outcomes that will tell whether you've succeeded. If you're lucky, this will require only you to collect the data. If you aren't so fortunate, you'll have to get colleagues to cooperate and provide you with the data you need and at the right reporting cadence.

Here's one example from a recent client engagement. The client wanted to know how an increased emphasis on publishing regular updates to their Facebook fan page with links to their website would impact that website's traffic. We worked with the client to find the right person in the organization to provide data on page views. Two weeks later, we got the data—but it was reported on a monthly basis and not a daily basis as we'd requested. We were told that reports on daily traffic would take a month or longer to produce. For our specific situation, it wasn't a terribly handy or workable solution. Only much later did we actually receive those reports, and then the data was 60 days old!

Fortunately, Facebook reports ad results as often as in real time should you need it, as does Google if you've integrated with Google Analytics. So, most people reading this book won't deal with the major delays that we faced with the enterprise customer referenced earlier. In some circumstances, however, it does take time to get reports about the performance of websites or landing pages. It's better to know earlier rather than later what dependencies you have in collecting metrics and what you can expect.

Let's turn our attention to a few measurements that will indicate success for your efforts. Assume for a moment that you are running a Facebook group. You'll add people, lose people, and interact with these people over time. You'll need a measure that tells you, at the end of the day, that you are consistently growing your Facebook group over time. The same goes for profiles, fan pages, and applications. Table 6.1 summarizes the statistics you can measure on Facebook and the derivative metrics that can be measured on an ongoing basis to tell you what is happening. You will measure progress over time—daily, weekly, or monthly—to see the impact of your efforts.

Presence	Core metrics	Derivative metrics
Profile	# of friends # of Wall posts	Net # of fans/friends added/lost per day # of "likes" per day
Fan page	# of fans # of "likes" # of comments # of Wall posts	Ratio of "likes"/Wall posts Ratio of comments/Wall posts
Group	# of group members	
Applications	# of daily active users # of fans	

If you are promoting a website with Facebook ads, you'll want to establish success criteria for the effort. Page views and unique users are two commonly used metrics designed to measure the increased attention that a site gets. But in most cases, users will have a number of ways to find that website; Facebook ads may be one of many ways that people navigate there.

Overall, you're trying to understand how different parts of your marketing mix convert people to whatever business goal you want to achieve. Many marketers who are not "quantitatively oriented" fail when they don't try to isolate metrics at each part along the way. We call this the "customer walk": how we inform people of marketing offers and watch them convert at different stages along the way. Figure 6.2 illustrates the basic customer walk. Impressions inform target customers of an offer. They may or may not choose to respond to it by clicking an ad for that offer. A customer turns into a lead when they agree to an ongoing marketing relationship with your business by joining a mailing list, following a page, or affiliating with other social media account. Finally, a customer is a "purchaser" when they've made some sort of deep transaction with your organization, whether it is financial, volunteering time, or some other meaningful active commitment that goes above and beyond a passive relationship.

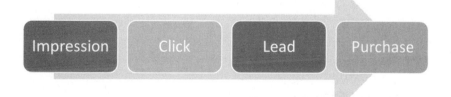

Figure 6.2 The customer walk—progressing users toward conversions

Now consider for a moment that if you are pointing people to a website or something else that is accessible in hundreds of ways, you'll have no idea what your Facebook advertising specifically does to generate the business outcomes you need. That's why we typically advise most advertising clients to set up an entirely new landing tab or page to measure how Facebook ads affect the customer walk. Why? You might discover that Facebook ads do a great job of generating leads or purchases for your business. Conversely, you may discover otherwise. It's hard to say, but if you isolate outcomes and create landing tabs that are accessible *only* by people clicking your Facebook ads, you can let the numbers tell you.

Get Your Baseline

If you're targeting your Facebook page, place, group, or app with Facebook ads, it's a best practice to understand how it is performing on its own without any demand generation. Know how many fans/friends your site attracts before and after advertising to make sure you know exactly what advertising does for you.

Wednesday/Thursday/Friday: Create Your First Ads

There are actually four ways to get started with Facebook advertising. We mentioned the easiest and most common earlier in this chapter: by accessing the Ads link under Apps in the left sidebar on Facebook. Another way to access the Facebook advertising interface is by going directly to www.facebook.com/advertising. Facebook also occasionally displays a Create An Ad link in the upper-right corner of fan pages that you administer with a green Get More Fans button. There is also an Advertising link on the footer of most web pages on Facebook. Any of these options will get you started.

The first time you visit the Ads page, you'll see a screen similar to Figure 6.3. If you've already run an ad on Facebook, the first screen you will see in the Ads page is a summary of results of ads you've already run (see Figure 6.4). You'll need to click the Create An Ad button at the upper-right part of the screen to put a new advertisement into the system regardless of whether you have already used Facebook advertising.

Note: If you want to advertise a fan page, group, or application, you will have to become an administrator of it first; otherwise, you'll have to provide Facebook with a URL. You have to be an administrator to get Sponsored Stories and other specialized ad types on Facebook.

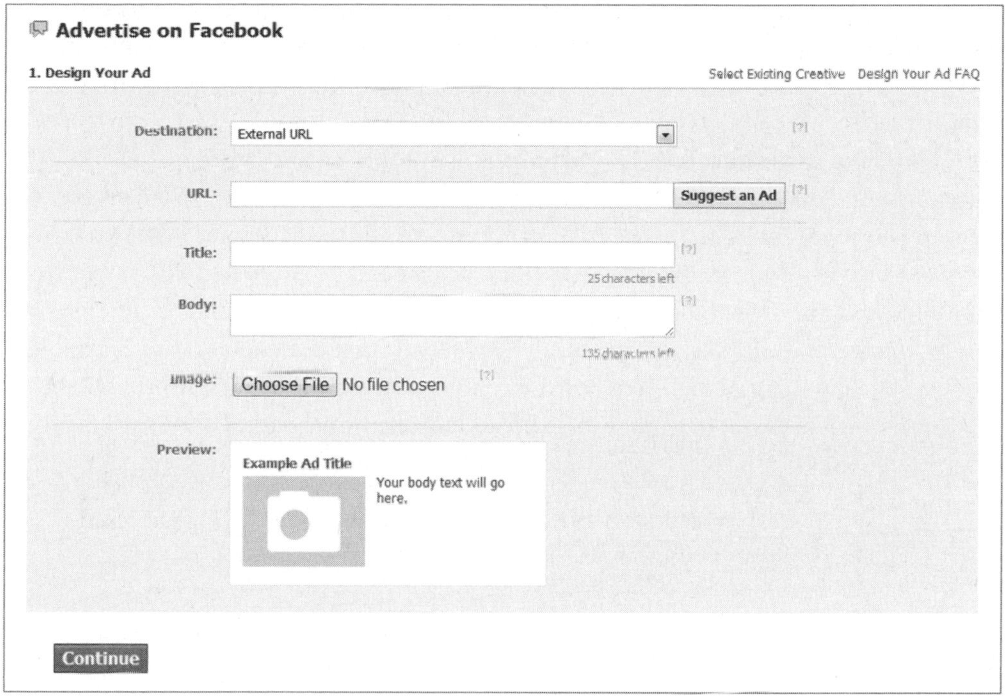

Figure 6.3 Facebook advertising, first visit

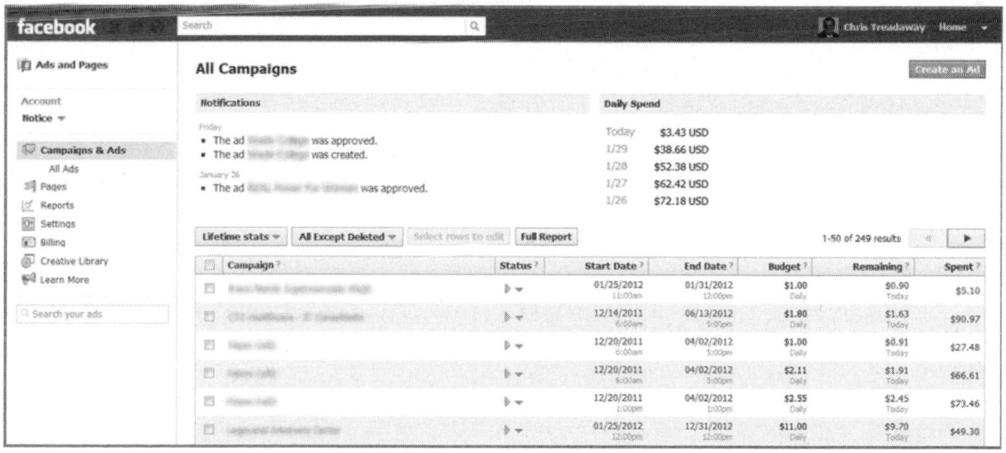

Figure 6.4 Facebook ad manager, results

On the ad entry screen, you will create your first advertisement by adding text to the fields on the left side of the screen. Meanwhile, your ad will update on the right side of the screen—this will show you how your ad will appear to Facebook users. You have 25 characters for your title and only 90 characters for the body of the advertisement, which are firm limits. This is a recent change, as Facebook ads allowed for 135 characters until March 2012. Be careful as you write your ad copy because Facebook won't allow you to add more characters once you reach your limit. We have certainly written our fair share of ad copy with partially written words because we weren't careful here!

If you're advertising a Facebook property—a page, an app, a group, or a place—you will have a few choices when determining the type of advertisement you want to place (see Figure 6.5). The two main types of ads for Facebook properties are Sponsored Stories and "traditional" Facebook ads. Sponsored Stories take content from your page and promote it with paid advertising, essentially guaranteeing your content will be viewed by your fans and friends of your fans. There are two types of Sponsored Stories: Page Like Stories and Page Post Like Stories. Page Like Stories inform friends of people who liked your page that their friend has liked your page. Page Post Like Stories tell their friends that they liked a particular piece of content on your page.

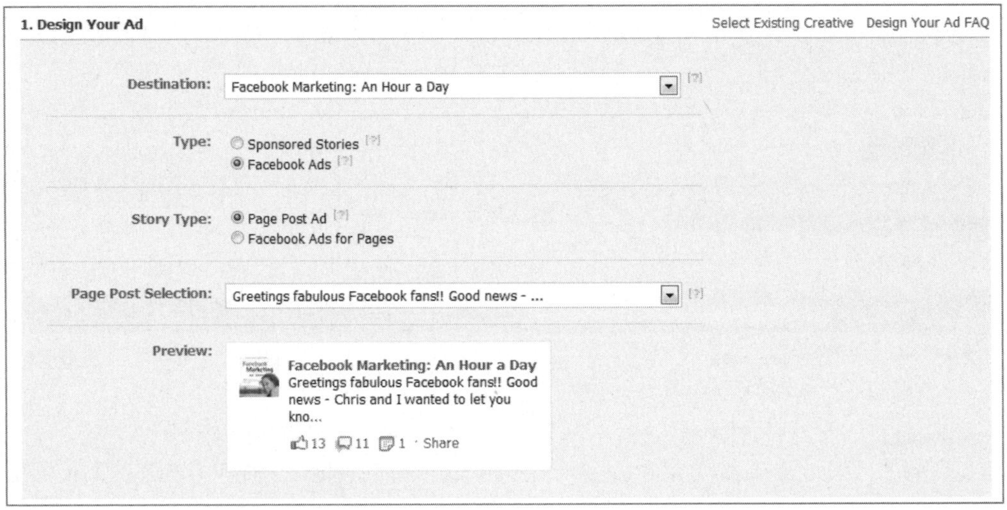

Figure 6.5 Types of Facebook ads for pages

"Traditional" Facebook ads allow you to control the body text of your ad as well as the imagery that you use. You can also use a Facebook Ad for Pages to send people directly to a tab on your page, which is helpful for those of you who have a custom landing tab experience for certain users. Alternatively, the Page Post Ad will post status updates of your choice as advertisements, effectively guaranteeing that you'll get visibility for your content. This is particularly helpful if your page's Edgerank is suffering and you need help exposing content to your own people.

You may also notice the links Select Existing Creative and Design Your Ad FAQ. Select Existing Creative takes you to a library of the pictures, titles, and ad copy that you've used in your previous Facebook advertising efforts. This helps you skip several steps in the process, get a faster approval for your ads, and run your advertisements faster. Use this feature to choose from the existing creative, if applicable. But be careful. Ad copy will be filled in automatically and will override any content that you had in section 1, Design Your Ad.

This is probably a good time to take a few moments to review the Design Your Ad FAQ, especially if you are creating your first advertisement. Facebook has strict rules about the types of ad copy it accepts, and it thinks nothing of rejecting your ad if it doesn't meet the guidelines. When you are finished, definitely add an image to your ad—this can be a logo, an icon, a picture, or anything relevant to the advertisement that you think will improve the chances of getting people to click it. Some studies show that the ad picture is the top factor that impacts your click-through rate.

After you've entered your ad copy, you'll have an opportunity to target particular users. Remember Chapter 4, "Month 1: Create the Plan and Get Started," when we discussed profile data? Here's where you get to tap into it as an advertiser! Figure 6.6 shows where you enter criteria of Facebook users that you'd like to target for your advertisement. Make the choices you'd like, and Facebook will automatically update the number of people who may see your ad on the upper-right side of the screen. Not much here has changed over the past several years except ZIP code targeting, which is a recent addition to Facebook's ad targeting options. This is the first step of many for Facebook ads to ultimately emulate ad targeting opportunities available in the offline world.

Buyer Beware When Targeting ZIP Codes on Facebook

Facebook's recent addition of ZIP code ad targeting has been met with much fanfare. Now marketers can target exact ZIP codes to reach customers like they would with direct mail campaigns.

But beware of the accuracy; it may not be there quite yet. On a recent client engagement, we targeted a single ZIP code near the downtown area of a mid-sized U.S. city. From other data, we knew that the ZIP code had approximately 40,000 residents. But according to Facebook, only 600 people lived in this very popular part of town.

Facebook primarily uses IP address and in-browser location settings to determine the ZIP code of a particular user. Unfortunately, those approaches don't necessarily mean the data is accurate. Over time, we expect Facebook to get much more accurate when determining a user's location. But for right now, it isn't quite as reliable as it could be, so make sure that if you do ZIP code targeting that you don't exclusively rely upon it (Figure 6.6).

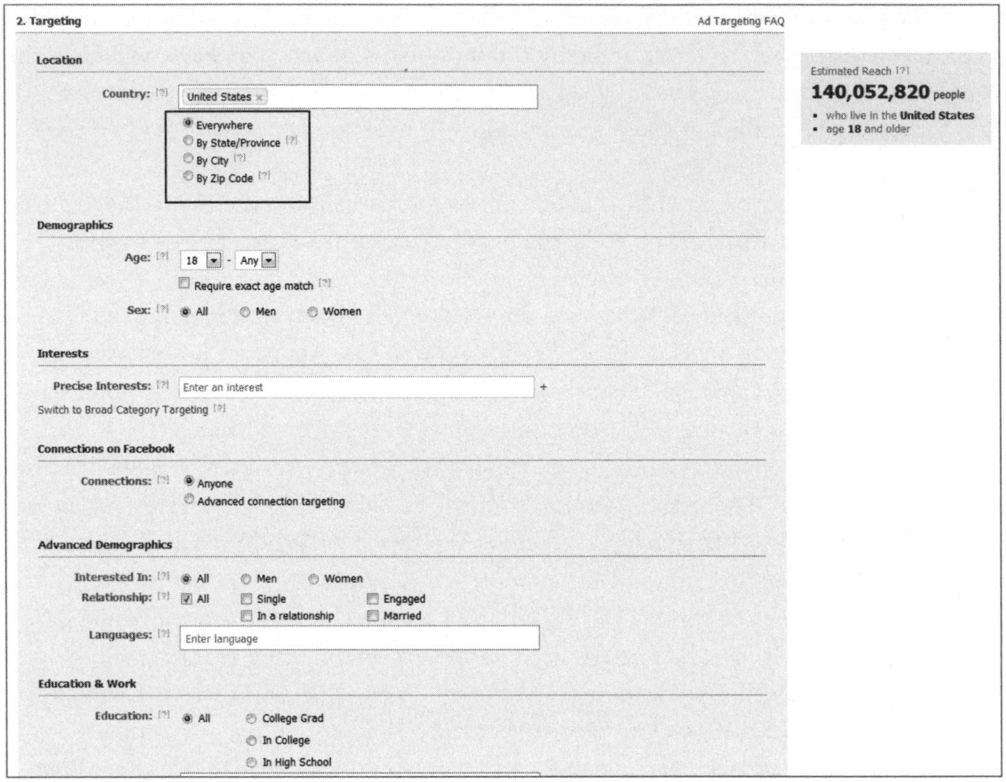

Figure 6.6 Targeting ZIP codes

Another relatively recent change to the Facebook advertising self-serve system is the simplification of interests targeting. These shortcuts allow you to easily identify target markets, people with kids, particular mobile users, and the like. It's a welcome change for many advertisers because these targets would take some creativity and precision to find otherwise (Figure 6.7).

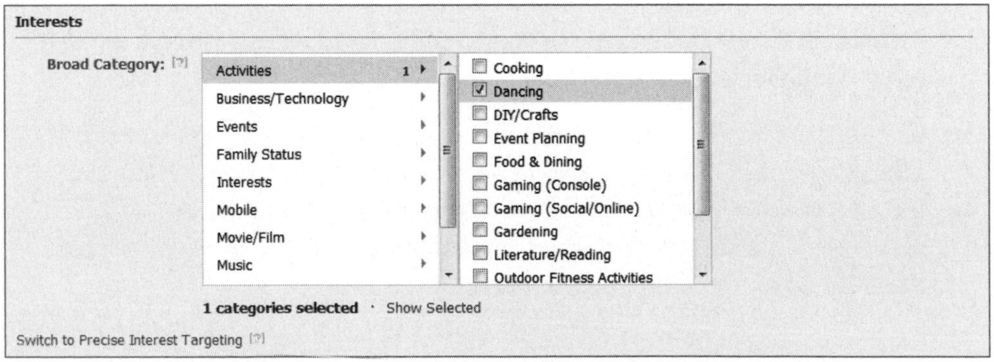

Figure 6.7 Broad category targeting

As you digest all this information, think of the permutations of targeted groups that you could create. You can target Facebook users in a variety of ways, including the following:

- People older than 65 in New York state
- Engaged women between the ages of 30 and 34 in Spain
- Male college graduates in Chicago
- Single people on their birthdays
- Employees of companies you want to target for business purposes

The possibilities are endless. In addition, Facebook will reportedly soon be launching additional ad types:

- Mobile user and deeper location-based targeting
- A more invasive "Sponsored stories" that is sold as a premium ad option and guarantees marketing messages are visible by users directly inside the News Feed
- The ability to target users in real time

These are huge prospective developments that may change ad strategy and opportunities for marketers.

The final step in the self-serve process is to define your campaign and set what you are willing to spend on advertisements. Figure 6.8 shows you the options you have in this final step.

Action-optimized CPM is a new option at the time of the publication of this book, and not much is known about it at this time. For more information, please check our Facebook Page for more information at http://www.facebook.com/marketingbook.

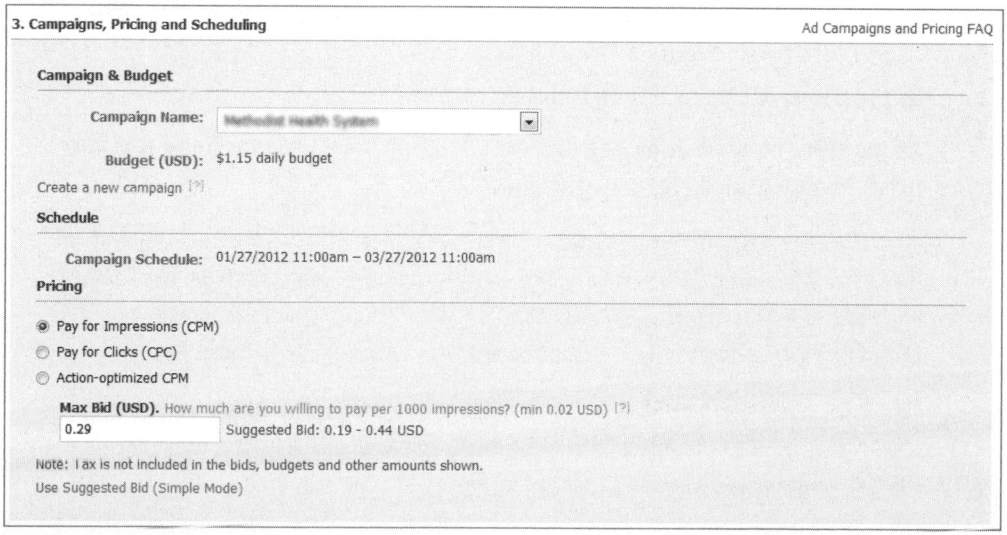

Figure 6.8 Campaign types and pricing

Three things are most critical here:

Set Your Daily Budget This is very important so your costs don't spiral out of control. Early in a project we like to set the daily budget lower than we've budgeted so we can learn and get an idea of what will happen.

Schedule Your Ad Campaign This is necessary if you have a date at which the ad is no longer relevant or the offer isn't available any longer. If the ads can run indefinitely and if you plan to monitor your campaign regularly, there isn't any reason to set an end date.

Pay for Impressions or Clicks Facebook gives you two options: impression-based advertising and click-through advertising. Based on the options you've chosen for targeting, Facebook will also estimate the cost and the number of impressions or clicks that you are likely to receive on a given day.

After you've paid for the ad, your ad is sent to Facebook for final approval. Facebook personnel will review your ad to make sure it meets its guidelines before "lighting it up" on Facebook. This process can take as little as a few minutes or as long as a few days depending on its queue and whether you've run a similar ad in the past. Either way, Facebook will notify you of its decision via email. If your ad is accepted, it will start running almost immediately. If your ad does not meet Facebook's standards, you will get a rejection email asking you to resubmit the ad. Facebook typically doesn't give you the exact reason why your ad was rejected, so if you're doing this regularly, you may ultimately become both a detective and an expert in Facebook advertising guidelines!

Note: When you get started, it's important to collect statistics on what is happening. So, get a few ads running as soon as you can and leave them alone. Once you get a week of data on your ads, you'll be in a better position to experiment and make changes.

Impressions or Clicks? Which Is Better for You?

Are you having trouble deciding between impression-based advertising and click-through advertising? The answer lies in what you're trying to achieve.

Impression-based advertising guarantees you a certain number of *impressions*, or placements on the screen. When you bid 50 cents for an impression-based advertising campaign, you are agreeing to pay 50 cents for 1,000 impressions. This is known as the cost per mil (thousand), or CPM. Because you pay only for the impressions, any clicks you get out of the deal are free.

Click-through advertising guarantees that the only time you pay for advertising is when a user clicks your ad. So, if you bid 50 cents per click, your 50 cents is spent the first time someone clicks your ad—regardless of whether it is the first impression for your ad or the millionth. This is typically the best way to guarantee that a certain number of people will act upon your offer every day.

Week 2: Build the Dashboard and Collect Data

By now, you should have at least one ad approved by Facebook and running for your customers to see. This week, you'll monitor the campaign, analyze results, make changes, create more ads for existing campaigns, and establish new campaigns. Why go to all this effort? At a minimum, you'll want to make sure you aren't just blowing your money. But if you're going to spend money on advertising, it also makes sense to make that spend as efficient as possible. Those of you who report to more demanding executives who want proof of at least something resembling a return on investment are particularly under pressure to show how dollars increase revenues and profits or save money you're spending on other alternatives. Remember also that you're experimenting with a variety of approaches designed to reach customers as effectively as you can. This takes a little care and feeding—your campaign won't optimize itself just because you took a half hour to create a single ad!

Monday: Know What Data Can Tell You

To truly understand the impact of your marketing approach, you need intelligence on what happens with your web properties before, during, and after an advertising campaign. The standard cocktail of Internet marketing metrics apply: page views, unique users, fans/followers/friends, conversations, and so on (see Chapter 8, "The Analytics of Facebook"). The metrics you choose are really up to you—and the right answer depends entirely on your specific business situation. Facebook Insights may also have given you some ideas of new metrics to consider. No matter what, you're trying to understand the impact of your marketing efforts:

Marketing Reach If you increase advertising spend by $X, you'll get Y more fans/page views/interactions/new customers.

Investment Every new fan costs you $X and generates $Y in lifetime revenue, for a lifetime return on investment of $Z.

Comparison Interactions on Facebook cost $X, which compares to $Y on Google, $Z through traditional print advertising, and $A on Yahoo!

Targeting Reaching fans in <insert country> costs $X on Facebook, compared to $Y on Google, $Z through traditional print advertising, and $A on Yahoo!

Competitive If you don't get 5,000 fans on Facebook as inexpensively as possible, your competitor will crush you.

Although different businesses have different pressures, just about all businesses today are looking for ways to do things as inexpensively and effectively as possible. Fortunately, you can set up your campaigns to understand the economics of Facebook advertising and optimize your campaigns to make the most of whatever resources you have.

Tuesday: Make Final Decisions about Your Data Reporting Cadence

First things first—you need to decide how often you'll look at your performance metrics. How is your page performing? How are your ads performing? Which metrics matter? And will you watch your competition? Some of this is achievable in Facebook Insights, and some requires creating a tool or dashboard in a spreadsheet to analyze campaigns. We tend to prefer collecting data in a spreadsheet, which you can later roll up into whatever view you need to inform yourself and your management team.

Last week, you decided the statistics that you'll track, and you probably also now know exactly what it will take for you to get the numbers you need. Make sure you collect the core metrics on a regular yet consistent basis—either daily, weekly, biweekly, or monthly. Otherwise, you'll analyze one set of data against a slightly different period of time than another, and it will make your analyses inaccurate. Consistency is critical so that you're always comparing like data day-to-day.

Daily data collection is generally the safest and most revealing way to go. By choosing daily reporting, you are collecting data in its most useful molecular form. You can go back to any day in the past and see exactly what happened, but only if you've committed to recording data in a spreadsheet or other format that you can save to your hard drive. Otherwise, you are leaving it up to Facebook, Google, or any other service to save data for you.

You can also roll up data over a period of time—say a week, a month, and so on—and analyze how your campaign improved or maxed out at various stages of the project. Most important, you can analyze it on any vector you choose, be it the net number of fans you've added, total cost of your campaign, cost per fan, click-through cost, or any other metric you'd like to see.

Now, there is one downside of choosing a daily reporting: like it or not, someone is on weekend duty! If you've missed a day, it may not be a big deal, though. If you're collecting data on the net number of fans you have each day, you can make some educated guesses for days you aren't able to get in front of your computer. Daily advertising data can be pulled into your dashboard in a variety of ways well beyond the day after. But don't make a common practice of this because it will poison your data over time and make assessments about how your properties do on different days of the week useless.

Wednesday: Set Up and Populate the Dashboard

For the sake of examples in this book, we'll show how to set up a dashboard of daily data for a hypothetical Facebook marketing and advertising campaign. We'll also assume a fairly common scenario—tracking the performance of a Facebook fan page alongside followers of a corporate Twitter account. If you refer to Table 6.1, you'll see that we should record at least one of a number of metrics: number of fans, number of "likes," or number of comments. Let's keep this one simple and record the number of fans this particular page has every day. We'll do the same thing with the Twitter follower count. We'll also add a column to track the number of new fans/followers we have added each day; this number is generated by subtracting yesterday's number for each from today's number. Figure 6.9 is the beginning of our dashboard.

	FB Fans	FB Fans/Day	Twitter Followers	Twitter/Day
27–Apr	516	5	449	1
28–Apr	517	1	453	4
29–Apr	522	5	461	8
30–Apr	523	1	460	−1
1–May	533	10	470	10
2–May	534	1	477	7
3–May	538	4	479	2
4–May	544	6	482	3
5–May	547	3	488	6
6–May	549	2	491	3
7–May	557	8	492	1
8–May	559	2	492	0
9–May	561	2	494	2
10–May	565	4	498	4
11–May	568	3	503	5
12–May	573	5	511	8
13–May	577	4	513	2

Figure 6.9 Basic dashboard

As you populate your dashboard, you may notice that Facebook records your data in a variety of ways. Some metrics are recorded automatically and are accessible for a long time via Facebook Insights or other parts of the platform. Others, such as the number of "likes" you create, are recorded only when you intervene and count them manually. Yet both sets of numbers are helpful at different times and perhaps might be useful later when you want to analyze your performance over time and compare the data to other situations. So today, and probably for the next few days, you'll need to get into the habit of collecting data that you think may very well be overkill. That's OK—you will want the record of what has happened later. For now, just make sure you populate the dashboard religiously at a consistent time of day as often as you can.

Thursday: Understand Moving Averages

Now let's review a concept that we'll use quite a bit—moving averages. *Moving averages* are a daily average of a consistent backward-looking period of time (7 days, 14 days, 28 days, and so on). They're calculated every day and then charted to give a longer-term perspective on what is happening. They're also good for reducing "spikes" in data that happen for understandable reasons (like weekends) and for reasons you'll never totally understand. Moving averages help clear up data that might ordinarily distract you from noticing the general trend of the impact of your marketing efforts.

Moving averages have a significant role to play in the dashboard and in reporting. We'll go through that later in this chapter. But for now, we'll add moving averages to our basic dashboard; we'll simply add two columns next to the FB Fans/Day column and label them 7 DMA and 28 DMA for a one-week and four-week moving average calculation. To do this, you'll need to average the current day and the previous six days to get your seven-day moving average. The same goes for the 28 DMA column; you'll average the present day along with the 27 previous days of data. This is all very easy to do in Microsoft Excel or other spreadsheet application. If you don't have enough data yet, hold off until you do. Otherwise, you won't have a full 7- or 28-day moving average, and it will skew your data. Take Figure 6.10, for example.

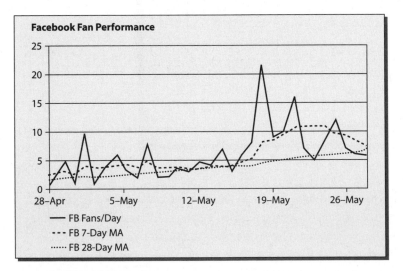

Figure 6.10 Moving averages chart

This is a chart of the number of Facebook fans we have attracted for a 28-day period; it's a common chart we like sharing with clients. Notice that the solid line is all over the map; that is the daily outcomes. If we determined success or failure by daily performance, we'd have some violent ups and downs—some really good and really bad days! Moving averages are much more insightful when looking at long-term trends to see whether your tactics are working. The value of 7- and 28-day moving averages is to share progress on both short-term and longer-term perspectives. If you've done this properly, your dashboard will look much like Figure 6.11.

A	E	F	G	H	I	J	K	L
	FB Fans	FB Fans/Day	FB7DMA	FB28DMA	Twitter Followers	Twitter/Day	Twitter 7DMA	Twitter28DMA
30–Apr	523	1	2.7	1.92	460	−1	2.0	4.64
1–May	533	10	4.0	2.23	470	10	3.3	4.85
2–May	534	1	3.6	2.19	477	7	4.1	4.93
3–May	538	4	3.9	2.25	479	2	4.4	4.82
4–May	544	6	4.0	2.46	482	3	4.7	4.79
5–May	547	3	4.3	2.57	488	6	5.0	4.93
6–May	549	2	3.9	2.64	491	3	4.3	4.96
7–May	557	8	4.9	2.93	492	1	4.6	4.64
8–May	559	2	3.7	3.00	492	0	3.1	4.25
9–May	561	2	3.9	3.07	494	2	2.4	4.07
10–May	565	4	3.9	3.21	498	4	2.7	4.04
11–May	568	3	3.4	3.32	503	5	3.0	4.07
12–May	573	5	3.7	3.50	511	8	3.3	4.21
13–May	577	4	4.0	3.64	513	2	3.1	4.07
14–May	584	7	3.9	3.89	511	−2	2.7	3.89
15–May	587	3	4.0	4.00	519	8	3.9	3.82
16–May	593	6	4.6	4.11	522	3	4.0	3.71
17–May	601	8	5.1	4.04	525	3	3.9	3.54
18–May	623	22	7.9	4.68	528	3	3.6	3.43
19–May	632	9	8.4	4.79	530	2	2.7	3.39
20–May	642	10	9.3	5.04	545	15	4.6	3.68
21–May	658	16	10.6	5.50	550	5	5.6	3.71
22–May	665	7	11.1	5.71	555	5	5.1	3.86
23–May	670	5	11.0	5.75	557	2	5.0	3.89
24–May	678	8	11.0	5.96	559	2	4.9	3.96
25–May	690	12	9.6	6.21	562	3	4.9	4.04
26–May	697	7	9.3	6.43	563	1	4.7	3.93
27–May	703	6	8.7	6.46	570	7	3.6	3.89
28–May	709	6	7.3	6.64	571	1	3.0	3.96

Figure 6.11 Dashboard with moving averages

One final note on the dashboard: we're simply tracking outcomes because most marketing managers want to be able to understand and communicate improvements to the most important metrics. Your specific situation may require you to add columns in your dashboard to track activity—how well you are doing your job to keep the presence fresh and how well customers respond with direct feedback ("likes," comments, and so on). The more data you have, the better; you can always ignore or hide certain columns in your dashboard when that data isn't necessary.

Note: Want to really impress colleagues with the depth of your analysis of daily data? After you've updated your spreadsheet for six to eight weeks or more, add a column in your spreadsheet with corresponding days of the week for each date. Then sum and average all the totals for each day of the week to see what days do well and which days don't. When you show your colleagues data that proves your Facebook presence does best on Tuesdays and worst on Fridays, you'll get that much more credibility for being on top of things.

Friday: Back Up Your Dashboard

Once the dashboard is established, it really does become your best friend—whatever you do, don't lose this file. It will contain all the data you need to create the insights you need to provide your colleagues on an ongoing basis, and it will answer basic questions. Where have we been? Is this working? What happened when I made a change? How does advertising impact our ability to attract new fans? Data from the dashboard can inform even the most routine decisions. Be sure to back up this file regularly—ideally you'd be running it from a secure online/offline storage service like Dropbox, or perhaps you prefer keeping your data in a Google Docs spreadsheet. You don't want a catastrophic computer hardware failure to annihilate your dashboard and all the metrics you've so painstakingly recorded. In the example in Figure 6.8, you should record all your key metrics and extend your moving average numbers to keep them up-to-date. As circumstances warrant, you can use this spreadsheet to create charts showing your progress or how different tactics have made you more or less successful.

Additionally, you may want to consider saving copies of the creative that you're using for ad copy. Spreadsheets are a good way to store imagery, ad titles, and other ad copy details that you've used in the past. Facebook is generally reliable in that it doesn't often "lose" your data. But after a few years, Facebook really doesn't have much of an obligation to keep your old ad copy, and it's feasible that Facebook may remove it without your knowledge. It's better to be safe than sorry. We will go into more detail on dashboards in Chapter 8.

Week 3: Refine Your Campaign Using A/B and Multivariate Testing

Now that you have a functional albeit basic dashboard and you know how to create an ad on Facebook, it's time for you to send your campaign into high gear. What do we mean by this? Running multiple ads and campaigns makes a lot more sense when you have the infrastructure in place to see how you've done and how you can improve. And that's what you've built with your dashboard—a simple system for you to test cause and effect. At the end of the day, you're looking to turn your efforts into a system where your every action can produce a somewhat predictable reaction.

Monday: Learn the Basics of A/B and Multivariate Testing

In its simplest form, *A/B testing* is understanding the impacts of doing things two different ways. We'll go through it in a little more detail here, assuming you are marketing a Facebook fan page. For example:

- What is the average number of net new fans on days you posted content? What is the average number of net new fans on days you didn't post new content?

- What is the average number of net new fans you get on days you post content about international politics? Other types of content?

- What is the cost per click on advertising run in the United States vs. the United Kingdom vs. Canada?

Notice that in each case, there is an either/or. You're evaluating two or more things but leaving every other variable consistent across all the things you test.

Answers to the previous questions are critical to optimizing a campaign, but only as long as you have enough activity to pass the "red-face" test of statistical validity. In other words, if you rely on a few days of feedback, you may just choose days when people are particularly unfriendly to your cause. Running things for a longer period of time will turn your hunches into knowledge. The bar is not true statistical validity but more of a feeling that you've run things for long enough, with different characteristics, and with enough eyeballs that you feel like you could defend the thought process to even the most demanding people in your organization.

Take the first example mentioned, for instance—if you never post content on Saturday, you are likely affecting what should be a totally objective outcome had you posted content every day of the week. If Facebook traffic turns out to be 25% lower on Saturdays than other days of the week, a 15% lower fan conversion rate may actually indicate success because you're doing better than Facebook does! Without randomness and context for your assertions, you can actually draw the wrong conclusions and make bad decisions for your organization.

Sometimes you don't want to test just two potential outcomes. Maybe you want to see how three or more different things can impact outcomes on a website. This is called *multivariate testing*. Here are a few anecdotal examples of multivariate testing as it relates to Facebook advertising:

- Jane is a product manager running an impression-based Facebook advertising campaign across four English-speaking countries: the United States, Canada, Australia, and the United Kingdom. These ads target groups and pages that are updated infrequently. Which ads generate the lowest cost per click?

- Tom wants to see how both ad copy and geography impact the performance of his nonprofit's click-through marketing campaign. Which combination of ad copy and geography does the best job of getting people to sign up for his newsletter?

- Jennifer has three different sets of images that she can use for her Facebook advertising campaigns, but she doesn't know whether one set is best. She'll set up the same ad copy across three different versions of ad copy. Which set gives her the lowest cost per new fan?

Multivariate testing is a great option when you have a number of criteria you'd like to test but no earthly idea of how individual elements impact performance metrics. It's good for a scattershot approach to give the marketer a quick idea of what works. The marketer can then drill deeper by isolating specific criteria with A/B tests to optimize an advertising campaign.

Tuesday: Understand the Basics of Great Ad Copy

Turn your attention now to best practices for creating great ad copy. As we've mentioned, Facebook's Ads page gives you 25 characters for a title for your ad and 135 characters for the body. Ads appear on the right side of users' News Feed, profile, events, groups, fan pages, and other major pages on Facebook, and they refresh upon every new click made within Facebook, including when a user clicks the tabs on a profile, group, or fan page. If you are advertising a Facebook fan page, the title will be the name of your page, and you won't be able to edit it. If you are advertising an application, a group, or a website, you will be able to edit the title.

All told, you have up to 160 characters to make your case to users that they should pay attention to you, along with the opportunity to present an image. Images that you upload will be resized to 110×80 pixels, and this will be presented to you on the right side of the screen after you choose the image you want. Be sure to take a look to ensure your image looks good at that size.

When it comes to effective ad copy, you need to do a few things:

- Be clear. Tell people exactly why your offer is compelling and why they should care.
- Be human. Your ad appears alongside ads from other companies. Speak to people as people and not as companies or large organizations.
- Appeal to segments of your market. Facebook ads can be created to reach very specific market segments. Use this to your advantage to see what works best.
- Don't oversell. Overpromising is a great way to make people angry about the fact that they've clicked your ad. Make it a positive experience.
- Try different things. Customers can view your company or brand in a variety of ways. Use different approaches to engage.
- Include a "call to action." Don't leave it to a customer to interpret what they should do if they like your ad. Tell them what they need to do next.

Facebook doesn't just run every ad you place. It has a set of guidelines that you must follow for your ad to be approved. We won't cover them in detail here, but you can check them out at http://www.facebook.com/ad_guidelines.php. You can also refer to Facebook's best practices at www.facebook.com/ads/best_practices.php.

We'll now show you an example of two different sets of ad copy for a local restaurant. The real name of the restaurant will be withheld to protect the innocent. Both of the following ads sent Facebook users of all ages near the restaurant to a reservations page on the Joe's Bar and Grill website:

Advertisement #1

Joe's Bar and Grill

> Joe's serves the area's best
> steaks, seafood, and other
> local favorites. Make a
> reservation today.

Advertisement #2

Eat at Joe's

> Nothing is the spirit of the
> Pacific Northwest quite like
> Joe's Bar and Grill. Come
> in today!

Let's break down these two ads. The first has a more formal flair, talks about the food, and suggests a call to action for people to make a reservation. The second is a little less formal but has a weaker call to action. Conventional wisdom says that ad #1 would be better. Which ad do you think did better?

This is a bit of a trick question. After 10 days of running both ads, it turned out that the second ad did better than the first. Owners of the restaurant speculated that customers did not respond well to formality. But at the same time, the first ad had a few good elements. The call to action was a lot stronger, and the owner liked that it mentioned the types of food someone could order at Joe's. So, what did we do to figure out how to best optimize this particular ad?

We scrapped ad #1, declaring it a loser in the A/B test for these two ads. But we decided to compare ad #2 to two additional new ads to create an A/B/C test across ads #2, #3, and #4:

Advertisement #3

Eat at Joe's

Enjoy the Pacific Northwest's
finest steaks and seafood.
Make a reservation today.

Advertisement #4

Eat at Joe's

Nothing is the spirit of the
Pacific Northwest quite like
Joe's Bar and Grill. Make a
reservation today.

In ad #3, we refer to the types of food that are served at Joe's, but we went with the casual title. We also changed the call to action. In ad #4, we kept the same call to action, but the remainder of the ad features the same ad copy as ad #2. So, we ran three different ads about the same restaurant in an attempt to isolate the exact words and phrases that optimize Joe's advertising campaign. We don't suppose anything; rather, we use the data that comes back after the ads run for long enough to feel confident in the outcome. This is typically a week or more if we have that much time to let things run and see what happens.

So, which ad do you think was the best? It turns out that advertisement #4 was the right combination of casual language and a useful call to action, but the results were close. We actually ran both advertisements #3 and #4, but we budgeted more money for #4. Joe was happy, and he increased traffic in his restaurant significantly through this advertising approach—but only after running a few tests to see how his customers responded to ads that appeared to be similar on first glance.

As you can see, slight variations in ad copy can play a very significant role in the outcome of a Facebook advertising campaign. You'd be amazed at how a single word can dramatically increase or decrease performance. Now, this matters differently for impression-based advertising than click-through campaigns. You are rewarded for creating great ad copy for impression-based or CPM ads, because your clicks are truly free. In the case of click-through ads, your clicks aren't free, but your impressions are. Bad or very specific ad copy targeting certain people can work in your favor because you can get a lot of free impressions when your ads don't compel people to click as often as they could.

Facebook Advertising Q&A with Marty Weintraub

Marty Weintraub has seen it all with Facebook ads since its inception. In his company, aimclear, he has managed Facebook ad campaigns of more than 30 billion impressions around the world and has worked with major global brands such as MarthaStewart.com, Siemens, and Second Life. He's also the author of *Killer Facebook Ads* (Wiley, 2011). We asked Marty to summarize his thoughts on social advertising and where things are heading.

Q: *You've been active in the social ads business for quite awhile. What's the current state of Facebook advertising?*

A: Facebook ads have claimed the birthright of being an 800-pound gorilla of the online display advertising universe. At the time of this writing, Facebook ads are being widely adopted by businesses, both B2C and B2B, and specialty agencies are sprouting up like weeds to service such clients. Sophisticated third-party tools have been created and are finally on par with search PPC management platforms. Because Facebook ads work so well when expectations are aligned with reality, advertisers are flocking to try it. The price has gone way up, though costs are beginning to stabilize.

To understand the state of the Facebook advertising ecosystem, it's important to appreciate just how far things have evolved. These are not your big sister's Facebook ads anymore. The DIY ads platform was first released in late 2007 and evolved rather slowly at first. Still, for the right products, services, and KPIs, Facebook ads were incredibly powerful right out of the gate. Things were a little messy at first because spammers, affiliates, and arbitrage artists clogged up the space. However, we noted that there were incredible impression counts early, even in some hyper-targeted social demographic spaces. Also, we noticed that Facebook was not just for kids anymore. For instance, in 2008, there were more than 25,000 users over the age of 30 who were interested in "Las Vegas Vacation." That's when we knew Facebook ads were going to be a fantastic ride. The huge impression count made Facebook ads very attractive for branding.

That April we started telling clients to get it while it was hot, that they should buy their 100 million impressions now to make their brand a household name to targeted users, at a $.04 CPM (50,000 to 100,000) lower than Google's Content Network was for many placements. At those prices, who cared if there were any conversions? We noticed that serving gazillions of branding impressions in Facebook seemed to drive users straight to the top of the Google search funnel. In other words, Facebook users "heard" of the brand, remembered, and then searched for it in Google later. Those were heady times, indeed. We knew the bargain would not last, as Facebook itself grew more massive. By 2010 the cost was rising, and in 2011 Facebook ads ceased to be such a huge bargain for early adopters. The short answer to where Facebook ads are at now is that Facebook ads are mainstream, baby!

continues

Facebook Advertising Q&A with Marty Weintraub *(Continued)*

Q: *Have advertiser expectations of Facebook changed significantly over the years?*

A: Because the ads cost more, advertisers are more concerned about ROI. That can be a disconnect because it's difficult, in a last-touch-conversion-measuring world, to quantify the value of socialization and attribution as opposed to last-touch direct-response KPIs. Also, as advertisers spend a higher percentage of their media dollars on Facebook ads, they expect better customer service. Facebook does not provide much personalized service, even to some advertisers that spend millions. Facebook's account rep structure is ever-evolving and not nearly as well run as Google's.

A positive development in advertiser expectations is that as a result of books like this, conference speakers, blog posts, and so on, marketers are setting more realistic goals. In Facebook, it's easy to seed friend making with Facebook ads. Facebook ads are really good for promoting content, which yields ROI that can be hard to measure. There are few better ways to build community than sponsored stories. The direct response sale that marketers covet is totally doable and tends to be more expensive, on a cost per action (CPA) basis, than search. PR efforts are totally useful in Facebook but harder to measure. Anyone who thinks Facebook ads suck is not using Facebook ads for the right goals. Advertisers are beginning to get real.

Q: *How do you think social advertising compares to search advertising?*

A: Search advertising, when keywords are filtered by "buyers' intent," is still the most focused online advertising in the world. Social PPC is more about targeting the whole user, by way of their interests, predilections, occupations, educations, and other highly personal nodes. Social PPC demographic targeting works hand in hand with search marketing, together tendering a radically effective one-two punch. They each have their place. Both search and social advertising are essential to the overall marketing mix.

Q: *How well do you think Facebook ads perform relative to other ad alternatives?*

A: Facebook ads, to my mind, is the most effective online display advertising channel on Earth. They transcend anything we've known before.

Q: *What other social media advertising options are available? How would you characterize alternatives to Facebook ads in the social advertising category?*

A: LinkedIn's ability to matriculate precise occupations with the companies those users work for and other attributes shows a lot of promise. YouTube placements via Google's contextual targeting tool are highly effective. Paid Stumbles (StumbleUpon) yields interesting results because the users can't tell it's paid, and StumbleUpon provides fascinating demographic data. Sponsored Tweets, while not available mainstream as of yet, offers some cool social amplification features, as do sponsored hashtags. The Google Display Network provides layers of placement tools including some social demographic targeting features, and the volume is massive. There are also a lot of junky placements that cause the Google

Wednesday: Create Ad Variations

Earlier in this chapter, we covered the basics of creating your first ad, so for the purposes of this day, we'll assume you have already created your first ad. Now it's time to create some variations on that first ad that you will later use to compare against each other for effectiveness. The good news is that Facebook knows this is a common scenario for marketers. So, there is a Copy An Existing Ad option on the Ads page that streamlines most of the process. Just go to the Ads page, and click the green Create An Ad button. It is accessible via the drop-down menu at the top of the screen.

Choose the ad you'd like to copy, and Facebook will import the settings from that ad into the screen for you; the destination URL, ad title/copy, targeting options, and bid will all be preserved for you. All you need to do is get into the self-serve settings and change whatever you'd like. Your old ad will serve as the control group, and the new ad will be the test, which is not unlike the scientific method. You just want to know which one performs best for the metric you'd like to optimize. Ideally you will run them at the same time for a true apples-to-apples comparison. Feel free also to create many variations; the key is to leave a few things consistent across all the ads so you can isolate the drivers of better/worse performance. There is no point in doing this if you don't get smarter.

Thursday: Judge Ad Performance

So, in the previous example, how did we determine that "Eat at Joe's" ad #2 did better than #1 and that #4 did better than #2 and #3? It all comes down to the numbers. Let's first take a look at the numbers that Facebook provides you in the ads interface and define what these different numbers mean.

Figure 6.12 is the summary view of ads that ran within a different sample campaign.

Figure 6.12 Basic Facebook ad statistics

For each ad, you see the following numbers:

Ad Name This is the descriptive name you've given your ad—be sure to name your ad accurately so you can know what you see at this summary view.

Status This is whether the ad has run for its allotted time, whether it is paused, or whether it is running.

Reach This is the number of people who saw an ad in the time period selected for the report. This is similar to the unique visitors metric for websites.

Frequency This is the average number of times each of the people in the Reach metric was provided with an impression of your ad.

Social Reach This is the number of people who viewed your ad and also had a connection to a friend who liked your page, used your app, or RSVPed to your event. This number will generally be low except in cases where either you're extremely popular or you are running ads targeting friends of your fans.

Connections This is the number of people who accepted the invitation to "like" your page, use your app, or RSVP to your event. This number will be zero if you are promoting a website outside of Facebook.

Clicks This is the total number of clicks that you've received for the time period.

CTR (%) This is the click-through rate, calculated as total clicks divided by total impressions. This tells you the rate at which people click your ad.

Bid This is the amount of money you are willing to pay for an impression or a click, along with the type of ad that you are running.

Price This is the effective, final cost of the ads you are running, which is oftentimes different from your bid.

Total Spent This is the overall spend for this particular ad for the time period; this is viewable in the overall summary but is not provided on an ad-by-ad basis in this screen.

This view is a great way for you to look at how individual ads do relative to one another, but only as long as you look at relative numbers instead of absolute numbers. Absolute numbers such as clicks, impressions, and the total amount of money you've spent on advertising really tell only part of the story. In other words, when analyzed by themselves, you don't know whether those numbers are good or bad. For example, you may have put a lower bid in for a particular ad, and it may not have gotten the traffic necessary to generate as many clicks as another ad. Instead, you should look at relative numbers like click-through rate, cost per click, and cost per thousand impressions to see how individual ads truly perform relative to each other.

But interestingly, several useful statistics were removed from this summary view in 2010. This quick view will not tell you the total number of impressions, the average CPC, or average overall CPM that you are paying. You'd have to drill down to individual ads to collect this molecular yet highly valuable information for when you want to optimize your ads. In a sense, Facebook took a step back here, but that's just all the more reason for you to keep track of the numbers yourself.

In Figure 6.12, we ran an impression-based campaign across all the ads (CPM). You may notice on the bottom right of the screen that the price is a bit lower than the amount we bid. Why does this happen? Bids are truly run like an auction on Facebook—this is also how it is done with Google AdWords, Yahoo! Overture, and Microsoft's adCenter. When you set up your ad, Facebook suggests bid amounts that will guarantee that your ad will get enough impressions to meet your daily budget. But if they can't find other advertisers that meet similar criteria to fill the auction, you'll pay less. Often, we have seen the effective CPM turn out to be anywhere from 10 to 75% less than the bid amount, which is all the better for the cash-conscious marketer! It's yet another advantage for impression-based advertising on Facebook; sometimes you'll pay far less than you actually bid, thus giving you more impressions for your dollar.

Here we can get the estimated reach and frequency of each ad, along with the click-through rate (CTR %). You'd compare the reach to the target market numbers that you estimated when you started the campaign to see the percentage of people in the target market that have seen your ad. Frequency gives you an indication of saturation, specifically how often the people in the reach category have seen this particular ad.

What's the Optimal Frequency for Running Facebook Ads?

It's a common question that we hear all the time from Facebook ad clients: what's the right frequency to target before changing ads, retiring them, or retooling the campaign? The correct answer is always that the numbers should tell you when to stop. Look at your CTR by week; once the numbers start to drop, it's a sure sign that your ad/targeting combination has fatigued, and it's time to try something else. There is a lot of variability from one campaign to another — we've seen some take 50 or more impressions before the ads started to fatigue!

But if you're looking for a starting assumption, our data suggests that approximately 12-15 ad impressions per person are necessary to maximize the performance of your impression-based ad campaigns.

The next step to analyzing your numbers is to look at your average (effective) CPC and average (effective) CPM. To see these numbers, click Full Report on the Campaign screen. You'll see the "full" ad report on this campaign, as shown in Figure 6.13.

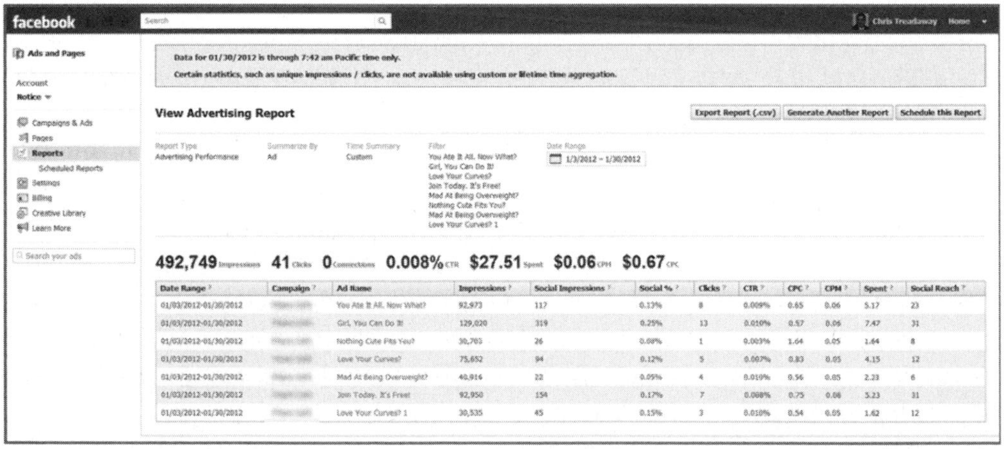

Figure 6.13 Full campaign ad report

In this particular case, we're running an ad campaign for a client in the weight loss products business. This is a breakout of the different ads that we're running, along with the impression count, social numbers (impressions, percent, and reach), clicks, CTR, CPC, CPM, and total amount of money spent. For the purposes of this exercise, we've blurred out the social numbers because we are not advertising a page or people with connections to the brand. Because it is an impressions campaign, you may notice that the CPM numbers are pretty similar. We're getting $0.05 to $0.06 CPM—not a bad deal! But there is a lot more variation in the CPC numbers. Some ads are attracting a lower cost per click because the ad creative is better or more appealing. Lower CPCs are good in CPM campaigns, because you're getting both the branding benefit and the click-through benefit at the same time.

In this case, we had three ads that got a 0.01% CTR. Not surprisingly, these ads got the lowest effective cost per click. Girl You Can Do It!, Mad At Being Overweight?, and Love Your Curves 1 (a variation of the first Love Your Curves ad) are the top performers. So, if you're looking to generate the most clicks you can per impression and thus get the lowest cost per click, you'll want to put more ad budget into these three ads and perhaps pause the others. But the numbers could also be misleading at the same time.

Check out the impression count on the ads again. Girl You Can Do It achieved a 0.01% CTR with more than 100,000 impressions—the most on the list. So, you can probably say that the ad is a keeper. But several of the other ads did not get as many impressions. Nothing Cute Fits You? appears to be an underperforming ad, but it has run less than 25% of the time of the Girl You Can Do It ad. Repetition matters in the impression-based advertising business, and you can't give up on ads that simply may not have run enough for you to draw conclusions.

Similarly, you may celebrate the other two ads that have a 0.01% CTR, but they have 40,916 and 30,535 impressions, respectively. It happens all the time that, over time, ads either improve or falter given more impressions and a more statistically valid amount of time to run.

So, in this particular case study, we'd try to get all the ads to 75,000 impressions or more before drawing conclusions. We can already see that the following ads are performing well with an adequate number of impressions: Girl You Can Do It, You Ate It All. Now What?, and Join Today. It's Free. So, we would create a second variant of ad copy, title, and imagery to see whether we could find combinations to perform even better. Finally, we'll retire the Love Your Curves ad because it has a suitable number of impressions and is underperforming relative to the other ads that have received at least 50,000 impressions.

Next week, we'll review the data again and see what happened. We typically kill the worst-performing ad when we test three ads against each other; then we tweak the best-performing ads and run A/B tests to verify outcomes. We will run all of these against each other and repeat the process to kill underperforming ads and gradually get better. This process, if repeated religiously, tends to optimize click-through rates in impression-based campaigns.

You can run this optimization any number of ways: gender tests with male vs. female targeting, geographic targeting, age targeting, interests, and so on. In all cases, the process is the same. We'll similarly look at the worst performance from a CTR percentage. In this case, ad #4, which targeted men, did the worst. Again, we'll look at ad copy and any further targeting to make a mental note that this ad didn't work well at all relative to the others. It could be because this particular offer doesn't resonate well with men, or it could be the ad copy. At this point, you can shut down the ad altogether, or you can run an alternative ad against the same demographic to see whether something else will work. Some people prefer experimentation even with poorly performing ads, while others are willing to make relatively quick decisions to retire underperforming ads. There is no right/wrong way to do it—either approach will work. At the end of the day, if you repeat the overall process, you will get gradually more efficient with your advertising spend.

Friday: Educate Stakeholders on the Process

Stakeholders likely cannot, and should not, understand the idiosyncrasies of running and optimizing a campaign. That's your job, right? But this is a good opportunity to educate your colleagues, especially as you kick off your first Facebook advertising campaign with ad copy and the beginning of A/B and multivariate testing. This has all the elements that demonstrate well: creativity, a reasoned approach to a difficult problem, a systematic means for collecting relatively unimpeachable feedback from customers, and data as the final arbiter of any dispute. When social media marketing disintegrates into people shouting opinions over each other with no data to support their assertions, everyone is wasting time.

This is probably the right time to sit down with supporters and hecklers alike to show them what you are doing. Think of it as a confidence-building exercise where you can explain things, answer questions, and, more important, educate folks on the fact that metrics and success criteria are indeed being watched carefully and that you're doing everything you can to make it work.

Regardless of what anyone in your company tells you, there is no way of knowing what the right answers are in advance. We remember one particular engagement where the client was convinced that a certain type of image was going to result in a better outcome, because it had always worked that way before. Ads run with these images actually created new fans at a cost of 3.5 times more than ads run without the imagery altogether. The clients didn't believe us until we showed them the statistics! This is the kind of insight you need—and another prime example of why you need to experiment. What you think will work and what actually works can be two entirely different things. Let data be the judge, jury, and executioner.

Week 4: Analyze and Adjust the Campaign

Last week, you spent a lot of time going through the analysis of a particular ad or series of ads. The great news is that you can "uplevel" all of that work, put ads into groups, and analyze everything at a campaign level.

Monday: Perform Basic Analysis of a Campaign

Let's perform analysis on a campaign that ran internationally several years ago. Several of the screen shots are a little dated, but the point here is to illustrate how we'd look at reaction to a brand's advertising internationally. Figure 6.14 shows the results of campaigns we created across several scenarios. We used the same ad copy across all five campaigns to compare its effectiveness in the United States, Australia, Canada, and the United Kingdom. We also ran a series of different subject-area ads to see how results would differ from more general ads we ran in different English-speaking countries. What you see in Figure 6.14 are the outcomes after running five ads for each campaign without having made any changes or edits.

All Campaigns

	Campaign	Status	Budget/day	Clicks	Impressions	CTR (%)	Avg. CPC	Spent
	US General Ads	Paused	$2.00	1,717	1,414,084	0.121%	$0.18	$313.72
	Australia Ads	Completed	$3.00	162	247,518	0.065%	$0.22	$36.00
	Canada Ads	Completed	$3.00	127	303,824	0.042%	$0.28	$35.95
	Subject Area Ads	Completed	$20.00	318	724,895	0.044%	$0.44	$139.15
	UK Ads	Completed	$3.00	251	163,325	0.154%	$0.14	$36.00
	Totals			**2,575**	**2,853,646**	**0.090%**	**$0.22**	**$560.82**

Figure 6.14 Assessing an international ad campaign

Overall, we spent $560.82 on 2,575 clicks for an average click-through cost of $0.22 per click. Although it isn't calculated on this particular screen, we achieved just under a $0.20 effective cost per thousand impressions as well. By dividing your click-through cost by the impression cost and multiplying by 1,000, you can calculate exactly how many impressions it takes on average to generate a single click. In this case, the answer is roughly 1,100. Why is this important? You can do the same analysis for individual campaigns or specific ads and use the metric to gauge the effectiveness of your ad copy. Generally speaking, if it takes fewer impressions to generate a click, the ad copy is more effective, and vice versa. If you're particularly obsessive about costs, you can convert ads with better ad copy to impression-based ads and those with worse ad copy to click-throughs as long as the economics make sense.

If you look at CTR percentage and effective cost per click, the most effective advertising was in the United Kingdom. Perhaps our brand or our message resonates particularly well there for cultural reasons or our ad copy works particularly well in the United Kingdom. No other experimental campaign did as well. Ads in Australia and Canada had mediocre performance relative to the United States and the United Kingdom. Look at the spend in Australia and the United Kingdom—it was exactly the same, $36, but we got almost 100 additional clicks in the United Kingdom! Now that's performance. Subject-area ads, with the second lowest CTR percentage and the highest average click-through cost, didn't fare nearly as well as the general ads we ran.

Looking at this simple chart, we'd first conclude that all the advertising was a pretty good deal for this advertiser, which was looking to extend its brand to Facebook. Very few advertising options anywhere give you such granular targeting and the interactivity that social media provides for the low cost of a $0.20 CPM—not email, banner ads, billboards, television, radio, or anything in print. It's unprecedentedly inexpensive to reach people on Facebook today.

We'd also conclude that if we wanted to optimize for efficiency, we'd devote almost all the ad budget to the United Kingdom. Clicks cost only 14 cents each, and one person clicks our ad for every 651 impressions targeting residents of the United Kingdom. That is by far the best overall performance of any of our campaigns. U.S. ads are also a good investment, while those in Canada and Australia need work.

Tuesday: Recalibrate Advertising

How confident can you be in the conclusions you draw from your analysis? It depends on what you are assessing. We like to run ads for at least a week or two to get enough data to draw conclusions. Similarly, it's nice to run a similar number of impressions across all ads before making comparisons. In the previous case, it's entirely feasible that we hit people in the United Kingdom on a good week and that the numbers will worsen if the ad is run for more time. Conversely, it's possible that the numbers should be even better in the United Kingdom. We don't know for sure, because in this case we got only one-tenth of the number of impressions that we got for the United States. So, in this case, you have two options:

- Leave it alone, and compare numbers based on the page views you have.
- Devote more budget to the United Kingdom, Canada, and Australia to even out the page views.

It isn't perfect—you won't quite have an apples-to-apples comparison with data from other geographies because you're running the ads at different seasons of the year, you're remedying one problem (discrepancy in page views) but creating another (discrepancy in when the ads run). But it is a judgment call that you'll need to make based on your hunch and what colleagues think you should do if they are involved in the decision-making process. Ideally, you would've noticed the discrepancy as you monitored the campaign all along.

In the case of the subject-area specific campaign, we probably have enough data with more than 700,000 impressions to suggest that these probably didn't work. But that isn't to say that some individual ads didn't do remarkably well. In each case, regardless of overall performance of the campaign, it makes a lot of sense to quickly drill down into the campaign to see what ads performed well and which didn't. You may find that the numbers are very poor at the campaign level, but you may have had one spectacular ad that holds the keys to success for that campaign. So, you'd undergo the same recalibration process again to make sure you can indeed draw valid conclusions from the data—pause some ads, increase budgets on other ads, determine whether you have enough information already, and so on.

Social Advertising Alternatives

By now, you may be wondering how Google, LinkedIn, and Twitter advertising compare to Facebook. Well, in most cases, they don't work as well, are more expensive, or may even fit both conditions.

Google, for example, has been around for a really long time, and so a lot of the click-throughs are very, very expensive. Why? Well, Google's ads are priced by an auction that has been running since 2000. So, the keywords go to the highest bidder, and it isn't uncommon to hear of clicks costing $5, $7, $10, and even $20 each these days. In many cases, these ads now cost far more than they are worth to the advertisers.

LinkedIn offers both click-through and banner advertising options to customers seeking business-to-business connections. These ads are currently much more expensive than those running on Facebook and, in our experience, do not generate great click-through results.

Twitter suffers from a few problems as well. Twitter does not capture rich profile data from its users, so the targeting options are fairly limited. Thus, the main thrust of Twitter's advertising efforts is Sponsored Tweets, whereby a popular Twitter user will mention a product or service as an ad unit. But there is a more fundamental issue with Twitter; it's in how Twitter works. Twitter is a constant and never-ending stream of contributions from all the people a user follows. So, it is really easy to miss a tweet. Ads may come and go without the user even having an opportunity to see them. By contrast, Facebook ads are on the right side of the screen—easily ignored, but at least you have a chance.

Wednesday: Review and Spice Up Your Dashboard

The previous examples illustrate yet another reason why you need to monitor your results through a dashboard and not through Facebook's interface. Facebook does a great job of showing you lifetime numbers and results over the past week, but currently it does not give you time-series results to show you when certain tactics and advertising campaigns are no longer optimal for you. It can't be programmed to help you isolate ads or campaigns that don't have sufficient budget or traffic to tell you that the data it provides is valid and comparable to results elsewhere. It also doesn't help you learn which marketing tactics provide you with the second- or third-level outcomes you need to be successful. If you use Facebook's tools to assess your progress alone, you'll be doing a lot of guesswork when you can know so much more.

Here are some features of Microsoft Excel that you can use regularly to help visualize data and isolate issues in a Facebook advertising campaign:

Heat Maps and Conditional Formatting Red, yellow, and green tell an analyst very quickly where there are problems and successes.

Standard Deviation Knowing the degree to which data spikes tells you whether you need to investigate why certain ads/tactics/days/approaches are succeeding and why others are not.

Charts/Graphs These are handy for reporting and further visualization of data.

This is where it is also handy to roll up data by week and month. There you can look for performance specifically to see whether the campaign, advertising, or tactics you're using are getting stale and are in need of some revision. You can also calculate a variety of derivative statistics inside Excel, usually in columns that are not visible to you until you want to view them later. These are also ideal places to use data analysis tools such as heat maps; derivative statistics can be difficult to understand without visuals to show how they compare to one another.

Thursday: Analyze Your Numbers Further with Moving Averages

So, how does all this work in practice? Let's take a look in more detail at how you can use your basic dashboard to assess your own performance. Figure 6.15 is a chart made from the data we captured in our basic spreadsheet on the number of Facebook fans added in a given day.

Figure 6.16 is an overlay of the seven-day moving average—the average of the previous seven days' worth of activity.

As we've discussed, this has the impact of smoothing out the outcomes to make the data a little easier to read. You can see peaks relative to the norm for the seven-day moving average on or around May 25, July 13, August 3, August 15, and again on September 17. This is an indication of the overall impact of tactics you undertake; this can be more attentive content posting, interactions with your customers, more effective advertising, new campaigns, or the result of additional advertising budget. So, be sure your dashboard has a record of the things you are doing differently at different points in the timeline. You'll want a good history of what you've done after the fact to better explain how things are changing.

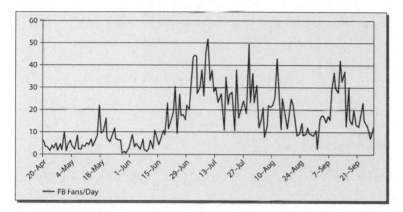

Figure 6.15 Fans per day

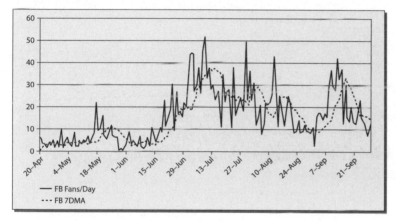

Figure 6.16 Fans per day with seven-day moving average

Now let's take a look at the 28-day moving average for fans per day in Figure 6.17. This is where the data gets a lot more interesting and provides greater insight into your performance.

Notice how the 28-day moving average creeps along early in May and early June. That's understandable—we didn't run any advertising in May and early June, but we did slightly increase the regularity with which we posted content. This can easily explain the 28-day moving average increase from approximately 4 per day to 8 per day. We launched advertising for this account in late June, so the 28-day moving average number increased dramatically. Ads ran on and off until early August, when they were shut down for more than a month.

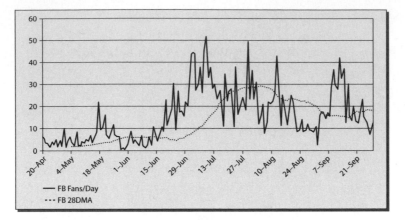

Figure 6.17 28-day moving average for fans per day

Notice that the 28-day moving average levels off around September 5. No ads were run in the preceding 28-day period. What does this tell us? It gives us an opportunity to measure metrics on our performance in several scenarios. Table 6.2 is another way of reading the numbers.

▶ **Table 6.2** Analysis of moving average chart

Time period	Approximate date	Estimated fans/day
Before daily content	May 6	3.5
After daily content	June 1	6.5
Advertising campaign	July 27	29
Post-advertising	September 4	16
Incremental fans/day as a result of daily content	3	
Incremental fans/day gained after advertising	9.5	

The net increase as a result of advertising gives us a sense of the lasting benefit of the advertising campaign. But how can an advertising campaign have a continuing impact if no impressions are being displayed to users or if we aren't buying clicks?

It stands to reason that as you have more fans or participants in your Facebook presence, you'll have more chances to impact people. Having more eyeballs on your content equals more reactions, more feedback, more sharing with friends, and so on. Take a simplistic case of the performance of a fan page with 100 fans compared to one with 10,000 fans. To get a single "like" or a comment, you'd need 1% of fans in the first case to respond, whereas you'd need only 0.01% of fans in the second case. If the same 1% of fans responded in the second case, you'd get a whopping 100 responses to your content.

Sharing has even a bigger impact. Let's say that 1% of fans in each case decided to share some of your content with friends—1 vs. 100. Let's also assume that each

Facebook fan on average has 75 friends. When 1% of fans shares your content with friends, that content appears on 75 News Feeds in the first case but on 7,500 in the second. So, the total impact of your piece of content is 100 of your fans + 75 random Facebook people for a total of 175 News Feed impressions in the first case. In the second case, you have 10,000 fans + 7,500 random people for a total of 17,500 News Feed impressions for a single piece of content.

Now let's further assume that you got 9,000 of the 10,000 fans in the second case directly through Facebook advertising, and you stopped advertising. You still have the benefit of reaching people through content after the advertising campaign has long ended because you don't just lose the fans after the advertising ends.

> **Note:** If you really want to learn as much as you can about how Facebook advertising impacts your success, you may want to consider making frequent changes. Run an ad campaign for a few weeks, and then pull it for a month. Observe what happened before, during, and after the ad campaign. Next, put your ads back on the network after making a few tweaks—ad copy or targeting options, for instance. Raise your ad budget to see how that impacts the seven-day moving averages, and then lower it again. If you mix your advertising tactics, you can begin to get a feel for how you can use ad budget to get the results you need.

Friday: Review Your Work with Advertising and Start Anew

Facebook advertising is a great way to generate demand for your Facebook presence. Ads are currently the most inexpensive option you have in Internet advertising on a CPM basis. If you can temper your expectations and make your advertisements fit the social context, you can be very successful. Just make sure you track what happens so you have the knowledge and insight you need to make your campaign work the most for you.

So, let's summarize the steps necessary to optimize a campaign:

1. Create multiple ads of similar themes.
2. Organize them into campaigns.
3. Let them run for a week or two while recording daily outcomes.
4. Analyze statistics/outcomes.
5. Retire underperforming ads, and run new A/B tests by creating variations on better ads.
6. Go back to step 3, and repeat until you have optimized your numbers.

If you haven't done some of these things, review that part of this chapter, and progress from there.

With each iteration, you should get smarter, and you should learn new things about your advertising approach. Over time, you should be generating outcomes more cheaply and efficiently. As long as this happens, you should continue to iterate.

But after a month or so of building and optimizing an advertising campaign, you may notice that the campaign isn't doing as well as it used to do. What happened? Just about all Facebook advertising has a bit of a "shelf life": an amount of time that the combination of your ad copy and the demographics that you target will provide great results. But as people begin to see your ad repeatedly (and some people see it even after having acted upon it), your numbers will naturally drop a bit. That's OK; it's the surest sign that you've captured the available opportunity.

Here you have a few options:

- Continue running the ads because even though your numbers aren't as good as they used to be, they're still acceptable.

- Run a different ad at the same demographic.

- Run the same ads at different demographics.

The possibilities are truly endless. Just keep in mind that you'll need to track how your ad performs over time, because at a certain point you've maximized the benefits from that specific campaign and it's time to make a decision—make changes, continue, or move on to something else.

Facebook Ads Changes of February 29, 2012

On February 29, 2012, Facebook announced significant changes to its ads offering. The biggest fundamental change is that ads will be much more integrated across Facebook than ever before. Prior to the implementation of these changes, ads sat on the right side of the screen for users experiencing Facebook through a browser on a computer or laptop.

- Facebook is introducing Logout Ads to brands, unlocking ad space for the 37 million people per day who actually log out. It's revolutionary because someone will be forced to see an ad, watch a video, or perform some task before logging out. Yes, it's a captive audience — but it's an activity that less than 5% of the total Facebook audience performs on a daily basis.

- Facebook will place ad units inside each user's News Feed alongside real News Feed stories. This premium ad unit will first be available to brands but will likely extend to companies of all sizes eventually. Exactly how this is executed will determine User acceptance and the ultimate fate of this type of ad unit.

- Facebook will allow advertisers to target mobile users —iPad, iPhone, Android—and will put these ads in the News Feed. Previously, Facebook allowed for this but did not actually display ads to users of these platforms who used the Facebook app. It would only display to people who actually went to www.facebook.com on the mobile device. This is a good development for two types of advertisers in particular — those advertising apps and those

Facebook Ads Changes of February 29, 2012 *(Continued)*

desiring a "location-based" advertising option from Facebook. Device targeting also puts Facebook ads at parity with Google's Adwords offering, which has offered mobile device platform targeting for some time.

All told, ads are about to get much more prominent in the Facebook experience. In the past, Users have briefly complained about major changes but have come to accept them. We'll see what happens this time.

Some of the moves are justifiable — Facebook ad CTRs are very low. Some of these changes are designed to address poor CTR performance by making the ads almost impossible to ignore. Others are designed to make ads more actionable. As a result, advertisers will see the raw performance of Facebook ads improve — and click-through rates will improve. But it could have the impact of reducing the number of impressions advertisers get for the money. These types of changes always involve a tradeoff, and that's the most likely scenario here.

It should be noted that Facebook is doing this at the same time it is preparing for its IPO. That is probably not a coincidence. Facebook is under pressure to not just nail their projected ads revenue numbers, but dramatically exceed them. Facebook is optimizing its ads system to generate the most money from the traffic they're generating as investor expectations become far more important.

Unfortunately, we won't know the full impacts on workflows, costs, and marketing campaigns for awhile. We also won't know how all of this impacts the type of ads that we see—whether smaller businesses will be able to effectively use Facebook or if they'll be drowned out by big brands. This is the emerging story of mid-2012 and one that certainly bears watching.

The big question is whether or not Facebook can pull off this ambitious set of changes elegantly. Our hunch is that you'll see Facebook increasingly littered with corporate ads/promotions, and User outcry will be loud at least at the beginning. Will it be enough for people to migrate away? Can another social network capitalize and put a dent into Facebook? Mark Zuckerberg's bet is a resounding "no." We shall see.

Beyond Pages: Groups, Apps, Social Plugins, and Mobile

Other than business (fan) pages, Facebook offers a variety of default apps and third-party apps, along with several additional features that most businesses would do well to take advantage of. In this chapter, we'll go through these features and apps and walk you through many of our favorite third-party apps.

Chapter Contents

Groups for Business

In late 2010, Facebook significantly changed up the format of groups. Previously, businesses were confused as to the best channel on Facebook through which to market. Profiles had much similarity to pages, and often businesses would set up a personal profile in the name of a business. (This is against the terms of use; if you have a profile in the name of a business, Facebook offers a feature to convert it to a fan page.) And, groups seemed too similar to fan pages. In many ways, groups were much easier than fan pages on which to build a large member base.

Facebook wanted businesses to focus on fan pages to promote their brands, products, and services. So, once Facebook rolled out the revamped groups—New Groups, as they are called—the differences between groups and pages were much more obvious. New Groups were designed to enhance communication between small groups of Facebook users, typically who would know one another, such as special-interest groups or small groups of close friends or family. The biggest difference with New Groups is that anyone can be added without their permission. In other words, anyone can start a New Group and add any of their friends. All manner of New Groups sprang up, and users experimented with adding many of their friends.

In addition, Facebook's groups have similar functionality to Google groups or Yahoo! groups, insofar as when any member posts to the group, that activity triggers a notification (and email message) to all members. If you get added to an active Facebook group, this can suddenly create a flood of notifications and new email messages. Groups can grow very quickly as new members are added and they, in turn, add their friends. This ability for users to add their friends to any group without their permission caused a great deal of backlash at first and much buzz in the blogosphere. The feature has not been changed in more than a year and is still one of the most challenging aspects of groups for users to understand and use responsibly.

Groups do have some similarity to pages and profiles (Timelines): they have a Wall on which users post content. Content can be in the form of updates, links, photos, and videos. In addition, members can create—and edit—docs. The functionality and editing features of these docs are somewhat limited, but they do offer a collaborative workspace, so to speak. Members can also create events.

Like the old format of groups, New Groups have three levels of privacy: open, closed, and secret.

- Open means that anyone can see the content posted in the group and see the list of group members. To join an open group, anyone can request membership.

- Closed means anyone can find the group and see the list of group members, but they cannot see any content. To join a closed group, anyone can request membership.

- Secret means the group is completely private; nobody can find the group or content—only its members know the group exists.

When you set up a new group, the default privacy level is closed. With all three types of groups, admins can edit the settings so new members have to be approved by an admin. Given that any group member can add any of their friends to any of the three styles of groups to which they belong, we recommend enabling the setting for admins to approve new members. This allows you more control over the growth of the group. Some group owners choose to set up an open or closed group so Facebook users can easily find the group and ask to join; then the admin switches the privacy level to secret. However, note that once a group reaches 250 members, it is not possible to change the privacy level. So, give careful thought to the long-term privacy choice.

Find and Join Groups

Joining industry groups can give you a significant competitive advantage. You might want to join some groups just to observe and stay up-to-date with trends, for example. Or, you could join groups that contain a large portion of your target demographic and then become active on a regular basis in such groups in order to network, add value, answer questions, and share valuable tips/resources. Doing so will give you prime visibility and help create top-of-mind awareness for your business. Keep in mind, you can participate in groups only via your personal profile, not your business page. Depending on the size and type of your business, the practice of joining and participating in active groups could prove very lucrative over time. The key point, though, is to understand the primary unspoken rule to which you will need to adhere: no outright soliciting. The same applies when you are actively posting on other fan pages. It becomes very apparent if you only step in when you want to make an offer and pitch your wares.

Some time ago, we came across a great phrase pertaining to Facebook in particular: *when the marketers move in, the members move out.* So, the best antidote is quite simply to become a member. Do not appear like a marketer. When you approach your networking on Facebook as a fellow member, people let their guard down and realize you are not there to pitch them. This approach is different than directly making offers and sharing calls to action on your own fan page. (Of course, these offers are always interspersed with valuable, educational content, as we discussed in Chapter 5, "Month 2: Establish Your Corporate Presence with Pages.")

Finding existing groups can be challenging. Using the main search box on the navigation bar, try typing in keywords for subjects related to your business that interest you. Groups show up in the initial search results on the drop-down menu, and if you click the magnifying glass, you'll go to the main search page, where you can drill deeper to find more groups, as illustrated in Figure 7.1.

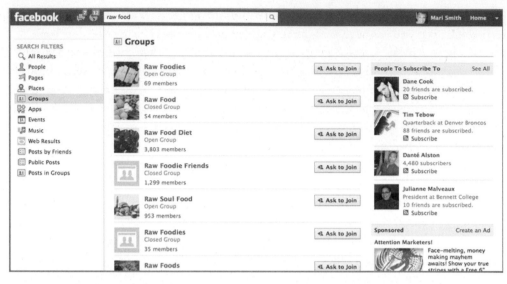

Figure 7.1 Searching for groups

In Figure 7.1, the groups without the Ask to Join button are old-style groups that have been scheduled for archiving.

Because content in open groups is visible to users on Facebook, it is also indexed on Google, so experiment with searching for keywords on Google and include "Facebook group" in your search. You might also seek recommendations from your friends, subscribers, and fans by posting a status update on your personal profile (Timeline) or fan page and asking which groups your network finds particularly valuable.

Create Your Own Group

By far, one of the best ways to take advantage of Facebook's New Groups is to set up one or more of your own. These are possible uses of such groups:

- A small mastermind with your peers
- A focus group to brainstorm new product ideas for your business
- A peer-to-peer support group that you supervise
- A group of industry experts who share and discuss trends with one another
- A value-added benefit of a group coaching/continuity program that you offer
- An ongoing networking group for attendees of any virtual or live event that you host

We own and belong to groups that cater to all of these uses. By offering membership in a secret Facebook group as part of various training programs, live events, and virtual events, we have increased our customer satisfaction and retention rates considerably. There is a certain type of magic that happens with secret groups on Facebook. It's one of the few places on Facebook where members can truly feel comfortable with exactly who is seeing what content. When you post content on your Timeline (profile) to specific lists, you might second-guess yourself at times and have to go back and double-check which friends are in that list and who can see what content. Also, your friends do not know which other friends are on the list—it's not like a discussion list. (Friend lists/smart lists are designed to help you manage your incoming and outgoing content.) However, with secret groups in particular, it's very much a private discussion forum. Nonetheless, we strongly recommend that members exercise caution and do not share extremely private and sensitive information.

How to Set Up Your Group

Go to http://facebook.com/groups and click the green Create Group button. Type in the name of your group; this can be edited later if you change your mind. The default privacy setting is Closed; select Open or Secret if you want to set up one of these types. You'll need to add a minimum of one friend to get to the next step. For now, select one of your team members/assistants, for example. Your new group will be instantly created. Then, you can tweak your settings as you want; click the gear icon in the upper right and click Edit Group. Add a profile picture, select an icon, and add a description. For open and closed groups, the description will be visible to potential members.

You can also set up a special email address for your group. This makes it easy for you and your members to post content to the group via regular email. Be sure to also edit your Notification settings to your liking. You may want to turn them off completely and just receive notifications via Facebook and not email.

If ever you need to delete a group, it's not that easy. First, you need to remove all members one by one and then remove yourself. Facebook automatically deletes groups once they have no members.

Create Your Group Terms

Just as you should have clear guidelines for what users can and cannot post on your page Wall, we recommend setting up similar guidelines for your group. The following is an example guideline from one of Mari's groups:

WELCOME!! This is a special, private group for all SANG members to continue the networking between events! Let's keep the spirit of "How may I help you" going virtually. Feel free to post support you'd like to receive, help that you can offer, news about upcoming events you may have, special occasions you're celebrating etc. etc. As with the live SANG events, this is a "no-pitch" zone. :) NOTE: All posts and comments go out to all members as an email notification unless and until members change their preferences. To edit which email notifications you receive, just click the "Notifications" button at the top.

You may also want to add a minimum of one or two additional admins and assign specific moderators, depending on the size of your group.

Grow Your Group

There is a certain etiquette with Facebook groups. The way they are designed, any member can add any friend (unless the group owner has set it up so that admins have to approve members). Often, even if you're very close friends with someone, they may not be very happy about being automatically added to a group without their permission, especially if it's a particularly active group with a lot of email. Our recommendation, therefore, is to always seek permission first before adding anyone to a Facebook group. You can do this by contacting them privately via email on Facebook, or through regular email if you have access to the person's email address.

For open and closed groups, you could certainly encourage members to post the URL on their profile or fan pages and invite their friends to request membership. Plus, promote the link to your group through other social channels such as Twitter and Google+, along with including an invitation in your email newsletters.

As your group grows, you'll want to assign one or more moderators. Keeping the spam and any inappropriate content to a minimum is critical to the livelihood of the group.

Facebook Default Apps

Facebook's default apps have remained fairly constant over the past five years or more. On pages, these are the default apps:

- Photos
- Videos
- Events
- Questions
- Notes

To generate the maximum visibility and the most engagement (people talking about your page and your content) in the News Feed and Ticker, we recommend making the best use of all types of apps. Experiment with status updates that are short, medium, and long. Share photos and videos, because these types of posts tend to get the best visibility in the News Feed. Run a few polls via the Questions app. Then track and measure your response rates. Refer to Chapter 6, "Month 2: Establish Your Corporate Presence with Pages," for how to interpret your metrics through Facebook Insights. Also, refer to Chapter 5 for more on content strategy.

Use the Events app for your virtual and live events. The Events app creates a "subcommunity" within your page and is somewhat similar to a group. Your event has a wall that you can post on and so can your fans. You and your fans can share updates, links, photos, and videos (Figure 7.2). All activity generates new content for attendees' News Feeds and Tickers, so be sure to encourage your attendees and invitees to get active on your event Wall! Plus, attendees can check in to your event, which provides more visibility in the News Feed and Ticker.

Figure 7.2 An event Wall

Discussion and reviews were removed in fall 2011. Facebook wants to encourage page owners to do all their posting and engaging directly on the Wall; Wall activity creates "story activities" that, in turn, go out into the Tickers (and News Feeds) of your fans and their friends. At some point, Facebook may remove the Notes app, too, given the increase in status update character numbers. The character limit for status updates was 420 for the longest time; then Facebook had no sooner begun to increase the limit to 500 characters when it jumped way up to 5,000. Facebook did not make a big announcement about this change; it just suddenly seemed to appear not long after the F8 Developers Conference in September 2011. It may be that this large increase was in response to Google+; the ability to write much more extensively seemed to spark significantly more conversation and engagement on Google+. And, true to Facebook's constant changing, just as we were writing this chapter, Facebook announced it had increased the status update character limit to a whopping 63,206 characters. Presumably this move was made to increase time on the site and to ensure its product continues to be very competitive with Google+. (Google+'s character limit is apparently 100,000.)

Third-Party Apps

In Chapter 5, we discussed all the basics of setting up your Facebook fan page. To make your fan page more compelling and engaging for your fans, you can add any number of third-party apps. All fan pages come with the default Facebook apps as mentioned in the previous section: Photos, Videos, Notes, Questions, and Events.

App discovery for your Facebook page can be rather elusive these days. Facebook used to have an apps directory but removed it in early 2011. Now, you basically need to know what app you're looking for and search for it in the search bar. Keep an eye on active Facebook Pages to see what apps they use.

To search for an app, just begin typing the name of the app in the main search bar at the top. You'll see in the search results different categories: People, Places, Pages, Groups, and Apps. Click the app you want to add, and then look for the Add to My Page link.

Once you've added an app to your page, it's not always obvious what to do next. Go back to your main fan page, click the Edit Page button at the top right, and then click Apps, and you'll see all apps added to your page in alphabetical order. Go to the app you just added and click Go to App to configure your settings. Each app is different as to how you can configure the settings. Usually there is a help section or a simple tutorial.

You'll also want to click Edit Settings in the Apps section of your page and make sure the tab has been added. Plus, in this section, you can add your own custom name for the tab.

There are many categories of third-party apps, for example:

- iFrame, where you can add your own custom content
- Contest apps
- Contact forms
- Commerce/shopping apps
- Scheduling apps
- RSS Feed apps
- Live video apps
- Live chat apps

See this blog post for an extensive list of more than 75 apps: www.socialmediaexaminer.com/facebook-apps/.

Here are just a few suggested apps for fan pages:

Static HTML Facebook phased out its Facebook Markup Language (FBML) app and replaced it with iFrames. Since this change, there has been a plethora of new iFrames apps available. We like the simplicity of the Static HTML app, though you do need to create the raw HTML/code in a WYSIWYG editor. You can even introduce the "fan-gating" element where nonfans see different content from fans.

One of the most popular uses of any iFrame app is to create a custom content to enhance the user experience of fans and non fans on your Page. On such apps, you can also include rich media such as a video and perhaps an opt-in box for a free give-away. Another benefit to the Static HTML app is you can install multiple iterations of the app. In other words, you might have one landing tab as a welcome message and another with details of your services.

TabSite This is a full fan page customization app with templates, plus easy drag-and-drop widgets. See http://tabsite.com and http://facebook.com/tabsite.

Facebook to Twitter This is Facebook's own app that allows you to post to Twitter. There's great potential leverage in using this app to bring your Twitter followers back to your fan page. You have up to 60,000 characters in the Facebook publisher to create content, and when you have this app applied to your fan page, your posts get truncated at about 120 characters and posted out as a tweet with a shortened (on.fb.me) link to your fan page. You can find Facebook to Twitter at http://facebook.com/twitter.

Selective Tweets To reverse the process in the previous app (posting *from* Twitter *to* your Facebook fan page), this app works wonders because if your tweet volume is high, you don't need to clutter up your fan page with excess content. Rather, you can select which tweets get posted as your fan page status update. If you're also using the Facebook to Twitter app, you can temporarily adjust the settings so as not to double post. You can find the app at http://apps.facebook.com/selectivetwitter.

For additional Facebook fan page apps, visit the Resources section on Mari's website, which she keeps fairly up-to-date with the latest apps to enhance your fan page: http://marismith.com/resources. See also http://socialmediaexaminer.com and search for "Facebook apps."

Social Plugins

In addition to optimizing your fan page with apps, you want to optimize your website with Facebook's array of plugins. See this web page: https://developers.facebook.com/docs/plugins/. The current list of available plugins you can add to your website is as follows:

Like Button The Like button is the small ubiquitous button that lets users share pages from your website back to their Facebook profiles with one click. This is one of the easiest buttons to get visitors to your site to click. There isn't much thinking involved; when someone likes your content, they feel compelled to click the Like button. Facebook used to have the activity that posted back to the user's profile just be one line item. Now, it's a full story with thumbnail.

When installing the Like button to your website, we recommend including the feature that shows faces of friends who have "liked" the post; this provides valuable social proof. Figure 7.3 shows a Like button I (Mari) often place in the middle of a blog post; the Like button is set to like my Facebook fan page. Because I'm the admin of my fan page, you can see there is a link to the admin page and Insights; only admins see this on the plugins.

Figure 7.3 Example Like button

Send Button This is a fairly new addition to the social plug-in collection and allows users to send your content to their friends via Facebook email. It's a wonderful tool because some studies show that one of the most popular methods of sharing content online is still email. You visit a site and see an article that your friend James would find particularly interesting; click the Send button and email only to James. *Voila.*

There is a wide array of WordPress plugins that include the Facebook Share button. We recommend adding both the Like button and Share button; this gives you the greatest flexibility for sharing your content. Visitors to your site can go for the simple one-click Like. Also, the Share button allows users to post the content to their own profiles (Timelines), to any friend's profile, to any fan page for which they are an administrator, and to any groups to which they belong, as well as allows them to email it to any friend.

Comments This has become an increasingly popular plug-in used on all manner of blogs, websites, sales pages, "squeeze" pages, and more. The beauty of how this plug-in works is that the user can choose to post their comment to their profile (or to their fan page, if posting as their page). Then, the thread of comments remains intact and trails wherever the comments end up. In other words, when a user's comment posts to their Facebook profile and a friend of this person also leaves a comment underneath, that same comment posts back to your website. You might also consider adding this plug-in to your custom iFrame app to bring more visibility to your fan page.

Like Box This is another must-have plug-in for your website. You can edit the dimensions and choose whether to show the faces of some of your fans (randomized depending on the visitor's social graph). You can also choose to show the stream (your latest Wall posts). Figure 7.4 is an example of a large Like box on my (Mari's) blog where I have the stream showing and a large number of faces. The faces always randomize depending on who is viewing the page, because Facebook's social graph displays each person's friends first.

Figure 7.4 Facebook Like box

Login Button This plug-in allows visitors to your site to sign up via their Facebook credentials. Allowing access via Facebook is becoming increasingly popular. A recent study by Sociable Labs revealed that, on average, 50.8% of traffic was logged into Facebook while visiting e-commerce sites. This means sites can really tailor the shopping experience using the Facebook plugins and API. See `www.simplyzesty.com/facebookover-50-of-online-shoppers-are-logged-onto-facebook-while-on-ecommerce-sites/`.

Registration More and more businesses are starting to use the Registration plug-in as a lead capture tool (Figure 7.5). Use this plug-in as an opt-in box, and when anyone already logged into Facebook visits your website, they will see their own details pre-populated, which may compel them to sign up. Plus, using the social graph, Facebook displays some of the user's friends who have already registered. Some users may feel apprehensive about sharing their data, however, so it's best to provide an option to sign up without Facebook integration as well.

Example

To save you time, the registration form below has been prefilled using your Facebook profile.

Name and Public Information:
Mari Smith
4822 friends

Birthday: Aug 12, ▮▮

Gender: Female

Current Location: San Diego, California

Email Address: ▮▮▮▮▮▮▮

Register 31 friends have registered.

Terms of Service · Privacy Policy · Clicking Register will also give Developer Site access to your Facebook friends list and other public information. Nothing will be shared with Developer Site until you click Register. **Learn more**

Figure 7.5 Facebook registration box

Activity Feed The Activity Feed plug-in shows users what their friends are doing on your site through likes and comments.

Recommendations The Recommendations plug-in gives users personalized suggestions for pages on your site they might like.

Facepile The Facepile plug-in displays the Facebook profile pictures of users who have liked your page or have signed up for your site.

Live Stream The Live Stream plug-in lets your users share activity and comments in real time as they interact during a live event. This is a tremendous feature, and you may have seen it accompanying a live video-streaming show such as Livestream.com offers or on http://facebook.com/fblive.

Featured Case: Q&A with Rick Wittenbraker, VP of Marketing for YETI Coolers

Rick Wittenbraker is the VP of Marketing for YETI Coolers, a manufacturer of premium coolers for hunters and outdoorspeople. Their loyal and enthusiastic following, the YETI Nation, is the center of many of their brand and marketing efforts, including social media.

Q. *First, tell us a little about YETI Coolers.*

A. YETI Coolers, founded in 2006, designs and manufactures the highest-quality coolers available. Its coolers are designed to outlast and outperform any other, providing the ultimate in ice retention, durability, and design across a wide range of uses, including hunting, fishing, camping, boating, tailgating, rafting, catering, and commercial cooking.

Featured Case: Q&A with Rick Wittenbraker, VP of Marketing for YETI Coolers *(Continued)*

Q. *Who is YETI's target market, and what is your philosophy for engaging with your target market?*

A. Broadly speaking, our target market is anyone whose activities include using a cooler. In reality, we are more focused on the outdoors activities markets such as hunting, fishing, fly fishing, rafting, camping, tailgating, and other similar activities. We engage with those target markets through a variety of activities including traditional media (TV, magazines), social media, trade shows, and more. As with marketing any other product, it is really about finding out what your audience is doing and then figuring out a way to get in front of them.

Q. *How important is Facebook in your marketing plan?*

A. At the end of the day, we manufacture a premium consumer item. We also have more than 1,700 brick-and-mortar retailers that proudly sell our coolers across the country. So, most of our marketing efforts are spent on building the *brand* and not just trying to create online sales. Facebook is a huge part of that given its enormous audience and reach, the affinity that people show for brands/products that interest them, and the ability to create campaigns, activations, and other community activities. Our fan base, the YETI Nation, is very active on Facebook.

Facebook is also a great way for us to collaborate with other brands, the TV shows and magazines we sponsor, our Pro Staff, and our dealer network. Recently, our Facebook page has also taken on an element of customer service as fans post questions regarding product, how-tos, warranty, and so on, on our Wall, so much so, in fact, that our customer service team now has admin privileges to the page so that they can respond to such inquiries.

Q. *What features of Facebook do you use more often than others? Pages, advertising, events, photo albums, access to Open Graph/APIs, and so on.*

A. Pages are the biggest piece for us. That is the rally point for YETI Coolers on Facebook. Photo albums are a big part of that, as we often post new photos and hold monthly photo contests where fans send us their images, and we post them in the albums. On a lesser scale, we have also used advertising (small monthly budget) and events.

Q. *In your opinion, what are the strengths and weaknesses of using Facebook for marketing purposes?*

A. Strengths: Efficiency, cost, access to market, facility in collaborating, availability of apps and other customizations, interaction with fans.

Weaknesses: Inherent platform limitations, does not replace other activities so not a direct cost savings, requires frequent monitoring, and so on.

continues

Featured Case: Q&A with Rick Wittenbraker, VP of Marketing for YETI Coolers *(Continued)*

Q. *How do you see social media marketing as a part of YETI's longer-term marketing plan? Will you use more/less over time?*

A. Looking forward, social media will take a growing role in our overall marketing plan. We will continue to grow our Facebook presence, specifically with richer features, more interactions, and deeper engagement. We will continue to seek new ways to engage with the YETI Nation as Facebook makes advances. We will also continue to utilize other social media sites such as YouTube, Flickr, Twitter, our blog, and more.

Create Your Own App

At the time we wrote the first edition of this book, apps were necessary for writing pretty much anything other than a status update to the News Feed of your fans. Marketers therefore used apps to place custom messages, imagery, and the like on the News Feed, primarily for promotional purposes. The effort was particularly successful for casual games. Those of you who have used Facebook for a few years may remember all the News Feed updates you'd get from friends playing casual games. For example, "Jane wants to send a big 'Thank You' to her generous friends in Farmville. Click to get a Farmville bonus."

Facebook did two things to counter the proliferation of annoying messages from apps and casual games. First, it gave users more control over News Feed content by allowing people to block apps from the News Feed. Then it altogether removed app notifications from the News Feed and placed them in a separate section of the left navigation—under App Requests and Game Requests, respectively (see Figure 7.6).

Figure 7.6 App Requests and Game Requests sections

So, the primary justification once used for building Facebook apps to promote a product or service is now more or less moot. Marketers cannot easily "hack" the News Feed by creating a clever app. And consumers are not eagerly clicking links in their News Feeds as they once did.

Nonetheless, custom Facebook development is actually alive and well. The difference is that the paradigm has shifted from apps to APIs and from FBML to standards-based web languages that are approachable for anyone with a background in web development. Apps are still used for custom experiences inside Facebook and as infrastructure for advanced products and services that run outside of Facebook. In either case, apps are probably beyond what most people will need to do—and many of you will get what you need from Facebook's social plugins.

Facebook makes these plugins (mentioned in the previous section of this chapter) and rich APIs available to developers to help extend marketing and social messages from Facebook to the Web, and vice versa.

All of that said, there are still a few cases where it may make sense for you to create a specialized Facebook application to enhance a marketing campaign:

Launch of a New Product or Service You can introduce a product through an application that shows off the value of your product in a creative manner.

Immersive Branding Apps can provide a multimedia, interactive, or gaming experience that gives a user a positive and reinforcing experience with your brand or product.

Logical Brand Extension via the News Feed and/or Profile Certain businesses have products or services that more naturally lend themselves to specialized applications that reinforce the overall value proposition.

In each of these circumstances, you're looking to use the application as a clever call to action that makes the user do something that reinforces your business or brand message. The applications themselves can serve an entirely different purpose, but at the end of the day, users of the application will be exposed to one of your marketing messages in a clever way, assuming you don't force the brand or the product onto the customer too aggressively. This is where creativity really comes into play as much as any other place in Facebook marketing. It is rare to find an application that succeeds virally without some humor or interesting angle on a product or service. You can't just overtly sell your product to consumers via a Facebook app and expect it to be a viral hit. The execution of a clever idea is a necessary success factor in creating a successful marketing initiative through Facebook applications.

Conceptually, it's also good to think about what you want to achieve with your application. Most folks are motivated by one of the following goals:

Building a Viral Hit You may want to create an engaging application that people will enjoy using repeatedly and will recommend to friends, either directly or by allowing messages to propagate via the News Feed.

Introducing New Functionality An app can offer an experience through Facebook that provides relatively unique new social features or provides similar benefits, but with a unique distribution angle that makes Facebook users more aware of it than competitor applications.

Extending the Brand in a New Way An app can also utilize brand assets in a slightly different way that is engaging or interesting to the target market.

Providing Entertainment for the Sake of Brand/Product Loyalty Some apps help people enjoy themselves or pass time by interacting with your brand or with other consumers through games, interactive experiences, and so on.

Best Practices for Apps

Whether you get an internal team or a third-party vendor to build your Facebook application, you'll still need a solid understanding of best practices when it comes to designing, building, and deploying Facebook applications. After all, you can't possibly expect to effectively manage this project if you don't have a reasonable foundation when it comes to understanding the core tenets of what it takes to build a good Facebook application. We're going to briefly cover three major areas when it comes to this topic: speed, user experience, and terms.

Speed

It's important to make sure your application is built to run efficiently on the Facebook platform. As with any application that you build on the Internet, the speed at which a page loads into a user's browser is one of the single most critical elements of execution when it comes to the user's perception or enjoyment of your application. Because you're dealing with an application programming interface when building Facebook applications, paying special attention to the techniques used to cause your application to render quickly on a user's profile is especially important. You need to pay close attention to this aspect of your application, because the fact that you're going through an API means the web browser has to wait twice as long to retrieve information and display it to your user than it would with an application that doesn't use an application programming interface.

Granted, in many cases we are dealing with seconds or even milliseconds when talking about transactions between applications. However, users have little to no patience on the Web, and the time adds up quickly when someone is waiting for their browser to render the web page they are waiting on. It's important that you take the most efficient path possible to grabbing data and processing information you need and bringing it back to your web pages so your users are presented with the most responsive experience possible.

User Experience

User experience (UX) is defined as the quality of experience one has when interacting with the design of something. This is not limited to Facebook applications or even web pages. For example, a person has a bad user experience when sipping out of a leaky travel mug. You want to make sure your users have a good experience with your application.

When taking into account user experience as it relates to the design of your Facebook application, you must think about the needs of your user, any constraints your company has from a business or brand point of view, and any limitations or needs technically related to the application and your goals.

Generally, you should always consider ease of use, information design (intuitiveness), the structure of the elements on your page, aesthetics, and overall functionality. When designing a Facebook application, there are several specific elements to ponder:

- Make sure your application doesn't require users to install third-party applications to use your application.
- Don't force users into logic loops if they opt out of performing a task that you deem valuable.
- Don't force users to spam their friends in order to enjoy the features of your application.
- Engage with your users.
- Allow users to engage with each other.
- Keep your application fresh by fixing UI issues that inevitably arise, and update the app on a regular basis to encourage repeated use.

Terms

Lastly, you need to make sure Facebook is happy with what you're doing with its platform. After all, it's just good manners to understand the house rules and abide by them. After you've come up with a concept for your application, it is well advised that you read the developer principles and policies (http://developers.facebook.com/policy), including the statement of rights and responsibilities listed at the top.

On a very high level, you need to know that Facebook takes user privacy, spamming, lying, cheating, copyright, pornography, hate speech, and intellectual property very seriously. Stray into any of these areas in a manner that is counter to Facebook's guidelines for acceptable use, and you should expect swift, unapologetic action from Facebook to correct the situation for its users and remove your application from Facebook altogether.

Complicated Apps, Simple Plugins

Facebook continues to de-emphasize apps for developers who want to tap into the social graph in lieu of social plugins. The good news is that as you consider hiring technical talent to support your marketing initiative, you don't really need top-notch developers today to do the basics. Facebook has simplified many of the most common integration scenarios so that even entry-level web developers can do the job. That said, you'll always need top-tier web developer talent to do deep customization and to stretch Facebook for all it has to offer.

Hire a Programmer

Now that you have some understanding about what you need to be considering when designing and deploying your shiny new Facebook application, let's talk about getting someone to build it for you. Hiring a really good programmer who specializes in any language is a difficult process. We don't want to overwhelm you, but at the same time, this process needs to be taken seriously. There's a very high price to be paid for hiring a low-quality programmer. Do your homework, check references, and be sure candidates can back up any claims they make in regard to success and experience.

Assess Your Candidates

Qualified developers should have the expertise and the experience to be able to discuss any aspect of the Facebook application development process covered in this chapter. Furthermore, they should be able to expand on any of these topics with relative ease. Now, we're not looking for perfection here. If a programmer doesn't define UX exactly as we do here but clearly shows that they understand that UX is the practice of designing something to the benefit of the user, you're probably in good shape.

The candidate needs to have a fairly deep understanding of these principles, which in turn will show their level of experience and, ideally, success. Ask the programmer how she would enhance the performance of a Facebook application.

Next, you're looking for technical competence. Have the programmer show you at least three applications they have built in the past. The applications should be live on the Facebook platform. Use these applications, and let your gut tell you whether the performance is where it needs to be. Does the navigation make sense? Is there a logical progression in the data structures or the application's narrative?

On a more fundamental level, have some basic tests that you give to all applicants in order to consider them seriously for the position. These should include the following:

- Embed a live video feed in a Facebook profile.
- Allow comments on a live video feed.

- Pull some basic profile information (name, city, and ZIP code) from the Facebook friends of a logged-in user account.
- Connect to a third-party data source, pull data from it, and display data in a Facebook application.

If you have any peers or acquaintances with Facebook development experience, ask the candidate to give you some samples of the Facebook-related code they have written and have your friend review it. Although there are many "right" ways to skin a cat when it comes to programming, making it difficult to identify the "best" code, it is certainly easy for an experienced programmer to identify poor programming practices.

One more thing—ask the candidate questions that will give some insight into their work ethic and habits. Questions should be direct and clear, such as "If you committed to a deadline and started to realize that hitting the goal would be a challenge, how would you react?" You are looking for a two-part answer here. First, the programmer needs to communicate to you and the rest of the team that the deadline is in jeopardy, with some explanation about why the issues have arisen. Second, the programmer needs to indicate that unless the situation is an impossible one, they will still work diligently to hit the original deadline. Change is inevitable, so communication is key.

Manage a Development Project

Best practices for project management have been written about in a dozen formats or more. But at the end of the day, it's not which project management method or project development method you choose that determines success. The management of the overall project life cycle, the work ethic of the team members involved, leadership, and discipline have a much greater impact on the success of a project than the project management philosophy that is employed.

If you don't have any project management background or experience, then you don't want to take this part lightly. As critical as the programmer's job is when it comes to building your Facebook application, the manager on the project arguably has a much larger impact on the overall success of your endeavor. If you're going to take on the role of project manager for your Facebook application projects, it's critical that you manage the crucial steps in the project life cycle.

Scope and Goals

Before you run off expecting to build an application that will solve all your company's problems, first come up with some tangible, realistic goals that you want the application to reach. These objectives will determine features that will direct the development of your app. Specifically, what technical features of your Facebook app support the business objectives you have? What is the minimum bar necessary to achieve those goals and to give users a good experience with your application? What can users do with the Facebook app and how? How will communication flow through the app, email, Facebook notifications, and the Facebook News Feed?

It isn't an academic exercise to do all of this up front. It's a necessary task that you'll need to conduct to avoid building the wrong thing and then rebuilding it later. Every hour of a developer's time is costly, especially if you make a mistake and have to make changes. Start with a good idea of what you want, and document those requirements. You may need to make a change or two as you go, but at least you'll cut out a lot of unnecessary time having your developer help scope your application and write your requirements.

Research as many apps as you can in the genre you're planning to build, as well as apps with features you want to emulate. Make a list of such apps—with the URLs to the app pages—and a corresponding list of features you like so you can present this information to your developer.

As you consider what you're going to build, also remember to use the right tool for the job. Facebook applications are great experiences inside the social network/social graph. So, you can succeed if your goals are about acquiring users or monetizing through virtual goods or third-party advertising inside your app. But Facebook apps won't solve all your problems, especially if you are looking to drive product sales, extend the reach of email marketing campaigns, or drive traffic to your website. You often will need a combination of Facebook and other social media tools or your own website to make your marketing campaign work as designed.

For example, let's say you have a mandate from your management team to create a Facebook application that will generate an additional 120 online sales of your product. That's a great idea, but if you're asked to do this exclusively through a Facebook application, you may have some trouble. One reason is that Facebook does not currently allow you to add a shopping cart to a person's profile. So, a goal of having your Facebook application drive the immediate sales of your product may be asking too much of the Facebook application, no matter how good it is. It makes more sense to use the Facebook application to drive traffic to a landing page on your website.

So, in this case, you actually need both your Facebook application and your landing page to work properly. The Facebook application can be measured for the effectiveness of pulling people into the website, while the landing page itself must be optimized separately with different copy and layout to ensure that customers convert at the highest rate possible. This difference is important to understand when defining goals and ensuring that the application *and* supporting cast members are scoped properly. Sometimes you need more than just a one-man band.

Additional Deliverables

In addition to the functions of your application, you will need to ask your developer for a number of other things to ensure that a new developer can take over the project in a worst-case scenario or in case you choose a different developer for the next version. Be sure to include the following as you define the scope of your project:

- A copy of any source code created to build the application
- The addition of one of your employees as a developer of the application so you can conduct administrator tasks
- Project files and documentation related to the project
- Hosting information for your application
- Database structures related to your project

Your developer should also perform any configurations necessary through the hosting provider to ensure that the app is up and running properly before finishing the project. Facebook requires all new apps to be approved before communications propagate across Facebook and before the app can be found in a search. Oftentimes, Facebook disallows apps from being approved because of violations of the developer terms of service mentioned earlier in this chapter. Don't sign off on completion of your application until the approval process has been completed. Otherwise, you may build an application that never launches to its intended audience.

Project Planning

Project planning involves not just hiring people for tasks you can't complete but also securing necessary resources, assigning responsibilities, and defining and securing a budget, if it is necessary. Depending upon the size of your project, it is important that you define what specific tasks are required in order to produce the finished product. You should estimate the time and effort required for each task, identify dependencies between different activities, and map out a realistic schedule for the overall project. Make sure that you involve your team when estimating how long the different activities will take and the inconveniences associated with them. Define critical dates and associated milestones. Make sure all this information is written into the project plan, including any relevant budget information, and get sign-off for the overall project from your key stakeholders.

Communication and Project Tracking

After you've done all this work to determine the scope, define your deliverables, and create a project plan that all necessary parties agree to, you must have open and effective communication if your project is going to be successful. Transparency and leadership are critical. It doesn't do anyone any good to have a well-defined project plan with the scope and tasks assigned if no one on the team knows what those tasks are or when the milestones hit.

As the project plan is being executed, you must track the actual results of your team's efforts and the specific tasks completed by the different members of your team as they are mapped out in the project plan. Not only are you looking for individuals who are hitting their goals according to the project timeline, you are also herding cats. In more complex projects, there are many times when some tasks intersect with other tasks being completed by different team members. If someone on the team gets off track and falls behind, it can hold up the efforts of the entire team and create a negative impact across the entire team in a cascading manner. Not only does this cause the project to fall behind schedule, but this can also create monetary and morale issues. Your job is to motivate team members to stay on track. When problems crop up, it's your job to mitigate the negative impact on the entire team by reassigning resources or making changes to the project plan.

Change and Risk Management

This brings up two other important responsibilities related to project management: change and risk management. Even when scope and project planning are conducted under the best of circumstances, stakeholders often change their minds about what they want out of an application. This could be because they see changes in the marketplace, because the underlying business changes, or because they had a barbecue at their cousin's house this weekend and Uncle Frank came up with some great ideas that the team hadn't considered.

Sometimes situations demand changes in your approach that may impact scope, timelines, or deliverables that you once thought you needed. Changes like this and other events can adversely affect the successful outcome of your project. When possible, it's critical that the project manager identifies risks and notifies the appropriate stakeholders of the situation as soon as possible. Sometimes you're willing to take a risk to make a change, and other times you won't be willing. The project manager, more than any individual on the team, can have a great deal of impact on the ultimate success of the project. Communication is key to making it work.

Debug Your App

If you are relatively new to the software development business, you are probably not familiar with bugs—identifying them, classifying them, and prioritizing them. It's an art to find them, so if you have a talented tester nearby, you'll certainly want some help. Once you've found your bugs, two main concepts help drive changes to applications: severity and priority.

Severity is assessed by determining what happens for a user, without making any qualifications about the veracity or importance of the bug. In other words, what does the user experience? A numerical scale is used to classify each bug, and numbers are assigned independently of priority

Debug Your App *(Continued)*

and before it is assigned. For example, we use the following broadly defined scale for our applications:

- *Severity 1*: Browser or app crash, data loss: a fatal bug that causes the app or browser to terminate or data in the application to be lost.

- *Severity 2*: Usability problem: app too difficult to use and/or too little information given to the user.

- *Severity 3*: Feature loss: important feature from last version inadvertently left out in current version.

- *Severity 4*: Inconvenience/layout problem: process in the app not streamlined, poor layout, too much information given to the user.

- *Severity 5*: Personal preference: no apparent problem for the user, but someone on your team (or you) prefer(s) that the app behave differently.

Once all bugs have been identified in a sweep of the app, you can sit down with your team to assign a *priority* to each of the bugs. Priority is a determination of how quickly you'd like to fix the bug, and it is usually assigned in a group setting where people with different opinions can share their thoughts on the importance of each bug. We use the following priority scale for our applications and websites:

- *Priority 0*: Urgent, must fix immediately.

- *Priority 1*: Very important fix but not immediately urgent.

- *Priority 2*: Important fix that should be completed in the current version before official release.

- *Priority 3*: Not a necessary fix for this version. Fix it if we can get to it; otherwise, add to next version and reprioritize alongside other bugs.

- *Priority 4*: Feature enhancement or change that should be part of the next version.

- *Priority 5*: Feature enhancement or change to consider for a future version.

Finally, if you are seeking the perfect application or website, you may be disappointed by just how long it takes to release. Most commercial websites have minor issues that the developers or business managers don't like on the site. The reality of the Web today is that there really is no such thing as the perfect app or website. Conventional wisdom in the software business is that if you've released an application or website without minor bugs, you've released it too late. So relax, but make sure you knock out major issues so you're happy with the outcome.

Monetize Your App

It's one thing to create a fun, popular, and viral app. It's another to create an app that actually makes you money. Of the 300,000+ Facebook apps, only a small%age of them are currently being monetized. You may be happy with the viral visibility and user data your app provides. But we suspect you'd also like to know about ways to generate revenue from your app!

It should be noted that your efforts may be better spent utilizing Facebook's primary features, such as the fan page, social ads, Facebook Connect, and existing apps to further expand your reach and monetize your own products and services. However, if you do go the route of developing your own app, Facebook suggests five popular business models for monetizing your app, detailed at this web page: http://wiki.developers.facebook.com/index.php/Common_Business_Models_for_Facebook_Applications.

In brief, the five models are as follows:

Advertising By optimizing the data that Facebook provides its app developers, you can serve highly targeted ads on the canvas page of your app.

Freemium (by Subscription) You provide the basic access to your app for free but offer an upgrade level that users need to pay for.

Virtual Credits/Virtual Goods Users purchase or earn virtual credits.

Affiliate Fees Earn a commission from items users buy via an affiliate link on your app. For example, the Virtual Bookshelf earns money when users purchase books linked to it on Amazon.com.

Merchandising Offer items such as mouse mats, mugs, caps, T-shirts, and so on, with your brand/app/logo.

The Future: Applications on Mobile Devices

We've covered the present of Facebook apps; certainly we're beyond the early days when there weren't many rules. Some of the opportunities for fast viral growth are gone. The bar is higher today than it was. But it doesn't mean that Facebook apps will necessarily fade into obscurity. In fact, they may enjoy a renaissance.

Remember that Facebook has more than 350 million users, and the social network continues to grow at a rapid pace. The installed base of the Facebook platform is rivaled only by the Web, by Windows, and by SMS today. No other platform comes close to the reach of Facebook. At the same time, smartphones are continuing to grow in popularity. Increasingly, consumers want a mobile web experience regardless of where they are.

The popularity of Apple's iTunes and the App Store tells us that there is already a huge market in third-party mobile applications. Google has created a similar applications marketplace for Android phones, and Microsoft is doing the same with Windows Mobile. When three industry giants all go after the same market, you have to think there is truly an opportunity! Many of these apps run outside the social context that Facebook so uniquely and comprehensively provides.

Similarly, a variety of third-party apps have attempted to build a social network around mobile applications such as location-based services. These applications allow the user to invite friends to join through the phone's contact list. It is a social network of sorts, but it isn't anywhere near as comprehensive. Many active Facebook users have far more Facebook friends than cell phone numbers.

Consider these Facebook mobile stats:

- More than 65 million active users are currently accessing Facebook through their mobile devices.

- People who use Facebook on their mobile devices are almost 50% more active on Facebook than nonmobile users.

- More than 180 mobile operators in 60 countries are working to deploy and promote Facebook mobile products.

There are a few possibilities for the evolution of mobile apps that utilize social graph data from Facebook:

Facebook Connect–Enabled Sites that Behave like Mobile Apps There is nothing keeping developers today from building sites that are purposely optimized to run as apps on mobile devices. Facebook Connect (which was covered in Chapter 7) would pull in required social graph data and allow for communication with friends and across News Feeds.

App Compatibility through Facebook Mobile Facebook Mobile runs on a wide range of mobile devices (iPhone, Blackberry, Palm, Android, Sidekick, Windows Mobile, and others). This app displays a wide range of data that is exposed on Facebook—the News Feed, status updates, profiles, and other friend activity. But Facebook Mobile does not allow third-party apps to run through Facebook Mobile and run on the mobile device as they run on Facebook. Should Facebook see an opportunity in extending the dev platform fully to mobile devices, we would expect future compatibility between third-party Facebook apps and Facebook Mobile.

A Mobile Facebook App Container Alternatively, Facebook could release a simple "app container" for each type of mobile device that taps into the user's social graph on Facebook. This container would be fully customizable to a particular brand or look and feel. It would act as a "platform" of its own but would allow for Facebook and mobile development with one simple, comprehensive effort. This would reduce the confusion and effort necessary to target different mobile devices, and it would also allow developers to focus on creating better apps that users will enjoy.

Facebook applications are a great way to extend your brand experience beyond the provided features of the Facebook platform. It just takes a little creativity and patience to navigate the rules and standards that have evolved after the first few years of third-party social application development. It is truly multidisciplinary—you'll need to scope an app properly, enforce a great customer experience, and manage a development effort to get it in the right place. If you don't, your time, money, and energy will be wasted, and you'll have to find a new Facebook tactic to engage with your audience.

Facebook Mobile for Business

If you are a local business owner, your Facebook fan page will be a Place page, complete with a map and feature for customers to add reviews. Plus, most businesses can take advantage of Check-in Deals, which is where a mobile user comes into your physical location and checks in to Facebook (adds their location). When they select your location from the menu on their smartphone, if you have a Deal set up, customers can take advantage of this on the spot. Deals help you reward your customers and build loyalty. To set up Check-in Deals for your business, you need to go to your Place page on Facebook and click Edit Page at the top right. When you see Deals listed in the menu on the left, click and then follow the tutorial.

There are four types of Check-in Deals:

Individual Deals These are great for a one-time offer, such as 20% off any purchase or buy an entrée and get your appetizer for free.

Loyalty Deals This is ideal if you have the type of business where customers come back time and again, such as a coffee shop, gym, bookstore, and so forth. Your customer can claim the deal after no fewer than two and no more than 20 check-ins to your location.

Friend Deals These deals are perfect for any business where customers tend to come in with a few friends, such as a restaurant or bar. Groups of up to eight people can claim these deals.

Charity Deals Each time someone claims this type of deal, you make a donation to your favorite charity.

You can have only one type of deal running at any given time. But they are tremendous for incentivizing existing customers and getting more prospects in the door. Be sure to train your staff to educate your community that you have the deals available. Watch for clientele coming into your location with their smartphones, and encourage them to check in to get the current deal. You never know how many Facebook friends someone walking into your premises may have; when they check in, they're also giving your business free word-of-mouth marketing on Facebook!

To find out more about how to set this feature up, go to https://www.facebook.com/deals/checkin/business/.

The Analytics of Facebook

Social media is the latest big thing in marketing, but it's even better when impact can be shown not just with strong opinions but with numbers to demonstrate successes in customer engagement, satisfaction, increased page views, and even return on investment (ROI). In this chapter, we'll review the basic concepts of analytics and how you can make them part of your decision making process so you know what to track, what is important, and why.

Chapter Contents

Keep Score with Metrics and Monitoring

Imagine this scenario for a moment. You are sitting outside a conference room waiting to give a presentation to senior executives of your company about the progress you've made with social media. They want you to present one slide with all the details of how you've done, and they want you to speak about how your company has fared relative to your competition. What belongs on that one slide? Better yet, how can you communicate the value of what you do in 5 minutes? What will convince them that you've succeeded and that they should trust your plan? This is why metrics or key performance indicators are so important. Although a cynic might say that numbers can be distorted to tell whatever story you'd like, statistics is also the preferred language of executives. So, what statistics matter most in social media? To understand all the metrics that truly matter, you need to step back and learn the basics of Internet marketing.

First you should understand that everything your customers, partners, and so on do on your websites is recorded in a massive log file. This log file is a bit cryptic, but fortunately you don't have to interpret it. Web analytics tools take care of this for you by generating readable reports by date and metric. Figure 8.1 is an example of such a report from Google Analytics. If you don't currently manage or get reports on your company's website traffic, you should try to get your hands on one to understand what appears in reports, how often they are generated, and how your company views them. For years, Internet-based businesses have watched these numbers very closely. But now, businesses of all kinds have concluded that the Internet says a lot about the health of a product, brand, or business unit. The best way to get familiar with the nomenclature, reporting, and intelligence generated from these reports is to dive in headfirst.

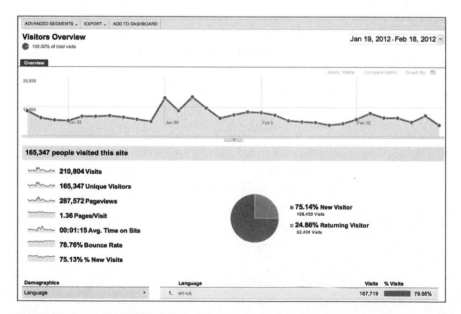

Figure 8.1 Sample Google Analytics report

Table 8.1 summarizes the basics of unique users, page views, and abandonment or bounce rates. When someone visits your website or social media presence on a given day, that person is regarded as a new unique user. With that unique user, you (by definition) also get your first page view; this can be a visit to a landing page, your home page, or any other page on your site that is indexed by a search engine. Some of these users will find something else of interest on your site and click another link to go to another page. This gives you another page view but not another unique user. Other users will get what they need from the page they found on your site, or they'll be disappointed in what they see. So, they'll move on to another destination on the Web or shut down their browser altogether. This behavior is known as a *bounce* or an *abandonment*.

▶ **Table 8.1** Basic Internet marketing metrics

Statistic	Definition	Meaning
Unique users	# of distinct people who visit your site on a given day	Awareness of your site
Page views	# of distinct pages viewed on a given day	Stickiness of your site, value of site's content
Bounce rate	% of people who view one page on your site and then leave	Whether people are truly interested in your site/content
Time spent on site	Amount of time in minutes the average user spends on your site	Whether your site is truly a destination or a pass-through

Measure Your Facebook Marketing with Insights

Just as Google provides analytics for your websites, Facebook provides a similar level of analytics on your page. These analytics, which give you detailed views of the things that are happening and not happening on your pages, appear only when an administrator views a page.

When analyzing your Insights data for your fan page, we can assume your primary objectives are to increase the total number of fans and to increase the engagement rate (frequency of interactions) of those fans. With a creative Facebook ad campaign and integrated Twitter promotion or other social media platform and promotion on your blog, websites, e-zine, emails, direct mail, and other channels, you should see an increase in fans. But that's just part of the equation. You need to provide consistent, relevant, quality content; otherwise, most Facebook users who join your page may never come back after that initial action.

As Facebook points out, "Page admins who post meaningful content will retain fans, while admins who post spammy or low-quality material will lose fans and subscribers."

And, to quote TechCrunch, "…that's really the big difference between Facebook fans and Twitter followers. On Twitter, you follow someone because you want to hear what they have to say. On Facebook, you fan them just to show your support or affinity. Too often, it's a throwaway gesture." Though this may be true for certain fan pages and for certain individuals, we tend to disagree.

The secret to creating a highly active fan page that ultimately drives other key performance indicators, such as opt-ins (email subscribers), blog subscribers, product sales, and paying clients, is to demonstrate you genuinely care about your fans. Definitely update far more often than the average of every 16 days! Respond promptly to fans' questions, comments, suggestions, reviews, and so on. Plus, involve your fans by asking questions and conducting surveys and polls. You can even ask them what types of content they most want from you or, if you were to run a contest, what prize they would most want to win.

The in-depth Insights data appears only on pages for which you are an administrator. If you wanted to also review your competitors' performance data, given Facebook allows access to its Insights API, there are a large number of third-party service providers that offer these types of metrics, namely, PageLever.com, CrowdBooster.com, EdgerankChecker.com, PolygraphMedia.com, SocialBakers.com, and BlitzLocal.com.

Now we'll explain the vast range of numbers and labels under Facebook Insights. Facebook is in the midst of upgrading the Old Insights to New Insights. At the time of writing this chapter (February 2012), Facebook has not yet fully rolled out the New Insights to all pages. Many pages still have the Old Insights. So, we will do our best to cover both for you in this chapter, starting with the New Insights.

New Insights

Along with the main Insights tab, there are three subcategories (tabs): Likes, Reach, and Talking About, as shown in Figure 8.2. If you have a Place page, there will be a fourth subcategory for Check-ins.

The main Insights tab shows at a glance the reach and engaged users for each individual post you made on your Wall. This is where a marketer can get a quick and immediate glimpse of the overall performance of a page.

When reviewing your Insights report, you can navigate through different graphs and data visualizations that show trends in user acquisition.

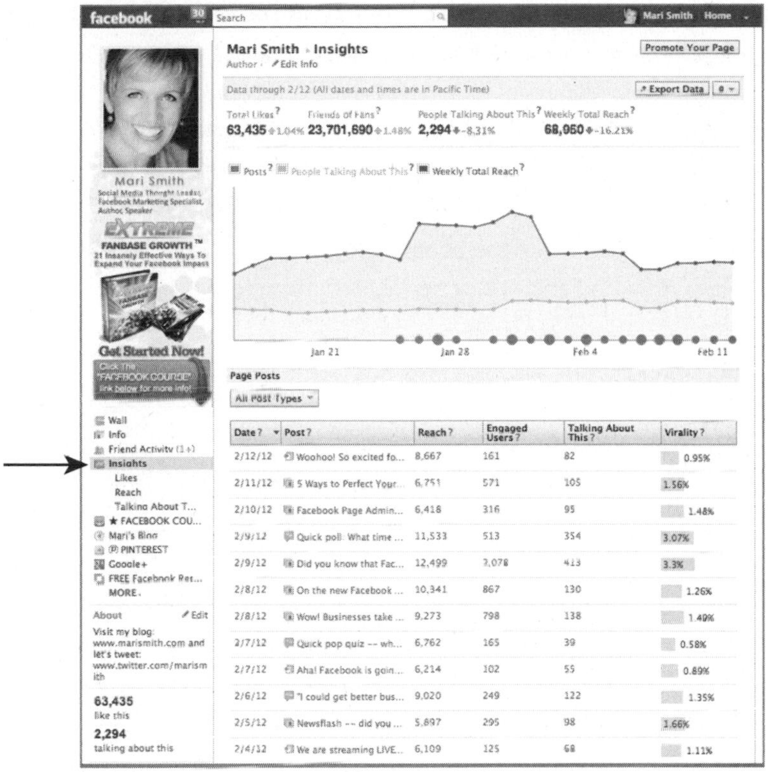

Figure 8.2 Facebook page: New Insights

Insights Tab

The following is the information on the Insights tab:

Initial Stats As shown in Figure 8.2, across the very top of this tab, you'll see the following:

> **Total Likes** This is the number of unique people who "like" your page (otherwise known as fans). Note that these are always individual Facebook users; even though other fan pages can "like" your fan page, they are never counted in your total likes. This number is always public-facing—anyone can see how many total likes you have without having access to your Insights data.
>
> **Friends of Fans** This is the number of unique people who are friends with people who "liked" your page.
>
> **People Talking About This** This is the number of unique people who created a "story" about your page. A story is created when someone likes your page; posts to your page Wall; "likes," comments on, or shares one of your page posts; answers a question you posted; responds to your event; mentions (@ tags) your page; tags your page in a photo; checks in at your Place page; or recommends your Place page. This stat is always calculated on a weekly basis but is refreshed every

24 hours. Along with Total Likes mentioned earlier, this People Talking About This (or PTAT as we often refer to it) stat is the only other public-facing stat and is a relatively new addition to the array of metrics that Facebook provides. Any Facebook user can see the PTAT figure just below the total number of likes on any fan page. In fact, given that Facebook pages are public and indexed on Google, even those people without a Facebook account can view these stats.

Weekly Total Reach This is the number of unique people who have seen any content associated with your page, including any ads or Sponsored Stories pointing to your page.

Next to each of these four stats mentioned, you will also see a percentage and an up or down arrow. If your stats are positive, they show in green with an up arrow. If they are negative, they show in red with a down arrow. It won't necessarily be possible to always have these numbers positive; because your page activity fluctuates from week to week, you'll see a natural undulation.

Graph Below the initial stats at the top, you'll see an attractive and interactive graph. This shows your posts (as purple "bubbles"—the size of the bubbles represents the number of posts your page published each day), PTAT (as a green line with dots on the graph), and Weekly Total Reach (as a blue line with dots on the graph). When you hover over each dot and bubble, you'll see they contain additional information for that day.

Page Posts Insights The most detailed part of the main Insights tab is the lower section, where you can see a significant amount of additional metrics for every post. Click any of the column headers to sort the data by that column. Stats in each column are tracked from the day you published the post until 28 days after.

Just above each column, you have an option to select from a drop-down menu and view only specific post types. The types are Post, Photo, Link, Video, Platform Post (posts made via a third-party app), or Question.

The following is detailed information about each column; this same information is available any time you hover your mouse over a question mark throughout Facebook Insights.

Date This is the day you published the post to your page (in your time zone).

Post This is a small extract of the post. Click any of the post links to see the full post in a small pop-up. On the pop-up, click View Post to go to the permalink of the full post with its thread of comments, likes, and shares (opens in a new tab/window).

Reach: This is the number of unique people who have seen your post. Click the number for a pop-up bar chart showing the total Organic, Paid, and Viral. Organic is the number of unique people who have seen your post in their News Feeds or on your page; this includes people who have liked your page and people who haven't. Paid is the number of unique people who have seen your post from ads and Sponsored Stories. Viral is the number of unique people who have seen your post as a result of one of their friends interacting with your page or post.

Engaged Users This is the number of unique people who have clicked your post. Click the number for a pop-up pie chart showing a breakdown of clicks per post: 1) Stories Generated, which are when someone likes, comments on, or shares your post, responds to an event, or answers a question you asked. 2) Photo Views pertains only to posts you make with a photo and shows the number of times the photo has been viewed at full size (meaning that the user has clicked the image). 3) Link Clicks are only for posts you make that include a link or a video; this stat shows the number of clicks on your link or video. 4) Other Clicks is everything not counted in the first two stats, such as clicking @ tags, clicking the permalink, clicking the number of likes, or clicking the number of shares. Facebook states that these types of clicks are strong indicators of attention to your post. If a visitor or fan is interested enough to check out who else has liked or shared your post, they are likely spending more time interacting with your post than someone who just clicks Like on the post.

> **Note:** There is an extremely important stat on the pop-up pie chart when you click Engaged Users, and that is the number of people who gave "negative feedback." This number reports the number of people who have chosen to hide your post in their News Feeds or have reported it as spam. We are amazed that Facebook has this critical number so buried in its Insights data. In the Old Insights, this number was referred to as Unsubscribe. However, when Facebook introduced the Subscribe option for personal profiles (Timelines), it changed the wording on this stat.

Talking About This This is the same stat we mentioned earlier. However, in this column, the number now shows the PTAT for each post. It is the number of unique people who created a "story" about your page. A story is created when someone likes your page; posts to your page Wall; "likes," comments on, or shares one of your page posts; answers a question you posted; responds to your event; mentions (@ tags) your page; tags your page in a photo; checks in at your Place page; or recommends your Place page. Click the number for a pop-up pie chart that shows the individual number of likes, comments, and shares. If the post is a question, you'll also see the number of responses. If the post is about an event, you should see a set of stats for responses to the event.

Virality This stat shows the percentage of people who have created a story from your page post out of the total number of unique people who have seen it. One of your goals is to work on increasing this number by experimenting with a variety of types of posts, days of the week, and times of day. Plus, consider taking out ads and Sponsored Stories targeted to your fans and friends of fans in order to boost overall engagement and increase your stats.

Likes Tab

This tab shows a breakdown of the demographics, locations, and sources of all your fans, as shown in Figure 8.3. The top bar graph shows gender and age as percentages. The middle section shows countries, cities, and languages.

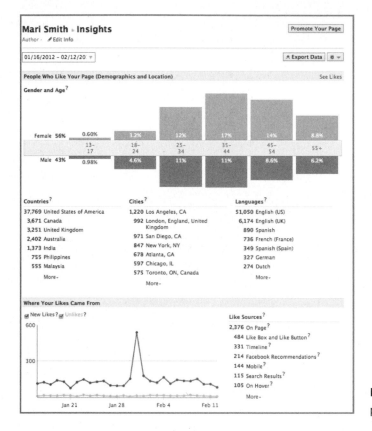

Figure 8.3 Facebook page Insights: Likes tab

It's important to review these demographics regularly to get a sense of what times of day are best to get maximum engagement. For example, I (Mari) live in the Pacific time zone, and although the majority of my fans live in U.S. time zones, a significant portion of my fans live in the United Kingdom, which is 8 hours ahead, and in Australia, which is 18 to 19 hours ahead. So, I need to take this into account and really mix up the posting times to get maximum News Feed visibility and engagement with my fans around the world. This means using a third-party posting tool, such as HootSuite, to preschedule. However, it can also mean hiring a moderator/admin in a different part of the world. My main moderator lives in the Netherlands.

The bottom section shows where your likes (fans) came from—that is, how and where your fans discovered your page in order to like it. These could be directly on the page, via a Like box or Like button, on your (personal) Timeline, on hover (hovercard), from ads, and so forth. This is critical data to analyze in order to do more of what's working and less of what is not.

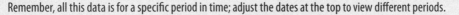

Note: Next to the list of sources, you'll also see a chart of Likes and Unlikes. In addition to closely tracking the number of people who hid your post in their News Feeds (see earlier "Engaged Users" section), it's vital to keep a close eye on your number of unlikes. You need to become aware of what is causing fans to hide your posts and unlike your page. The top reason is usually that you are posting too often. The second reason is that you're posting content that is not relevant to your fans.

Remember, all this data is for a specific period in time; adjust the dates at the top to view different periods.

Reach Tab

Similar to your Likes tab, this section now drills deep into the demographics and locations of all the unique people who have seen your page and your posts.

Who You Reached As with the Likes tab, you'll see gender and age as percentages and a bar graph and then, below that, the countries, cities, and languages. This can be very fascinating data to compare to the people who "like" your page; it could be that you're reaching a much broader and more diverse audience than just your fans. In addition, pay close attention to which time zones the people you reach live in and continue adjusting your posting times accordingly until you reach your magic "sweet spot" (optimized engagement on your page).

How You Reached People In this section, you'll see two very useful charts that show how you reached people and how often, as shown in Figure 8.4. This includes Organic, Paid, and Viral values, as mentioned earlier. You can also view this data in any of three sections: All Page Content, Your Posts, and Stories by Others. Each of these three sets of data reveals additional data useful to you, such as whether user-generated stories are reaching a wider audience than your own posts.

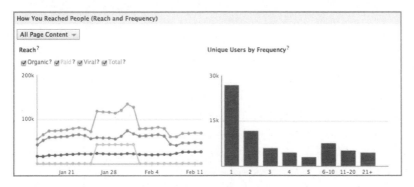

Figure 8.4 Facebook page Insights data: how you reached people

Visits To Your Page This is a simple line graph showing Page Views and Unique Visitors metrics, meaning the number of times your fan page was viewed on any given day during the time period selected, along with the number of unique people who visited your page. The unique visitors will almost always be lower than the page views because often fans and visitors will return to your page more than once a day.

The bottom two sections under this one are Total Tab Views (an important one to check and see where visitors and fans are landing) and External Referrers (much like Google Analytics, it's very useful to know where most of your traffic is coming from). As part of your marketing plans, make it a point to reach out to your top sources (or up-and-coming sources) and nurture those relationships.

Talking About This Tab

This section shows demographics about all the people who have "created stories" about your page, not just visited it as in the Reach tab. Data on this tab shows only when you have more than 30 people talking about your page. Along with the demographics, you'll see a section with details on how people are talking about your page. There are two charts: one showing the numbers of people talking about certain types of content and the other showing viral reach. Viral reach is the number of people who saw a story created by a friend of theirs about your page.

Check-Ins Tab

This tab will appear only on Place pages (for local businesses or businesses that have entered a street address in their About section). As with the Talking About This data, demographic data for Check-ins is available only when more than 30 people checked in at your Place page in the 7 days preceding the last day of your selected date range. This tab also includes a graph showing how people have checked in to your Place page: via mobile device or website.

Some of the data in the various Insights tabs can get a bit mind-boggling. We encourage you to start with the basics, and you can always drill deeper as needed.

Old Insights

As mentioned at the beginning of this chapter, it may be that many pages do not yet have access to the New Insights data. This section now covers the Old Insights, because they are quite different in layout and in some of the vernacular.

Insights is broken down into three main categories: Overview, Users, and Interactions. Overview summarizes Users and Interactions data, which is provided in greater detail on the other two tabs. This is where a marketer can get a quick and immediate glimpse of the overall performance of a page.

Users Tab

The Users tab includes the following information:

Daily/Weekly/Monthly Active Users This is the number of people who have been active on your page once a day, once a week, and once a month. The actions of daily active users are broken down further so you know how they behave, whether they've viewed the page, viewed a post, liked a post, commented on a post, or posted to the Wall (if you've given your fans permission to do so).

Likes/Unlikes This is the total number of fans over time, overlaid with the total number of fans who have unliked your page.

Demographics This is the percentage of your fan base that belongs in various age and gender demographic groups.

Top Countries, Cities, Languages This is the growth of your fan base over time, broken down by country, major metropolitan area, and spoken language.

Page Views This is both the total number of times your page was viewed per day and the total number of unique people who viewed your page. Both numbers include those people who have "liked" your page and those who have not.

Media Consumption This is the total photo views, audio plays, and video plays for the content you have uploaded to your page.

Interactions Tab

The following information is available on the Interactions tab:

Daily Story Feedback This is a summary of the interactions taking place around different pieces of content that are made available on the Wall of the page. Note that this is where your "unsubscribes" show, that is, the number of people who have hidden posts by you in their News Feeds. (In the New Insights, this data is now reported under Engaged Users and is referred to as people who "gave negative feedback.")

Daily Page Activity This is a summary of the interactions taking place with the page itself over time. Activity includes Mentions, Discussion Posts, Reviews, Wall Posts, and Videos. (Facebook has since removed both the Discussions and the Reviews features, but they are still showing as labels in the Old Insights.)

Insights for App Developers

Insights is also used by marketers and application developers to measure the success of Facebook applications. The same suite of demographic data is available, along with other metrics specific to the application. To get this information, you must first be listed as a developer of a Facebook application. Then, go to www.facebook.com/developer, and click the application that you want to learn about. On the lower-right side of the screen, you should see Insights and a See All link. There, you can find Usage Statistics—the number of active monthly users for your application, the total number of users you've earned for the lifetime of the application, the number of Wall posts people make about the application, and the number of reviews you've received. The User Response tab includes information on how certain metrics pertain to the application relative to the statistical norm across Facebook. For example, some apps are better than others at getting people to respond to real-time notifications. Other apps inspire people to respond to those same messages and report them as spam. These are important marketing insights that can give you an idea of how well your application is meeting customer needs. The problem is that this data is currently made available only to "official developers" of an app, and it's buried alongside a variety of numbers that would be interesting only to a techie. Ah, the joys of being a 21st-century marketer.

The Importance of Derivative Statistics

These basic Internet marketing metrics are important, but they don't even begin to tell the entire story about the health of your Internet presence. Analysis is necessary to look at a few of these numbers in combination with other metrics or on a time-trending basis. Individually, we call these second-level metrics *derivative statistics* because they are created by looking at some of these numbers on a relative basis or by combining some of the statistics to see how the site performs over time.

If you're confused by the concept of derivative statistics, consider that many of you use derivative statistics just about every day. For example, when you drive your car, you want to know several things. How far have you traveled? That's measured in miles or kilometers. How long have you been in the car? That's measured in time. But speed—how fast have you gone? That requires miles or kilometers per hour—a derivative statistic that is measured by dividing distance by time. It isn't such an esoteric concept; we use derivative measurements all the time.

Some social media examples of derivative statistics are page views per unique user, money per subscriber, click-through rate, cost per click, clicks per hour, fans per day, and so on. These things tell you, in different ways, how efficient you are at achieving certain business goals and how quickly you are achieving them.

How do derivative statistics help you learn more about the use of your website? It's really a matter of looking at your performance critically and as objectively as possible. If you are hoping for a particular outcome, you're less likely to consider that your site isn't performing as well as it could. We tell people all the time that most Internet marketing and social media campaigns are not optimized, no matter how much you think they are. So if you start with the assumption that you have to improve something in your presence, you'll be more likely to find things to fix.

Note: Whatever you do, don't be a cheerleader for your Internet and social media effort. Your job is to find problems and fix them proactively. Think critically about what you're doing. Look for hints of declining performance or ways you can make great performance even better. If you're creative and thinking critically about your job, you'll identify issues before your colleagues do. That's a much better situation than the alternative.

For example, you may have a directive to make your website more engaging for users. You get a report saying that you've had a 40% increase in unique users, from 1,000 to 1,400 per day, over the last month. Page views are up from 2,225 to 2,661. It's time to celebrate, right? Wrong. Although your unique users metric is up, your page views per unique user metric is actually down 17%. You've attracted more people to your site, but they're also not sticking around! So, you've succeeded with one metric but failed in the one that actually matters to you. Digging another level beyond the obvious is the key to figuring out what is really happening.

Advanced Statistical Analysis

For many of our readers, basic analytics will only create more questions, which require answers you can really only find by analyzing data further. There are two ways to draw deeper conclusions from the data than Facebook Insights provides. You can work with a Facebook analytics company that can mine the data out of your Facebook pages to provide a richer set of analytics that may impress your superiors. This is typically the low-touch approach—just spend a few hundred dollars, and a third party will give you many of the answers you need.

Why Should You Analyze the Data?

Statistics can give you a much better idea of how you are performing. If you harness them properly, you can learn about your advertising and demand generation campaigns, the health of your page, or the effectiveness of your marketing efforts, whether they are internal or outsourced to consultants.

Alternatively, you can collect the data yourself and perform your own analysis. Fortunately, Facebook Insights allows you to export data to Excel or CSV files for your own records and manipulation. Just open Facebook Insights (click your Insights tab), then click the Export Data button in the upper right, and select a date range in the pop-up window (Figure 8.5). It won't take long before you have Insights data on a spreadsheet in front of you.

It is important to note that this is not a full export of the data on your Facebook page but rather an export of the analytics that Facebook Insights provides. So, it's Facebook's summary of the analytics that matter to you. The downside of this is that you may not agree with or even understand Facebook's interpretation of metrics that matter to your business.

So, how do you begin to collect all the data that you will need to generate derivative statistics and gain intelligence from all the numbers? The easiest way to get started is to create a dashboard in a spreadsheet such as Microsoft Excel. This dashboard will be the one place where you keep a daily record of everything that has happened from the start of your project. Suffice it to say that your dashboard will be your best friend and the one file you simply can't afford to lose, so be sure to back it up regularly or keep it in an online backup service like Windows Live Mesh.

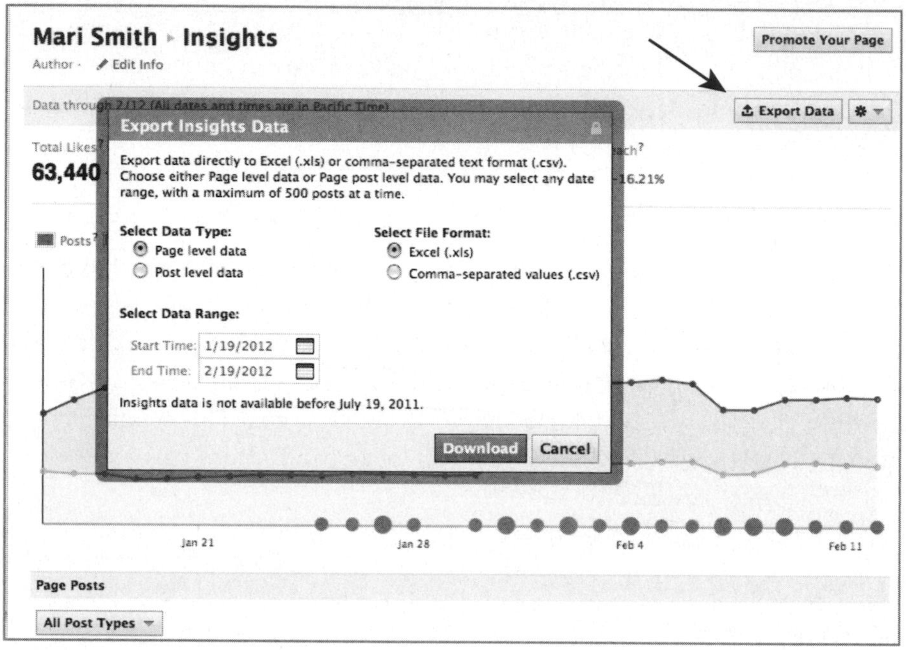

Figure 8.5 Facebook Insights Data Export button

Every piece of data you can collect about your website and social media effort belongs in the dashboard. What are those metrics that are so handy? We've covered them throughout this book, so odds are you are already aware of what you'll need. If you're running a fan page, you'll want to know what your fan count is at the same time every day. The same metric applies to groups or friends of a profile. If you're running advertising campaigns to drive traffic, you'll want to know how much money you spent, how many clicks it generated, and how many impressions you got for your money. Remember, it's all about having the discipline to collect numbers every day so when the time comes, you'll be able to analyze outcomes and drive intelligence from a cryptic set of numbers.

If it's a multichannel marketing effort—such as using Facebook ads to drive website hits or using Google ads to increase your Facebook fan count—you'll want to collect those numbers individually by using the interface provided for reporting. Different analytics services (Google, Facebook, and so on) keep daily data for different periods of time, so if you don't get data on a timely basis, you can lose it altogether. Therefore, make a commitment to capturing all the data you can every day. You can always disregard unnecessary data later, after you determine what you really need. Different services also automate parts of the process for you. Google Analytics, for example, can be set up to generate reports for you and automatically send you updates via email or on demand.

Executive Management of Internet Marketing and Social Media Progress

If you're an executive managing an Internet marketing or social media effort, you are in a tough position. On one hand, you are ultimately responsible for the success or failure of this marketing program. On the other hand, you don't have time to become an expert. That's why you've hired staff, a contractor, a consultant, or an agency to help you. You are almost entirely reliant upon these people to make it work.

Nonetheless, you really need to understand the basics of Internet marketing metrics and derivative statistics. Those responsible have all the incentives in the world for telling you that things are going well and have all the tools at their disposal to tell whatever story they'd like. Make sure you ask probing questions to learn exactly what is happening. Here are a few other tips:

- Learn the process. How exactly is success and failure judged by your people?

- Ask for time-trending data. What is your performance over time? Week by week? Month by month?

- Demand comparative data. How do you do versus your competitors? Understand that you won't get comparative metrics across the board, but you should have a basic idea of how your competitors drive traffic.

- Seek iterative improvements. How are your people assessing themselves critically and making improvements on the fly? And do they do so in a way that keeps the data consistent and comparable on an apples-to-apples basis?

- Look for numbers that show progress. Your people should be able to tell you which data indicate progress. Make sure you understand what they're saying, and probe!

If you're working with someone in your company who is assigned to this work for the first time, you may need to be patient with them while they're learning. Experts, consultants, and contractors should know most of this already—if they're the caliber of professional that you deserve for your business. Ask difficult questions, and apply the correct level of understanding based on the stated qualifications of the person responsible.

And finally, keep in the back of your mind a few important quotes about statistics:

"Facts are stubborn things, but statistics are more pliable."
   —*Author unknown*

"Statistics are like bikinis. What they reveal is suggestive, but what they conceal is vital."
   —*Aaron Levenstein*

Now the same thing is available to you for your social media properties as well. Every post, comment, like, content share, fan, subscribe, and so on is similarly logged by Facebook and is quantifiable. You can get a lot of this data manually by recording the individual actions that take place yourself, but it would get awfully tedious after a while and just about impossible for bigger properties that get thousands of individual interactions per day. Facebook makes some of this data available in Facebook Insights and, as we mentioned previously, allows you to export some of it to Microsoft Excel. This is perfect for those of you data junkies out there who want to crunch and analyze the numbers, perhaps using Pivot Tables. So, in that spirit, we thought we'd give you a few pointers on doing that and some of the data analyses that we've found useful in helping people determine the health and success of their Facebook assets over time. Going into this, you'll just want a good strategy for acquiring voluminous data on a consistent basis and with a consistent time period in mind. You may not see the benefits of this up front, but you'll be happy you did it when the time comes to analyze your progress.

First let's walk through building a dashboard together. Figure 8.6 is the beginning of a dashboard we built for a client with an established brand name that was interested in increasing the community on its Facebook fan page.

	A	B	C	D	E	F	G
1		FB/Unique Users	FB/Page View	FB Fans	Twitter Followers	FB Fans/Day	Twitter/Day
30	28–Apr	9	30	517	453	1	4
31	29–Apr	11	26	522	461	5	8
32	30–Apr	23	54	523	460	1	–1
33	1–May	12	32	533	470	10	10
34	2–May	4	6	534	477	1	7
35	3–May	10	22	538	479	4	2
36	4–May	8	23	544	482	6	3
37	5–May	4	8	547	488	3	6
38	6–May	3	7	549	491	2	3
39	7–May	5	8	557	492	8	1
40	8–May	4	14	559	492	2	0
41	9–May	2	3	561	494	2	2
42	10–May	2	4	565	498	4	4
43	11–May	6	20	568	503	3	5
44	12–May	3	4	573	511	5	8
45	13–May	10	27	577	513	4	2
46	14–May	4	16	584	511	7	–2
47	15–May	10	27	587	519	3	8
48	16–May	3	5	593	522	6	3
49	17–May	2	4	601	525	8	3
50	18–May	8	25	623	528	22	3
51	19–May	7	21	632	530	9	2
52	20–May	16	36	642	545	10	15
53	21–May	6	11	658	550	16	5
54	22–May	8	17	665	555	7	5

Figure 8.6 Basic dashboard for Facebook and Twitter

In this simple case, we wanted to capture the daily total number of Facebook fans (column E) the client had, along with some metrics on how the Facebook fan page was being used through unique users and page views (columns B and C). At the time we started the project, the team had a secondary objective, to see how increased social media engagement on Facebook would impact the company's Twitter presence, so we added column F to track the total number of Twitter followers per day. That's it—the basics of a dashboard. Pretty simple, eh? Better yet, you can export some of this data from Facebook Insights to help you get historical data quickly.

If that were it, the job would be very easy. But these numbers by themselves offer a lot more insight when you keep up with the data collection process and update the dashboard regularly. Take, for example, the incremental fans per day metric. This is one that simply helps you determine how many net new fans you are adding per day: new people who have "liked" your page minus any who are tired of you and want to remove their association with your organization. Figure 8.7 shows the basic dashboard but with new columns for net new incremental fans per day. It's really pretty simple—all you do to calculate this derivative statistic is subtract the total number of fans you had yesterday from today.

1		FB/Unique Users	FB/Page View	FB Fans	Twitter Followers	FB Fans/Day	Twitter/Day
30	28–Apr	9	30	517	453	1	4
31	29–Apr	11	26	522	461	5	8
32	30–Apr	23	54	523	460	1	–1
33	1–May	12	32	533	470	=E33–E32	10
34	2–May	4	6	534	477	1	7
35	3–May	10	22	538	479	4	2
36	4–May	8	23	544	482	6	3
37	5–May	4	8	547	488	3	6
38	6–May	3	7	549	491	2	3
39	7–May	5	8	557	492	8	1
40	8–May	4	14	559	492	2	0
41	9–May	2	3	561	494	2	2
42	10–May	2	4	565	498	4	4
43	11–May	6	20	568	503	3	5
44	12–May	3	4	573	511	5	8

Figure 8.7 Dashboard with fans/day metric

Figure 8.8 is a chart of this basic metric over the first month of the project. What does this simple chart tell you? It says you inherited a presence that was generating somewhere in the ballpark of four fans per day. It says that you did "something" right starting around May 17. It also says that the impact of that "something" appeared to wear off a bit about a week later, but the overall effort appeared to, at minimum, double the number of incremental fans you could generate for the fan page per day. Not bad at all.

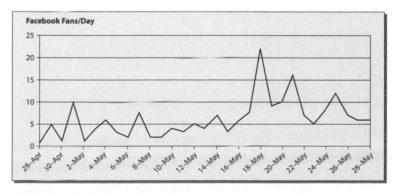

Figure 8.8 One-month chart of Facebook fans/day

One other observation you may have made regarding this chart is spikes in the data. This is both a positive and a negative. It is good to see spikes because you can see the direct impact of things you do on individual days. We like taking notes in the comments field for a cell in a dashboard spreadsheet just to remind ourselves what happened on that particular day. It certainly helps after you've run a campaign for a long time and you can't remember what you did on what day! One negative of this chart, however, is that you can get distracted by the high and low spikes. Sometimes, you didn't have to do anything at all to see a major spike upward or downward. Someone who closely manages or scrutinizes the process may want an explanation, when in fact this is just normal noise. If you are looking at the data every day, keep in mind that you are just going to have good days and bad days. You'll also have days of the week or holidays that naturally just don't do as well. You may notice in Figure 8.8 that there are dips in the data on May 2, 9, 15, and 22. What is the one thing these dates all have in common? They are Fridays and Saturdays—two days when you'd expect people to spend less time online and on Facebook.

Now how can you gain intelligence from the data? You can drive yourself crazy looking at daily spikes in data, which may drive you to "overoptimize" your site. Trends are perhaps better detected when you employ the use of moving averages. We talked about moving averages in Chapter 6, "Month 3: Creating Demand with Facebook Advertising." The idea behind moving averages is that they can help you see and visualize longer-term trends. If long enough, moving averages also help you largely eliminate circumstances such as weekends, holidays, and so on, which can skew results, and give a clearer picture of the health of a site or campaign. The key is to get a moving average for a long enough period of time. For example, a four-day moving average wouldn't work because some of the moving average data would incorporate weekends while others wouldn't. Because you want your data to be as clear and consistent as possible, we recommend 7-, 14-, and 28-day moving averages for almost all Internet marketing work.

Note: To calculate a moving average, simply pick the amount of time you want and take the average outcome for that metric over that period. For example, a seven-day moving average would be calculated by averaging today and the last six days of results. That number would be "today's seven-day moving average metric," which you will then need to recalculate tomorrow and every day thereafter.

Figure 8.9 shows the same one-month chart of new Facebook fans as Figure 8.8, but it includes another line with the smoothed-out seven-day moving average (DMA). Now the chart gets a lot more interesting. You can clearly see that the fan page was minimally effective with little to no maintenance in the first half of May. The campaign work done in mid-May was very effective, but the 7 DMA line is trending downward. If your goal is to get a consistent eight new Facebook fans per day, the jury is still out regarding your success. If the goal is 10 to 12 new Facebook fans per day, you'll need to employ at least one new trick to consistently reach your goals. Longer moving averages, such as 28- or 56-day moving averages, help you determine the success or failure of campaigns that are designed to run for a long period of time. As with all your data, be sure to collect as much information as you can on the various externalities that take place—things that happen either inside or outside the Internet marketing campaign that can impact results. You'll want to know exactly how certain activities impact performance.

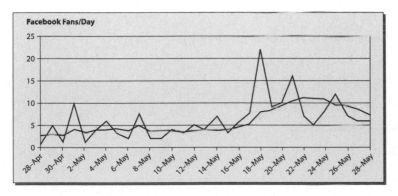

Figure 8.9 One-month chart of Facebook fans with seven-day moving average

Over and above moving averages, we also like to compartmentalize important data into weekly, monthly, and quarterly views to analyze the success or failure of a project. Take, for example, Figure 8.10, which is a summary of advertising outcomes for another client that wanted to grow its number of Facebook fans. For this particular campaign, we recommended Facebook advertising as a means to get the word out about a revamped Facebook fan page. You'll notice that in the first few weeks we learned a lot about what customers liked and didn't like about our advertising. In weeks 3 and 4, we raised the advertising budget with the lessons learned from weeks 1 and 2. We found opportunities to get more efficient with ads, so we pulled back some ads and added others in week 5. Over time, we found more fans with less advertising spend, and we acquired those fans more efficiently over time at a small marginal cost. When you can find fans at $0.27 each and you can communicate with them *ad infinitum* for years to come, you've done a great job! We don't know whether it is coincidence, our great partnership, or dumb luck, but our primary contact at the client company was promoted during the middle of week 5!

	Ad Spend	Clicks	Cost/Fan	Fans	Fans/Clicks
Week 1	$ 52.50	213	$ 0.59	117	55%
Week 2	$ 47.50	201	$ 0.39	151	75%
Week 3	$ 97.72	475	$ 0.43	255	54%
Week 4	$ 80.00	458	$ 0.39	231	50%
Week 5	$ 35.00	202	$ 0.27	160	79%
Week 6	$ 35.00	236	$ 0.22	188	80%
Week 7	$ 35.00	194	$ 0.27	160	82%

Figure 8.10 Summary advertising data by week

But it goes beyond looking at how fan count is impacted by various marketing activities. There is so much more that you can do to analyze your content effectiveness/strategy. The following list is a summary of the top metrics for assessing the quality and performance of a Facebook marketing effort:

Audience Growth: How the Fan Count of a Facebook Page Grows Over Time

- Absolute Fan Count
- # of Fans Added per Day
- % of Fan Growth per Day

Page Maintenance: Measurement of the Use of Best Practices to Keep a Page Maintained

- All-Time Admin Posts
- Daily Admin Posts
- All-Time Admin Posts by Day of Week
- All-Time Admin Posts by Hour
- Deleted User Posts/Comments

Overall Engagement: High-Level Overview of How Much People Interact with a Page

- User Posts (if you've enabled them)
- Likes
- Comments
- Comment Likes
- All Engagement (User Posts, Likes, Comments, Comment Likes)
- Unique Contributors

Fan Participation: User Participation Levels as a Function of the Page's Total Audience

- Engagement per fan
- Posts per fan
- Comments per fan
- Likes per fan
- Comment Likes per fan
- Likes per comment
- Active Fan %

Content Effectiveness: How Content Gets People to Interact Regardless of the Number of Posts

- Likes per post
- Comments per post
- Most Engaging Content

- Most Commented-on Content
- Most Liked Content

Influencers: The Top Fans of a Page

- Most Engaged Fans
- Most Commenting Fans
- Most "Liking" Fans

Numbers from Facebook Insights and perhaps your own observations will help you generate some of these derivative metrics. You can then roll up the data into weekly, monthly, quarterly, or annual views to tell you how things happen on a longer timeframe.

Other data sets, such as Influencers data, are not currently made available to you and are accessible only by buying third-party analytics reports. The same goes for competitor activity; Facebook Insights allows you to track your own page but not those of competitors. But it is nonetheless helpful. For instance, if you are the social marketing manager or agency for Coca-Cola, all of this data may be helpful for you to watch on a time-trending basis. But you also may want to see how you perform against Pepsi—that's why you'd invest money in a reporting or analytics product.

Featured Case: Kevin Hillstrom, Ambassador for Social ROI

Kevin Hillstrom spent more than 20 years in the retail industry, including stints as vice president of database marketing at Nordstrom, director of circulation at Eddie Bauer, and manager of analytical services at Lands' End. Today, he is one of the most outspoken advocates of social media analytics and ROI, and his blog, MineThatData (www.minethatdata.com/blog), is one of the most-read database marketing publications of any kind in the world. In his company, also named MineThatData, Kevin has helped more than 65 companies and their CEOs understand the complex relationship between advertising, products, brands, and channels. We caught up with Kevin recently to learn his perspective on social media ROI in 2012 and beyond.

Q: *You've been an outspoken champion of ROI across all marketing channels (online, offline, social) for many years on your blog, MineThatData. What do you think the state of marketing is today as it relates to return on investment? Is social ROI achievable?*

A: I think the state of marketing and ROI is not in great shape. We have trained a generation of analysts and marketing experts to analyze "conversion," providing them with free tools (Google Analytics) to measure conversion. This is exactly the opposite of what is needed to measure social ROI. Social ROI falls in what I call "annual analytics," meaning that ROI is best measured as the outcome of many small activities. With social, you're looking at summing the value of hundreds of pennies. Instead, we try to measure a specific penny, and that is really, really hard to do. Social ROI is achievable, and honestly, it isn't terribly difficult to measure. We simply aren't measuring the right things.

continues

Featured Case: Kevin Hillstrom, Ambassador for Social ROI *(Continued)*

Q: *What do you think is currently the most promising opportunity for companies in social media?*

A: It certainly isn't tweeting "Today we're offering 20% off plus free shipping!" It has been my experience that opportunities are plentiful for individuals and small organizations. I generate 70% of my annual revenue from my blog. However, social media, as a sales generator, doesn't scale for mid-sized or large brands. If it did scale, we would read story after story about how socially savvy brands (i.e., Best Buy or Victoria's Secret) have comp store sales increases that are +15% or +20%, and that simply hasn't happened. The opportunities, to me, are fourfold. First, social media is like the "prospect list" that catalogers kept in the 1990s; they allowed you to request a catalog for free, and then they obtained your name and address and were able to market to you going forward. Social media offers the same opportunity. Second, social media to the "winners club" that casinos use to reel in customers and experience a relationship or to various retail loyalty programs. It is a way for "brands" to have a relationship with customers and to learn what customers care about and are interested in. Third, social media is a spectacular customer service channel, and, unfortunately, this aspect of the medium is underutilized and somewhat disrespected. Fourth, social media can be "built into" the fabric of a business. In other words, it is not a "feature" or "channel" that you bolt onto a brand (like email marketing, for instance), but instead, it "is" the product.

Q: *Do you have any examples of companies that you think are approaching social media the right way? Or the wrong way?*

A: Too many people talk about the wrong way. Here's an example of a positive outcome. Read this post from Bob Lefsetz: `http://lefsetz.com/wordpress/index.php/archives/2011/12/11/nic-adler-in-aspen/`.

Twenty percent of sales come from social media; that's a positive ROI. But read the post carefully. Social is built into the fabric of the marketing strategy of the club owner. As an example, I had an obscure link to this post in a paragraph of a blog post. The club found that story and followed me on Twitter within 24 hours. You know, if you're willing to work from 12:00 a.m. to 3:00 a.m. every day for a year and you're willing to build social into the fabric of your experience, it just might work. Again, there is a stark contrast between tweeting "25% off plus free shipping" once a day and doing what this individual does. This individual builds social into the fabric of the experience.

Q: *What do you make of the rise, peak, and slight downturn of the group purchasing frenzy?*

A: We do a terrible job, as a marketing community, of understanding customer segments. Terrible. There are "x" customers who crave discounts and promotions. These are the folks

Featured Case: Kevin Hillstrom, Ambassador for Social ROI *(Continued)*

who are at Wal-Mart at midnight of Thanksgiving/Black Friday. They represent maybe 20% of the population. When you offer them a new way of enjoying discounts and promotions (Groupon/Living Social), they're going to go "all in," and they're going to tell their friends. Group purchasing isn't the issue; it's a new way to win at discounts and promotions that is the issue here. Once there are hundreds of brands doing the same discounts and promotions, well, the fun is gone. Now, it's time for somebody to do something new. Innovation in discounting will always draw a crowd. Sustaining the audience, however, is much more challenging.

Q: *What is your outlook for traditional marketing in a world where so many things are measurable online?*

A: Things are very measurable offline as well. Online, you have a free tool like Google Analytics that makes it very easy to measure things. Offline, well, you don't have that. But plenty of people do the hard work to measure things in my world. Many retailers measure in-store conversion rate, they estimate how many people enter the store, and they measure how many people purchase merchandise, so they have the same measurements that online folks have. Many retailers integrate online data and offline data; these folks have an enormous competitive advantage over online-only folks. I work with companies that are able to measure that a customer visited a website via Twitter on Monday and purchased in-store on Tuesday. The type of analytics work you do offline is different than the work that online folks do; it simply isn't talked about as often.

Q: *Have we seen the peak of Facebook, or do you think it will continue to grow?*

A: This is only an opinion. Facebook, to me, will become an Internet utility. Microsoft won the desktop, Google won search, Facebook won social. There will be something that comes along that fuses social and retailing in ways we can't imagine at this time. In fact, I think there will be tons of niche-based startups that cater to groups with unique interests; these businesses will thrive and will be happy not to achieve 800 million in scale. When technology allows for what I'd call "helpful holograms," well, then things really change. Until then, Facebook will grow at a slower rate, in my opinion, and will continue to dominate social in the way that Google dominates search.

Q: *Do any other social networks interest you from an ROI perspective?*

A: I am very interested in how people/brands use social networks. I think we are in the top of the first inning in terms of how people leverage social networks. We can't measure ROI in so many cases because we haven't figured out how all of this stuff fits in with retail skills we've honed over 100 or more years.

When the Standard Facebook Experience Isn't Quite Enough: Landing Pages

Let's now turn our attention to landing pages. Landing pages are web pages or custom Facebook tabs on your page that are explicitly set up to encourage visitors to take an immediate action. It can be a simple action ("like my page") or can require a bigger investment from the user ("purchase my product" or "join my mailing list"). Usually there is an attractive enticement on the landing page—sign up for free information, a newsletter, free quote for something, and so on. These aren't new; they've been around for a long time. But as the Internet has matured, people have focused more time and energy on landing pages because they are the best way to map a campaign to a clear business objective.

Like landing pages on the Internet, successful landing pages on social media are based on conversions to a business objective. On Facebook fan pages, it might be the conversion of the visitor into a fan. On a Facebook profile, it's the conversion of the visitor to a friend. On Twitter, it's the conversion of the visitor to a follower. If you've failed to convert the person, it doesn't necessarily mean you've lost that person forever. You may have caught the person on a busy day. That person may be back another day to visit your site and make the commitment you want them to make. This is why thinking too short-term can be dangerous with social media; positive reinforcement of your brand works online just as well as it works with print media. Sooner or later, repeated positive interactions with your brand or product will have a great impact on your business and future marketing plan. Unfortunately, those benefits are not quite as quantifiable as those you get from immediate conversions; not everything can be effectively measured, as much as we'd all like that to be the case.

In the context of social media, marketers often build landing pages on the Web for Facebook advertising and through a custom Facebook tab for when people land on a Facebook page. Here are a few best practices that you should consider when building your landing page:

- Make the call to action clear. Have a single call to action that the user must perform to take the next step.

- Don't let the user get confused. What you want the user to do next should be immediately noticeable and visible to the user without scrolling the page in the browser.

- Use positive images. Positive imagery generally performs better than images of frustrated or angry people.

- Don't overwhelm the user. Too many words or a complicated form will only alienate the user and make him or her abandon the site. Keep it concise.

- Test with friends before launching. Use the 5-second rule to determine how usable and understandable your landing page is. Our favorite tool for this is fivesecondtest: www.fivesecondtest.com.

A few examples we've alluded to earlier in this book are for companies that effectively blend social media with other web properties. In those cases, customers are informed about a marketing program via social media, but the landing page actually resides elsewhere on the Web. Why is this the case? For one, Facebook and Twitter offer limited platforms for a new web presence. Some things are just easier to build on the Web than on a proprietary social network. The Web is also much more accessible than Facebook or Twitter. Companies want to reach as many consumers as possible, even the Luddites who aren't on social networks yet. Finally, if a landing page lives on the Web, a company can point numerous demand generation/advertising approaches to the campaign. This helps the company learn more about who responds best to the marketing offer and how different types of Internet media can be used to reach customers more effectively and inexpensively in the future.

Conduct Tests for Greater Results

Success with landing pages depends a great deal on tweaking your conversion rates using a variety of tactics designed to let data drive your decision making. The great thing about the Web is that sites, buttons, layout, and advertising can be updated or changed quickly, and you can track outcomes based on those changes. The science and process behind optimizing your site based on these changes is known as *A/B* or *multivariate* testing, which we covered in detail in Chapter 6.

To review, A/B testing may sound like a complicated concept. But in reality, the concept is simple. It's used to test the effectiveness of two pieces of creative to see which one results in a better, faster, or more inexpensive response from customers. This isn't particularly difficult when you can change the design of a logo or an e-commerce website and see what the outcomes are with data from your web analytics reports. Contrast this with the physical world. If you owned a storefront, you'd have very little data to rely upon unless you monitored the activity of every customer *and* you found a way to read their minds!

Take, for example, A/B testing for advertising. Your objective is to see which of two ads are more effective than the other. Effectiveness in this case will be measured by total cost, clicks, cost per click, and ultimately lead generation cost (measured as total cost divided by form submissions).

You want to test two ads to see which performs better than the other. These two ads are henceforth known as A and B, and you treat them as subjects to which you have no particular emotional attachment. The different advertising copy points to a single landing page on the Internet—a page that is kept consistent throughout the entire A/B test. It's critically important to isolate a single variable for an A/B test to work properly. Then it's simple: you run the advertising for long enough to know conclusively which ad is superior. The collective response of your "subjects"—that is, customers—will tell the tale, and the results will come in the form of relatively unimpeachable statistics.

Ideally, you'd like to see tens of thousands of impressions over at least a week before drawing any conclusions. If you're running smaller campaigns with far fewer subjects, you may have to come to conclusions with far less data. Although that isn't preferable, it's probably OK in most situations. Just understand that the more you run an A/B test, the more reliable your data will be. And if you're doing some A/B testing, you are better off than someone who is doing no A/B testing at all.

Note: If you have a few different options, feel free to run them all at the same time. Although it's called A/B testing, you can run an A/B/C/D/E all at the same time. Just keep a single outcome variable so you can see whether A, B, C, D, or E wins.

Your Facebook fan page has its own landing page too: existing fans always land on your Wall by default unless you have 10,000 fans or more. In those cases of more popular pages, you can choose to set the default landing tab people see when they arrive at your page. It's an important feature that allows marketers of larger pages to run A/B tests by watching the performance of different landing tabs to see how people convert to fans. Additionally, because custom landing tabs each carry a different URL, you can test the effectiveness of two different tabs by shortening the URLs and using tracking links with a service such as bit.ly. That provides you with the number of clicks per tab (though it won't count traffic coming from any other sources where you're not using the bit.ly links). Then, if you had an opt-in box on each of the tabs, you could conduct a reasonable split test to see which opt-in is more effective. You wouldn't be able to tell which tab (landing page) was most effective in converting fans, though; that test may be best conducted one tab at a time.

Multivariate testing is similar to A/B testing in that you are testing to see which landing page is more effective. The difference is that you are simultaneously testing for a number of variables. This can be any number of things: the placement of your Buy Now link, the text you've included on your site, the design or layout of the site, and so on. You'll need to randomly serve different landing pages at the same time—so a user at a particular point in the day can be served different iterations equally. You just need to maintain randomness, so things such as time of day, geography, or day of week don't impact the data. Remember, you are looking to keep as many things equal or consistent as possible.

We really like using multivariate testing when we first assess what is happening on an existing web property. It is a scattershot approach that helps you quickly test new ideas or theories that people have about improving important customer metrics on your website once they get there. You can try different combinations of text, imagery, icons, and the like to determine the mix that gets the right customer response. Data will often let you know what things don't work. This will narrow down your multivariate testing to the best ideas, which you can then isolate in individual A/B tests where you keep everything else consistent, with the exception of the creative that you are trying to analyze. The advantage you get from this approach is that you move beyond opinion and into facts backed by data.

What all of this implies is that you can spend a lot of time tweaking your web properties to optimize for the outcomes that are important to your business. Some people probably think that is terrible, but others may think this is a great opportunity. It's why we spoke earlier in this chapter about the importance of truly knowing your strategic objectives for your website. What metrics are important to your business? Why do you have a website or social media presence? Every business has a different answer to these questions. You can be the person who aligns your web presence and social media effort with things that truly matter at the executive level.

Addressing Common Marketing Problems

9

You can follow all the advice given in this book and from other sources and still very easily hit road bumps that make it tougher for you to execute your marketing plan. In this chapter, we'll cover a number of the most common ones that we've experienced and been asked about and offer tips, tricks, and considerations that will help you.

Chapter Contents
My Fan Page Won't Grow, and My Fans Can't See My Content
Creating Appropriate Content for International Audiences
Managing Negative Comments and Feedback
Can't Measure, Determine ROI, or Understand Metrics
Reach Business Customers on Facebook
Migrate Fans from One Page to Another
Low Response Rates for Facebook Advertising

My Fan Page Won't Grow, and My Fans Can't See My Content

Probably the most common problem that marketers encounter on Facebook is a stagnant Facebook page that doesn't attract more users and doesn't earn social interactions (likes, comments, Wall posts, @ tags). It's demoralizing—you spend time carefully selecting content that you think people will like, only to get little to no response from users. But what's worse is that you can't show your friends, colleagues, and customers that your page is indeed interesting to other people. You lack social proof and can't get the flywheel to start turning. So, you get no viral marketing benefit, no increased awareness of your product or service, and nothing more than family and friends participating in your community. It's a virtual ghost town!

In almost all cases like this, we counsel people through this thought process:

Think about Who You Are and Your Marketing Plan Step back for a moment and think about your page—not in a panic, but rationally and in the context of the user. People can interact with a lot of different things on Facebook. Remember, you're competing with all manner of apps, games, close friends, acquaintances, the Ticker, chat, and other pages and groups—some of which are simply more interesting or more recognized worldwide.

One client, a local nonprofit, asked us to help with their Facebook strategy back in 2010 because they had a copy of the first edition of this book but were not seeing results about six months in. This client was aghast that they were not growing their Facebook page by leaps and bounds. But it was a relatively new nonprofit that had little to no name recognition. It was a local group whose work had just received its first bit of free publicity, 60 seconds of coverage by the morning show of a local television station that they didn't even post to their Facebook page. This organization had no partnerships with local businesses to help promote the nonprofit or the cause. They were just getting started, but expected that doing basic maintenance on their Facebook page would create a huge marketing success story by itself.

Who you are and the "brand" you've established for yourself definitely contribute to success on Facebook. It's why brands such as Coca-Cola, Ford, and Alicia Keys can establish a huge following doing many of the same things that other people do routinely to maintain and update Facebook Pages. The power of the brand really helps.

A common mistake marketers make when they are immersed in the day-to-day marketing of products that they grow to love is thinking the broader consumer market shares the same passion. But in a market where everyone is a publisher, there is just a ton of content for people to read.

Consider and Reconsider Your Target Market All hope is not lost for the rest of us, however. We just have to play to our strengths. Your organization likely has "brand affinity" among a smaller but just as passionate market. Your favorite Mexican restaurant may have "brand affinity" among salsa lovers because the restaurant makes the best salsa in town. Play to that strength. A local charity may have great "brand affinity" from its volunteers and early supporters. Play to that strength and build a plan there that helps you reach those people in ways that make them want to support and promote you.

Typically this means you need to narrow your focus, not broaden it. Trying to be all things to all people is a really tough way to build loyalty and repeated engagement. If you had to narrow it down (and you probably do if you're reading this chapter), who is your target market? If you had to generalize the characteristics of people most likely to share your perspective, affiliate with your page, and respond to your messaging, what would those characteristics be? Earlier in this book, we discussed the value of *personas*: anthropomorphizing the types of people you want to reach with marketing. This is the place to pull out those personas and ask yourself some tough questions:

- Am I effectively reaching these people? If not, why not?
- Is my content carefully thought out and relevant to my audience?
- Am I posting only during business hours?
- What days and times of day is my target market most likely to be active on Facebook?
- If I am reaching my fans, why aren't they responding?
- Is my content too self-serving?
- Is it interesting to them and their peers?
- How can I reach more of them?
- What would be the ideal experience for them?

Then of course, repeat the same exercise with secondary and tertiary market segments that you think you should reach and those you want to influence.

Perform a Quick Content Audit Oftentimes, poor engagement results from not delivering an interesting experience that is meaningful to your community. If you do things in a way that prioritizes your business processes over customer satisfaction, you'll fail, especially in something like Facebook that requires you to bring people together to share experiences and observations. Yet very often, people launch and operate their pages with first thoughts and considerations given to internal processes and workflows.

Earlier in this book, we recommended that you spend time on a thoughtful and detailed customer segmentation exercise to understand the different types of people who are likely to interact with your page. It isn't an academic exercise but rather a good way to put yourself in the shoes of the very people you expect to interact with your page. This segmentation is the first step to producing a good content audit.

Content is and has been the main driver of interactions in social media: photos, videos, blog posts, articles, and so on. It is what makes people comment, like, share life's happy moments, argue with each other, and so on. All of these things affect Edgerank, which drives visibility on the Facebook News Feed. But if you're missing the mark with a large part of your audience, you won't get the interactions, you'll damage your Edgerank, and you won't get the virtuous cycle "flywheel" working in your favor.

A content audit is necessary to understand a few things. You need to know what you've done, what has succeeded, how you've satisfied different parts of your target market, and ultimately what you need to do to turn the tide. There are several steps to a content audit:

- Look at your most successful posts. In the world of optimized News Feeds, the best content is that which creates the most social interactions. Do you know which pieces of content have earned you the most social interactions? If not, you should. Figure 9.1 is an example of the top-performing content for a page that we've managed for a client. We pulled out the total number of interactions for each piece of content and sorted by the total number of interactions that each earned over a period of time using a polygraph report from Polygraph Media (www.polygraphmedia.com). You can get the information there, or you can get your most recent, most popular content using Facebook Insights—review the Reach, Engaged Users, Talking About This, and Virality percentages for each post. This data can easily be exported to an Excel or CSV file for further analysis to discover your best posts.

	Date	Type	Comments	Likes	Comment Likes	Total Interactions
Mothers increasingly move to goat's milk to help allergic children	10/3/2011	Link	1,410	428	76	1,914
How is everyone doing today?	11/15/2011	Wall Post	331	875	138	1,344
Meet Susan Jones, Supermom	6/17/2010	Photo	209	866	30	1,105
10 Keys for a Healthy Youngster	4/15/2011	Link	371	321	211	903
Should you teach your child Mandarin Chinese?	7/31/2011	Link	510	177	34	721
What do you do to make a healthier Thanksgiving dinner?	11/11/2010	Wall Post	416	31	26	473

Figure 9.1 List of top-performing content

Here, you'll want to pay close attention to the dates of your posts, the types of content (photo, Link, Wall post, video, and so on), and the subject matter of each piece of successful content to understand the things that make people react. Get a good idea of the types of things people respond to. Ideally, you'd have a list of the 20 top-performing pieces of content or more.

Tip: If you want to get super-analytical, get an average of the number of social interactions you earn from each type of content. Then you can see how photos perform relative to links, Wall posts, videos, and community contributions.

- Cross-reference your best posts with your segmentation. Now, take a look at the content through the filter of your top three demographic market segments (for example, females 25–34, males 45–64, males 35–44, or moms, grandmothers, and so on). Are you performing best with the same market segments? Are you appealing well to multiple market segments? Or are you hitting a market segment that you aren't actually trying to reach?

- The best way to do this is to look at these successful posts by going to each one individually. Get a sense of what people are saying and how they are responding to the content and to each other in the community. If you can't learn enough by looking at the comments, click the link for each user and scan their publicly available profile information. Make sure you begin to get a mental model of your community, how/when they respond, and the users who respond. As you scan what has happened, take notes on what you see. Use your observations to craft hypotheses about what you think is happening.

- You may also notice some commonality, as certain individuals may emerge as your "top fans" as well. Oftentimes, the people who comment the most (and the most intelligently) are the top influencers on your page. They're respected voices, if you will. You may want to take extra steps to make them happy and to include them in your social media marketing. Even a direct message just thanking them for their continued support can go a long way to achieving customer loyalty and continued participation.

- Revisit your editorial calendar. If you've followed our suggestions, you probably have the next month of posts planned out in your bright, shiny editorial calendar. Or maybe you just maintain a spreadsheet with the types of content that you are planning to post in the future. Either way, take a look at it now that you know more about the performance of your content. Would you make any changes to the content you are posting or the types of content that you think people will like? Are there any pieces of content that you'd rather not share now?

- A wide variety of major brands optimize their Facebook content for social sharing. It happens all the time in the search engine marketing world, where companies such as Demand Media and others optimize their content for visibility in search engine results. It's no different here on Facebook, in an increasingly popular field known as *social content optimization*. Oddly enough, if you do social content optimization right, you will become that much more visible in search engines as well. For more information, check out David Armano's insightful summary of Edelman's work in this field at `http://darmano.typepad.com/logic_emotion/2011/07/sco.html`.

- Generate demand with Facebook ads. If you've improved your content mix and still do not have the results you need, you can always throw gasoline on it and create a massive fire. Fortunately, Facebook makes this a lot easier now than ever before with its recent changes to Facebook advertising. Pages with problems breaking into the News Feed can promote stories to their own fans by creating what is called a Page Post Ad (Figure 9.2). The Page Post Ad is just what it sounds like—an ad unit that is constructed from one of your page posts. Instead of relying on Edgerank to post your content to the News Feed of your fans, the Page Post Ad places it above the fold, guaranteed, for a small fee. You can select who can see the ad, choosing from anyone, nonfans, current fans, friends of fans, and advanced targeting (users who are or are not connected to a particular page, event, or app of yours).

Figure 9.2 Creating a Page Post Ad

Creating Appropriate Content for International Audiences

As Facebook draws nearer to a billion users, one thing is certain. A vast majority of Facebook users now don't live in your country...no matter where you live. And even if you are marketing a local business, product, or service, your Facebook presence is open to the world of Facebook users. So, no matter what you're marketing, on Facebook it's open for the people of the world to comment on, engage with, interact with, and enjoy.

This is arguably the next step in a broader trend of internationalization, where our world is becoming a smaller place very rapidly. Think about how the exchange of ideas and communication has changed over the past 100 years. In the 20th century, people shared experiences in person, locally, at coffee shops, restaurants, and the like. Geography constrained us because it was difficult to travel long distances. Telecommunications advancements had not yet taken place, and telecommunications infrastructure was not in place for us to communicate casually.

It wasn't long ago—20 years or less—that long-distance phone calls were expensive! I (Chris) remember being in college less than 20 years ago. I was on a budget, so I was really careful when I called my parents, who lived 150 miles away, or my grandparents, who lived only 45 minutes away. Those calls were expensive at 10 to 12 cents per minute. At the same time, Internet access through Prodigy or AOL was metered. It cost money to write email messages! So, the very idea of sharing life's mundane details or perspectives on current affairs was simply out of the question.

But today, we log in with our computers and our cell phones, and we can both read and comment on the news in the new town square, Facebook. Facebook has become the international community where we all come together to share ideas and life's experiences. The only thing that is lost in translation is local language, colloquialisms, and social standards that simply don't translate well on the international stage. Even though we all come together and live on a single planet, we do not share common sensibilities on the comments that are appropriate. Acceptable content for one culture may very well be objectionable to people from another. It isn't a value judgment one way or another; cultural differences are OK. But consider the recent case of the country of India, which is now seeking to ban offensive content from being displayed (http://news.yahoo.com/india-asks-internet-giants-screen-user-content-073908727.html). Cultural sensitivities are a huge that is only getting bigger with every passing day.

How should marketers who attract fans from all around the world attack this problem? Well, to some degree, this is a question of what your target market will find acceptable/unacceptable.

Social media gives you an opportunity to get personal: to attach a deep personality to your brand, product, or service. Think also about what your brand communicates and how. If it were a person, how would it respond to current affairs? Would it comment? Would it have a voice? This isn't feasible with all Facebook marketing efforts, but you may have an opportunity to create a real personality around your product or service.

For example, broadly marketed consumer brands go out of their way to not be terribly objectionable in other forms of media. Governments behave similarly. In these two cases, social media shouldn't be regarded any differently; it is another extension of the brand, so why change the voice? But other organizations—cause-based organizations, those with a specific agenda, or brands that are built around specific types of people—have a lot more opportunity to experiment with their voices.

Think of "Keith Stone," the "spokesman" for Keystone Light, a beer brand marketed primarily in the United States to the budget-conscious consumer. Although Keystone Light is a consumer brand, managers have taken on the brand's irreverent approach with status updates that reinforce the positioning of the brand and the product (see Figure 9.3).

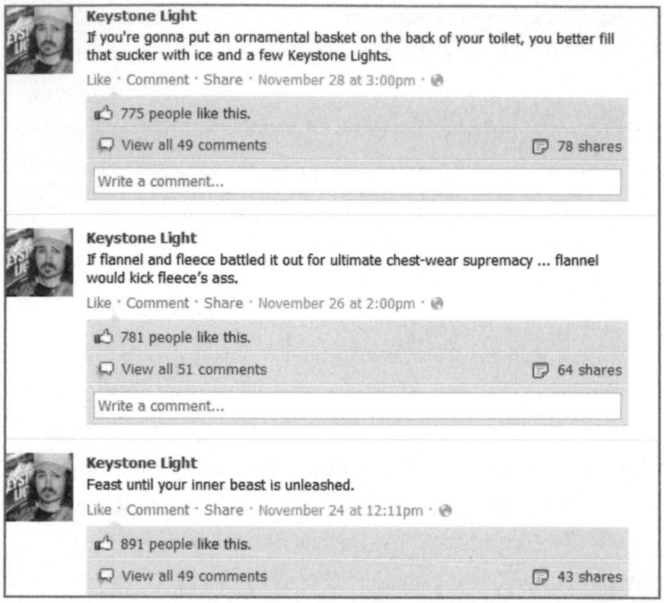

Figure 9.3 Irreverent Keystone Light status updates

But generally speaking, the best way to internationalize your content is to just avoid things that could be insulting or controversial in the first place.

- Avoid local and regional references, jokes, and insults. Instead, consider using things that are universally funny or straightforward.

- Stay out of politics, religion, and contentious current affairs. Passing judgment on other people is typically a great way to alienate part of your customer base.

- Consider posting content that speaks to the universal human condition.

The point here is not to sanitize your page of anything that might be objectionable to some segment of your market. But it is a good idea to avoid alienating your target market or people who can influence decisions that matter most to your organization.

The counterargument is, of course, that there is no such thing as bad publicity. Anything that promotes a brand for free in media can potentially "go viral"—and if it does, is it such a bad thing? You be the judge of that.

As far as reaching your international audience in their language, good news! Facebook does provide a couple of solutions for you that you can use on a post-by-post basis. As you can see in Figure 9.4, before you make any post, you can click the Public button next to Share and select Location/Language.

Then in the pop-up box (shown in Figure 9.5), type in the country or countries (and city/cities as well, if you want) and/or language(s).

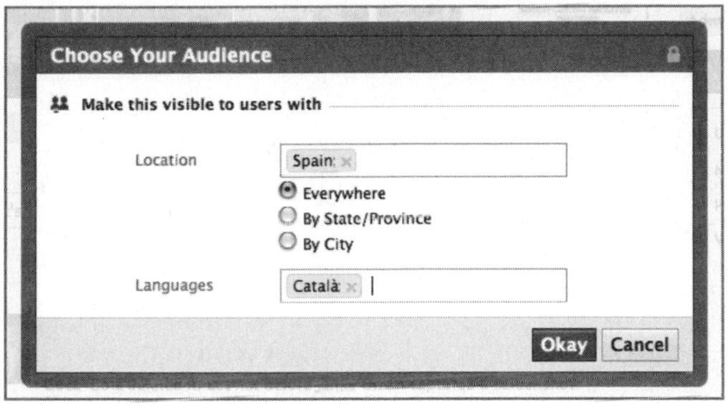

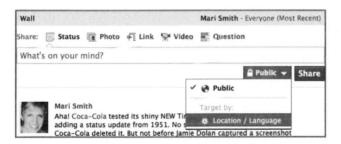

Figure 9.4 Selecting Location/Language

Wall   **Mari Smith** · Everyone (Most Recent)

Share: 📝 **Status**   📷 **Photo**   ✂ **Link**   🎥 **Video**   📋 **Question**

What's on your mind?

🔒 **Public** ▾   **Share**

✓ 🌐 **Public**

Target by:

⚙ **Location / Language**

Mari Smith
Aha! Coca-Cola tested its shiny NEW Ti[...]
adding a status update from 1951. No [...]
Coca-Cola deleted it. But not before Jamie Dolan captured a screenshot

Figure 9.5 Fan page audience selector

Then, when you post the update on your Wall, only the Facebook users in your chosen location or those who have their Facebook set to your chosen language will be able to see your post. This is a terrific feature for managing multiple-language audiences within one fan page. For example, your English-speaking fans don't need to see your Spanish updates, and vice versa. You may need to do some testing with this feature and see how your fans respond. You could have a number of bilingual fans who like the different languages.

Plus, Facebook is slowly rolling out an inline language translation feature for comments, which we think is fantastic. Right now, we're seeing this feature mainly on personal profiles (Timelines), where any comment made in a language other than the language in which you view Facebook has a little "translate" link beside the comment. The on-the-fly comment translation feature is coming to business pages too. Interestingly enough, Bing powers the individual post language translation feature, despite the fact that Facebook has its own internal language translation capabilities.

Probably the bigger issue for people administering pages is managing comments from your own fans, if you've opted to turn on that feature in Facebook (which we highly recommend). It's far easier to control outbound messages from your page than the contributions of others, who are not constrained by the shackles of messaging, brand standards, and decency. That was a joke, of course. Facebook's moderation tools can help with this effort.

There are currently two moderation options built into Facebook for page administrators: keywords and profanity. Keywords allow you to enter individual words or phrases that you'd like to be sent directly to spam on your Wall. You can enter several words or phrases at a time, and Facebook will take care of the rest. On the profanity side, you can choose from No profanity filtering, Medium, and Strong. All of these are simple and lightweight solutions to what can be a hairy problem. If you're interested in more options for monitoring and moderation and real-time updates, investigate offerings from a variety of vendors that provide monitoring and moderation services. A quick Google search will help you investigate the various options and price points available.

Finally, also consider that if you are running Facebook advertising campaigns, you are sensitive to local issues, words/phrases, and vernacular as you try to get people in local markets to respond to your ads. Nothing can quite kill a marketing campaign like being the next Chevy Nova, marketed in Latin America (in Spanish, Nova is pronounced exactly the same as "no va," meaning "it won't run").

How the F*** Marta Kagan Succeeded in Social Media

Marta Kagan both ruffled a lot of feathers and got a ton of attention for her comprehensive "What the f**k is social media?" presentations in 2009-10. You can check them out at www.slideshare.net/mzkagan/what-the-fk-social-media and at www.slideshare.net/mzkagan/what-the-fk-is-social-media-one-year-later. We sat down with her to get her opinions on the best ways to market yourself and get attention, because she clearly got attention.

*Q. You're the creator of the extraordinarily popular "What the f**k is social media?" presentations that have circulated around the Internet, getting millions of page views in the process. Did you hold your breath as you released a presentation with such a controversial name?*

A. Nope. Not for a f**king minute.

Q. What do you think made the presentations so popular?

A. I think it was a combination of good timing and the right blend of steak + sizzle. It was also probably one of the first times that a widely shared "business" presentation dropped F-bombs (repeatedly).

Q. Do you think you would've been as successful if you did not use profanity in the title of your presentation?

A. No.

How the F*** Marta Kagan Succeeded in Social Media *(Continued)*

Q. *How much feedback did you get—both positive and negative—from the presentation?*

A. *Lots.* More positive than negative, but not surprisingly, there were plenty of folks who felt the excessive use of asterisks was offensive.

Q. *What do you think the implications are for marketers? Did you trip across something that marketers can use?*

A. The implications are simple: whatever you do, make it remarkable. Remarkable = "worthy of remark." If your work doesn't elicit an immediate emotional response (positive or negative), go back and try again. My personal "litmus test" for whether or not a new idea is awesome is simple: does this scare the hell out of people? If yes, then we're on the right track.

Q. *How do you view Facebook in the social media marketing mix today? How do you see it evolving?*

A. Facebook is becoming the lowest common denominator of social media, yet the "rules of engagement" are so counterintuitive to most businesses that I think we have a long road ahead.

Managing Negative Comments and Feedback

We all like to believe that customers will have nothing but positive experiences with our companies, but we all know that isn't realistic. People use Facebook, Twitter, and other social media properties to cry out for help all the time when a customer experience is not what it should be. As marketers, we pay attention for good reason. According to Cone Inc.'s 2011 Online Influence Trend Tracker report, 89% of consumers find online channels to be trustworthy sources of product and service reviews. This number was up from 68% in 2010.

I (Chris) am reminded of a trip my wife and I took to Las Vegas in mid-2010 for my sister's wedding. We were on the last flight leaving Las Vegas to return home one evening when our airline abruptly cancelled our flight. There we stood in line at the ticket counter waiting for what seemed like an eternity. One agent at the counter was processing the travel plans (and the fate) of more than 200 passengers, all of whom were displaced by this rather inconvenient change in the itinerary. Disgusted, I turned to my wife and said, "Can you believe they have a single agent handling all of us? It will be an hour after our original flight before they tell us what our plans are for the evening!" Naturally, I turned to social media to vent my frustrations—hitting both the Twitter account for the airline and their Facebook page.

How could you possibly handle the last flight out of Vegas with only a SINGLE agent!!! #airlinefail*
*name of airline withheld

And, of course, friends read the post and chimed in with their own experiences about the airline, stoking a frenzy of negative feedback on my profile and in the global Twitter feed.

Cooler heads eventually prevailed—we were stuck overnight in Las Vegas after all. It could have been a lot worse. But the damage was done from a social marketing perspective. Tens of thousands of people may have been exposed to my frustration.

Dealing with negative feedback is probably the most misunderstood problem that marketers encounter on Facebook. If you're running something like an airline, then delays, flight cancellations, and weather impacts are an inevitability—a natural course of action that just happens every now and then. Sadly, people get caught in the crosshairs. People going to important business meetings, visiting family for the holidays, and attending weddings and funerals are those most likely to panic in the event of a travel disruption. With social media, impassioned, negative feedback is an occupational hazard. It's the tricky side of the social media "revolution"—how do you deal with it?

There are generally two drastically different schools of thought about dealing with negative feedback. One school of thought says that you should eliminate whatever bad feedback you get by deleting comments that people make if you can do it, which you can on Facebook Pages where you have allowed people to write Wall posts. That said, it's a highly frowned-upon practice to forcibly remove legitimate feedback from your social media properties. Check out the Word of Mouth Marketing Association's ethics page at http://womma.org/ethics/ for more information.

The other approach is to deal with negative feedback directly and to not shy away from it. Listen to what people have to say and address their concerns publicly so other people can see your response—and see that you are listening. It's better to attach your spin or your voice to negative feedback for a few reasons. First, there may have been some misunderstanding by the customer that needs to be addressed, not only for the complainer but for other people who may have a similar experience. Second, it can be an opportunity to build more confidence in other people who may be interested in your product or service. Responding to customer feedback is a sign that you are indeed paying attention and always striving to provide better service. Finally, the complaining customer may just be unreasonable, and you might have to address the problem directly. It's uncomfortable but sometimes necessary.

Just because someone provides negative feedback to your company on social media doesn't mean you have to ignore it. You can use this as an opportunity to react to what your customers are saying, and you can turn it into a positive. Whatever you choose, it should match the voice of your brand and should be compatible with your workflows and customer expectations.

Can't Measure, Determine ROI, or Understand Metrics

The funny thing about all the time, effort, and money we've spent on social media marketing is that it seems at times that we're no closer to understanding how it affects the top and bottom lines. Whether you have a team, an individual manager, or a consultant, it's hard to tell whether the dollars you spend in direct costs, salaries, benefits, monthly retainers, fees, and other expenses are worth it.

Conceptually, we think a vast majority of us understand and acknowledge two things about social media marketing. One, there are enough people interacting on different social media properties to suggest that it is a worthwhile endeavor to participate at some level. Secondarily, marketing is and always has been one part art and one part an inexact science. Only with the last decade of innovations in click-through marketing have we been able to put a fixed cost on actions taken on the Internet, because we now can calculate cost per click and cost per conversion if we set up to do it. As such, pressures have been put on marketers all around the world to justify campaigns and activities and to gather meaningful metrics from marketing.

But let's step back for a moment and think about the analog world. Let's use a hypothetical situation and assume that you work in marketing for a multinational company that is deciding whether or not it should participate in an important industry trade show. You have to put together materials for a booth—displays, eye candy for a table, product information, brochures, demos, and so on. You have to decide which level of sponsorship you would like for the event. A colleague has suggested that you use some of the budget to hire a well-known but B-list comedian to roam the halls and promote your business. How do you spend your money? And at the event, are you planning to track each individual action to understand the return you are getting from each individual brochure, white paper, and minute that the comedian is helping to market your business?

The fact is that you aren't going to measure the effectiveness of your marketing spend at a molecular level. It wouldn't be practical to demand ROI metrics on every piece of marketing collateral you or your team produced. Even if you could measure it, would you spend time obsessing over the return on those individual investments? In a practical sense, successful marketing at events is generally measured at a much higher level—from "we had a very successful event!" in the least demanding organizations to "we collected 187 business cards and have 72 warm leads as a result of our participation" in more metrics-oriented organizations.

As much as chief marketing officers would like to know return on investment for all marketing activities, most know that marketing is far more inexact than that. There is simply too much to account for that can't be explained, and people make purchasing decisions using a wide range of considerations—of which marketing is just one. Take, for example, the Snickers candy bar a friend of ours bought the other day. We asked him, "What made you buy that Snickers bar?" He said, "I don't know. I just needed something to satisfy my hunger." For those of you who are not aware, Snickers has run the "Snickers satisfies you" campaign now for several years. The integrated marketing campaign probably had something to do with his purchase. But what specific marketing activity should be credited with return on that investment? It's impossible to say.

For larger companies, social media is critical as part of an integrated marketing campaign. CMOs are demanding metrics on success, but not necessarily for purposes of understanding return on investment. CMOs want to understand costs and outcomes. But most understand that holding individual activities to specific return on investment metrics is too demanding and too low-level for its marketing managers to focus on. Rather, marketing managers are encouraged to scale programs in a cost-effective manner that engages fans and encourages them, oftentimes worldwide. Metrics are also used as a way for the entire team to keep a scorecard—to ensure that the team works toward a meaningful goal and to make sure that people responsible are keeping tabs on things that are taking place.

In all the conversations that we have had with marketing executives in bigger companies, that's been the recurring theme in social media. Most people want to establish meaningful metrics that can be captured—both a snapshot of where things are at the moment and a time-trending look at how actions are improving key performance indicators.

Only in the most "transactional" businesses—where money is spent not for branding, awareness, or to spread a message but rather to make the cash register ring—do marketers focus specifically on incremental revenue, profits, and purchases.

So, to summarize, in general you need to get regular reports on *something* that your organization believes to be meaningful. ROI is the buzzword that everyone speaks of, but most organizations are far from being able to determine their social ROI. A vast majority need to start with a less ambitious goal—to effectively measure *something* on a regular basis to align everyone around the same goals. That something can be looking at fan/follower count over time, the number of comments or social engagements that you earn every month, traffic to your Facebook Pages, and so on. The same report, in charts and graphs, and delivered at regular intervals, can tell you how you are improving to hit those goals. You need consistency in the data that you can gather and your commitment to gathering it in a regular cadence. And you need to make sure that the people working for you commit to this so they don't sabotage you, because it unfortunately does happen. Pick out meaningful metrics for your organization, get everyone on the same page on how success will be measured, and commit to keeping tabs on what is happening.

For more details on the exact metrics you should use, please refer to Chapter 8, "The Analytics of Facebook."

Plus, for an excellent social media ROI framework, refer to our friend Jeremiah Owyang's "pyramid," where he describes the need to report three different sets of metrics to three different sets of staff: www.web-strategist.com/blog/2010/12/13/framework-the-social-media-roi-pyramid/.

Reach Business Customers on Facebook

Reaching businesspeople on Facebook is one of the most misunderstood parts of social media marketing today. Conventional wisdom is that you can't effectively conduct business-to-business marketing on Facebook. We can't tell you how many times we've heard people say, "You can't reach business audiences on Facebook. They're on LinkedIn, right? That's the place for businesspeople!"

But the numbers are telling a different story. Reed, a U.K. jobs website at www.reed.co.uk, commissioned a study in June 2011 called "Social Networking at Work" to get the answers. In that study, it was revealed that no less than 33% of employees use social media at the office. Almost half of them access Facebook during that time. More stunning is that an estimated 65% of people are alternatively accessing social networks from their mobile devices while at work. The highest concentration of social media users were in the marketing and information technology fields. Palo Alto Networks released data on its customers' social networking traffic in late 2010 and stated that Facebook was responsible for a whopping 80% of all social media traffic on its corporate customers' networks worldwide. When you consider that LinkedIn (at the time this chapter was written) has less than 20% of Facebook's audience worldwide, it's arguable that there is a larger corporate audience on Facebook currently than on LinkedIn.

This has not gone unnoticed in corporate IT departments around the world. Palo Alto Networks also claims that one-third are already blocking social media sites at the corporate firewall. And Panda Security's Social Media Risk Index study claimed that a similar number of small and medium businesses blocked social media sites. Who knew our employers wanted us to work and not hang out all day with friends on Facebook?

Note: Facebook is so addictive that a product has been created to help workers appear to be working when they are actually on their favorite social media site. Excelbook takes content from Facebook and displays it in a Microsoft Excel document so passersby won't see you browsing on Facebook. For more information, check out www.addictivetips.com/windows-tips/secretly-use-facebook-at-work-by-disguising-it-as-an-excel-sheet/. And for other tips on not getting caught using Facebook at work, this article from AllFacebook can help as well: www.allfacebook.com/how-to-use-facebook-at-work-without-being-caught-2011-08.

But remember, the opportunity is not just about reaching businesspeople while they are at work. People spend anywhere from 7 to 12 hours a day at their offices. The same businesspeople you're trying to reach are using Facebook at least half their time outside the office: at home and coffee shops and via their mobile devices and tablets. So while the Facebook experience is ostensibly a consumer experience, it doesn't matter. A large number of Facebook users are one-half consumer, one-half business decision maker. In fact, we often like to say that the acronyms B2C and B2B can be replaced with people to people (P2P). So, B2B messaging is entirely appropriate for Facebook, and in our opinion it's a very much underutilized tactic that many marketers unfortunately ignore.

Seven Keys to Successful B2B Marketing on Facebook

What are the keys to successfully marketing business products or services on Facebook to reach businesspeople specifically? Here are a few best practices that we've seen from the best B2B companies on Facebook:

1. Remember that B2B marketing on Facebook isn't the same as consumer marketing on Facebook. A key rule here is this: don't be something that you are not. Consumer brands look to entertain to earn social engagement from their audiences. Entertainment is of value to some business customers, but more often than not, the B2B customer is much more interested in getting things done, being more productive, and, quite frankly, using products and services to make it easier to get away from work altogether. Some consumer marketing principles are certainly in order to keep the content lighthearted, but remember the motivations of your B2B customer, and make your Facebook campaign—content, creativity, and engagement—appropriate for your audience.

2. "Like" complementary products, services, and publications. Odds are that your partners, your customers, and complementary products and services are on Facebook trying to do the same things you are doing. In the spirit of "coopetition," find such pages and "like" them from your page. (To do so, click the small down arrow next to Home in the top right navigation bar, and then select "Use Facebook as:" and choose your fan page.) When in "page mode" like this, you can also join conversations and strive to be valuable to everyone who reads it. Ideally, when posting and commenting as your page on other pages, we recommend always signing with your first name to humanize your business. Also, try to be useful, personal, and friendly. In so doing, you'll create great visibility for your own fan page, and others can easily like your pages using the "hovercard" (hover over any hyperlinked fan page name and the Like button is right there). This gives you more exposure to the very people you'd like to approach somewhere in the sales cycle.

3. Don't be too sales-y. There's a fine line between over-promoting yourself and doing it just enough not to annoy people. Ideally, your products, services, and the press will do the talking for you—so you can point to third parties who have had successes and who can vouch for you. If you say too much about yourself, your efforts might just backfire. Be careful.

4. Promote your people. Many successful brands are using Facebook as a means to give customers and other interested parties a "behind-the-scenes" look at the business and the people who work on it every day. Find people in your organization that make things work and promote them. Something as simple as sharing pictures of staff members or having one of your team host a live Q&A chat on your Wall can really help boost morale internally and externally with your fans. First, this practice can help with any content problems you may have, especially when you are having trouble filling your editorial calendar. Second, it can be genuinely entertaining and compelling content for someone to read: a break from more serious news like current affairs or industry developments. Third, it's more personable. Rather than posting as a brand, you can use this as a reminder to your customers that your business is comprised of people like them with the same joys, concerns, and feelings about life. An occasional picture of a team member celebrating a landmark birthday, a pregnant mom, a pet, or a new baby is a great reminder of the humanity we all share, irrespective of whatever we're marketing. Finally, it will give your employees a reason to promote your business themselves, albeit indirectly, by having them talk about themselves and share content about themselves that is published on Facebook. Don't underestimate the power of vanity!

5. Take a "quality over quantity" approach to managing the Facebook page, both in who your fans are and in the content that they're sharing. Remember that in business-to-business marketing, a single and verifiable customer is generally worth a lot more than, say, a business-to-consumer customer that may provide a few transactions worth $100 or less over the course of a year. So, if you have only a few hundred people on the page but they're all customers, then it is a pretty big success for most B2B marketing situations. Targeting is key here. Think of it differently: if your numbers are good but you aren't reaching prospective customers, is it worth it? Or will you just make people more skeptical about the value of your work in the long run when it doesn't amount to much?

6. Keep the conversation professional. Earlier in this book, we shared a number of tips for using content to engage with audiences. Certain types of content are likely to create passionate responses that might make the conversation take an unfortunate and unprofessional turn. In most business-to-business marketing scenarios, you'll want to keep the conversation above board. That might take

some work in your content strategy, in how you watch the page, and in the commenting options that you choose to make available to users.

7. Utilize Facebook ads to directly target your audience. Many people, especially those in larger companies, join "workplace" networks in order to have more access to other people who work at the same company. You can target specific workplaces in Facebook advertising, which is a huge benefit to people targeting individual big companies. This type of targeting is not quite as precise as, say, LinkedIn ads targeting, which allows you to target people known to be working at specific places. But it is a lot cheaper on a cost-per-impression basis and a little cheaper on a cost-per-click basis. Use this to your advantage, and if you'd like, compare numbers across the two social networks. As it stands today, you'll get a lot more bang for your buck using targeted Facebook ads.

Migrate Fans from One Page to Another

Sometimes, for whatever reason, you may have to ask your loyal fans to get up *en masse* and move to a new destination, such as getting fans to move from one page to another or moving people from one social network to another. It is most typical of bigger companies to, as a course of business, generally give business groups or units a significant amount of autonomy to do whatever they need to do to promote their business. The pattern is always the same. A business group creates a page with a great vanity URL, only for people in another business unit or a central authority to later realize its value. So, a transfer is ultimately necessary, although not even remotely ideal. Why? We've never heard it put more succinctly than this:

> You do not "move" audiences.
>
> Keith Olbermann, reflecting on his 1993 move from ESPN to ESPN2
> in Those Guys Have All the Fun: Inside the World of ESPN by James
> Andrew Miller and Tom Shales

Migrating audiences in any form of media is probably one of the most difficult things you can do. First, people are creatures of habit. Take, for example, your favorite websites or blogs. Start naming a few of them and keep going until you can't think of any more. If you're like the rest of us, you can probably only think of maybe 10 to 12 destinations before you start to have to think about it more. With the deluge of information that we've all experienced during the social media revolution, our brains can remember only a few things. So, if you move an audience on TV, the Internet, social media, and so on, you'd better do it in a way that makes people not have to think about what you've asked them to do. Second, no matter what you do, some percentage of people just simply won't do what you need them to do. They join your page or Twitter account and often don't think twice about it afterward. You're just a sentient part of their stream that contributes alongside everyone else. If you're gone all of a sudden, are they really going to both remember and go to the property that you've asked them to use instead? In most cases, no. Asking audiences to move is on par with starting over and rebuilding your assets from square one.

So, in the short term, and possibly longer, your numbers will suffer. It might be worth the trade-off in the end, but if you're going to migrate your audience, you need to be prepared for the worst. Major brands such as Microsoft, Clorox, and others have attempted to migrate fan page audiences and have seen only 25–35% move from the original page to the new page.

The number one golden rule of migrating fans from one page to another is this: don't do it.

Moving Forward with the Migration

If you've decided that you have to move fans to another page, here are a few other tips to make the transition as easy as possible:

Involve the Community Right or wrong, people who participate in online communities gain a sense of ownership of them. In our minds, it's good because you want people to be invested in things related to your product or service. As such, it makes sense to tell the community about your plans. Explain why. Get feedback, even if you don't intend to change your opinion. Treat your fans with respect, maybe even more than they deserve. They'll be a lot more likely to listen to you.

Communicate Early and Often Unfortunately, you're going to have to repeat the call to action to get people to move for a few reasons. Edgerank will not prioritize your content for all your fans—that's a fact. In addition, your fans aren't necessarily logging in every day. Although more than half do so, a large percentage do not. Facebook does not currently make this easier by allowing you to designate to certain Wall posts, persist or be "sticky" at the top of your Wall. So, you'll have to repeat yourself maybe a little more than you and your top fans are comfortable with just to make sure everyone sees your message. You might also consider including the CTA on your page image because that's always seen at the top of your page by visitors and fans.

Populate the New Page with Content before Launch It probably goes without saying, but most users wouldn't respond well if you requested that they move to another page only for them to see absolutely nothing there. So, before you launch your new page or even announce its existence, populate it with content as if it were live. What's the bar you need to hit? Two weeks or more of daily posts, a populated About section, and a half dozen photos would do the trick. Be sure to hit Facebook's minimum of 25 fans so you can secure a good vanity URL that is easy for people to remember. And if you want to get fancy, include a custom landing tab for your page that helps people make the transition when they arrive. Make sure that when people arrive, it's warm, it's inviting, and the call to action is conveniently communicated (Figure 9.6).

Figure 9.6 Landing tab for Fanta soft drinks

Supplement the Announcement with a Promotion Nothing motivates people like a good promotion. Contests, sweepstakes, and giveaways with the condition that people "like" your page are a good way to get people to respond. Then, of course, you must promote the winners with a Wall post picture when the contest has ended! (Just be sure to adhere to Facebook's promotion guidelines: www.facebook.com/promotions_guidelines.php.) See also Chapter 5, "Month 2: Establish Your Corporate Presence with Pages."

Make Your Users Vote Involve the community by making your fans vote with "likes" for decisions that you make about your page. This can help you in multiple ways. For one, "likes" improve your Edgerank. But perhaps more importantly, voting gives people a vested interest in things that take place on the new page and also gives them a reason to return or think positively of your product or service.

Remind Them Forcibly with Facebook Advertising Remember in Chapter 6, "Month 3: Create Demand with Facebook Advertising," when we discussed augmenting Facebook's Edgerank with Page Post Ads that would promote your content to users using paid advertising placements? This is a great way to hit people you can't reach, even though they like your page. This is a tactic you'll have to pull out for your less enthusiastic fans, but hey—a fan is a fan, and we all want to convert as many as we can to the new page, right?

Converting Places and Profiles to Pages and Combining Them

You might have the nasty situation of trying to combine multiple assets into a single one. Sometimes businesses start as profiles and may have a place or a page as well. It becomes untenable to actually maintain multiple assets on Facebook at the same time, and so it is decided that these things should be combined to reduce confusion for users, friends, and fans. Unfortunately, as much as this makes perfect sense, it isn't terribly straightforward either.

The best answer currently is to move to a page and announce the retirement of the other assets 90 days in advance. Then, perform the exit plan that we suggested earlier, but don't run ads targeted at people on your profile, because you can't target profile friends in Facebook advertising. Facebook has made a long-term commitment to the page as the primary means for organizations to use the platform. So, just run with it.

A more straightforward process is involved in converting personal profiles to pages. Simply go to https://www.facebook.com/pages/create.php?migrate to turn a Facebook profile into a Facebook page.

If you have a Facebook business page and a Facebook Place page with identical street/mailing addresses, we recommend you go ahead and merge these two pages. The page with the least "likes" will be merged into the page with the most likes. Go to your Edit Page admin dashboard and look under Resources for the Merge option. If needed, refer to Facebook Help for further support on this process. Go to http://facebook.com/help and type in merge to find the right section.

Low Response Rates for Facebook Advertising

An occasional complaint from people who run Facebook advertising campaigns is that they don't quite get the response that advertisers want in certain situations. Many people approach Facebook ads as a great alternative to other types of advertising because the cost of impression (CPM) is so comparatively low while the targeting options are so comparatively rich. It only stands to reason that if you can target people better—geographically, by interests, by age/gender, and so on—you'll get both cheaper rates *and* better performance.

Oh, if it were only that simple.

The term *performance* means different things to different people. Some advertisers are happy with clicks. Others want people to convert to fans upon clicking an ad. Others are even more demanding and want people to convert to email subscribers, leads, or even purchases. And then others are not looking at absolute costs but rather how this particular type of advertising compares to others, such as traditional advertising, print advertising, direct mail, search engine advertising, or other lead generation programs that do not have a paid demand generation component. So, it's critical to first know what the expectations are of the performance of your ad campaign; ideally you'd know this before you start your ad campaign. But the concept of performance varies from person to person, and you may not even have agreement within your organization as to what that is.

A wide range of criteria determine whether something as relatively inexpensive as Facebook advertising actually performs well for you:

- Who you're targeting and what you're offering in your advertising. If there is a mismatch between your targeting criteria and your offer, you can't possibly succeed. Maybe your ad performance is telling you that a particular target market is not appropriate for your offer.

- "Catchiness" of your image. Does your imagery grab a user's attention aggressively?

- Title. Is the title of your ad working well to make people want to learn more?

- Quality of your ad copy. Does the ad copy adequately explain your offer and entice users to seek more information?

- Type of ad unit. CPC ad units get a higher click-through (CTR) rate because they are placed more consistently "above the fold". In Figure 9.7, notice the ad unit at the bottom right of the screen. It is "above the fold" because it is visible on the screen without requiring the user to scroll to view it. For this figure, two other advertisements sat below the screen. This is the biggest problem for impression-based Facebook ads: many are displayed on the screen but never actually viewed by Facebook users.

Figure 9.7 Ad unit above the fold

A/B testing and multivariate testing are critical to assessing how individual differences in your ad campaigns contribute to or detract from performance. Similarly, you have to construct your campaigns properly to isolate individual variables that affect advertising performance. For more information on campaigns, A/B testing, and multivariate testing, please refer to Chapter 6.

If you're not getting the bang for your buck that you expected, it may be a good time to change your approach. We've seen some cost per click (CPC) advertisers have more success with cost per impression (CPM) advertising, and vice versa. Click-through rates in the United States for CPM ads typically range from 0.007 to 0.015% although there is significant variation by industry, advertiser, and call to action. Advertisers can expect to get clicks for $1.50 on average in CPM campaigns. With CPC campaigns, you can get closer to $1 clicks in many cases, but with a much higher CTR. That means your ad was very efficient at getting clicks, but you won't get as many impressions for your money.

If you're outside of these ranges, you may want to reconsider what you're doing. But be forewarned, poorly targeted ads or ones that are not promoting a compelling offer can do much worse. Put yourself in the shoes of the reader, and be honest with yourself. If you were in the target market, would you find this particular ad compelling? If you can honestly answer yes, tweaks may get you where you need to be. If not, major changes may be in order. Whatever you do, don't be afraid to be nimble. And, be sure to reread Chapter 6 all about Facebook ads!

Unique Facebook Marketing Scenarios

We've spent a vast majority of this book focusing on the concepts behind effective Facebook marketing. Create a page, maintain it with great content of interest to your fans, measure your outcomes, create custom Facebook experiences if the basics don't work for you, and use advertising to hit the accelerator on your efforts if it is warranted. All the while, establish a good workflow for getting the job done. But certain kinds of organizations have particular concerns and unique situations that must be considered when using Facebook for marketing. We'll now turn our attention to specific, proven marketing tactics that work in organizations that you wouldn't typically expect to use Facebook for marketing purposes.

Businesses Appealing to Tourists

In the summer of 2011, my family and I (Chris) took a weeklong beach vacation to Orange Beach, Alabama. It's not a widely known fact outside of the South, but Alabama has miles of great beaches and is a tourist destination for much of the year. Even though the condominium we rented had a full kitchen, several nights we instead decided to enjoy the conveniences of a local restaurant. Much to our surprise, it was tougher to make an informed decision than we expected. We weren't exactly on vacation with "foodies," but we did want to enjoy a good local dining experience instead of the standard chain restaurant that we could get back home.

As in any resort area, all the tried-and-true marketing approaches had been used by many of the various local restaurants. There were flyers downstairs in stacks in the main lobby of our condo. Several had even gone to great lengths to produce four-color brochures for their restaurants—quite a costly endeavor but probably necessary for inclusion in the rack of flyers for tourist traps, entertainment venues, and swamp tours. I asked the concierge at the condominium if she could suggest a few places for us to consider. She rattled off a few of the most popular places in Orange Beach. But as I walked away with a handful of menus, flyers, and her suggestions, I couldn't help but think that we would do better by looking online for reviews and customer comments about some of these places. And maybe I could find other places that would suit the varied interests of our relatively large party.

So, I opened my laptop and started searching. First, I hit Google to see whether there were any websites that highlighted the various restaurants of the area. I didn't have a lot of luck, although I emerged with another handful of restaurants to consider. I asked people in our group what they wanted to eat and then narrowed my choices to find the best seafood restaurant I could. Naturally, I then decided to research each of them. I hit Yelp and Google Reviews to get an idea of what fellow tourists were saying about the various choices. I ran a few more detailed searches on Google to see what local bloggers had to say about each place. I looked at the menus of each establishment that posted them online to get an idea of their offerings and the cost. And finally, I went to Facebook to see whether they had any dialogue with customers and to see whether I could perhaps find a coupon or learn about their daily specials.

After all my research, we settled on the Shrimp Shack—a small but very comfortable restaurant a few miles from our condominium (Figure 10.1). In the course of my research, I also found a popular local chain called Wintzell's Oyster House that had been featured on the Food Network. We ate a meal later in the week there. All told, we were all very satisfied with the meals we had at both places.

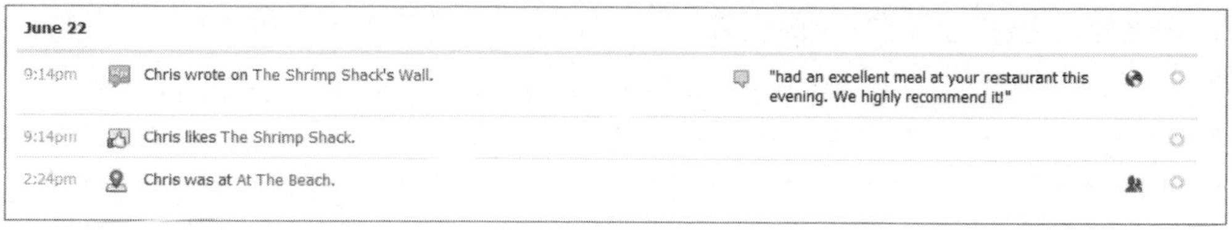

June 22				
9:14pm	Chris wrote on The Shrimp Shack's Wall.	"had an excellent meal at your restaurant this evening. We highly recommend it!"		
9:14pm	Chris likes The Shrimp Shack.			
2:24pm	Chris was at At The Beach.			

Figure 10.1 The Shrimp Shack

Now you can certainly argue that I spent way too much time and energy looking up details on the local restaurants. I am, after all, a veteran of all things Internet and social media, and I have come to trust the "wisdom of the crowd" to aid with occasional everyday decision making. But consider this about your marketing efforts and the various segments of your market—people will find you in ways that is most comfortable to them. Some of your audience will make decisions on a snap judgment, almost capriciously. Others will do significant research to make a decision that is as seemingly minor as picking a restaurant. Personally, I am going to spend a ton of time researching a seafood restaurant only because the implications of a bad decision are so terrible—from having an unsatisfying, expensive meal to food poisoning. And I took a lot more time making the decision because we traveled with a party of eight. One bad decision would negatively impact the vacation experience of many.

But this experience highlights the difficulties and opportunities for seasonal businesses like those in beach towns that have to effectively market to people who may visit, at most, one to two times per year. Location and reputation are always going to be huge for businesses operating in a popular tourist community. But how can you effectively market your business so people are aware of you—either before they arrive or while they're visiting and making decisions? And how can you do it repeatedly so that every week you continue to appeal to a new group of tourists visiting your area? The challenge, of course, is that you're in a unique marketing situation that requires you to convince people to choose you over the hundreds of different things they can choose to do in a resort area.

Research is the first step. Most major tourist areas will release statistics on who is visiting, such as the 2010–2011 Visitor Profile released by the Alabama Gulf Coast Convention & Visitors Bureau (www.gulfshores.com/stats/GSANNL11.pdf). Figure 10.2 is a summary of the tourists, where they are from, and what they're spending on local accommodations. This rich, detailed report has some other great nuggets of information, including how people get information about local businesses before and upon arrival, which attractions they've visited, how they've spent their money, and activities they enjoyed during their visit. Find a report like this for your area and analyze it to understand the following questions:

- Where are my customers visiting from?

- What do they typically spend?

- How do they find information on local attractions, restaurants, and tourist activities?

- What do they like about the area? What do they dislike?

2010 – 2011 Visitor Profile and Occupancy Statistics — Alabama Gulf Coast Convention and Visitors Bureau				
Regional Distribution of Visitors	Fall 2010	Winter 2010	Spring 2011	Summer 2011
Alabama	44.6%	39.4%	37.2%	35.5%
Southeast	39.7	25.9	41.0	46.1
Northeast	0.7	2.0	0.5	0.6
Midwest	8.6	27.5	14.1	8.8
Southwest	4.2	2.7	5.6	7.8
Markets of Opportunity	2.2	2.5	1.6	1.2
Total	100.0%	100.0%	100.0%	100.0%

Economic Impact Estimates	Fall 2010	Winter 2010	Spring 2011	Summer 2011
Occupancy Condominium Market	33.7%	16.4%	47.3%	69.2%
Occupancy Hotel/Motel Market	51.6%	28.5%	64.8%	78.6%
ADR Condominium Market	$100.96	$67.04	$146.79	$228.97
ADR Hotel/Motel Market	$116.11	$80.47	$128.17	$138.64

Top U.S. Feeder Markets (By Season)			
Fall 2010		Winter 2010	
Core Origin Markets		Core Origin Markets	
1. Birmingham	23.1%	1. Birmingham	19.1%
2. Huntsville/Decatur	7.7	2. Mobile/Pensacola	7.5
3. New Orleans	5.0	3. Huntsville/Decatur	5.4
4. Nashville	4.7	4. Montgomery/Selma	4.1
5. Mobile/Pensacola	4.5	5. New Orleans	3.6
6. Atlanta	3.7	6. Atlanta	3.3
7. Montgomery/Selma	3.5	7. Nashville	3.1
8. Baton Rouge	3.2	8. Jackson, MS	2.7
9. Jackson, MS	3.0	9. Baton Rouge	2.6
10. Memphis	2.5	10. Chattanooga	2.2
Total	60.9%	Total	53.6%

Top U.S. Feeder Markets (By Season)			
Spring 2011		Summer 2011	
Core Origin Markets		Core Origin Markets	
1. Birmingham	18.1%	1. Birmingham	19.8%
2. Mobile/Pensacola	6.8	2. New Orleans	6.6
3. Huntsville/Decatur	5.3	3. Huntsville/Decatur	6.4
4. New Orleans	5.2	4. Nashville	5.2
5. Montgomery/Selma	4.7	5. Mobile	4.3
6. Atlanta	4.4	6. Memphis	4.0
7. Nashville	4.2	7. Montgomery	3.7
8. Baton Rouge	3.8	8. Baton Rouge	3.7
9. Jackson, MS	3.0	9. Jackson, MS	2.9
10. Columbus/Tupelo	2.4	10. Atlanta	2.8
		11. Lafayette, LA	2.8
Total	57.9%	Total	62.2%

	Fall '10 (Sept. – Oct.)	Winter '10 (Nov. – Feb.)
Number of Visitors	278,000	241,900

Spring '11 (Mar. – May)	Summer '11 (Jun. – Aug.)	Annual '10 – '11
275,900	593,600	1,389,400

Figure 10.2 Alabama Visitors Bureau statistics

Traditionally, this type of data has helped businesses perform offline marketing and has given marketers a broad understanding of tourists. But increasingly, we see local businesses using this information to accentuate online marketing efforts. For example, over the past several decades this data might have helped businesses better understand where they should put flyers. But now, astute marketers are using this information to better highlight the local business through social media. They're "liking" the pages of complementary attractions and posting/reposting content that highlights them. They're encouraging Yelp and Google Local reviews in exchange for discounts. They're using video cameras to capture the experience of attractions they visit and posting them to YouTube. They're posting pictures to Facebook and publishing menus there along with details about attire, hours of operation, contact information, and directions. Some are even running Facebook ads to nudge customers into a visit or into printing a coupon.

In these situations that require marketers to reach visiting customers, loyalty really takes a backseat to visibility. Local tourist businesses must make sure that marketing campaigns are comprehensive enough that tourists can't help but find them. Top performers do this by doing three things: optimizing search engine visibility, aggressively maintaining social media properties, and running local demand generation campaigns to reach people while they are in town. Advertising can be the "shot in the arm" your business needs to make the never-ending stream of tourists aware of what you have to offer. Make sure all your bases are covered and maintained, and you'll maximize your ability to reach people regardless of how they want to find you.

Religious Organizations

Local churches, synagogues, and other religious organizations are the "bedrock" of many communities all around the world. For many years, they've offered their communities a wide range of "life to death" services—from child care to education, weekly services, social ministries, and ultimately care for the sick and dying. As such, they're serving a demographic audience that really has only two things in common: locality and faith. People young and old from a wide range of backgrounds and with significantly different interests come together to celebrate their religion and in some respects their cultural commonality.

Churches with a younger audience tend to dominate in most local markets for a few reasons. Congregations appealing to younger people tend to have more younger people in leadership positions. So, it's easier to rationalize social media as an important part of the church's outreach to the broader community. Congregations serving an older demographic group are typically slower to adopt Facebook and other social media outlets because many of the administrators and leaders are just now understanding why they and perhaps the church should participate. Additionally, the adoption rate among younger demographic groups is very high relative to older ones. So, social media can be a good way to not just communicate what is happening at the church but to also attract new, younger members to the congregation. Astute churches recognize that social media is an effective marketing vehicle that can embrace younger audiences, which is vital to the continuing growth of the community.

The biggest issue that many churches encounter with Facebook and social media marketing is the additional work involved in maintaining it properly. From a purely mechanical standpoint, you don't want to "overpost," lest you annoy the congregation. You will need to keep the content fun, interesting, and relative to people in the community as you would need to do for any other Facebook page.

But then there are practical realities that make the commitment more complicated. People running various events, ministries, and volunteer groups will want to promote their activities, but with everything going on, you may not have enough opportunities to talk about everything that is happening. The page should not be simply a means to remind people of important events, but it could easily become that if you aren't careful.

Should the page be a place where anyone can post or comment to the Wall? There are certainly positives and negatives associated with opening up contributions from individuals, but some of those may have inappropriate content or profanity. Moderation becomes a big issue for any page that allows people to contribute or communicate among themselves.

Successful churches are also prescriptive about the types of content different people are allowed to post. The church that I (Chris) belong tochurch had a particular concern about doctrine; our pastor and a few of the priests were the only people allowed to comment on church teachings. Getting the pastor's time for posting content, responding to people, and reviewing other staffers' contributions was and remains a big and somewhat complicated barrier to adoption. If you're involved in some way in establishing a social media presence for your church, follow these steps to get off on the right foot:

Identify a Leader/Editor Put a single person in charge, with oversight from a committee so they have checks and balances in the editorial function. Be sure to give the editor enough day-to-day responsibility to do their job, however. The committee is not in place to scrutinize but rather to help think through difficult problems and gray areas.

Establish an Approval Process for Content Make sure there is a clearly communicated process for posting content (review and approval) before it goes live. Give people enough time to submit content, but don't require so much time that special urgent issues can't be accommodated.

Distribute Ownership Whether it's posting or reviewing for governance purposes, it's better to have multiple people involved in the effort necessary to get the job done. Do this to ensure that the workload does not overwhelm anyone and that you have multiple people trained in case of staff or volunteer turnover.

Establish an Editorial Calendar Give a day of the week to each type of content you'll have— youth, singles, school, care for the sick, and so on, and consistently post once a week on each. Save a few slots also for urgent and timely posts/reposts.

Set a Limit to Promotional Content Allow for a set number of posts about events or other promotions that need to be communicated. Fund-raising is a great cause but should not dominate posts on the page. The same goes for special events or any other single type of content that you may want to share. Keep it fresh!

Featured Case: Bill Leake, Apogee Results

Bill Leake has seen it all in his almost 20 years in Internet marketing. Bill has been driving provable revenues through Internet marketing techniques since the mid-1990s when, as part of the management team at Power Computing, he built the first company to sell $1 million of product over the Internet. The ex-Dell Computer and McKinsey & Company consultant has built a thriving business as CEO of Apogee Results, which provides a wide range of Internet marketing and social marketing services to its customers. Bill also serves as president of the Austin Interactive Marketing Association and was the chairman of the Search Engine Marketing Professionals Organization (SEMPO) North America committee. Bill received a master of business degree with honors from the University of Texas at Austin and a bachelor's degree from Yale University. We caught up with Bill to get his opinion of social media and Internet marketing in 2012 and beyond.

Q. *Your company got started in search engine marketing. How much has moved to social media over the last few years?*

A. Though our foundation of provable search engine marketing excellence has propelled ApogeeResults.com to be one of the largest independent metrics-focused digital agencies in the Southwest, more and more of our work has been moving to social-informed, if not social-focused, campaigns over the past several years. Probably 40% of our client billings have some sort of "earned media" component to them these days, up from almost nothing several years ago. This comes in several forms, from social advertising to socially infused SEO efforts to using traditional digital paid media (for example, Google AdWords or displays ads) to promote social media ecosystem "wins" (favorable blog posts/comments). More and more of our link-building efforts, also, encompass blogger outreach as part and parcel of the approach.

In fact, we keep meaning to produce two infographics, the first one being about the top 10 mistakes social media "experts" make when it comes to search, the second being about the top 10 mistakes search experts make when it comes to social. Far too many social media campaigns never manage to get around to the "Show me the money" step and encourage all these great discussions going on to take a small baby step inside the store, sales funnel, or whatever the ultimate client goal happens to be. Far too many folks crying out that "social media drives SEO" fail to understand even the most basic elements of SEO, such as how to choose keywords or how to build links that last, rather than ephemeral content that gives a short-term, one-time rankings pop that fades quickly (a typical blog post, for example).

Q. *How does social advertising compare to search advertising?*

A. They are kissing cousins but far enough apart so that they can safely marry, as there's plenty of different DNA in the two of them. I view social advertising as straddling midway in between display ads and search ads in terms of immediate direct response potential.

continues

Possibly it's even closer to display ads. The reasoning behind this is that people engaged on a social site are engaged in social activities. They aren't searching, they are socializing (and browsing) as their primary activity. Social advertising, done incorrectly, is very interruptive and annoying, much like a waiter who keeps inserting himself into a deep discussion you're trying to have with your lunch date. Search ads, by contrast, are often helpful, as people on a search engine are searching. Folks rarely go to Google to kill time, unlike Facebook. There are some sites that are midway in between, like Twitter, YouTube, and Wikipedia—all of those can be massive "Here's another shiny penny" time sinks but also serve tremendously useful information retrieval functions. And of course, with the exception of Twitter, most social advertising is graphical, rather than textual, so that plays into things. Much more than Google AdWords, it's highly important to vary your social advertising frequently, just like display ads.

Q. ***What are the biggest mistakes you see with clients who approach you for help with their Internet marketing problems?***

A. The biggest is not having clearly articulated goals. If they don't know what success looks like, we're not likely to stumble across it. Ensuring that both our client and the team we provision them with are aligned on how victory is defined is fundamental. Sometimes our initial goal can simply be to get out there, do some market research, and set some agreed goals. The second biggest mistake is not having the commitment to metrics to measure progress toward the goals. It's hard to hit a goal flying blind or flying with the wrong metrics. Probably the third biggest mistake is not having realistic, achievable expectations; we still see far too much of folks who want the equivalent of a 10-day Mediterranean cruise for $50. The Internet can be cost-effective, but it still takes investment, whether it be time, talent, or treasure (dollars), or some combination thereof. And the last mistake we see far too much of is a failure to integrate digital marketing channels and a failure to integrate online with offline. There's lots to be learned from PPC that applies to SEO. There's lots to be learned from social that applies to PR, there's lots to be learned from email conversions that applies to website development, and so on.

Q. ***How do you evaluate the current competition in social media between Facebook, Twitter, Google+, and others?***

A. I am a fan of competition, as it keeps all players on their toes and innovating. Wasn't it amazing how fast Facebook rolled out some "new" features once Google+ launched— features that seemed very similar? It was almost as if they had those features "on the shelf and ready to roll" on a moment's notice just in case they ever needed them. Once a company has "won," they tend to slack off and focus on ever smaller improvements. Before Facebook came on the scene a few years back, Google's main innovations seemed to be heading down the path of minor tweaks to its comparison shopping engine aimed at slowly putting the likes of BankRate, LowerMyBills.com, Realtor.com, and other lead aggregators/affiliates out of business. Now with Apple and Facebook as viable competitors, Google has once again become an innovation engine, with significant revamps to its search engine algorithms several times over the past 18 months. Twitter is and will remain an also-ran that tests features for others to implement.

Q. *Looking in the crystal ball, how do you think Internet marketing will evolve over the next five years?*

A. Several years ago, in 2007, I was honored to be tapped by South by Southwest Interactive to give a solo keynote speech on "The Future of Search" in the big room in the convention center. SXSW Interactive back then was nowhere near as crazy as it is now, but it was a full room, and the speech was well received. This was the same year that SXSW Interactive was panned (largely on Twitter) for doing a soft-core, only-lob-easy-pitches interview with Mark Zuckerberg of Facebook.

In my session, I accurately called out mobile as being, finally, nearly *ready* for prime time, and also called out the rise of video and the death of second life (thank goodness). However, I missed a bunch of things too, so I'm always wary of crystal balls. As one example, I've been in the digital world since 1995 and have been building companies that depend on measurable digital marketing success since that time, including several Inc. 500 companies and one software 500 company. I have owned one Internet Retailer 500 company, and I have helped build multiple other Internet Retailer 500 companies, in addition to many, many, many VC-backed successful high-growth firms that depend on the Internet for their revenue pipeline. Despite all that and despite being a geeky student of business history, had you asked me in 2006 who Google's major competitors would be five years later, I'd have totally missed the mark. I would not have named Apple and Facebook.

That's the wonderful thing about this ecosystem in which we live; it's still fluid, and for those of us who like to be kept on our toes, it's fun. We must adapt or die. That being said, here are my predictions:

- Google wins display and local search.
- Facebook stays atop social for several more years.
- Twitter fades and gets acquired. (In my mind, Twitter is like Friendster in that it is an early form that points toward something in the future that we don't quite know yet.)
- Apple stumbles, badly. (I hope I'm wrong here.)
- Mobile remains open and highly contested.
- Rich media remains competitive, with Google in the lead.
- More people "search" in ways that only peripherally involve classic "search" engines.

Government

All around the world, government employees and management are beginning to understand the power and the opportunity of using social media where traditional communications have dominated for many years. The reasons are similar to a lot of the themes we've covered in this book: immediacy of communications, low cost, reach, the ability to edit or change something if a mistake is made, and so on. Social media usage is already as pervasive as email in some demographic groups. All of it makes social media very appealing, especially for communities where citizens are more "tech-savvy."

The meme of Government 2.0 has emerged to cover these issues broadly as the concept grows in popularity. We're in a perfect storm for social media in government for a few reasons:

Maturing Social and Web 2. 0 Technologies Facebook, Twitter, and other social media technologies are ostensibly competing platforms, and they are beginning to mature, so there is less technical risk associated with using these products.

Increased Pressure on Government to Modernize Senior government officials are beginning to read about cases where the private sector has saved money or increased revenues using social media, and they look to employ similar practices for their agencies.

Potential for Cost Savings New technologies, if properly harnessed, can dramatically reduce the cost of traditional marketing and communications.

2008 Election of Barack Obama It can be argued that the 44th president of the United States was the first elected with the support of social media as campaign officials mobilized millions of people to vote.

But interestingly, government policy has not exactly caught up to the realities of social media, crowdsourcing, and user-generated content. For instance, many government agencies forbid employees from blogging because of the risk that an employee will say something that may be perceived to be official government policy. Then the statement or position taken by the blogger/employee becomes a potential legal liability for the government. The more you see situations like this, the easier it is to understand that policy makers aren't necessarily trying to get in the way of progress as much as they are trying to balance risk with opportunity while minimizing unintended consequences. But again, overall it is a big weakness of social media that none of us can truly divide our professional and personal lives without a lot of work and care.

So, what types of government projects can Facebook and social media assist? Earlier in this book, we suggested that social media can in some ways be considered another marketing channel—akin to email, a phone line, or a paper brochure—except that social media is inherently interactive and provides a means for people to communicate with each other inexpensively and in real time. In that sense, the government can use Facebook and social media to quickly and effectively communicate via the social graph—both to citizens and to spread the word from citizens to one another. Take, for example, the work that NASA has done with its Facebook presence; you can find its fan page at www.facebook.com/nasa. NASA has achieved quite a following, with more than 700,000 fans who receive regular updates on what is happening there, stunning photos (Figure 10.3), articles, and other information on space and aeronautics science.

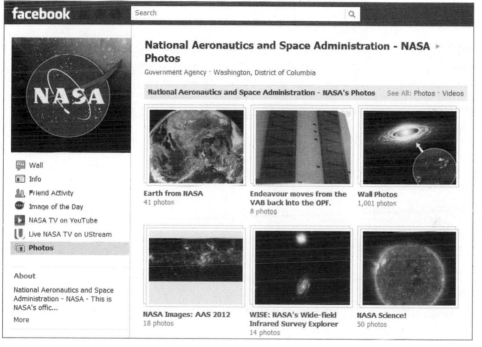

Figure 10.3 NASA photos

NASA also shares a variety of links to other sources of information on the Internet and in social media. It shares the "wonder of space" by selecting an Image of the Day (Figure 10.4) to encourage repeat visits to the page. Video of major events are promoted as well; NASA has linked to its live uStream content and its YouTube channel as well (Figure 10.5).

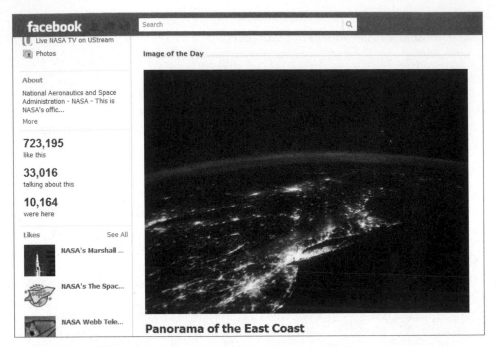

Figure 10.4 Image of the Day

Figure 10.5 NASA videos

Similarly, government organizations can use social media as a platform for people to communicate with one another. Take, for example, the U.S. Air Force page at www.facebook.com/USAirForce. The page defaults to the Wall, where a variety of people from all over the world comment on their love for the Air Force or their loved ones who are serving. But interestingly enough, there are two U.S. Air Force fan pages currently—the other is at www.facebook.com/pages/US-Air-Force/134276840326. One is apparently backed by folks in the Pentagon, while the other originated from Colorado Springs, the home of the Air Force Academy. One has more interactivity, the other more content. Same organization, two official Facebook fan pages. Hey, nobody said that coordinating efforts is easy and that social media actually brings people to a consensus.

Often an early-adopter government employee who uses a social media product will introduce an idea for how the government agency can use Facebook or a competing product. But it may not necessarily have the attention of senior officials because the effort is early, has very few users initially, or just simply isn't on the radar of important issues. A "pilot" project will be run because interested employees have a passion about the opportunity, and they want to take the initiative to try something new. This employee will get approval from the manager, who is often a progressive, forward-thinking person.

We've seen it happen numerous times in government agencies that a project like this will then get popular—it will gain traction through citizen usage or appreciation by a supportive niche of citizens. But unlike businesses that may see something like this as an opportunity and perhaps become overzealous about using it as a marketing channel, popularity tends to have the opposite effect in government agencies. A large following or fan count demonstrates success, but ironically senior government officials will want to then step back to ensure that it fits into other government initiatives and that many of the risks are identified and mitigated. The attorneys enter, and ultimately the project looks a lot different than it did originally. In the end, it sometimes then misses the mark with the very people the project was intended to serve.

So, what do you do if you are a government employee looking to inject Facebook or other social media into your outreach to citizens? First, make sure it can work in your community. Although social media is becoming increasingly popular worldwide, your community may not respond well to government communications through social media. Second, talk to citizens and solicit their feedback as you would for any other new program. Even small focus groups with friends and family can tell you a lot about how people will perceive your ideas for social media. Next, stay focused, and set attainable goals for your effort. Part of the solution is making sure that you are doing things the right way, and as we've mentioned previously, this may require some experimentation along the way. Finally, understand the internal environment in your agency. Anticipating future problems early in the process will help you make good decisions that will benefit you later.

Nonprofits

Facebook has undoubtedly contributed greatly to a huge surge in nonprofit awareness, fund-raising, and causes. According to the 2011 Nonprofit Social Network Report (available at www.nonprofitsocialnetworksurvey.com), a jaw-dropping 89% of nonprofits have a Facebook page. Additionally, the average nonprofit Facebook page fan count increased 161% in 2011.

The strategies for successful fan engagement are essentially the same as those for for-profit businesses: provide consistent valuable information, invite fans to contribute their thoughts freely, respond promptly, add photos, videos, and other types of multi media content, and so on. Plus, you can regularly make fans aware of fund-raising activities, providing clear instructions for how fans can help and get involved more, both online and offline locally.

A common trend among nonprofit organization leaders in social media is their devotion to the medium as a communications vehicle. The best nonprofits perform best practices in social media and use it to grow their fan base. Then, when it is necessary, they mobilize this fan base to do things such as volunteer their time, donate money, or share ideas with their friends. Note how different this is from brand marketing; very few people will act on their connection with Clorox bleach the same as they will with the Susan G. Komen Foundation.

It's a huge opportunity and somewhat of an unfair advantage for cause-based nonprofits. Remember, we're all participating to share life's joys, concerns, and frustrations. Many nonprofit groups support people who need help in some way. So, it's a hand-to-glove fit in some ways. Nonprofits can use social media to remind people of a cause by sharing deeply personal stories that can connect with a Facebook user, either through personal experience or by witnessing the trials of a loved one. As Simon Mainwaring said in *Fast Company*, "Facebook enables nonprofits to be better storytellers." (See www.fastcompany.com/1758575/how-non-profits-use-facebook-to-build-awareness-community-and-fundraising). Truer words have not been spoken about the possibility for nonprofits to use Facebook to do deeper and more sophisticated marketing.

Facebook has built a special page as a resource for nonprofits and other organizations for social good at www.facebook.com/nonprofits.

To quote Facebook on this special resource page, "We built it to help you harness the power of Facebook and bring positive change to the world. Facebook empowers nonprofits by enabling them to mobilize communities, organize events, increase fundraising, reduce costs with free online tools, and raise awareness through viral networks."

Example Nonprofits on Facebook

Beth Kanter, a respected nonprofit technology and social media writer and author of *The Networked Nonprofit* (Jossey-Bass, 2010), wrote an informative case study on her blog about the Red Cross's social media journey. Red Cross came under public attack for the way it handled disaster relief efforts after Hurricane Katrina. The organization then hired a social media manager (Wendy Harman), who helped to roll out a comprehensive, fully integrated social media policy and develop a powerful operational handbook. You can find the full case study, along with an excellent 109-page slideshow, here:

http://beth.typepad.com/beths_blog/2009/07/red-cross-social-media-strategypolicy-handbook-an-excellent-model.html

Check out Beth's ongoing commentary on nonprofit social media marketing at www.bethkanter.org.

The following are several examples of nonprofits of all sizes successfully using Facebook to heighten awareness, strengthen their support, and raise funds:

Red Cross: www.facebook.com/redcross

UNICEF: www.facebook.com/unicef

Susan G. Komen for the Cure: www.facebook.com/susangkomenforthecure

continues

Example Nonprofits on Facebook *(Continued)*

LIVESTRONG: www.facebook.com/livestrong

Greenpeace: www.facebook.com/greenpeace.international

Weston A. Price Foundation: www.facebook.com/pages/
Weston-A-Price-Foundation/58956225915

Pancreatic Cancer Action Network: www.facebook.com/JointheFight

Modest Needs Foundation: www.facebook.com/pages/
Modest-Needs-Foundation/46172034338

Electronic Frontier Foundation (EFF): www.facebook.com/eff

The good news for those of you working in the nonprofit area is that you can use Facebook to help with three objectives generally common to most nonprofits:

Issues Advocacy Trying to get people on your side? There is no better way to do so than to share your perspective. Put your spin on articles other people write, or use a long status update to share your opinion. Increasingly, organizations are treating status updates as they would write blog posts—to create conversation through Facebook likes and comments.

Volunteerism It's a huge hassle to find people to fill volunteer slots. A number of nonprofits are using social media to find new volunteers and ensure that time slots are filled. Check out VolunteerSpot (www.volunteerspot.com) and Sparked (www.sparked.com), which are two tools that can further help you bridge social media and your needs for volunteers.

Fund-Raising Fund-raising as a broad goal is always tough. But social media can help you humanize the reasons that you need money and the cause you support. Use storytelling to bring your cause and your nonprofit to life. Tools such as Rally (www.rally.org) and HelpAttack (www.helpattack.com) can give you the infrastructure necessary to collect money and understand how different campaigns and content generate donations.

Featured Case: Worldwide "Cause" Marketing

If you're trying to start a petition or simply draw attention to a cause that means something to you, you're in luck. There are several options to get you started. Causes.com (Figure 10.6) allows anyone to start and promote a cause, and Facebook is the primary promotional vehicle. Just go to Causes.com and click Start A Cause. You'll be asked to log in with Facebook (Figure 10.7), which will help you promote your efforts to your friends. Interestingly, Causes used to run as a Facebook

Featured Case: Worldwide "Cause" Marketing *(Continued)*

app but converted to a website enhanced by Facebook Connect. These changes and further development of the app resulted in significant improvements to the performance of the service, as reported by TechCrunch (see `http://techcrunch.com/2010/10/15/new-features-help -a-birthday-wish-set-a-new-causes-record-10k-in-24-hours/`).

If you want to be a little less aggressive with promoting your cause on Facebook, you can opt to use Change.org instead. Change.org allows you to log in with Facebook or create an account on its service—it's your choice.

Figure 10.6 Causes home page

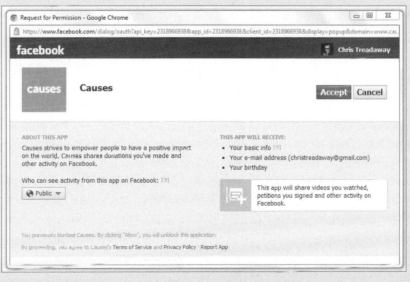

Figure 10.7 Causes login

Education

Given that Facebook was started at Harvard University (in 2004 by three Harvard students) and for the first two years of its existence only those people with a `.edu` email address could access and create a profile on Facebook, it stands to reason that education is a large part of the Facebook ecosystem. When Facebook opened its doors to companies and ultimately the general public starting in 2006, many students who were active on the site in those first couple of years were very resistant (at first!) to the masses coming onto the site and changing the overall user experience of this "walled garden." However, as time wore on, tens of thousands of fun third-party applications sprang up, Facebook kept adding useful new features, and the original members found they could expand their networks as they wanted and control their experiences with the granular privacy settings.

Now, in 2012, with the sheer volume of users, the amount of time they spend on Facebook, and the vast range of personal information they share, more and more organizations, including schools, colleges, and universities, will find themselves using Facebook to coordinate activities and distribute information.

Facebook's primary features of events, groups, and fan pages all work just as well for the education field as they do for the commercial and nonprofit sectors. With consistent, relevant updates and proper engagement, schools, colleges, and universities can easily expand their reach to recruit more students for full classes, boost morale, bolster student/teacher relationships, and even help improve grades.

As with nonprofits, Facebook also has a specific resource page to support educators in making the best use of Facebook. See `www.facebook.com/education`.

Featured Case: Emergency Notification via Facebook

Communicating with students via text messaging has been an integral part of school systems for a while. Now, with the prevalence of social networks, being able to reach thousands of students via Facebook and Twitter is more important than ever.

Oregon's Pacific University (`www.facebook.com/pacificu`) integrated student notification via Facebook and Twitter using Ominlert's e2Campus (`http://e2campus.com`). Along with alerts via email, RSS feeds, and text messaging to mobile devices, a service like e2Campus includes the ability for institutions to reach thousands of students and teachers with one click via Facebook and Twitter. As we talked earlier in this section about the sheer amount of time users/students spend on Facebook, with the ability to send alerts via Facebook, schools can increase their outreach for important communication. The following is from a CampusTechnology.com article:

According to Lee M. Colaw, vice president of information services at Pacific University, letting e2Campus contact students in

Featured Case: Emergency Notification via Facebook *(Continued)*

> *emergencies through Facebook made sense. In fact, students had already requested it. When he conducted follow-up assessments on how the e2Campus system was working, Colaw said, students had suggested that the best way to reach them was via Facebook. Students said that they themselves were already re-typing and sending out university messages via Facebook. "We thought it would be more professional," Colaw said, "if the message came straight from the university instead."*

http://campustechnology.com/Articles/2009/01/23/University-Links-
Twitter-Facebook-with-Notification-System.aspx

Achieving Marketing and Recruitment Goals

Some schools may not be as hip to all the new Web 2.0 and social media marketing strategies. Or, they'll at least have a presence on Facebook in the form of a group or fan page, but the school may not know how to optimize their social network activity to achieve measurable results. There is a fine art to utilizing Facebook to connect with current students, empower teachers, promote the school to gain more enrollments, and track and measure your success. This is a specialty field that we're now seeing specialty services cater to. For example, BlueFuego, Inc. conducts a "social web audit" for colleges and universities to see how they're currently utilizing the social Web, and then it provides a social web strategy, training, and implementation support, with a heavy focus on the Facebook platform. Clients such as Abilene Christian University (http://facebook.com/welcometoacu) and Bentley University (http://facebook.com/bentleyadmission) are now engaging with hundreds of incoming students, attracting new leads, and providing customer service around the clock! Learn more at http://bluefuego.com and www.facebook.com/BlueFuego.

Example Schools, Colleges, and Universities on Facebook

Here are a few examples to learn from:

- Stanford University: www.facebook.com/stanford
- University of Michigan: www.facebook.com/universityofmichigan
- Harvard University: www.facebook.com/Harvard
- Thunderbird, School of Global Management: www.facebook.com/ThunderbirdSchool

- Sewickley Academy: www.facebook.com/SewickleyAcademy

- Fresno Pacific University–Graduate School: www.facebook.com/graduatedegree

- Fresno Pacific University–Student Activities: www.facebook.com/pages/
  Fresno-Pacific-University-Student-Activities/110898556037

- SuperCamp, an academic summer camp for sixth grade through college students: www.facebook.com/SuperCamp

Startups

Social media is a potentially huge opportunity for startup businesses, especially those that need to sell or market to consumers. Startups are often the most cost-sensitive organizations of any you'll find. But where startups are poor in cash resources, they are generally willing to try anything and work hard at new things that may help the business succeed. Social media is a good fit because much of it is built to be self-serve. Everything we've discussed in this book is designed to help you cut your learning curve and be effective as quickly as you can.

Generally speaking, marketing for a startup isn't about perception or the basic blocking and tackling associated with communicating messages to customers around the world. It is a much more surgical approach—how do you reach customers who are willing and able to adopt or buy your products and services? It's about transactions and finding qualified leads. It's about introducing new concepts to the marketplace that are bigger, better, faster, or more efficient than alternative ways of doing things. And all of that needs to be done cost-effectively.

For unrecognized brands created by new, often unproven startup businesses, it can be very difficult to make a big splash. Consumers generally don't know who you are or what your products do unless they have experience doing business with you. Your brands are not yet established, and they carry little to no meaning once you get outside of the relatively small and friendly group of family, friends, business colleagues, and early customers who keep up with you and want you to succeed.

So, all in all, you are a relative unknown fighting against all the other noise on Facebook, not to mention competitors who may be engaging with customers on Facebook and social media. In that sense, it is relatively easy to get a small and loyal following for your efforts early, but it is decidedly more difficult to scale once you've exhausted people who are at least a little familiar with you. How do you go beyond that first 100 or so people? You'll need many more than 100 people to show the world that your product is at least minimally important.

With a hat tip to Geoffrey Moore, we suggest that the answer certainly begins with your early adopters—people who will appreciate your work well before others realize on their own just how wonderful you and your products or services are. How can you identify and branch out from your early adopters?

Focus to Keep Early Adopters Happy Fill a niche, do it very well, engage regularly, and listen intently to your customers. Grow after you do one thing well, and don't get too ambitious early, because it may dilute the message you are trying to promote.

Ask for Support to Get Them Involved A lot of people like to be associated with a success story from its humble beginnings. Appeal to them by asking for their help to promote you or your company to their friends and colleagues. Oftentimes, you'll get assistance. Don't be afraid to ask for support—just don't overdo it because you may offend someone if you're too persistent.

Enthusiastically Represent Your Product/Service Startups are exciting—the possibilities are endless for you and your cofounders as you embark upon your mission to change the world. Why not communicate your enthusiasm to your fans? Your "voice" is critical to inspiring and energizing your fan base. It will encourage people to share thoughts and ideas with you and will help fans see your company in a positive light. Be positive and communicate consistently, and you'll turn people who passively "like" your page into true evangelists who share your message with others who may not have heard about your company.

Advertise to Find and Target New People As discussed in Chapter 6, Facebook advertising is perhaps one of the most effective and inexpensive ways available to target specific people based on profile data that they have entered voluntarily. Fortunately for you, this means you can run ads aimed at people who live in a particular city, aimed at people who work in a company you are trying to sell, or aimed at people of a certain age who fit the profile of early adopters for your product.

Be Consistently Useful for the Customer First All too often, companies get so focused on their own needs that they forget to focus on the customer. The temptation is too great to send more marketing messages out through social media, and soon enough the ratio of marketing messages to useful content gets out of whack. Then customers abandon the social media effort. Just be sure to help the customer first and sell last. Make it a soft sale, and you'll do a lot better.

Finally, some companies don't use social media specifically as a marketing channel as much as they use social media to enhance an existing or new product. Social media isn't just the social graph—it is the social context through which you can deliver or receive real-time communications, identify validated users, and bridge between the Web and social relationships. In certain cases, use of a product or service that is integrated with social media can help sell the very product you're trying to market. There are also opportunities to create new products and services using the social graph and data that can help modernize old businesses. If you go down this path, just remember that Facebook is similarly looking for new and interesting ways to make money. Facebook will always have competing interests between fostering a healthy, vibrant developer ecosystem and creating economic value for itself, not unlike Microsoft in the early days of the PC platform. You'll have to pay attention to industry news and events to know exactly how and where you can innovate.

Facebook in the Future

Trust us, our knowledge of Facebook the platform combined with marketing on Facebook is extremely deep. However, we don't profess to know everything there is to know about Facebook. We wanted to reach out to our community of esteemed fellow Facebook experts and passionate users of the world's number-one social network to invite them to contribute their thoughts on where Facebook is headed in the coming months and years. This chapter contains several interviews we conducted with our valued contributors; we invited each expert to provide answers to his or her choice of three or more questions from our selection. We trust this chapter adds extra value to you, our readers, and helps to create an even bigger vision of just what is possible with the whole world using Facebook.

QUESTION 1: Walled Garden?

Some people compare Facebook to the efforts of AOL in the 1990s to create a "walled garden," where interactions take place primarily on Facebook, eschewing the Web broadly. Is this a fair comparison? And if so, will Facebook succeed in doing this?

Chad Wittman: Absolutely. I believe Facebook is one search revamp away from finally securing search engine dominance from Google. Facebook is now in a position where they've achieved a dominant critical mass. Every generation is using the platform, from children to grandparents.

AOL succeeded in a "walled garden" approach because they simplified cutting-edge technology for any user at any age. They made email easy to understand and use. The Internet user of today inherently understands search engines, social media, and email. Facebook must also simplify the technology of today for any user at any age. They've already started the process with Open Graph, enabling users to experience media with the simple click of a Play button. If Facebook continues in this direction, it will be a dominant force for the next 10 years.

Brian Massey: From the point of view of marketers, Facebook is its own world. It is a world with a dark blue sky and a stark white earth, and it is populated by familiar faces. Marketers see that when we invite Facebook users out of this world, to our own websites, they respond negatively, converting at lower rates. When we invite them to places within the Facebook world—an app, page, or profile—conversion rates are higher. Just as AOL was the Internet to so many in the 1990s, Facebook is the primary place to hang out for hundreds of millions of members. As businesses find new ways to extend Facebook, we will expand the walls of the garden, immersing friends and fans into new but unmistakably Facebookian worlds. Just as Branch Out brought a form of LinkedIn to Facebook, users will find themselves entering richer applications. Will we participate in a second life–like world populated by our families and friends? Yes, we will.

David Foster: I feel that in a way Facebook has succeeded in making the Web a much better place, and yes, it is rather similar to AOL, which is it was a place everyone went to connect, whether it be through messages or chat rooms...wow, remember chat rooms? Up until 2:00 a.m. talking to strangers all over the world? At least now they are called "friends."

Ben Pickering: I believe this comparison is valid in the sense that AOL embodied the Internet for many people in the mid-to-late '90s, as Facebook appears to be doing more and more today. However, the concept of "openness" was not part of the Internet lexicon in the heyday of AOL. In the past 10 years, the Internet has changed fundamentally, thanks to open protocols, including widespread use of public APIs, open source software, and easy sharing of content across platforms. By virtue of this, I don't think Facebook will ever create a "walled garden," but they may very well succeed in being the primary aggregator of content and the starting point for many people's online experiences.

Andrea Vahl: Facebook has done a much better job of integrating itself into the Web at large. They have implemented Facebook Likes boxes, Like buttons, the Facebook blog comment plug-in, and Facebook authentication to log in, just to name a few. Facebook continues to drive the interaction back to Facebook, but they also do a good job of blending in to where people are hanging out. I believe they will continue their outward reach and tear down more of their walls with the integration of apps and utilizing the Open Graph.

Nick Unsworth: Yes, I do agree with the comparison, and Facebook is doing an excellent job at continually improving their platform to make their users' lives more convenient and connected.

For Facebook to succeed with this strategy long-term, they will need to continually update their platform to incorporate technology that ultimately helps make their users' lives more and more convenient. Just think about the convenience of having photos on Facebook. This not only keeps the users engaged, but it also increases the barriers to entry for other networks to win over consumers.

Chase McMichael: Facebook's greatest challenge is staying relevant. They have created the world's largest web overlay ecosystem, and with use of their social graph, they have linked almost every piece of published content on the Net. The same goes for brands that have created Facebook Pages with the Like widget disseminated onto multiple home pages. However, all of this is a thin connection to consumers/followers since all of the major content publishers, such as bloggers and content-rich media sites, fight to stay relevant, while brands are increasingly using Facebook as their primary landing page. In order for Facebook's "walled garden" strategy to work, they need to retain their advantage by offering more than what current social platforms have to offer.

Facebook was very quick to stop Google+ users from transferring their friend data. Facebook feels a clear threat to their existence by being an open network; this activity could see a mass migration of followers like we saw with MySpace. While Facebook approaches 1 billion users, the big question is whether they can retain their current number of influencers who drive the bulk of the social conversations. It's been highly publicized that they are losing the influencer core. With the rise of Google+, which has search integration built into its platform, the question remains, will this continue to drive users/followers to a more open platform?

The competition to capture the social-consumer interactions is heating up. Twitter is becoming stronger, with every publication and media outlet pushing their Twitter handle over their Facebook page. This is a clear indication of the paradigm shifting. Facebook was approached by Google to be included in the Google+ personal search feather, and this was a radical move, but they chose to increase the pressure and put a higher level of disruption in the marketplace, since Facebook won't let Google index most of its content. The facts are simple: SEO/search and display still grab the bulk of ad dollars that are spent, and this will always have a predominant role in a brand's online presence. Facebook is trying everything to monetize their current audience, but the potential cost of alienating the users is a high risk they must take to go IPO.

Facebook doesn't make your content any better or get more people to like your product; it just simplifies the ability to disseminate information on a social graph. Facebook didn't invent the social graph; they just made it work efficiently from an interaction perspective. Facebook's desire to be "the Web" is without question; however, Google is going to continue to fight and protect its primary revenue stream: SEO/search and display.

Jan Rezab: I don't think that the Facebook model is a fully "walled" garden, as they have quite an open API and allow interactions to happen outside (Facebook Connect).

Scott Ayres: Very fair comparison. The success of AOL when it started was that it was pretty much the only Internet service provider for households across the globe. Where they failed was when they tried to do too much and lost focus of what got them there. I get why Facebook wants people to stay on their site. It's all about the ad dollars that result in eyes staying on Facebook. But I fear that by attempting to do this, many people will either get bored with the site or be fearful of the site owning too much property online. People love variety, so sitting on the same site all day for everything while in theory sounds great, in reality will cause people to leave. Facebook needs to balance this and figure out how not to become the next AOL. (I do miss the connecting sound our old dial-up modems made! And the wonderful message of "You've Got Mail!")

QUESTION 2: **Privacy?**

How can Facebook users take full control of protecting their privacy as Facebook evolves?

Dave Kerpen: Facebook users who are concerned about protecting their privacy should diligently check their privacy settings and their sharing settings, in general and on each individual post. While Facebook's privacy settings will only get more complex as

Facebook evolves, it is sharing settings on content, which will cost people their jobs and relationships over and over. There will be legal battles about whether it's a fireable offense when users' status updates complaining about bosses and employers get into unintended hands. In the meantime, in the face of changing and often complex privacy settings, my word to the wise remains: Never share anything on Facebook you wouldn't want your mother or boss to see.

Ching Ya: Through identification of the things they can share and whom they are sharing with. As much as I like to compliment Facebook's recent efforts to improve their privacy settings, the truth is a lot of general users are still unaware of the privacy options available, especially when some are hidden and some are updated without the public's consent until widely broadcasted by popular social media sites or industry leaders. The good news is, ever since their settlement with FTC, all future privacy changes will be made opt-in. But even so, Facebook will continue to undergo rapid changes. Timeline is a good example of how a feature can lead to intense debates on displaying someone's life story in one place, even with all the privacy settings available. So, always be ready for worst-case scenarios in case one day your Timeline is exposed to unwanted viewers—either by mistake, carelessness, or a system bug.

No one can protect your data better than you can.

Chad Wittman: Privacy is an adult problem. The youth of today care little about privacy. They were born into a world of constant information at their fingertips. Each of their friends, teachers, and favorite brands are accessible online at any time. Youth are more interested in the benefits and value of casting away privacy, which ultimately allows them to participate in online social circles. When the youth of today join the workforce, privacy will be a shell of its current self.

Additionally, current privacy is an illusion. Most widely used Internet tools (Facebook, Google, Gmail, Twitter, and so on) are "free," but just because a tool is "free" doesn't mean it doesn't cost anything to use. The hidden cost is your privacy. As long as the most widely used Internet tools remain free, the user has little leverage. Regardless of laws or acts of Congress, these companies will still use private data in ways outlined by terms of service and privacy policies. This is the true cost of a free tool.

Andrea Vahl: Facebook privacy settings have gotten easier to set and understand recently in my opinion. But it can be hard to control what your own network shares. I think people are demanding better privacy controls, but they also need to fully utilize the ones that are already available by checking in periodically to see what's changed and knowing their current Facebook privacy settings.

Nick Unsworth: Facebook will always be after the consumer data, and they also tend to have poor communication with their users about how new updates affect their privacy settings.

It's important for consumers to check their account settings and make updates to their privacy settings on a monthly basis. At the end of the day, the consumers are in control of their privacy, but they have to be willing to keep on top of it.

Jan Rezab: I think it's the role of users to educate themselves and the role of Facebook to make sure everything is really clear to the users. I think with the recent changes, it got really good!

Scott Ayres: I think an educated Facebook user is a secure Facebook user. With the constant changes to Facebook that will likely never end, users need to take their privacy into their own hands and not just assume Facebook will protect them automatically. The latest rounds of Facebook changes have given the user the broadest amount of control over privacy we've ever seen. But, it's up to users to set the privacy settings to their preferred settings.

Brian Massey: The erosion of privacy is Web-wide, and Facebook will continue to gather more and more information on us as we move about Facebook and other sites across the Web. This is true of Google and hundreds of other ad networks as well. There will be a significant event: a company will abuse their access to this data in such an appalling way that these companies will be forced to conceal more of the information they collect on us. It will be temporary. Instead, it will be the public's understanding of how cookies are being used to track them and what advertisers have access to that will help change policy and behavior. What Danah Boyd said will continue to be true. To paraphrase: "Those who are in trouble in real life are the ones getting into trouble online." For many, the bright light of transparency will be *too* bright, and they will not be able to participate in the Facebook economy. It will be another disadvantage for those who already are at a disadvantage in the real economy.

David Foster: I think that people need to realize that if they put info out there, it will never be 100% protected. The only way it really ever is, is if we never give anyone our information...including our insurance companies, our banks, our cable companies. We give them more sensitive data than we give Facebook and never really question where that is going to go and how it will eventually be used in the case that a company goes out of business or is taken over by another company. I think people just focus way too much on this topic. If you don't want your cell number out there, don't add it to Facebook. Period.

Chase McMichael: We have witnessed every privacy blunder through the lens of Facebook. With that said, Facebook needs transparency on how it uses its consumers' data and should provide us with a simple notification for opting out when we do not like the projects they are pushing. A good example is the Politico project, which gives them access to every mention of a political candidate name in the News Feeds, public and in private, without Facebook users aware that they have been tracked. The most evident blunder Facebook made was sharing data on users' private and public mentions of the Republican presidential candidates without providing them with the opportunity to opt out.

Data sharing, if done right, matters and could be the biggest, and most dynamic, census of human opinion and interaction in history. From a holistic perspective, they can get away with these blatant violations because they are a proprietary closed community (a walled garden). As soon as any part of the platform gains traction without opportunity for monetization, their privacy restrictions tighten around consumers; hence, consumers' voices are minimized.

There is a major generation gap between those who don't care about what is being shared and sold and those who do. Facebook has been slow to respond and has put in a few controls enabling you to protect your data, but is it too late? The masses still use Facebook, so currently there is really no incentive for them to do a better job. We're now seeing the FCC getting in on the game, as well as European and Canadian groups pushing for a greater degree of transparency. This will always be a tug-of-war game as long as consumer data is the primary key to making money.

QUESTION 3: **Personal Data?**

How will Facebook's gathering of more and more personal data impact the users? And advertisers?

Nathan Latka: Many users of Facebook are using it to craft their online personas. This persona is almost never an accurate depiction of the user in life, including the economic drivers of that user's life.

As an example, a marketer may post photos to Facebook to depict success so that more people want to associate with them. Others may depict success by checking in to places they may be near but are not actually in. As an example, "Nathan checked in to Trump Tower" depicts success more than "Nathan checked in at Hotel XYZ" (the hotel across the street from Trump Tower).

This is where an agency conflict arises. The Trump Organization may then sink many thousands into Facebook ads targeting these "successful" users who Trump believes have the money to buy a Trump hotel room. In reality, Facebook has qualified these targeted users through user-provided, persona-driven data.

This significantly decreases the potential return for Trump Organization because the users that their ads target don't actually have the money to stay at a Trump hotel.

Facebook has to more closely tie real-life persona with online persona if it wants to continue to add value to its advertising platform.

Dave Kerpen: Facebook's gathering of more and more personal data will allow advertisers to target users even more precisely than they can today. Already, Facebook's advertising system allows for significantly better demographic and psychographic targeting than any ad media in history. In the future, this targeting will only get better. While some argue that the net effect of this precise ad targeting is an ill effect on users —the "creepiness" factor—I believe that great relevance in advertising creates a better experience on Facebook. I like to see what my friends like and are doing, especially if I'm interested in those brands, locations, or activities. Don't you?

David Foster: I happen to like the fact that I can go to Facebook and only see ads that are relevant to me. I, like many others, happen to like shopping, and I would much rather see ads based on my interests than to see ads that have nothing to do with me. So for me, I think the more data about movies, etc., that we give them, the more advertisers will be able to cater to the markets that truly want their products instead of wasting a ton of money on trying to find their demographic...and again, just don't give them more than you want them to have.

Ben Pickering: More data is undeniably a boon for advertisers. The holy grail of online advertising (or any advertising for that matter, but something uniquely possible on the Web) is one-to-one personalized marketing. I believe that this is ultimately a good thing for users: if you are going to be shown ads, don't you want to receive messages that are relevant to you? Of course, the trade-off is the sharing of more personal data. So long as the advertising systems place a barrier between the advertiser and end user such that the matching of ads to users takes place in a "black box," then I think users' privacy can remain protected at the same time that marketers are able to reach their target demographic without knowing who these people are at an individual level.

Andrea Vahl: The Facebook advertising platform is so successful because of the personal information they have available to advertisers. A bridal store can target all the identified engaged women in a particular ZIP code with their Facebook ad. It's amazing. As advertisers become more savvy at getting people to click the ads, the price of advertising on Facebook will go up. Facebook will continue to find more ways to subtly integrate the ads into the Facebook platform with mobile ads, News Feed ads, and more. Ideally, people will tolerate these ads as the price to pay for a free social platform.

Nick Unsworth: Many people enjoy Pandora because over time it gradually understands your taste in music and plays only songs that you're likely to enjoy. The same is true with Facebook; the more user data they have, the more they will be able to tailor the experience to their users' behaviors and interests.

I truly believe that Facebook will start to connect into commerce outside of just Facebook. Imagine checking into a hotel, and when you get to your room, it's playing your favorite music. What if your favorite movie was on the TV? All of that is possible today, and we are going to see more and more Facebook integration that takes place on Facebook, throughout the Web, and even in brick-and-mortar businesses. This may seem a little creepy, but it will lead to enhanced user experiences, and in the future we will look back one day and say, "How could we have ever lived without Facebook connected to businesses?"

The plethora of user data creates a "dream come true" environment for advertisers. There already is a massive shift in ad dollars flowing to Facebook as corporations realize that they can now target their advertising messages to their ideal prospects. As Facebook sprawls into more areas of consumers' lives, their ad platform will continually be optimized. To many people this all seems creepy, but I welcome it. How about you? Wouldn't you rather receive advertisements that cater to your likes and interests than see ads that you don't care about?

Scott Ayres: There will always be users who feel that Facebook (or any other site for that matter) are out to "get them." Unfortunately, they are always the loudest to voice their opinions on the matter as well. Users have to be conscious of what they are posting and how those posts are showing to their friends and the public. I foresee users sharing less personal items than they once did, as they are too leery of everyone seeing intimate details of their lives. For advertisers it's like getting the Golden Ticket to Willa Wonka's Chocolate Factory! What I mean by that is because people have shared and will share so much information about their interests and activities, ads on Facebook can be pinpoint targeted, unlike any other site in our history. The smart marketers will find those activities that they can target to convert their ads into sales.

Chase McMichael: As it stands, advertisers can't handle the amount of data being pushed at them; it's like drinking from a fire hose, and that's impossible. For the users, as specific targeting and relevance increases, the user experience gets better. But we have seen Facebook fail in attempting to "filter" the content they think is best; their results have been abysmal. On the flip side, advertisers have found this to be a gold mine of epic proportions.

Never before in history has the average business had the power to target this many people specifically, 900+ million users, and target by demographic, as well as location, and use the followers' likes at a low cost to the brands. The rise of Bid-Data and social analytics for brands is a major game-changer, because it allows brands to truly understand their audience based on behavior and intent. Social intelligence is paving the way to help them become more relevant based on the consumers' known behaviors.

Jan Rezab: I don't think the average user actually is seeing how much data Facebook is gathering. I think if it accounts for better user experience and more relevant ads, it counts. Remember, Facebook is free for members, so they have to make money off the service.

QUESTION 4: **Facebook Pages?**

What is the future of Facebook Pages? Will they make websites obsolete, or will they be a companion?

Chase McMichael: Today we're seeing brands use their Facebook page as a destination, and for good reason. If their consumers are on the social graph, they need to join the party, or they will be left out. The fact is with one click, brands are able to empower their consumers with the feature of showing their friends "I like this brand" or "See what I said." It's organic reach nirvana like never before. For inbound marketing, you can't get any better than this. Brands must still get consumers to do an email opt-in, but for some products as well as generations, email is "so my parents' thing."

Brands have a major conundrum between embracing things they can't control, and they are having a hard time finding direct ROI within social. The competition is dealing with the same issues, but brands see their competitors that have higher engagement, causing them to go into a reaction vs. strategic planning mode.

Phyllis Khare: The prevailing practice of having a website as a "hub" and having all your social accounts feed into it is still a good practice. But there are a lot of small businesses that don't have the time or staff to manage that type of setup. Having a Facebook business page act as your "website" is a great alternative.

You can do everything on a Facebook business page that you can do on a website: capture email addresses, show company information, tell the story of the company, have conversations, provide customer service, post press releases, showcase product videos, and more. You can have an e-commerce (or F-commerce) tab and sell your products or services to new and existing customers without taking them off Facebook at all. And the integration of the social graph with third-party apps creates an automatic (free) marketing machine on the largest social platform.

To answer the question directly, I think for the next few years both a website and a Facebook business page will be important for small businesses, but the "hub" will slide over to Facebook as more businesses are educated as to its value.

Scott Ayres: Depending on the business, the answer to this question will be different. The problem with websites is most small businesses tend to spend too much money creating them, and once they do create them and add content, they never change it. So, the sites become stale, old, and irrelevant. The beauty of a Facebook page is you can easily and quickly add new content to it or have it added by your fans. The fact that pages are free and require no hosting is very appealing to the small-business owner. Plus, it allows them to focus on one space, rather than spreading themselves too thin. As F-commerce evolves and becomes the "norm" for pages and users, this will greatly change how businesses view and use Facebook Pages. So, will websites be obsolete? Likely not, as most businesses want to ensure they have control over their online presence, but I do think less time, energy, and money will be spent on them.

Nathan Latka: This definition is from Wikipedia: "A set of related pages containing content (media), including text, video, music, audio, images, etc." That definition belongs to the term *website*. You'll notice the paradox immediately. Facebook presents text, video, music, audio, and images in a more relevant manner due to its social layer.

Users feel very comfortable on Facebook due to familiarity of navigation, images of their close friends and family, and other settings personal to them. A website can't offer this. Facebook would like to remain as a "platform," not as a website replacer. I think they will execute this flawlessly while they let applications replace websites.

Facebook presents music content better because of Spotify integration. Said in a different manner, I think Facebook won't ultimately replace websites, but applications built on top of Facebook will.

David Foster: I think they will always have to be a companion. I do see them playing a very crucial role in the future of online business, but I do not see them being the end-all solution nor do I feel they want to. Way too much support for them. Plus, they understand there are far too many other great options out there that give you a bit more flexibility (at this point anyway). I think they like where they are, and that is a hub to help us business owners brand ourselves and give them traffic.

Ching Ya: Facebook Pages will continue to be hotspots for brands and businesses to expand their reach to potential customers, as long they stay free and reachable—if not to all, to at least a portion of Facebook's humongous user base. Brand owners will find favors in third-party commercial apps for storefronts, custom tabs to enhance page presence, and social sharing among fans. Fans' engagement level on pages will be prioritized more than ever because it affects how the page updates will be sent to fans' News Feeds (and to their friends), based on Edgerank algorithms.

However, I don't think pages will ever replace websites until page owners have better control over the data obtained and the stability of the platform. An unexpected system bug on Facebook Pages can easily cause panic attacks to admins because they wouldn't have known what hit them and how long the problem will last. Some new admins may unwittingly violate Facebook terms of use and inadvertently send their pages to removal. No direct contact to reach Facebook support except bug forms is a problem. Facebook will have to provide substantial evidence that they are taking care of the bug instead of just an autoresponder claiming they will read the form but won't send a reply or notify users about the fix. Until Facebook improves customer support on pages, relying solely on a Facebook page, when one can't have full control, is still too risky compared to running a self-hosted website.

Ben Pickering: The past several years have witnessed the massive move of businesses establishing their presence on Facebook, largely through the creation of Facebook Pages. While there are a handful of businesses that may exist entirely on Facebook, for the majority of companies their websites will not become obsolete. In fact, I think that in the next two years you will see a bit of a pendulum swing back in favor of owned and controlled websites. I don't think Facebook will ever offer the full flexibility that your own website provides, and given the amount that most organizations have invested in building their web presence, it would be foolish to throw that all away. With that said, I think you will see more and more integration of Facebook platform features into third-party sites, thereby allowing Facebook Pages and owned websites to coexist and support each other.

Nick Unsworth: It's bold to say that websites will eventually become obsolete, but you can't help but toy with the idea when you start seeing Fortune 500 brands marketing their Facebook Pages instead of their own website pages. I think we are a long way from that, and Facebook would have to make all of the right moves to get there. Oh, and that little company named Google is going to put up the fight of the century to make sure that it doesn't happen.

Jan Rezab: Facebook is in the position where they cannot possibly do any harm to Facebook Pages. Facebook Pages, from my perspective, will always be there.

Dave Kerpen: Facebook Pages will never eliminate websites. Instead, they will become a strong companion to them, along with other social media profiles. In the future, branded content and applications will be largely portable and platform agnostic, so that that same module that lives on a Facebook page also lives on a company website, a Twitter brand page, and a Google+ brand page. This will be easier for companies and users alike.

QUESTION 5: **Gamification?**

Will more businesses integrate gamification on their fan pages?

David Foster: I think so, and I think it would be smart. We are actually looking at a way to do this—to make a virtual shopping experience on Facebook. I think it just makes things more interesting, and if you can get people excited to keep coming back, whether online or off, you have a great thing!

Ben Pickering: To me "gamification" is a mechanism for deeper consumer engagement. Brands are always looking for ways to engage their audience, so I definitely foresee more game, contest, and competition elements emerging everywhere.

Nick Unsworth: Absolutely, advertisers are starting to realize that consumers don't care about their ads as much as they care about what their friends think. Who do you trust more, an ad from a faceless corporation or a review that you see on your News Feed that comes from your best friend?

Gamification will continually evolve, because true word-of-mouth marketing is still the best channel. The only challenge for the evolution of gamification is Facebook's continual efforts to reduce spam. This is going to be a constant tug-of-war between the two.

Chase McMichael: Yes, using incentives to drive consumer Pavlovian-type or respondent conditioning and hitting a consumer's hot buttons will always be the major play. Essentially, this is Marketing 101. Marketers will always seek to evoke passion and a desire of belonging that pushes consumers to be advocates with no regard for what they truly are interested in or what they ultimately need. Gaming behavior has long been used in Las Vegas–style environments and will see more psychological manipulation in applications and use of data in the future.

Jan Rezab: Definitely, within the rules on Facebook, businesses will try to do more and more to gamify the experience with their profiles.

QUESTION 6: F-Commerce?

How big will Facebook commerce, "F-commerce," become in the next five years?

Nick Unsworth: It will play a serious role in our lives. With mainstream adoption, it has the potential to make our lives more convenient. They already have the audience, and once consumers start enjoying the convenience, it won't take long for it to reach critical mass and sprawl into many areas of commerce.

Scott Ayres: F-commerce, in my opinion, will result in the largest shift online in the next five years. Now not only can we get recommendations from friends about items to purchase, now we will be able to purchase those items without leaving Facebook. Facebook is slowly creating a space where people can connect, be informed, purchase, and run their businesses, all without leaving Facebook. Facebook's goal seems to be to become "all things to all people." And F-commerce is the largest piece of that puzzle.

David Foster: I see this being a great idea for games, and so on, but not for businesses to use as their sole merchant. It will be interesting to see where they go for sure, but I do not think Facebook would want to have to deal with the support issues of nonwork- ing carts on that mass a scale. I think it will be something they will try and it will fail, except in the game and app market.

Chase McMichael: To date Facebook has done a poor job with their credits, but it's no secret that F-commerce has monster potential. As for the gaming companies and vir- tual goods on social platforms, this current model works for Facebook as the primary source of their revenue success. Mobile carriers have created short codes and the abil- ity to purchase with them, so you can pay for goods and services on a mobile device and push the cost onto your carrier bill. This has not taken off because the carriers were taking too much. Their greed killed the potential revenue of this major outlet. Ultimately, who handles the payment exchange will become a major player, and cur- rently Amazon is the company poised to take F-commerce in the right direction.

Jan Rezab: We will see how this part gets big, but for me as a user, it's really interest- ing to know what my friends have recently bought. Maybe I'll want to buy it also!

QUESTION 7: Facebook Mobile?

Where do you see Facebook Mobile headed?

Andrea Vahl: Facebook Mobile is vitally important. Mobile use is expected to surpass desktop use by 2015 according to a study by IDC (www.idc.com/getdoc .jsp?containerId=prUS23028711). Facebook is preparing for that change by updating its mobile interface and making navigation easier. Facebook needs to add advertising into the mobile application to keep their revenue model.

Jan Rezab: I don't think people will differentiate between mobile and normal usage; I think it will be just usage of a particular service, for example, communicating with friends. You won't know if you send that message to your friend over the computer or mobile Facebook.

Brian Massey: The next great frontier for mobile advertising is text messaging. With high open rates and greater public acceptance, the only barrier is the cost of the messages themselves. Unlimited messaging plans will be the key. With their incredible membership, Facebook will have the power to influence the carriers to offer such plans.

Scott Ayres: As more and more people access Facebook primarily on their mobile devices (phones and tablets), Facebook will need to tailor the experience to these users. Mobile users have been sheltered from seeing ads, but this is changing, and businesses need to learn how to target mobile users via ads properly. Page owners will also need to be conscious of how their pages and content are accessible on mobile devices. As of this writing, the amazing custom tabs/apps people make for their pages aren't seen by mobile users. So, a page owner needs to find a way to get the content and context of those tabs in front of mobile users.

David Foster: I think it will be the main source of traffic for them. I mean, you can check in when you are out, share a photo of what you just ate and who you ate it with, and review the place where you're eating. We are such an "on-the-go" society that they will not have a choice.

I mean, have you seen teenagers these days? If they didn't have their cell phones, I think they would stop breathing!

Chad Wittman: Facebook Mobile is hopefully moving in a more intuitive direction. I believe Facebook needs to continually examine the value they bring to the user. The current value of Facebook Mobile is to check and update status. This is the first (and obvious) layer to the mobile challenge. I believe Facebook will either work more closely with mobile device creators or develop their own device to bring idiosyncratic value to the mobile experience.

I envision a future where using Facebook on a mobile device brings a different set of values to the user than using it on a desktop. Mobile allows some unique advantages over desktop-based browsing such as location, mobility, creating a photo/video, and so on. Leveraging these advantages into the mobile experience is the next step to bringing value to the user.

Nick Unsworth: This is a huge growth area. I think that as advertisers become more aware of the opportunity, there will be more dollars flooding into this industry. The result is continual growth and development.

Dave Kerpen: Facebook mobile has a strong future, as does the mobile web in general. Facebook executives realize both the growing trend of people accessing the web from their mobile phone, and emerging countries using smart phones in lieu of computers altogether. Consequently they're building more and more tools for users and developers to use Facebook from smartphones and mobile phones. In the future, Facebook will definitely have its own smartphone devices and mobile operating platform with its own application store (a la Apple and Amazon). In the near future, more people will access the Internet from phones than from desktop computers, and this trend will only grow. You can be sure Facebook will be along for the ride.

Chase McMichael: The explosions of smartphones and high-speed access via these devices have the ability to change everything. More websites are seeing that a major portion of their consumers are coming in through a mobile device.

Currently Facebook's biggest challenge is innovation and entering a crowed space. Facebook could acquire T-Mobile and LG to move into position and compete where others have a clear lead. Facebook on its own is not a mobile application; it's more of a platform/outlet that acts as a content destination. Creating collaborative applications that leverage location, content capture, and syndication to friends is the next big opportunity. There has yet to be a leader in this area, since Google pushes the Android OS, and Apple not opening their mobile OS creates a void in this area since there really is no standardization. Facebook has not created a unique OS so therein lies their major problem. Nothing unique means that not much can be gained in this area.

QUESTION 8: **Businesses on Facebook?**

Do you foresee that more businesses will make Facebook the center of their online presence? Please explain.

Jan Rezab: Yes, we are seeing that in many examples, with OREO, for example, putting their entire landing page for their global campaign on their Facebook page. We will be seeing more of that.

Chase McMichael: For most brands, Facebook is just a way to communicate with their consumers and drive engagement. However, more and more brands desire custom communities or using blog communities to drive increased engagement. The major concern brands have is loss of control or that Facebook changes the game and that beloved fan page that has millions of followers now has cost associated with it if you don't buy ads on Facebook. There is no question Facebook is under the monetizing gun to sustain its $100 billion valuation. With Google making about 10X on revenue vs. Facebook, the valuation numbers for Facebook do not add up. However, with close to one billion users on Facebook, brands must embrace all that this platform offers. Brands have a choice; they can integrate with the consumers' conversation and become a part of it and increase their overall consumer/follower engagement. Brands have an opportunity to own their content voice and be a leader in their own vertical via intelligence curation. InfiniGraph calls this *hypercuration*. Due to this fact, brands need a way to bring together what's the hottest piece of content tending within their vertical. Using this inertia in their favor will increase a brand's consumer traction. Brands that understand they can be the center of conversation will benefit by becoming the thought leaders and are no longer late to the party.

Ben Pickering: I think Facebook will be a central part of any company's online presence. However, I think that smart marketers will not rely on Facebook as their sole channel for reaching consumers. Instead, I think brand websites and Facebook Pages will coexist. There will be deeper integration through the Facebook platform to tie experiences on and off Facebook together.

Scott Ayres: In 2011 I think businesses embracing Facebook hit its peak honestly. As Google+ pages grow and expand, I feel that this could decrease the number of businesses adding pages and having a presence on Facebook. As Facebook changes how posts show constantly, many businesses are frustrated with Facebook, and rightfully so. That being said, I think perhaps fewer businesses on Facebook could be a good thing. In 2011 so many pages were created that added no value to our daily lives, and hopefully more legitimate pages will remain and be created.

Nick Unsworth: Yes, without question. The way that I think of the shift here is similar to what happened in telecom. There was a time when everyone was asking, will cell phones really make long-distance and landlines obsolete? The indicator was new home sales and apartment rentals. When someone would purchase a home and decide that they were going to simply use their cell phone, that's when I knew landlines and long-distance service would eventually be obsolete. At this point in time, they basically are, with the exception of cable companies desperately hanging on and forcing consumers to bundle. Even businesses are opting to use VoIP and Internet phone to conduct business because of the cost savings.

That relates to Facebook because when I have a new client that is starting a business, I'm finding that many of them will decide to build a Facebook business page and will elect not to build an additional website. If you think about it, why would they? They can build a website into their Facebook page in addition to all of the other benefits.

David Foster: I feel that businesses are starting to understand that you must have an online presence as well as a Facebook presence. Now being a Facebook app creator, of course it is the center of our presence, but it would really be hard, I feel, for attorneys, doctors, and so on to make it the center. I feel it will play a major role in customer service, loyalty, and engagement, but I think for a while yet people will still depend on their websites as their main site that leads people to their Facebook page, and vice versa.

Andrea Vahl: Some businesses have been tempted to stop using their website and make Facebook the center. But as Facebook changes without warning, sometimes with big consequences for Facebook Pages, businesses are realizing that they can't build their empire on rented property. They need to continue to use their own website as their main hub so that they have complete control over content, branding, and search engine data. Facebook can be an important part of reaching their customer base daily but must never replace a company website.

Brian Massey: Businesses will continue to be disinclined to make Facebook the center of their online presence. It will continue to be a source of traffic like search and display advertising. It will not be acceptable to these businesses to spend money building a social graph on Facebook only to have it deleted due to changing terms and conditions or Facebook's decision to enforce those terms and conditions. Thus, businesses will continue to extract information on users from Facebook and place it in their databases on servers that they own. Only then is it truly a business asset.

QUESTION 9: Third-Party Apps?

What is the future of third-party apps now that Facebook has introduced the Open Graph and seamless sharing via the Ticker and Timeline?

Nathan Lakta: "I am singing with Lady Gaga" holds more social capital than "I like Lady Gaga." And "I am building a fan page with Lujure" holds more capital than "I like Lujure." For these reasons, the future of third-party apps will be branded actions.

As they say, actions speak louder than words. "I am LEARNING from MARI SMITH" holds more weight than "I like Mari Smith."

What we are going to see in the future are brands competing to own branded actions. Nike and Adidas will fight for the verb *running*. Speedo will want *swimming*. Netflix and Hulu will fight for *watching*. You get the idea.

The only way for a brand to win these verbs is through sticky applications. Nike will develop software for its shoes that autoposts to Facebook: "Mari RAN 8.3 miles with NIKE." Better yet, Nike will acquire third-party developers who already have applications that track how much you run. RunKeeper is an example.

Brands are going to be forced to close the "psychological" loop with their brand advocates as well to drive more online credibility.

If Nike does put on health clinics that encourage running, that means fewer branded action posts to Facebook.

The idea of branded actions is great for the economy. Entrepreneurs will create software that measures and tracks actions in certain vertices, and then major players in those vertices will acquire the corresponding software to own their desired verbs.

The idea of branded actions is also great for humankind. It forces brands to be socially responsible. Nike will have to actually improve the health of people. Hulu will have to take the viewing experience to a top-notch level. Mari will have to continue to provide top-notch content if she wants "I am LEARNING from MARI SMITH" posts to overwhelm Facebook.

Branded actions. Economy wins. Humankind wins. Facebook wins.

David Foster: I think the Open Graph has the potential to be a real game-changer in how apps communicate for sure. I think that the language you can now speak on people's Walls makes it more interactive. It is genius really; however, I think that the Ticker and Timeline have some time left to grow on people. There are days I like it and other days I don't. I feel like I have lost a lot of communication since the change, and I have to go out of my way to find it now. Maybe it will grow on me. And as far as the Ticker...I have yet to even use it. See, I am 41 years old and still prefer my information to move slowly. That Ticker moves way too fast for me!

Chase McMichael: Brands and publishers will always need some type of API interfacing since Facebook cannot be their only access point on the social graph, so the data aggregation from a different graph can be linked back to web analytics and other performance-tracking mechanisms. Brands themselves need to take from the Facebook strategies of content engagement to insert them into their own properties in order to achieve success in today's world.

Jan Rezab: The methods and ways of sharing will continue to evolve. Timeline, Ticker, and frictionless sharing are just some of the examples of how this can evolve, and I am sure more will be coming. I think apps will move from gaming to more utility apps, which will help the people with their everyday needs.

Scott Ayres: Frictionless sharing will be the most talked about change to Facebook over the next few years. As I type this response, I'm listening to music via Spotify, and it is automatically sharing it with my friends! What this does is create more conversations, more common interests, and so on. And what it also does is make it so that people don't have to leave Facebook to get their music, news, and more. No longer do I have to copy and paste a link to a news article or song. Now I can just look at it or listen to it and my friends will see it, if I allow the app to share automatically, that is. We will see so many new apps that allow frictionless sharing moving forward. The downside of this is that too much automatic sharing could lead to cluttered and clogged News Feeds for users, which leads to frustration as they might feel their News Feed is full of fluff and garbage. But, third-party apps using Open Graph will be the biggest news story of 2012 for Facebook.

QUESTION 10: Monetizing?

Where do you fee; developers should be focusing to best optimize and monetize Facebook?

David Foster: I personally think that it will be in the Timeline app market. We have already been looking into ways to allow people to launch their Facebook Pages on their Timeline to their friends and family in a way that makes it fun and interactive but not obtrusive. You definitely have more options now as a developer, and I love the fact that Facebook loves its developers and leaves so much open for us to get in there and start our own business using their platform. For that, we are forever grateful.

Nick Unsworth: I'm not a gambling man, but I'm betting on gamification trends and Facebook application development. That's exactly why I'm building www.smashitsocial.com to create applications that enhance the consumer experience on Facebook and lead to increased results for business owners.

Chase McMichael: Developers have the greatest opportunity in understanding consumer interaction and creating software that crowdsources these actions in a way that has built-in intelligence to adapt to a user's interactions and become more personalized to them. Extracting social content and using that in an actionable way to drive greater engagement will separate the winning applications from the losers. For the platforms, this is true as well; however, the requirements are to integrate a brand's data with the social interaction/context to deliver more adaptive marketing.

Jan Rezab: Obviously through games and applications and, other than that, through marketing.

QUESTION 11: **How to Stay #1?**

What will Facebook need to do to continue being the number-one social network?

Ching Ya: Apart from evolving, Facebook should continuously listen to users' experiences on introduced features and improvise, if not to satisfy all, then remedy the concern people have in the two biggest concerns to date: privacy and account management. General users are less prone to rapid changes, and they occupy a huge portion of the Facebook user base. Facebook needs not only to educate on the features and how-tos but to reassure users that they are committed to putting users' interests first and how the new change will benefit them in the long run. Also, they need to enhance their support in bug issues and provide reachable contact information, besides bug forms, for important matters such as page hacks.

Nathan Latka: To remain the number-one social network, Facebook will have to find a way to make its user-generated content more closely aligned with accurate depictions of that user's life. Currently many Facebook users create pages and profiles to construct an online persona of what they desire to be instead of presenting real, accurate information.

Facebook can create this alignment of real life and "virtual life" through the development of technology like RFID tags or NFC.

Think about a world where Facebook recognizes, as you shop, that you are checking out a box of Kraft Mac n' Cheese or a Dole Fruit Bowl because your RFID tag is associated with the RFID tags on the boxes of these products.

Wal-Mart is already installing RFID technology on products to replace bar codes. Old Navy already uses RFID tags on infant clothes to prevent theft. This is advantageous to Facebook because the hardware (RFID) aspect of connecting products with people is already in place. NFC could be another approach but is only being used in the payments vertical right now.

Imagine not having to click an archaic accept button to tell Facebook you have a new "friend." The truth is, the people in my life don't just consist of "friends" and "not friends." There is an infinite number of degrees my relationships take on. RFID technology could be developed so that Facebook qualifies relationships based on how long you've spent next to someone else in the past year. Facebook would recognize family because I spend the holiday periods in close proximity with them. The challenge is: how do you connect RFID software (through a phone?) or RFID hardware to people? If Facebook goes the hardware route, they should follow Square's lead.

Facebook has excelled at connecting people. Now it needs to connect people to products. Facebook's Presence experiment is the beginning of this. Pedram Keyani and George Lee, the creators of Presence, say it best: "Roads? Where we're going, we don't need roads."

Chase McMichael: Facebook is still growing globally. However, for them to continue, there needs to be more innovation. Just relying on them being a social graph pipeline will not keep them in the number-one spot, and the battle is on with Google+. Just as Apple is the king of the smartphone, you now have Samsung and other Android devices knocking on their door. These competing forces to own the consumer relationship will never stop, regardless of who is competing within the marketplace.

Scott Ayres: At some point Facebook has to figure out how to better push out the changes it makes. I don't feel they need to ask me what I want, because with 800 million users that's impossible to do. And it would be foolish, honestly, of Facebook to try to do that. I think they do a good job with focus groups figuring out what might or might not work. But, when changes are made, Facebook needs to give more notice and more education to its users. This will lead to less complaining and quicker adoption. But, that being said, I think Facebook thrives on the complainers. Every post, whether for or against a Facebook change, is another ad impression. It's another opportunity for an ad to be clicked. It's another chance for Facebook to make money. It's pure genius when you think about it. By complaining, people actually make Facebook more money. So, my feeling is they are willing to risk hacking off half of the user base, as that means a massive amount of posts griping about the change, which means more ads were shown and Facebook made more money.

David Foster: Just stay consistent and listen to users, which they do. When they change something and people hate it, they tend to change it back, but when they see a vision and it makes sense to them, they sometimes change it anyway, and after a couple months of complaining and threatening to leave and go back to MySpace, we boot up our computer, open our browser, and fall in love all over again. It's not necessarily because we love Facebook but because we miss seeing our friends, which in the great scheme of things is what it's all about anyway. It would be too hard for people to walk away in large numbers anyway because most of us do not want to spend another 30 hours teaching our moms and dads how to upload photos to another platform!

Chad Wittman: In order for Facebook to stay on top, they must continue to bring value to the user. Their implementation of social games was a move in the right direction. Facebook should also target implementing ubiquitous search engine functionality within the Facebook framework. Facebook has been trying to revamp the email process (they're getting closer), but it's still not there yet. They need to bite the bullet and allow users to import their email addresses into the Facebook world. These steps could secure a long future for the social network.

Facebook's biggest enemy is developers who may create technologies that bypass the need for Facebook. The current process to utilize the Internet is actually a cumbersome operation. First, the user must obtain access to an Internet connection, navigate to a social network (i.e., Facebook), update their social profile, and then exit the system. Technology developers have an opportunity to streamline this process. Apple has already started the process with an iPhone and a Facebook app. But what if your phone/tablet enabled you to connect with people without taking all of those steps? Would you still need Facebook?

Andrea Vahl: Facebook will need to watch for feedback. Listening isn't always the best strategy because people like to complain. They will need to watch what people are doing, where they are logging in from, what apps are being used most frequently, and so on. Google+ has pushed them to introduce new features that have improved Facebook. Watch other networks to see what features are getting the best reviews and being used well.

QUESTION 12: **Coming Trends?**

What trends do you see affecting Facebook in the next two years?

Ben Pickering: One of the biggest trends will be the continuing mobile shift. As more and more people access the Web from their mobile devices, Facebook must not only optimize the user experience but also ensure that brands are able to effectively reach customers through the Facebook mobile platform. This includes fan pages and apps along with advertising. Getting the user experience right and effectively monetizing mobile are essential for Facebook's long-term success.

Chase McMichael: Greater use of agile marketing. (Agile marketing is the ability to adapt or refocus marketing efforts quickly and successfully in response to changes in customer behavior, market conditions, and business direction to benefit market share or share of wallet. It sounds simple, yet the means of achieving this agility are more complex.)

Facebook's challenge is being the largest community and having to monetize the audience in a world where a consumer being social is not about being monetized. Facebook not owning a mobile OS or being a commerce hub like Amazon and Apple are huge problems. Relying on the social graph as an application and not innovating fast enough is the biggest conundrum they face. Smaller, more scalable applications coming out that can disseminate information without consumer fatigue is the way for them to win, although given how Facebook works, their current size might prevent them from achieving this type of innovation.

David Foster: I am hoping *not* the SOPA bill! It seems as though there is a growing need to mess with our freedom of information and speech, and more and more it is carrying over to the online world, and that is something that really bothers me. My livelihood depends on the Internet. I see that potentially affecting Facebook much like it does in China and other countries. I really hope I am wrong, but if the way things are going is any indication, I am definitely concerned.

Phyllis Khare: The growing grandparent market and the nonprofit world are to my mind the fastest-growing trends online. If Facebook can create an integrated experience for these two groups, they will be leading all the other social platforms in the world.

How does Facebook do that? The grandparent market is a consumer market, and nonprofits are potential advertisers. Both sides of the commerce fence need some focus.

I think the grandparent market will really start to be more apparent in the next year, whereas the nonprofit world is really starting to be important right now.

For example, there is an alliance on YouTube called Project4Awesome that has created some amazing support for nonprofits. Facebook could organize something similar once a year and raise money and awareness for organizations such as Water.org, Freedom from Hunger, Autism Speaks, Doctors Without Borders, and so many more!

And for the grandparent market, if Facebook could curate businesses on Facebook that have products for the grandparent market—products that could be visited much like you would an online mall—an older demographic could find great value in that. But as it stands, the ability to search for appropriate G-commerce to buy baby things is basically nonexistent. So sales are lost. Figuring out a way to provide a portal or a curated list of links for grandparents would be doing something that no other social platform is doing right now.

Jan Rezab: They will definitely be affected by the competing Google+, though they have put most of the features inside the platform already, so it's going to be fun to watch both platforms really fight. The benefit of Facebook is still that you have your friends there.

Scott Ayres: 1) I think Facebook will be greatly affected by Google search. Currently it's rather difficult to find anything on Facebook unless you already know what it is you are looking for. Facebook doesn't need to become a search engine, but there need to be some major improvements to the search abilities on the site. 2) Mobile devices will change how Facebook is used. A larger amount of people do not even have computers now and are migrating to their smartphones and tablets. This shift will cause Facebook to have to gear the experience to these users. The hard part will be figuring out if the experience should be completely different or simply complement the browser version of Facebook. 3) While I've never been one to be concerned about privacy, I think most people are. Facebook has fallen short on this a few times in the eyes of users, and I think now they have taken it seriously. They will need to be careful to ensure a user's personal information remains secure. For many, it's too late, and they don't trust Facebook any longer.

QUESTION 13: **Biggest Threat?**

What is Facebook's biggest threat as it continues to grow?

Dave Kerpen: Facebook's biggest threats as the company continues to grow are Google+, Twitter, and Facebook itself. Google+ as of this writing has already topped 100 million users in less than a year, way ahead of Facebook's early growth schedule. Despite Google not calling Google+ a social network, it is a competitor to Facebook, and Google has major assets to support the product: Gmail, Google.com, YouTube, Chrome, and boatloads of cash in the bank. If people tire of hearing about what their second cousins are up to on Facebook, look for increased time spent on Google+.

Twitter is a threat to Facebook as well. Twitter's user numbers continue to grow, and its late 2011 redesign finally helped the typical consumer better understand its value proposition: Keep up with what your favorite celebrities, media, and experts have to say—even if you yourself don't want to "join the conversation." Twitter's major advantage over Facebook is its simplicity; as Facebook gets more and more complex, if Twitter is able to remain as simple as it's always been, it could pose a threat to Facebook.

But the biggest threat to Facebook's growth is Facebook itself. As a newly public company, it will be facing more scrutiny than ever before. Facebook will need to drive more and more revenue, and have to prove that it can do this without saturating users with advertisements. Just as Microsoft and Google did before Facebook, it will face government regulators, who must protect people from the effects of a possible monopoly. And Internet users have proven time and time again how fickle they are: Witness the rise and fall of Netscape, AOL, Friendster, and MySpace.

Ultimately, if Facebook is able to continue putting its billion plus users first, and serving them with a great user experience, they will remain the leader in social networking for years to come.

Phyllis Khare: To my mind, two things are Facebook's biggest threat; one is a personal aspect, and the other a business aspect. For the personal threat: I think Path is going to take away some of the old-timers on Facebook. There is a trend that I see among a 25 to 35 demographic who have gone through seemingly endless Facebook changes and have had enough. They want to go back to a simpler time and just have a small, a intimate group of friends. Path provides that to them. Facebook will need to address this in some way. As Facebook gets bigger and more complex, they need to figure out a way for users to modify an account to be bare-bones for those who prefer it that way. Otherwise, they will continue to see people leaving for simpler pastures.

For the business threat, I think obviously it is Google+. If a business has a completely filled-out Google Place listing and a Company page, the search advantages are just amazing. I can see many reasons why certain small businesses would prefer to have Google+ as their social platform of choice. To counter this, Facebook needs to get its Places and Check-in act together. Small businesses want those customer-originated marketing posts that Check-ins provide. Check-ins need a more prominent location and showcasing on a business page. And page admins need a way to repost those on the page. And most importantly, admins need to be able to target ads to people who have already checked in.

Ben Pickering: I think Facebook's biggest challenge is growth itself. This is not something unique to Facebook but is a challenge for any rapidly growing enterprise. Becoming a publicly traded company will expose the company to an increased level of scrutiny and pressure. Recruiting and retaining top talent will likely become a greater challenge when the prospect of huge IPO gains disappears (and the top talent in Silicon Valley is always searching for the "new-new thing"). From an execution standpoint, Facebook appears to have thus far continued to operate in the manner of a smaller company: introducing product changes quickly and reacting nimbly to any challenges.

If the company can avoid the bureaucracy and slowness in decision making that often comes in larger organizations, then they will be much less likely to risk losing their market leadership position.

Scott Ayres: Itself...Facebook is at that AOL stage in its shelf life. Facebook needs to be careful and not attempt to try to become all things to all people. This principle is true in every form of business that exists. It's always better to do one thing and do that one thing well. I fear that Facebook is trying too hard to hold people's feet to the site and by doing so watering down what it was created for. And that was to connect friends and family in an online manner that let you share what you were doing and so on. AOL originally was just an Internet service provider. Once it tried to do too many things, we saw what happened to it. It's the same with MySpace, Yahoo!, and so on. I think the simpler Facebook can keep things, the better for its long-term success. But, it could be too late to go back to a simpler Facebook at this point. Time will tell.

Nick Unsworth: Greed. They need to keep their users happy and always keep them as their number-one priority. It's easy to get greedy and listen to the advertisers and app developers who want more and more access.

Brian Massey: Google is the primary threat. Facebook must provide a greater number of services such as transaction processing, ratings and reviews services, and location-based services for businesses to connect with customers. Currently, Google is advancing into all of these areas, including the core social network offering through Google+. In short, to maintain customer growth, Facebook must use its data to make the entire Web easier to use for consumers and businesses alike. If Facebook remains an advertising-supported destination site, it could go the way of Yahoo!

Chase McMichael: From a security perspective, the virus and worm attacks and onslaught of spam will be ongoing issues. Since Facebook is a single connected network, any flaw can be exploited at a cataclysmic rate. In the content world of online business today, a mega merger that includes the social graph, mobile, and linked brand commerce, including a way to drive measurable advertising to create real ROI, is going to be the winner. The last major threat is other competing social graph applications leveraging group interaction models and user-generated content. No question, Google+ is going to push and erode away at Facebook's dominance in social, and vice versa. The winner of this battle will be the platform that embraces change, listens to its followers, innovates, and incorporates all of the elements I have mentioned.

Jan Rezab: As mentioned, that would be Google+, and of course themselves. Too many or too few changes could kill them.

David Foster: I would have to say support and just overall user experience when issues do arise. I personally have had an issue for months now that I cannot get fixed, and they have not responded. It is not on the Known Issues page, and it is really frustrating. I feel that they need to provide some sort of support, but when you have that many users using many different browsers with many different settings in many different parts of the world on many different Internet speeds…how would you do it? You would have to employ all of California! So, I think size is their biggest threat because the bigger they get, the worse user experience could get.

Perry Marshall's Crystal Ball for Facebook and Social Media

Perry Marshall is author of *The Ultimate Guide to Facebook Advertising*, published by Entrepreneur Press. He weighs in:

The immediate future of Facebook can be summarized in four words: social media grows up.

The Internet as we know it caught fire in 1997, and it took about four years for the chaos to give way to actual, sensible business models. In 1998 I had a profitable website, making me perhaps one of the 1,000 most profitable people on the entire Internet. The rest of the world was cluelessly kiting stock prices.

Social media during the last three to four years has been no different, and that's about to change. There was a dot-com bubble, and there's been a social media bubble.

The number-one thing that happens when opportunities "grow up" is you pay to play. It's not 160 free acres anymore; it's a real estate market. In Facebook, growing up means being willing to spend money on ads, even to market to your own fans.

While it may seem perverse to pay money to advertise to your own fans ("Hey, those are *my* fans, not theirs, aren't they?"), if you're a business, they're really Facebook fans.

Facebook similarly has been playing patty-cake with their advertising system, but that will change too. As of this writing, they are still a privately held company, suspended by venture capital and optimism. Right now, it's good enough to have 1 billion users.

Every single one of those people costs money in terms of server time and bandwidth, right? Eventually, 1 billion users will be a liability, not an asset. Shareholders will demand profits, and Facebook as a company will have to grow up. Mark Zuckerberg will not always be in his 20s.

This means that Facebook's precision of targeting, user interface, and tools will all dramatically improve in the next couple of years. It also means right now is the time to learn it backward and forward so that you have a "feeling for the organism."

The most immediately valuable thing about this, to advertisers, will be *data*: the ability to deeply understand what your customers want. Here's an example: We used Fanalytix software to analyze my own customers and discovered that a disproportionate number of my subscribers love...photography.

My business has nothing directly to do with photography. I'm not into photography. But my coauthor, Bryan Todd, is. It's an obvious bias in my customers. So, we easily generated a dozen ideas about how we could emotionally connect to our customers by talking about photography. We also found new ways to acquire customers, affordably, by advertising to photographers. In some cases, it's less expensive than getting them more directly.

Amazon kept a level head during the dot-com boom and bust, building a solid company all the way. Clearly they knew what they were about. My advice to you is to keep a similarly level head in what you are doing, capitalizing even on irrational behavior to build your foundation for the future.

Biographies

Scott Ayres is Affiliate/Social Media Squad Leader at Hubze. Scott has been an avid user of social media since the days of AOL chat and Yahoo! chat. Now he is always connected to Facebook, Twitter, LinkedIn, and Google+. Before falling into social media, he spent nearly 20 years in retail and 10 years in youth and sports ministry. Scott has degrees in both business management and church recreation. Connect with Scott at www.hubze.com.

David Foster is CEO of Hubze and the co-creator of FanPageEngine. Before entering the world of social media and becoming an entrepreneur, David spent time playing music, building houses, and selling cars. Now he gets to "do what I love and love what I do." David has been an Internet marketer for more than 14 years and a social media marketer for more than 4 years. Visit David's sites at www.hubze.com and www.fanpageengine.com.

Dave Kerpen is the cofounder and CEO of Likeable Media, an award-winning social media and word-of-mouth marketing firm. Dave runs his company alongside his wife and COO, Carrie Kerpen; they are backed by a team of social media thought leaders who collectively have managed over 250 accounts on Facebook and other social networks, for brands such as Verizon FiOS, 1-800 Flowers.com, Neutrogena, Uno Chicago Grill, The Pampered Chef, and Heineken. Dave has been featured on CNBC's "On the Money," ABC World News Tonight, the CBS Early Show, the *New York Times*, and countless blogs. Dave's book, a New York Times Best Seller, is *Likeable Social Media: How to Delight Your Customers, Create an Irresistible Brand, and Be Generally Amazing on Facebook (And Other Social Networks)*. Dave is proud of his Likeable business accomplishments but prouder of Charlotte and Kate, his two daughters at home in New York. Connect with Dave at www.likeable.com.

Phyllis Khare along with co-authors A. Vahl and Amy Porterfield is the author of two comprehensive books on social media marketing: *Social Media Marketing eLearning Kit for Dummies* (a four-color book with DVD and online learning environment) and *Facebook Marketing All-In-One for Dummies*. Phyllis has been a featured guest on Social Media Examiner, eMarketingVids, and Social Media Manners Twitter Events. She is a regular columnist and social media strategist for *iPhone Life* magazine at http://iphonelife.com and a writer for all four magazines published by GSG WorldMedia. Phyllis is a dynamic speaker and trainer, memorable and engaging for all social technology events. See all her publications at http://ow.ly/7n6pL.

Nathan Latka is a software entrepreneur who has empowered 40,000+ Facebook users with a do-it-yourself fan page customization tool called Lujure. He is the cofounder and CEO of this rapidly growing company. Visit Nathan's website at www.lujure.com.

Chase McMichael is CEO and cofounder of Infinigraph.com. Chase is an experienced entrepreneur in the cloud (big data) social intelligence space. He enables brands to measure social behavior and interaction around trending content that integrates with their paid, earned, and owned media. Chase is co-inventor of Hypercuration and a leader in real-time collaboration technologies. With more than 18 years of experience working for major corporations like Chase Manhattan, Sprint, Oracle, and Hearst Corporation, Chase's case studies are featured in *Social Media Analytics: Effective Tools for Building, Interpreting, and Using Metrics* and the upcoming *Facebook Marketing Secrets*. Chase has been awarded numerous patents, Fast Tech 50, and MarketingSherpa Viral Hall of Fame. He is a frequent speaker on social media. See more at www.infinigraph.com.

Brian Massey is the Conversion Scientist at Conversion Sciences, and he has the lab coat to prove it. His rare combination of interests, experiences, and neuroses was developed over almost 20 years as a computer programmer, entrepreneur, corporate marketer, national speaker, and writer. "Conversion" is the process of turning web traffic to leads and sales, and Conversion Sciences brings this ability to businesses of all sizes.

Brian is the author of *The Conversion Scientist* and is a columnist for ClickZ.com, Search Engine Land, and the Content Marketing Institute. He lives and works in Austin, Texas—where life and the Internet are hopelessly entwined. Connect with Brian at www.conversionscientist.com.

Ben Pickering: As CEO of Strutta, Ben guides the strategic direction of the company. He joined Strutta in September 2009 and has been involved with online media for more than 10 years. Prior to Strutta, Ben worked at Yahoo! where he held a variety of strategic roles within the company's display advertising business. While at Yahoo!, Ben played a key role in the first large-scale consumer promotion utilizing user-generated content (Doritos' "Crash the Super Bowl"). Now he's thrilled to be able to offer marketers of any size the ability to create powerful customer-engagement experiences using the Strutta platform.

As a writer, Ben has appeared on Mashable and as a featured contributor to Social Media Examiner. He has also been asked to speak on the topic of social media contests and promotions at events such as Likeable Media's #Likeable U Summit and Social Media Examiner's Facebook Success Summit. Find out more about Ben's company at www.strutta.com.

Jan Rezab is the CEO and cofounder of Socialbakers, a company focused on social media marketing and measurement. Jan's role is to actively push Socialbakers' global strategy. Socialbakers is one of the largest social media statistics resources worldwide, and its goals are to provide the best social profile monitoring and measure every social object there is in the world, in the context where it belongs. Socialbakers is also one of the Facebook Preferred Developer Consultants. Prior to joining the social media marketing world, Jan Rezab was CEO and founder of a mobile company called Redboss for eight years in the mobile content/games/services business. Visit Jan's website at www.socialbakers.com.

Nick Unsworth is a social media consultant, national speaker, and leading Facebook application developer who teaches entrepreneurs, service professionals, and business owners how to build profitable tribes of raving fans, followers, and customers. Connect with Nick at www.nickunsworth.com.

Andrea Vahl is a social media coach, speaker, and strategist. She is coauthor of *Facebook Marketing All-in-One for Dummies*. She uses her improv comedy skills to blog as an entertaining character named Grandma Mary: Social Media Edutainer. She is also the Facebook community manager for Social Media Examiner, an online magazine with more than 70,000 Facebook fans. You can find more information at www.AndreaVahl.com.

Chad Wittman is the founder of EdgeRank Checker. After finally hearing the word *EdgeRank*, many of his social media questions finally had an answer. Chad has been dedicated to the study of EdgeRank ever since, and he has developed a Facebook analytical tool to help measure its effects: EdgeRank Checker. He hopes to help pull the curtain back for people to succeed in social media marketing. Test out Chad's tool for yourself at www.edgerankchecker.com.

Ching Ya is a social media enthusiast and prolific blogger. She enjoys being a freelancer in writing, Facebook fan page customization, and blog setup. Connect with Ching Ya at http://chingya.com.

Recommended Resources

This appendix contains a wonderful roundup of many of our friends in the business—a whole range of blogs on Facebook marketing and social media marketing that you can add to your reader (and follow on Twitter, Facebook, LinkedIn, and Google+!). Plus, there are fan page design services, app developers, and more.

Appendix Contents

People, Blogs, and Businesses to Follow

Facebook Page Template, Design, and App Providers

Advanced Facebook Marketing Solutions

Facebook Contest and Promotion App Providers

Facebook Analytics Service Providers

Facebook App Development

People, Blogs, and Businesses to Follow

AllFacebook.com

AmyPorterfield.com

blog.Hubspot.com

BrianSolis.com

ConversationAgent.com

ConvinceAndConvert.com

CopyBlogger.com

DanZarrella.com

DigitalBrandMarketing.com

DennisYu.com

DuctTapeMarketing.com

eMarketer.com

FamousBloggers.net

FlowTown.com

GigaOm.com

HeidiCohen.com

Hubze.com

HyperArts.com

iMediaConnection.com

InsideFacebook.com

InspirationFeed.com

JeffBullas.com

JeffKorhan.com

JohnHaydon.com

KissMetrics.com

Likeable.com

LostRemote.com

MariSmith.com

MarketingProfs.com

MarketingTech.com

Mashable.com

MediaBistro.com

ProBlogger.net

PushingSocial.com

ReadWriteWeb.com

ReelSEO.com

Scobleizer.com

SearchEngineLand.com

SEOmoz.com

SimplyZesty.com

SiteProNews.com

SmallBizBonfire.com

SociableBlog.com

SocialMediaB2B.com

SocialMediaExaminer.com

SocialMediaExplorer.com

SocialMediaToday.com

SocialMouths.com

SocialTimes.com

SocialStrand.com

Soshable.com

SparringMind.com

SplashMedia.com

StaynAlive.com

TechCrunch.com

TechiPedia.com

TheNextWeb.com

TheSalesLion.com

TopRankBlog.com

ViralBlog.com

wChingYa.com

WebProNews.com

ZDnet.com

Facebook Page Template, Design, and App Providers

AppBistro.com

CustomFanPageDesigns.com

FanAppz.com

FanPageEngine.com

FanPageGenerator.com

Lujure.com

NorthSocial.com

ShortStack.com

SocialIdentities.com

Sprout

TabFusion.com

TabSite.com

Advanced Facebook Marketing Solutions

FanGager.com

BuddyMedia.com

Involver.com

Likeable.com

SproutInc.com

Vitrue.com

Facebook Contest and Promotion App Providers

LikeOurBusiness.com

OfferPop.com

Strutta.com

Votigo.com

WildfireApp.com

Facebook Analytics Service Providers

CrowdBooster.com

EdgeRankChecker.com

PageLever.com

PolygraphMedia.com

Socialbakers.com

TwentyFeet.com

ZuumSocial.com

Facebook App Development

AvenueSocial.com

MomentusMedia.com

Roles and
Responsibilities

In any organization—large corporations, government agencies, sports teams, startups, and so on—the difference between good and great is in the people who make up that organization. It's critical that people be properly evaluated and that they have the room to make decisions on behalf of the organization based on its goals and management philosophy. So, it stands to reason that one of the most important first steps to making your social media and Internet marketing campaigns succeed is picking the right people.

Appendix Contents

Job Functions

Here are the functions that someone must fill at various points of the development of a campaign to ensure that different perspectives are heard throughout the process:

The "General Manager" The person responsible for overseeing the overall campaign. This person should be able to do any of the business tasks necessary to conduct a social media marketing campaign, although the person doesn't necessarily need to be an expert in all of them. General managers should know enough to manage the process and be willing to learn things they do not know. In larger organizations, this person should also be available to "backfill" someone who is out because of illness, maternity/paternity leave, disability, or another reason.

The "Brand Manager" The person responsible for the stewardship of the brand. This person is the spokesperson for the brand. The brand manager ensures that the tone of the campaign or social media presence is in line with what the brand represents. This is also the person who makes sure that the campaign doesn't go too far and threaten brand sanctity or customer perception.

The "Business Requirements Gatherer" The person responsible for understanding the broad needs of the campaign across different stakeholder groups in the organization. This person is in tune with things that are happening in the organization and is probably the one colleague who does the best job networking within the organization. This is the person who collects all the feedback and translates it into a product that everyone can enjoy, but sometimes the result of this work is a compromise that nobody really likes. But possibly the most important role of business requirements gatherers is that they can integrate the social media campaign into other marketing efforts for maximum benefit. As we've discussed earlier in this book, you are much more likely to succeed when you use social media to enhance your marketing across different channels.

The "Creative" The person responsible for turning rough business concepts into something interesting, edgy, and engaging. This involves a process of brainstorming, conceptualizing, and presenting ideas to management for a new campaign. It's a role that demands both the creation of new ideas and the wherewithal to bring them to life through the use of imagery, icons, graphics, and sometimes text. The person is oftentimes a loud and vocal critic of the brand manager, who is decidedly more conservative about the use of organization assets, trademarks, brands, and so on.

The "Reporter" The person responsible for gathering statistics on the performance of the campaign across all types of media (social media, websites, others) and for sharing coherent reports on results. This is a role that is highly analytical and almost requires a stats junkie in a best-case scenario. Reporters should have enough skills with spreadsheets and with data analysis to create compelling reports and perhaps come up with some of their own that clearly tell the tale. It is often handy to make this person agnostic about the success or failure of the campaign. Just the facts, Ma'am.

The "Technical Lead" The person responsible for managing staff, consultants, or vendors responsible for custom web development required to support your marketing campaign. Much like the general manager, who is responsible for turning out a coherent marketing campaign, this person is responsible for communicating with developers and other technical personnel to ensure that customizations are done as effectively and inexpensively as possible. This isn't necessarily the person you'd invite to your next cocktail party, but the technical lead can help you do amazing things with Facebook apps, Facebook Connect, and your website.

The "Executive Sponsor" The executive at the organization who is ultimately responsible for the success or failure of the effort. This is a little tricky—in some organizations, failure is defined as an embarrassing problem that results from the execution of the campaign. In other organizations, failure is defined as falling short of very specific numbers—number of leads, costs per touch, and so on. As you can imagine, in the former case there isn't as much pressure to perform, but there is more pressure to "draw between the lines." In the latter case, there is more pressure from a marketing metrics perspective and more scrutiny over whether social media is a viable marketing tactic. You'll have pressure in your role if you are overseeing your campaign—exactly where will depend on how your organization views social media.

These roles don't need to be filled by different people; most organizations won't have the luxury of a large qualified staff to handle different roles. But the responsibilities are fairly consistent across just about all campaigns regardless of organization type or scope. And sometimes these roles are filled by third-party vendors or consultants who have specific expertise that is not available in your own organization.

Vendors vs. Employees

Everyone is likely busy at your company. So, you probably have a choice to make: do you assign tasks to employees, or do you hire vendors to fill gaps in your organization? The first and most fundamental question is always, "Do you have enough money and knowledge to hire a vendor that you can trust to do the job?" If you're lacking the budget, you'll have no choice but to get colleagues to share the workload. There is certainly a risk inherent in that approach—if your project is the lowest priority of a group of tasked colleagues, it probably won't succeed. There are also advantages to having vendors you trust, because you've worked with their employees in some other capacity over the years or because you have gotten a good recommendation from a friend.

But the choice of vendor or employee is really a strategy just like any other. If you believe social media to be the future of marketing like we do, you can easily justify bringing the capability in-house. It's a long-term investment, and it's better to keep that knowledge around the watercooler. However, you can accelerate the learning curve a bit by hiring the right vendor or consultant to share what they know with you and your team. Few people in most organizations have run successful social media marketing campaigns in the past, and even fewer have the breadth of career experiences that make them ideal candidates for a new campaign. But your colleagues probably have skills here and there that easily transfer with a little assistance.

Aside from the reasons mentioned, there are a few other considerations for your decision to seek help from a third party or choose to run your own Facebook marketing or social media campaign. We'll explore these next.

Use In-House Staff

Using in-house staff may be a viable option for your campaign if any of the following are true:

- You have faith in your people to figure it out.
- Social media execution is not critical to your success in the short term. You can endure some failure and experimentation without significant impact to your business or your brand.
- You want a long-term capability, and you suspect that your employees will not leave. If you think that institutional memory will indeed stay with your company, it's a good idea to invest in your people.
- You think your team can handle it without help.

Get Help from a Vendor or Consultant

On the other hand, you should consider getting outside help for the campaign if any of the following are true:

- You are skeptical about your team's ability to get the job done effectively without assistance.
- Social media is important in the short term but not terribly important long-term, so you need a quick shot of immediate expertise.
- Your employees simply don't have time. Social media maintenance can be very time-consuming if done well. A vendor or consultant can be a good "gun for hire" to help alleviate stress on your people.
- You need insurance—someone who can provide help if it is needed. Of course, you can always use this insurance to deflect blame if you need to, although it's rarely a great idea and not generally good business, but it happens.
- You've tried but failed to meet business objectives using social media, and you need someone to fix your problems.

If you do decide to hire a third party to assist with your effort, consider that social media is now established enough that most qualified professionals will have demonstrable success stories. Find out what companies they've helped. Talk to a few of their clients. Ask difficult questions about expertise, work style, and responsiveness. Keep in mind that a cottage industry of social media professionals has sprung forth over the past few years. Some consultants are truly qualified and can do a great job for you. Others are shameless self-promoters who do a better job of marketing themselves than they could ever do for you. It's far too easy to make a mistake and hire the wrong person if you haven't done your due diligence.

Three Tough Questions for Vendors

The world of social media consultants, experts, and the like can be very difficult to navigate. How do you know you're really dealing with someone who has the skills and talents to help you? Ask three probing questions to get the answers you need, and dig deeper if necessary:

- "What are your qualifications as a social media expert?" Find out exactly why the vendor thinks they're qualified to represent your business. You're looking for a few things here— time in the business, skills, and third-party validation that you're dealing with a true expert.

- "What problems have you solved for your clients?" Learn the breadth and depth of the vendor's expertise. Ideally, you'd be dealing with a vendor that has shown the capacity to create innovative solutions for a wide range of problems.

- "Who have you helped, and can I talk to a few of your former clients?" Success stories usually create rabid fans. Ask to talk to a few of them. When you do, probe to get a sense of exactly how the project went and whether the client and vendor are still on good terms.

A quick search on a popular search engine will also tell you quite a bit of information. Look for blog posts, articles in various web publications, and social media activity. If someone isn't terribly active on the Web and social media, that's probably not the right person to help you. Find out by doing your homework before you agree to sign a contract.

Glossary

@tags Facebook's syntax for creating hyperlinked profile names, page names, app names, and event names in Wall posts, photo or video descriptions, or comments throughout the platform. Though the @ tag often works by typing an uppercase letter only, the @ symbol works best to show a drop-down menu of choices from which the user/page can select. The "tagged" name will show in a shaded gray color, and then once published, the @ tag will be a clickable link as well as having the hovercard.

A/B testing Approach for determining how different designs of a single part of a web page or landing page impact a desired outcome metric. A/B testing is generally used to tweak a site once a design or overall approach is already determined. See also *multivariate* testing.

ad approval Process undertaken by Facebook to ensure that ads created by advertisers meet Facebook's quality standards. All Facebook ads must undergo ad approval before being presented to Facebook users. The process takes as little as an hour or as long as a week, depending on whether the advertiser has created an ad before and whether the ad is similar to other ads that have run on Facebook. Failing to pass ad approval means the process starts over again, and the ad must still be approved.

ad copy Text used to convince Facebook users to click an advertisement at the upper-right part of different pages on Facebook. Ad copy is created in the Ads and Pages application on Facebook and is presented to the user after an advertiser bids to run ads in a campaign and enters payment information. In Facebook, ad copy is currently limited to 25 characters for a title and 135 characters for the body of an ad.

API Application programming interface; the code that is run by a social network or other platform company that allows developers to integrate third-party code with the platform. Facebook, Twitter, and a wide range of other Web 2.0 and social media services maintain a developer API.

approved app A Facebook application that has been reviewed by Facebook to assess whether the application meets Facebook's guidelines for acceptable standards, quality, relevance, and notifications. Once approved for inclusion, the app can propagate messages to the News Feed, and the app will appear in Facebook search results.

bid Advertising metric that is the amount of money you are willing to pay for an impression or a click, along with the type of ad you are running.

blog Web log, or self-serve publishing technology used by people and organizations to share thoughts, opinions, and reactions to current events. Facebook allows blogging via its Notes feature, which is available via the Facebook profiles or fan pages.

bounce rate Percentage of people who view a web page and immediately leave it, usually after not finding what they want. Bounce rates are usually calculated as a metric to indicate the overall success of an ad—clicks that are generated on an ad that result in a high bounce rate rarely provide the business metrics that are desired. A high bounce rate indicates that the traffic generated from an advertisement isn't "high-quality" traffic, while a low bounce rate conversely indicates that the ad does indeed target the right people.

buzz A term used to describe lots of activity, virality, and people talking about a subject, page, event, and so forth. A brand may want to create "buzz" about a new product launch, or an author may want to create "buzz" about a forthcoming book, for example. When you engage with fans, place ads, run contests, and integrate other promotions, the buzz is more likely to happen on a grander scale.

call to action (CTA) A term frequently used in online and email marketing where the business/brand places a well-crafted invitation for visitors/readers/subscribers/fans to take action on a certain piece of content. Examples are "Click here to find out more" or "Enter your name and email for instant access." For Facebook fan page content, including a compelling CTA can help heighten engagement and EdgeRank score.

campaign A marketing initiative that integrates a set of advertising, marketing, or public relations commitments aimed at achieving business goals.

Check-in A Facebook "location-based service" whereby users with a smartphone can check into a specific business or place of interest (as determined by the GPS on their phone) and let all their Facebook friends know their location. Check-ins are an excellent form of free viral promotion for local businesses. Such businesses can also take advantage of Check-in Deals (see *Deals*).

click-through Also referred to as a *click*, a user who has seen an ad and clicked it to get more information.

click-through rate (CTR %) The frequency with which a user clicks an ad or family of ads. This is an important metric for determining the effectiveness of ad copy and images used to entice a user. Generally speaking, ads with a higher CTR % are more effective than ads with lower CTR % metrics, which indicate poorer response.

Community page Users can create their own Community page around a generic topic of interest. In addition, Facebook released a large quantity of its own Community pages, which pull in content from Wikipedia in one section of the page and aggregate all public posts from Facebook users and display them on the Wall of the page. Often, businesses might find that a Community page exists in its name. There isn't much that can be done about claiming these "floating" Community pages.

connections (in advertising context) Advertising metric that counts the verified number of people who accepted an advertised invitation to "like" your page, use your app, or RSVP to your event. This number will be zero if you are advertising a website outside of Facebook.

content audit Process undertaken to learn how much an organization has of specific types of content for future sharing or posting via a social network.

cost per action (CPA) The amount an advertiser will pay for a user to perform a very specific action, usually a sign-up on a web form or some other call to action that the advertiser wants. Facebook does not currently make CPA advertising available to customers but may in the future.

cost per click (CPC) The amount an advertiser will pay for a user to click an advertisement, irrespective of what the user does afterward. CPC advertising is currently an available option through Facebook advertising.

cost per mil (CPM) The amount an advertiser will pay for 1,000 impressions of an advertisement, irrespective of whether the user clicks the advertisement or performs an action afterward. CPM advertising is currently an available option through Facebook advertising.

cover image The large graphic that sits at the top of personal Timelines and fan page Timelines where users and businesses can showcase photos and graphical depictions about themselves and their work/brand. The dimensions are 851×315 pixels. Facebook has tight restrictions as to what can and cannot be showcased on the cover images, including no contact information (which goes in the About section), and no calls to action.

dashboard A summarized view of all important metrics that determine the success of a campaign or set of campaigns over time. Usually built in a spreadsheet, dashboards are important for recording numbers that are usually lost over time because social networks and other third-party sites do not keep exhaustive records long-term.

Deals Local businesses with a Facebook Place page may offer Check-in Deals to their customers. There are four types of Check-in Deals: Individual, Loyalty, Friend, and Charity. The first three types of deals can be excellent ways to entice new clientele to come into your establishment or to reward existing customers. See https://www.facebook.com/deals/checkin/ for more information.

derivative metric The combination of two or more metrics that helps marketers analyze progress over time and opportunities for optimizing websites. Some examples of important derivative metrics are page views per unique user, daily moving average cost per lead/fan, effective CPM per week, and so on.

editorial policy Rules that an organization uses to govern the types of content and the frequency with which content is posted or shared via social media.

engagement ad Type of advertisement that relies upon users to perform an action—such as play a video, "like" an ad, and so on—and have that action appear visible to other friends on Facebook.

Facebook application A product created from a set of custom code that is designed to run and allow interactions inside Facebook. Applications come in a variety of forms—most notably social games, productivity apps, music/lifestyle-sharing apps, custom notification apps, notification apps, and so on. Facebook has its own set of applications, and there are hundreds of thousands of third-party applications.

Facebook Connect A set of technologies provided by Facebook to web developers for integrating Facebook features with a third-party website. Facebook Connect includes embeddable single sign-on using Facebook authentication credentials, social comments, fan boxes and widgets, personalization opportunities, "share on Facebook" functionality, and other features.

Facebook credits Purchased by users to be used toward buying virtual gifts or interacting with certain applications.

Facebook Markup Language (FBML) The language used by developers to create Facebook applications.

Facepile A plug-in that displays the Facebook profile pictures of users who have connected with your page via a global or custom action. It can also be configured to display users who have signed up for your site.

fan A Facebook user who chooses to identify with a fan page and show support. As a result, fan page updates are shared on the fan's News Feed, and oftentimes the fan can post updates to the fan page directly. Facebook no longer uses the term *fan* for its pages, but it is still commonly used by many social marketers.

fan box A Facebook "widget" that summarizes highlights of a Facebook fan page and is published to a website, blog, or other place on the Internet. Fan boxes can include the total number of fans for a fan page, small profile pictures of those fans, or the latest updates to the fan page.

frenemies People who are friended primarily out of courtesy or social pressure more than a real relationship.

frequency Advertising metric that communicates the average number of times each of the people in the Reach metric was provided with an impression of an ad.

"Friends of Connections" advertising An option in Facebook advertising that allows an advertiser to target people based on associations that friends have made. For example, an advertiser can target friends of people who join a group, are a fan of a fan page, or have installed a particular application.

group A popular Facebook product, providing users with a way to connect around topics or interests. Groups can be Open, Closed, or Secret depending upon the level of privacy the creator would like to set.

hemispheric dominance Scientific theory that one side of our brain dominates our thought process and makes us view the world in different ways. Left-brained thinkers tend to be more practical, logical, and "numbers-oriented." Right-brained thinkers tend to be more artistic, emotional, and impulsive.

hidden posts On fan pages, Facebook often flags Wall posts by fans and/or visitors as spam. These "spam" posts go into a separate section under the page Wall that only admins can see. In your daily fan page management ritual, it's important to check your hidden posts because frequently there are a large number of bona fide posts that have been erroneously hidden. To unhide (and place back on the main page Wall), hover and click the icon in the top right of the post, and then click Unhide Post.

hovercard Whenever a Facebook user hovers over a hyperlinked profile name, fan page name, app name, or event name, a "card" pops up with options such as liking the page or adding the person as a friend.

Insights Facebook feature that provides marketers with a high-level overview of the performance of a Facebook page. Included are charts and graphs on the popularity and usage of the page as well as a demographic breakdown of the people who use the page.

landing page/tab A page established on a website or tab on a Facebook page that is intended to get consumers to respond to a particular call to action, usually communicated with an advertising campaign. Landing pages are established by traffic source and are not replicated, so statistics on the effectiveness of the tactic can be isolated and measured against other tactics in the campaign.

live feed All Facebook activity from friends and fan pages in chronological order. Whereas the (default) Top News is a reflection of "popularity" according to Facebook's algorithms, the live feed (now called Most Recent) is a straight listing of every post.

Live Stream One of Facebook's many social plug-ins, the Live Stream plug-in allows Facebook users to share activity and comments in real time as they interact during a live event.

max bid The amount of money per click or per thousand impressions that an advertiser is willing to pay to advertise. Suggestions for bid price are provided by Facebook after considering demand for the advertisement and availability of impressions per criteria set by the advertiser. An advertiser will set a bid in advance of running advertisements on Facebook and other popular Internet advertising destinations.

moving average Average of outcomes for a particular metric over a period of time, usually a week or month. Moving averages are designed to smooth out the impact of holidays and weekends to provide a consistent trending view of data as a means to judge the overall health of a campaign.

multivariate testing Approach for determining how multiple design differences on a website impact a desired outcome metric. Multivariate testing is generally used as a "scattershot" approach to quickly learn what features are responsible for the most well-optimized web destination that is possible. See also *A/B testing*.

networks Groups based around a workplace, high school, or college that users can join so they can connect with those around them more easily. Facebook used to also have geographic networks but has phased out this feature.

News Feed Summary of the most important things that are shared by friends, fan pages, groups, and applications. Facebook's algorithms decide which posts users see and in what order. The more activity a post has from users' friends or joined fan pages, the more likely the post will appear toward the top of their News Feed.

Notes Application in Facebook that allows users to blog directly inside the Facebook platform. In Notes, Facebook users can "tag" each other, which sends a notification to the person being tagged. Along with generating their own note inside Facebook, users can use the Notes app to import an RSS feed, such as their own blog feed.

Open Graph An extension of the social graph. Open Graph includes third-party websites and pages that people liked throughout the Web. Developers can tap into the social graph via the Open Graph by creating apps.

page view Statistic generated when a user visits a web page. Multiple page views are created when a user visits multiple pages in a single website. Generally, sites with higher page views are considered "stickier" than those with lower page views. Looking at page view statistics over time can determine whether changes to a site result in a stickier site or one that is less engaging.

personas Fictional people who characterize segments of a target market. Many marketers, especially those in larger companies, create personas to better understand market segments.

privacy settings Part of Facebook that determines how users control incoming notifications, status updates, and personal data from other people on the Internet and on Facebook.

profile Arguably one of the most important features of Facebook. The profile is the place where users tell the world and each other about themselves. Demographic information, status updates, friends, and other customizations live in the Facebook profile.

publisher The box that appears at the top of every Facebook user's News Feed, personal profile Wall, and fan pages. On personal profiles, content can be published via the publisher by users and their friends, depending on privacy settings. On fan pages, the administrator can post content via the fan page publisher, and fans can also post content depending on the settings.

return on investment (ROI) The amount of financial gain that results from a campaign or other Internet marketing initiative.

search A feature on Facebook. Users may search for any keyword or phrase by entering their query in the search box on Facebook. On the search results page, the filters on the left side of the page allow users to view specific people, fan pages, groups, and applications along with posts by friends or posts by everyone.

Share link/button A feature on Facebook. Every piece of content throughout Facebook contains a small Share link allowing users to repost the content on their own Timeline, on a friend's Timeline, on any fan page they administer, in a group, or via email. Privacy settings always prevail, however. If a piece of content is shared with only friends, even if it is shared publicly, only friends of the original owner of the content could see the post.

social graph The mapping of friends, friends of friends, and other connections that is the basis of Facebook and other social media platforms.

social media policy Rules and guidelines for the use of social media technologies and applications as it relates to a business or organization. These policies may both dictate how the company's assets are maintained and provide guidance for how employees are expected to use their own personal social media accounts.

social plug-in Code that Facebook provides website owners for placing a variety of buttons on their websites, including the Like button, Comments plug-in, Like box, registration, and more.

social reach Advertising metric communicated in the Facebook ads interface. It is calculated as the number of people who viewed an ad who also had a connection to a friend who liked your page, used your app, or RSVPed to your event. This number will generally be low except in cases where either you're extremely popular or you are running ads targeting friends of your fans.

sponsored ad Advertising opportunity generally for organizations with larger advertising budgets to include a brief ad in the upper-right corner of the Facebook News Feed page.

Static HTML One of the most popular iFrame apps for adding custom content to your fan page. iFrame apps replaced Static FaceBook Markup Language (FBML) in 2011.

status update The field at the top of the wall on all user profiles (Timelines) and Facebook Pages where up to 63,206 characters of text can be published. If the text contains a link, typically this will be posted on the Wall as a link, not a status update.

Subscribe A feature launched in September 2011 that allows Facebook users to enable this new setting and have any user "sign up" to receive public Timeline posts in their News Feed. Previously, all public content was visible on anyone's profile (Timeline). Subscribe now allows users to hear from anyone in their News Feed who has the feature enabled.

suggested bid Amount of money Facebook suggests that an advertiser "bid" to get the desired number of clicks or impressions in an advertising campaign.

Ticker A real-time display of activity stories from your Facebook friends. The Ticker appears in the top right of your home page and is also appended to the chat sidebar if you have it open. Users can choose to hide the Ticker by clicking the small up arrow on the upper-right corner of the Ticker on the home page.

Timeline The new term for Facebook personal profiles that allows users to showcase their entire life's events in a timeline format. Users can go back in time to add all manner of activities and landmark (or minor) events from the day they were born to today. Activity posted on the Timeline goes into the News Feeds and Tickers of that person's friends.

Timeline for pages On February 29, 2012, Facebook launched the Timeline design for fan pages. Just like personal Timelines, on the new fan pages, businesses and brands can also go back in time, starting from the date the company was founded, and add in all manner of milestones.

unique user A visitor to a website who has not been to that site previously during the queried time period. Increases in the number of unique users over time indicate that marketing campaigns are successful at engaging with new customers, while those that see a decrease in unique users over time are perhaps engaging with an already informed customer base.

username A short name used to identify a fan page or profile on Facebook, using the convention www.facebook.com/*vanityname*. Vanity names are important for simplifying complex URLs that Facebook otherwise uses for fan pages and profiles. Users may create one username for their personal profile and one for any fan page they administer. Personal usernames can be changed one time; fan page usernames cannot be changed. To secure usernames, users should go to http://facebook.com/username.

vanity name See *username*.

workflow The collection of processes and divided responsibilities in an organization that are established for the maintenance of a social media property/properties.

Index

Note to the Reader: Throughout this index **boldfaced** page numbers indicate primary discussions of a topic. *Italicized* page numbers indicate illustrations.

Moore, Geoffrey, 274–275
Mosaic web browser, 4
Most Interesting Man in the World character, 94
motivators, **32**
moving averages, **152–153**, *152–153*, **170–173**, *171–172*, **220–221**, *221*
multivariate testing, **155–156**, **227**
mutual respect culture, 130
MySpace network
    demise, 12
    vs. Facebook, **11–12**, 28
    profiles, 9, *9*
    startup, **8–9**
myYearbook network, 30

N

name recognition as social media benefit, 63
names
    ad statistics, 162
    groups, 181
NASA, **265**, *265–266*
negative comments and feedback
    initial stats, 209
    managing, **241–243**
Net Applications data, 15
New Groups, **178–179**
new page content in fan migration, 249, *250*
News Feeds, **38–43**, *41–43*
    content editing, 121
    Edgerank algorithm, 130
    and fictional characters, 92, 94
    status updates, 98, *98–99*
Nielsen Online study, 39
Nigam, Shashank, **124–125**
nonprofit organizations, **268–271**, *271*
Nonprofit Social Network Report, 268
NorthSocial.com app, 127
nostalgia as motivator, 32
Notes app, **102**, 183
notifications, **272–273**

O

Obama, Barack, 264
objectives in POST method, 109
off-topic posts, 131
offline promotion, **128–129**
Olbermann, Keith, 248
O'Neal, Shaquille, 17
Online Influence Trend Tracker reports, 241
online services, **3–4**, *3*
Only Admins Can See This Page option, 112
Oodle ads service, 102
Open Graph, 294
open groups, 178, 181
operational realities of content, 117
opinions, 39
optimization
    overoptimization, 220
    social content, 235

organization
    editorial policy for, 118
    metrics, 56
organizational fit, 85
Orkut service, 12
Other Clicks metric, 209
outbound communications, 49
overadvertising, **116**
overfriending, **94–95**
overoptimization, 220
Overture, 6, 163
ownership of religious organizations, 260
Owyang, Jeremiah, 245

P

Pacific University, 272
packaging, 128
Page Like Stories, 144
Page Post Ads, 236, *236*
Page Post Like Stories, 144
Page Posts Insights metric, **208**
Page Views metric, 205, 213
pages
    fan. *See* fan pages
    future, **286–289**
    maintenance metrics, 222
    overview, **63–65**
Palo Alto Networks, 245
Pancreatic Cancer Action Network, 270
Panda Security, 245
Path network, 30
paying for advertising, **147–148**, *147*
people
    in POST method, 109
    as resources, **310**
People Talking About This (PTAT) metric, **207–209**
performance
    ad, **162–166**, *164*
    defining, 251
personal experiences vs. professional, **96–97**
personal information
    account setup, **37–38**, *37*
    interviews, **283–286**
    profiles, **85–86**
personas, **57–58**
    creating, 91
    fan page growth, 233
PETCO page, 129
Photo Views metric, 209
photos
    NASA, **265–266**
    posting, **121–122**
    sharing, 26, **100–101**, *100*
Pickering, Ben
    biography, 307
    businesses, 293
    gamification, 289
    pages, **288**
    personal data, 284
    threats, **302–303**
    trends, **299**
    walled garden approach, **278–279**